Global Climate Policy: Actc
and Enduring Challenges

MW00464528

Global Environmental Accord: Strategies for Sustainability and Institutional Innovation

Nazli Choucri, series editor

A complete list of books published in the Global Environmental Accord series appears at the back of this book.

Global Climate Policy: Actors, Concepts, and Enduring Challenges

Edited by Urs Luterbacher and Detlef F. Sprinz

The MIT Press
Cambridge, Massachusetts
London, England

This book was set in Stone Serif by Westchester Publishing Services. Printed and bound in the United States of America.

Library of Congress Cataloging-in-Publication Data

Names: Luterbacher, Urs, editor. | Sprinz, Detlef, F., editor.
Title: Global climate policy: actors, concepts, and enduring challenges /
    edited by Urs Luterbacher and Detlef F. Sprinz.
Description: Cambridge, MA : The MIT Press, 2018. | Series: Global environmental
    accord. Strategies for sustainability and institutional innovation | Includes
    bibliographical references and index.
Identifiers: LCCN 2017040420 | ISBN 9780262037921 (hardcover : alk. paper) |
    ISBN 9780262535342 (pbk. : alk. paper)
Subjects: LCSH: Climate change mitigation--International cooperation. |
    Climatic change.
Classification: LCC TD171.75 .G56 2018 | DDC 363.738/74--dc23
    LC record available at https://lccn.loc.gov/2017040420

10 9 8 7 6 5 4 3 2 1

Contents

List of Abbreviations

ADP	Ad Hoc Working Group on the Durban Platform
AGBM	Ad Hoc Group on the Berlin Mandate
ALBA	Bolivarian Alliance for the Peoples of our America
AOSIS	Alliance of Small Island States
AWG-KP	Ad Hoc Working Group on Further Commitments for Annex I Parties under the Kyoto Protocol
AWG-LCA	Ad Hoc Working Group for Long-Term Cooperative Action
BASIC	Brazil, South Africa, India, and China
BINGOs	Business International NGOs
CAIT	Climate Action Indicator Tool
CBDRRC	Common But Differentiated Responsibility and Respective Capabilities
CDM	Clean Development Mechanism
CERs	Certified Emission Reductions
CFCs	Chlorofluorocarbon
CMA	Meeting of the Parties to the Paris Agreement
CMP	Conference of the Parties Serving as the Meeting of the Parties to the Kyoto Protocol
CO_2	Carbon dioxide
COP	Conference of the Parties
EMF	Energy Modeling Forum
ERUs	Emission Reduction Units
EU	European Union
GATT	General Agreement on Tariffs and Trade
GCC	Global Climate Coalition
GCF	Green Climate Fund

GDP	Gross domestic product
GEF	Global Environment Facility
GHG	Greenhouse gas
HFCs	Hydrofluorocarbons
IAR	International Assessment and Review
ICA	International Consultation and Analysis
IETA	International Emissions Trading Association
INC	Intergovernmental Negotiating Committee (for the UNFCCC)
INDCs	Intended Nationally Determined Contributions
IPCC	Intergovernmental Panel on Climate Change
IR	International Relations
JI	Joint Implementation
NDCs	Nationally Determined Contributions
NGO	Nongovernmental Organization
OECD	Organization for Economic Cooperation and Development
OECD DAC	Organisation for Economic Cooperation and Development / Development Assistance Committee
OPEC	Organization of the Petroleum Exporting Countries
PFCs	Perfluorocarbons
SBI	Subsidiary Body for Implementation
SBSTA	Subsidiary Body for Scientific and Technological Advice
SF_6	Sulphur hexafluoride
TCG	Transnational Climate Governance
UNCED	United Nations Conference on Environment and Development
UNDP	United Nations Development Programme
UNEP	United Nations Environment Programme
UNFCCC	United Nations Framework Convention on Climate Change
WMO	World Meteorological Organization
WRI	World Resources Institute
WTO	World Trade Organization

Foreword

Global climate policy never seems to arrive at a logical endpoint to warrant a final assessment of its accomplishments. This has been the challenge we faced in editing this book over a decade.

Will the Kyoto Protocol survive and prove to be a harbinger of a new era of saving planet earth from the feared impacts of climate change—or will go down in history as a failed architecture? We held our first authors conference in January 2007 at Geneva, Switzerland, when this question shaped discussions. The hopes for a Kyoto-style architecture culminated in the ultimately doomed expectations for the conclusion of a successor to the first commitment period under the Kyoto Protocol at Copenhagen in late 2009. Our subsequent authors meeting in Oslo in 2012 was influenced by the outcomes of the dashed hopes that surrounded the Copenhagen Conference of the Parties. However, the outcomes of this conference also sowed the seeds of the new architecture that culminated in the bottom-up approach of the 2015 Paris Agreement—whose ultimate effectiveness has yet to be proven. For some observers, the Paris Agreement served as the long-awaited firework that global climate policy is still feasible. With the announcement of President Trump on 01 June 2017 that the USA intends to leave the Paris Agreement, some observers doubt that the global climate regime will survive the departure of a former lead country—while others are more sanguine. There never seems to be an optimal time to conclude a book that shall be of value to scholars and students for a decade to come.

From the outset of this venture, we have employed an architecture that focuses on the broad strokes of analysis, concepts, history, and methods while engaging scholarship across several disciplines in the social sciences. A range of our chapters attends to the history of global climate negotiations and legal architectures of global climate policy. Other chapters concentrate on methodologically informed analyses of the incentives and disincentives to coordinate and cooperate on global climate policy—while further chapters focus on the actors themselves in more detail. Throughout the book, readers will find concepts applied to global climate policy that are also of enduring value in other fields of international and global policy. Our wholehearted thanks go, first and foremost, to our authors who have shown truly academic marathon runner qualities as well as a breadth of scholarship that single authors can hardly summon.

Our volume benefited from a range of persons and donors of resources. The 2007 authors conference and colloquium received generous financial support from the Swiss Federal Office of the Environment, and we particularly thank Jose Romero who was responsible for international negotiations. Our gratitude also extends to Hans Joachim Schellnhuber, director of the Potsdam Institute for Climate Research (PIK), Germany, who not only provided financial support but whose institute also hosted the backoffice on which the book relied over the years. We are also very grateful to Philippe Burrin, director of the Graduate Institute of International and Development Studies in Geneva, Switzerland, for making the colloquium possible by providing space and resources. In addition, we would also like to mention the participants of the 2007 colloquium, namely Scott Barrett, Ying Chen, Graciela Chichilnisky, Chandrashekhar Dasgupta, Emilio Lèbre La Rovere, Urs Leimbacher, Jiahua Pan, Gulnara Shalpykova, and Henry Tulkens for their reflections on an initial draft - as well as Navitri Putri who helped organizing it. We are thankful for the tremendous advice offered by Nazli Choucri over the years who not only participated in the colloquium but who also heads the Global Environmental Accord series at MIT Press.

The 2012 authors conference employed what was then a comparatively novel combination of in-house participation at the University of Oslo, Norway, and remote participation by video. We are grateful to Prof. Arild Underdal and the Department of Political Science at the University of Oslo for facilitating this low greenhouse-gas experiment.

Over the years, we were blessed to benefit from the support of a range of now former students and scholars, hosted by the Potsdam Institute for Climate Impact Research, that have assisted us in keeping a global authorship virtually hosted. We are particularly grateful to Alexandra Goritz, who supported us at the early and the very late stages of this volume as well as Katharina Schleicher, Mareike Thielen, and Anna Peters.

Finally, we are grateful to Clay Morgan, at the early stages, and Beth Clevenger as well as Anthony Zannino, at the MIT Press, during the later stages for steering the book and providing valuable advice. We also appreciate the time and constructive advice offered by three MIT Press reviewers that make the book a better source for students and scholars.

Duisburg, Geneva, New Haven, Potsdam, January 2018
Urs Luterbacher
Detlef F. Sprinz

1 Our Approach

Urs Luterbacher

1.1 Main Issues and Major and Enduring Challenges

This book is about the international political context of climate change. It constitutes a novel set of analyses about the current international climate change regime. This international regime, despite some setbacks such as the recent decision by President Trump to withdraw the United States from the Paris Agreement of 2015, has already a long history, and it looks like that its growth pattern will continue. This evolution will in all likelihood happen in some sense despite and maybe even because of the American decision as other members of the international community will probably step in and seek to strengthen the Paris Agreement on their own.[1]

Institutionally, the international climate change regime goes back to the drafting of the United Nations Framework Convention on Climate Change (UNFCCC) in 1992 at the Earth Summit in Rio when almost all UN members acceded to it. Currently 197 parties have ratified it. Once a year, the state of the international climate change regime is reviewed by the Conferences of the Parties to the UNFCCC (COP). The first (COP 1) took place in Berlin in 1995. The second (COP 2) was set in Geneva in 1996, and the third (COP 3) in Kyoto in 1997. The making of the Kyoto Protocol to the UNFCCC resulting from COP 3 was supposed to enhance decisively climate change mitigation by introducing mandatory greenhouse gas reduction targets for industrialized countries.[2] Since the beginning of the new millennium, the initial hopes that emerged after the elaboration of the Kyoto Protocol to construct a strong international climate regime with mandatory reduction obligations have faded. Currently, global climate negotiations have reached a new dimension with the conclusion of the Paris Agreement at COP 21 in

December 2015. It remains to be seen to what extent this agreement, which still has to be worked out in some of its details, will achieve its goal of limiting the rise in global temperatures to 1.5 to 2°C. The Kyoto Protocol *system* has been seriously threatened through the defection of Canada, and the Paris Agreement has moved from country-specific reduction goals (Kyoto Protocol) to national voluntary target setting (called nationally determined contributions [NDCs]). However, the Paris Agreement sets a goal to limit global temperature increase to "well below two degrees Celsius." In some sense the Paris Agreement represents a return to the situation that existed before the elaboration of the Kyoto Protocol when only the UNFCCC established in Rio in 1992 was defining the structure of the international climate regime—but with the addition of a well-defined global target. This regime has thus evolved so far within three phases. The first one was dominated by the UNFCCC with the idea that additional protocols to the treaty would eventually be agreed upon. The second phase was characterized by the elaboration of the Kyoto Protocol and the third one now by the Paris Agreement. All three phases present their own specific challenges for international coordination and cooperation strategies.

The original UNFCCC treaty contained very few obligations (such as reporting on emissions) and mostly recommendations such as avoiding dangerous anthropogenic interference with the climate system (art. 2). The definition of what this meant was not clarified. In fact, the specification of these recommendations was left to future elaborations of principles to be adopted within particular protocols similar to the Montreal Protocol to the Vienna Convention for the Protection of the Ozone Layer. The principles that were adopted after the conclusion of the UNFCCC were the Berlin Mandate, which established the guideline that industrialized countries should make the initial efforts to mitigate climate change. Finally, at COP 2 in Geneva, the decision was taken that industrialized countries should establish and observe mandatory and binding emission reduction targets, a move that opened the way for the elaboration of the Kyoto Protocol. In summary, this phase is characterized by coordination moves aimed at reaching a certain goal, in part through cooperation among at least a group of countries.

Recall here that coordination moves are about establishing conditions to meet a certain endpoint that may or not involve cooperation. To illustrate such a process, it is useful to evoke the analogy about the issues that arise when some people have to agree on a place to meet for dinner. Agreeing on a place to meet is basically a coordination problem. If we want to draw a parallel with climate change negotiations, the two degrees limit increase agreed on in Paris represents the meeting place. On the other hand, cooperative moves are all about how to reach such a meeting place by having people collaborate with each other. Now it is possible that some people involved in reaching the dinner destination have a harder time than others getting there because they do not know the city or because it is more complicated for them to go there than for others. This makes the path to the meeting area more expensive for them. This inequality problem in reaching the destination can be solved by cooperation. Since it is essential that in the end most people reach the predetermined place, cooperation would be a desirable feature that would make sure that everybody gets there in a reasonable amount of time. However, establishing such cooperative moves can be quite hard to achieve in practice.

As emphasized by Bueno de Mesquita (2009), it is difficult to get countries to participate in a cooperative effort that entails significant up-front costs and only long-term benefits in the form of damage avoidance. It is already sometimes problematic to get countries to agree to cooperate when significant and relatively rapid mutual benefits are extant, as, for instance, in trade agreements. It might, however, be possible to convince international actors to embark on a costly enterprise if it provides quick and tangible side benefits that are independent of the avoided long-term damage which would eventually result from a strong climate change regulatory system.[3] This is what the Kyoto Protocol tried to accomplish but, as will be discussed later, failed to do. The Paris Agreement represents a return to a pure coordination strategy that largely eschews to make explicit the ways in which its ultimate goals of a global temperature increase limit of two degrees will be reached, as will also be discussed later.

The Kyoto Protocol was negotiated at COP 3 in Kyoto and entailed mandatory reduction targets for all industrialized countries. These were determined along different greenhouse gases and were taking into account the particular situation of each country.[4] The protocol was severely hampered by the fact that the Clinton administration that negotiated it for the United States did not send it for ratification to the US Senate. The George W. Bush administration that succeeded it refused to ratify it and got out of the Kyoto process altogether. Nevertheless, the other participants decided to continue and to obey its targets. Kyoto was clearly a major effort at cooperation with a relatively centralized organization that allowed countries to operate reductions via a variety of means, among them emission reduction exchanges with others. However, Kyoto failed to attract further members and so the reduction efforts were confined to a relatively small group of countries. Their initial intent was to prove to the rest of the world that their reduction attempts were possible and worthwhile. However this strategy of "leading by example" did not work. Global emissions kept increasing at an exponential rate mainly because of the industrialization of China and India as figure 1.1 shows.

Kyoto's goals were finally reached for the set of countries that were following it but this achievement was hollow. In some sense Kyoto was a local success but a global failure that revealed the difficulties of reaching climate change goals with cooperative strategies that require internationally defined commitments. In addition, the failure by the European Union to

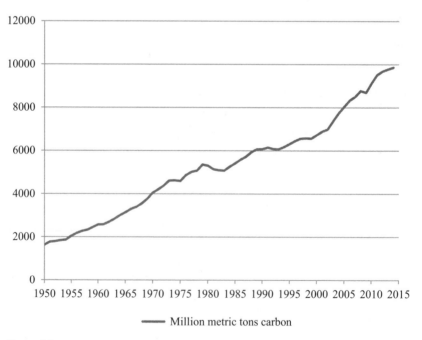

Figure 1.1
Global carbon emissions from fossil fuels 1950–2014.
Source: Data from Boden, Marland, and Andres (2017).

create an effective EU Emissions Trading System[5] helped to discredit such schemes at the international level as well. These failures revived the notion that systems based on decentralized coordination were better than those that rely on more centralized legally binding reduction targets. The Paris Agreement of 2015 can be considered as resulting from this conception.

In line with achieving coordination rather than cooperation, the Paris Agreement is more oriented toward voluntary reduction targets, which every country is supposed to undertake and which are subject to periodic reviews. The fragility of this arrangement is obvious with the election of Donald Trump in the United States and his efforts to undo some of the domestic commitments made by his predecessor together with Trump's decision to withdraw from the Agreement.[6] In order to achieve the dismantling of the US targets under the Paris Agreement, the current president did not even have to formally withdraw from it as it has neither rules nor binding obligations in terms of reduction efforts. The only expectation that the Paris Agreement provides is that each country will eventually implement some reduction commitment, a clear coordination goal. The fact that most countries have now embraced this concept leaves the European Union as the last guardian of the spirit of the Kyoto Protocol and the user of some of its mechanisms with the exception of some internal institutional actors such as American states or cities. These recent evolutions of the international climate change regime present major challenges in terms of evaluation and analysis. The authors of the chapters of this volume have been asked to provide further attempts to assess the current situation from a variety of dimensions and considerations.

The current climate change regime seems still to be at a breaking point despite the Paris Agreement: either the present institutional and negotiation structures will be preserved with the possibility that they will stagnate, die, or become irrelevant—or new forms of international cooperation will be created that will tame climate change. Our book examines these bigger and enduring challenges, especially chapters 3–5 are dealing with the "fundamentals" in terms of theory to help in the understanding of behaviors of national and subnational units involved in climate change negotiations. Subsequent chapters cover the methods and actors characterizing the global climate regime, as well as compliance and effectiveness. The book, on the one hand, attempts to give a detailed picture of the current situation and, on the other, tries to offer some answers to the question of the persistence of existing structures—or the emergence of new ones. In this sense, a good review of the Paris Agreement seems warranted to see to what extent it brings something new to the current negotiation structures.

In the following, we summarize the many issues investigated in the chapters included in the volume.

1.2   The Evolution of the Architecture of the Climate Change Regime

The evolution of the architecture of the climate change regime from its beginning until the Paris Agreement is undertaken by Daniel Bodansky and Lavanya Rajamani (in chapter 2). In their presentation, the authors examine the COPs of the UNFCCC to see if it remains an important forum, or if it will tend to be superseded recently by initiatives emanating from the G7 or the G20. The authors also provide an overview of the Paris Agreement, including the avenues of further elaboration of the agreement.

1.3   Theoretical Considerations

Michaël Aklin (in chapter 3) reviews a concise set of theoretical positions on climate change collaboration. He concludes that "since power is partly drawn from a solid economy, anything that might curb growth in the short run should be viewed with suspicion (Waltz 2000). To the extent that a climate treaty requires the reduction of industrial activities, realists would be skeptical about whether states could credibly commit to it." Thus, even if legally binding, the question remains if such international agreements can really be enforced. In contrast, he discusses whether the failure of cooperation in environmental matters is resulting from the lack of proper institutional setups as sometimes claimed by neoliberal institutionalists. He also evokes the position taken by constructivists who attribute problems of collaboration to a lack of common culture or language and also to the absence of epistemic communities to contribute to its development (Haas 1992, 2004). Finally, Aklin also analyzes the capacity of the interplay between domestic and international explanatory schemes to account for either success or failure of climate change cooperation.

One can reasonably conclude from this analysis that rather than seeing all these perspectives as rival, they should also be investigated in terms of their complementarity, each of them addressing different aspects of a social reality. The rational choice assumptions, common to realism and to neoliberal institutionalism, have to rest on the assumptions of common knowledge and consistent alignment of beliefs, all conditions to which constructivism may have useful things to suggest. Substantively, it is difficult to delimitate a strict realm of international politics, which is not influenced by domestic affairs, thus the necessity to study the interaction between these two domains. It thus appears necessary to look critically at some of the conceptions presented by the various schools of thought to explain climate change collaboration or the absence thereof.

1.4   Formal and Simulation Approaches of Climate Change Cooperation and Coalition Analysis

The book covers formal and simulation approaches in two chapters, one focusing on purely formal approaches based mostly on game theoretical considerations, and the other dealing with computer simulation and computational models.

In chapter 4, "Cooperation on Climate Cooperation: Insights from Game Theory," the authors Frank Grundig, Jon Hovi, and Hugh Ward analyze how theorists can actually explain the weak impacts of both the UNFCCC and the Kyoto process. However, even though pessimism about the lack of achievements of international climate change abatement procedures dominates the community of scholars dealing with formal models of decision making, some research points to possible ways of achieving substantial progress. The authors analyze the difficulties involved in reaching the path of a generalizable accord on emission reductions and examine how one can design such international processes.

Formal approaches of the kind discussed so far are often usefully complemented by the use of simulation methods. These are implemented via computational models in order to better anchor the kind of representations used by formal analysts into real-world situations. A whole literature devoted to these approaches has been emerging and is reviewed here by Thierry Bréchet and Urs Luterbacher in chapter 5. The approach provides useful tools to not only understand and illuminate current debates but also to assist negotiators of agreements on how to envisage alternative future possibilities. These models can help to evaluate future costs and benefits of climate change even broken down into different countries and regions.

Moreover, they try to assess which kind of coalitions between states will form, given advantages and disadvantages countries can extract from various kinds of international agreements.

1.5 The Climate Change and Trade Regimes

For international accords like the UNFCCC and the Kyoto Protocol, as well as future possible arrangements to work within the existing structure of international agreements, they have to be in tune with other legal regimes such as the world trade system. The legal structure of the trade regime has the advantage of relying on a strong dispute settlement mechanism, which may lead to an effective system of sanctions. It is therefore better to avoid any possibility of clashes between the two regimes. This is the object of chapter 6, by Urs Luterbacher, Carla Norrlof, and Jorge E. Viñuales, which is devoted to an analysis of possible contradictions between the two. The authors analyze the many areas of conflict for which countries, especially in Europe, could be tempted to use "green" protectionism to selectively help their industries. This could be detrimental to trade but perhaps also to environmental and climate change protection because it would deteriorate the status of internationally recognized property rights and thus encourage the overuse of natural resources.

1.6 Leadership Issues and Major Countries

Major countries, such as those emitting 2 percent of GHG or more, can influence climate change bargaining in a significant way. In chapter 7, Detlef F. Sprinz, Guri Bang, Lars Brückner, and Yasuko Kameyama set themselves to examine the situation of these major players in the evolving climate change regime. These include four emerging economies (Brazil, China, India, and Indonesia) as well as four developed countries or groups of countries (the European Union 28, Japan, the Russian Federation, and the United States of America). The authors study the positioning from the perspective of the interest-based explanation and domestic politics, and elucidate the relative power of both explanations and their limitations as applicable to major emitters. It remains important to evoke the nature of the interplay between domestic and international spheres. Major international agreements are not possible without some domestic acceptance.

1.7   Role of Nonstate Actors and Business

The role of nonstate actors is emphasized by Tora Skodvin in chapter 8. Their importance is not so much due to their weight at the international level. However, "if nonstate actors can influence parties at the domestic decision-making level that are pivotal in terms of forming a winning (or blocking) coalition in support of (or against) a particular policy, they may in fact have a significant impact also on the spectrum of politically feasible policy options at the international level." The role of nonstate actors may have even enhanced through the 2015 Paris Agreement. As a result of the bottom-up approach (NDCs) and the lack of enforcement mechanisms in the agreement, nonstate actors are crucial to hold governments accountable to their commitments.

In addition to the general question of the influence of nonstate actors, the special case of business and industrial interests and their leverage has to be evoked in this context. Matthew Paterson undertakes this in chapter 9. The author, taking a close look at the articulation of business interests, insists that these interests may be divergent as some might actually lobby in favor of climate change mitigation while others do the opposite. These divergent points of view might be explained by the various characteristics of the political economies of the countries in which they are imbedded. However, businesses are always seeking to develop new opportunities for their activities, and decarbonization might just present a novel one as compared with those of fossil fuels. Nevertheless the latter might prevail in the short run and help explain the current lull in establishing further reduction obligations.

Paterson underlines such business interests in conjunction with internal forces. As some domestic interests benefit either morally or materially from an international cooperative structure, they have an incentive not only to promote it but also to check that it is indeed implemented by state authorities. Domestic constituencies can thus play a major role in both initiating and then implementing an international environmental accord, a point made and explained by Dai (2007).

1.8   The Case of Developing and Emerging Countries

While the sharp differentiation between developed and developing countries subsided with the advent of the Paris Agreement, it remains important to focus on the situation of developing and emerging countries. The idea was that they have historically contributed much less to climate change than industrialized countries and should therefore only contribute marginally to mitigation (as within the framework of the clean development mechanism [CDM]). The special role of these countries is analyzed by Katharina and Axel Michaelowa in chapter 10. They point out that the differences between developing countries might sometimes be just as important as the difference between developing and developed countries. Moreover, they stress the ambiguity of the term *developing country* and the fact that it is hard to circumscribe it precisely. Equity questions concerning historical responsibilities for climate change might be as strong within as opposed to between countries. Finally, despite the vocal opposition of some developing or more precisely emerging countries to accept international obligations to diminish emissions of greenhouse gases, internally they are often inclined (e.g., China and India) to adopt climate change mitigation policies within their borders.

1.9 Implementing and Monitoring Climate Change Agreements

To set up an effective monitoring regime is difficult, as the controversies over the control of the financial system, both national and international, have demonstrated. Therefore, chapter 11 deals with the problems linked to implementation, compliance, and effectiveness of policies and institutions. Jon Hovi and Arild Underdal undertake a thorough analysis of this question within the context of climate change. The two authors detect major flaws in the design of the Kyoto Protocol with respect to compliance and effectiveness, which may account for its relative failure. They discuss the trilemma of "broad participation, deep commitments, *and* high compliance rates," a difficult task as they recognize themselves under the present circumstances. Whether the Paris Agreement comes close to this deal is discussed by the authors.

Chapter 12, by Detlef F. Sprinz, reviews the contributions of this book against the background of the announcement by President Trump on June 1, 2017, to leave the Paris Agreement or to renegotiate its contents. Subsequently, the Paris Agreement's main provisions are analyzed, and its architecture embedded in a "Sandwich Solution," which combines top-down with bottom-up components. The actors covered in this book are drawn together, as well as select aspects of international relations theories and the concepts used throughout this book. The chapter concludes by demonstrating the prospects of climate mitigation clubs and the tri-part challenge of time inconsistency, domestic fragmentation, and international anarchy.

The challenges presented to us by the current situation are multiple: How will negotiations to bolster the Paris Agreement progress now that the United States seems to have resumed its stance of obstruction? What will keep countries from shirking from self-imposed obligations? How can technological evolutions such as carbon negative procedures be agreed on and implemented? How can local and regional initiatives contribute to climate change control in the future? These questions concern developing as well as industrialized countries and are therefore at the core of the main questions addressed by our authors in this volume.

This brief review of the main issues surrounding the international climate change debate shows in some ways that answers to the dilemma posed in this introductory chapter are possible. In other words, organizing cooperation between states when costs are immediate and high, while benefits are uncertain and distant in time, is conceivable. However, it is an incredibly difficult task and it seems that the present institutional and political configuration is far from adequate in leading us toward such a goal. The current architecture of the international climate change regime might be able to solve some compensation questions, which are connected to helping some poorer countries to adapt to climate change.[7] To deal with the main problem of long-term mitigation seems, at least for the moment, an elusive goal.

Notes

The author is grateful to Jorge Viñuales for his help on disentangling some legal issues related to the Paris Agreement of 2015.

1. See the contribution by Sprinz in chapter 12.

2. The elaboration of a major international convention based on scientific observations is often followed by drafting subsequent protocols with additional obligations. In 1992 the scientific evidence about the reality of climate change and its dire consequences was far less established than in 1997. This evidence has become even sharper since as tangible consequences of global warming have appeared.

3. Fossil fuels have often significant side effects on public health either in their use or in their extraction processes. This is particularly true for coal burning but also

for so-called fracking of shale oil and gas. Limiting the use of fossil fuels for energy production also diminishes the negative side effects they generate.

4. For more details about this, see chapter 2 in this volume.

5. Too many reduction certificates were made available to firms that, combined with lower prices for fossil fuels, reduced the price of the ton of carbon to such low levels that it was not worth acquiring certificates for trading.

6. The Paris Agreement was engineered not to require the advice and consent of the US Senate for its ratification. This is manifest in a number of features. First, it is an "agreement," like other executive agreements that can be ratified by the president, rather than a protocol or a "treaty" that would require the Senate's advice and consent. Second, the entire system can be seen as organizing existing binding obligations that do not arise from the Paris Agreement itself but only from the UNFCCC or from sectorial US legislation. Third, the compliance committee envisioned in Article 15 has no "enforcement" dimension, hence reaffirming the lack of binding commitments arising from the Paris Agreement. For further information on the negotiation strategy followed by the US delegation to engineer the Agreement, see Wirth (2016).

7. The Green Climate Fund has been set up for that purpose. However, here also, US obstruction might make its working much more difficult than anticipated.

References

Boden, T. A., G. Marland, and R. J. Andres. 2017. *Global, Regional, and National Fossil-Fuel CO$_2$ Emissions*. Oak Ridge, TN: Carbon Dioxide Information Analysis Center, Oak Ridge National Laboratory, US Department of Energy.

Bueno de Mesquita, Bruce. 2009. *The Predictioneer's Game: Using the Logic of Brazen Self-Interest to See and Shape the Future*. New York: Random House.

Dai, Xinyuan. 2007. *International Institutions and National Policies*. Cambridge: Cambridge University Press.

Haas, Peter. 1992. "Introduction: Epistemic Communities and International Policy Coordination." *International Organization* 46 (1): 1–35.

———. 2004. "When Does Power Listen to Truth? A Constructivist Approach to the Policy Process." *Journal of European Public Policy* 11 (4): 569–592.

Waltz, Kenneth N. 2000. "Structural: Realism after the Cold War." *International Security* 25 (1): 5–41.

Wirth, David A. 2016. "Cracking the American Climate Negotiators' Hidden Code: United States Law and the Paris Agreement." *Climate Law* 6 (1): 152–170.

2 The Evolution and Governance Architecture of the United Nations Climate Change Regime

Daniel Bodansky and Lavanya Rajamani

2.1 Introduction

Although the general theory of greenhouse warming has been understood by scientists since the end of the nineteenth century, an international legal regime to address the problem of climate change began to develop only in the late 1980s.[1] In the nearly three decades since then, the regime has undergone a remarkable evolution. In 1992 states adopted the United Nations Framework Convention on Climate Change (UNFCCC), which took effect in 1994 and serves as the "constitution" for the international climate change regime. In 1997 the UNFCCC was supplemented by the Kyoto Protocol, which requires industrialized countries to reduce their emissions of carbon dioxide (CO_2) and five other gases that contribute to the greenhouse effect (greenhouse gases or GHG emissions). The 2001 Marrakesh Accords elaborated the Kyoto Protocol's regulatory regime, setting forth detailed rules regarding its operation.[2] After the Marrakesh Accords were negotiated, states turned their attention to addressing the post-2012 period, when the emission targets for the Kyoto Protocol's first commitment period were scheduled to end. The parties to the UNFCCC agreed in late 2007 to begin a round of negotiations pursuant to the Bali Action Plan, which led to the 2009 Copenhagen Accord and the 2010 Cancun Agreements. Meanwhile, the Kyoto Protocol parties negotiated an amendment establishing a second commitment period that extends the Kyoto Protocol emission targets through 2020. A new round of negotiations was launched in 2011 pursuant to the Durban Platform to develop a post-2020 climate regime. In 2015 the UNFCCC parties reached the historic Paris Agreement, an instrument that represents a step change in multilateral efforts to address climate change.

Several general features of the climate change regime are noteworthy. First, the regime has aimed, thus far, at the widest participation possible, because of the global nature of the greenhouse effect and the recognition that human-induced (anthropogenic) climate change is the "common concern of humankind" (UNFCCC 1992, preamble, para. 1). In the 2000s this aim was undermined by the withdrawal of the United States and Canada from the Kyoto Protocol, limited participation of developed countries in the second commitment period of the Kyoto Protocol, and the reluctance of developing countries to accept quantified limitations on their GHG emissions. The difficulty of agreeing on a universal approach can be traced to a number of factors, including differences in national circumstances and interests, domestic politics, and fundamental disagreements between developed and developing states over how the burden of climate mitigation should be shared. On the one hand, many developing countries argue that developed countries should bear the burden of dealing with climate change, since they account for the majority of cumulative CO_2 emissions.[3] In per capita terms, even today GHG emissions from developed countries are 2.5 times those from developing countries (IPCC 2014, 113). On the other hand, developed countries argue that developing countries cannot be exempt from taking action, since total emissions from developing countries have overtaken those from industrialized countries, and emissions from large developing countries are projected to continue to rise sharply (EIA 2013, 159–165). In 2005 China surpassed the United States as the world's largest emitter of CO_2.[4] Given these disagreements, the virtually universal international support for the 2015 Paris Agreement is remarkable.

Second, the climate change regime exemplifies the "framework convention/protocol" approach to international environmental law. As its title indicates, the UNFCCC established the basic framework for the climate change regime. The 1997 Kyoto Protocol then built on that framework by specifying obligations and mechanisms to control the GHG emissions of industrialized countries. The Paris Agreement created another framework, building on the UNFCCC, but with a different approach from that of the Kyoto Protocol.

Third, the climate change regime has an exceptionally broad scope, encompassing not simply environmental protection as traditionally conceived (that is, limiting emissions of pollutants), but economic and development policies more generally. Virtually the entire range of human activities contributes to GHG emissions. GHG emissions are inextricably linked to development aspirations, for instance. Indeed, the United Nations Development Programme (UNDP) has characterized climate change as the "the defining human development challenge for the 21st century" (UNDP 2008).

Fourth, the climate change regime is largely neutral regarding policy options. Climate change is primarily a problem of CO_2, which accounts for about 75 percent of current emissions (IPCC 2014); fossil fuels, which account for 57 percent of GHG emissions (Stern 2006); and ultimately coal, which represents more than three-quarters of the carbon in estimated fossil fuel reservoirs (IPCC 2001). While the climate change regime may place GHG-intensive sectors at a disadvantage, the UNFCCC, Kyoto Protocol, and Paris Agreement do not single out any particular greenhouse gas, economic sector, or technology for special attention. While attention has focused thus far on mitigation—an emphasis reflected in the Kyoto Protocol—the UNFCCC and the Paris Agreement address adaptation as well. As a result, states have significant flexibility in designing strategies to respond to climate change.

This chapter provides an introduction to the United Nations climate change regime. Section 2 reviews the development of the regime, from the emergence of the climate change issue in the 1980s through the adoption of the 1997 Kyoto Protocol, the 2001 Marrakech Accords, the 2007 Bali Action Plan, the 2009 Copenhagen Accord, the 2010 Cancun Agreements, the 2011 Durban Platform, and finally the 2015 Paris Agreement. Section 3 outlines the principal elements of the regime, and section 4 concludes with some brief observations about its future direction.

2.2   The Evolution of the Global Climate Change Regime

The development of the climate change regime in the late 1980s and 1990s rode a wave of environmental activity that began in 1987 with the discovery of the "ozone hole" and the publication of the Brundtland Commission report, *Our Common Future* (Brundtland 1987), and crested at the 1992 UN Conference on Environment and Development (UNCED) in Rio de Janeiro. This wave of environmental activity in the 1980s concerned longer-term, irreversible, global threats, such as the depletion of the stratospheric ozone layer, loss of biological diversity, and greenhouse warming, and focused not merely on environmental protection per se, but on the more general economic and social policies needed to achieve sustainable development (Clark 1989, 47).

The development of the climate change regime can usefully be divided into six periods: the *foundational phase*, during which scientific concern about global warming developed; the *agenda-setting phase*, from 1985 to 1988, when climate change was transformed from a scientific into a policy issue; a *prenegotiation period* from 1988 to 1990, when governments became heavily involved in the process; the *constitutional period* from 1991 to 1995, leading to the adoption and entry into force of the UNFCCC; a *regulatory phase*, focusing on the negotiation, elaboration, and implementation of the Kyoto Protocol from 1995 to 2007; and a *second constitutional phase* from 2001 to the present, building up to the adoption of the Paris Agreement and continuing now with the ongoing process of elaborating it. Table 2.1 provides a brief overview of the milestones in the evolution of the climate change regime.

2.2.1   Foundational Phase: The Emergence of Scientific Concern

Although the greenhouse warming theory was put forward more than a century ago by the Swedish chemist Svante Arrhenius (1896), climate change did not emerge as a *political* issue until the late 1980s. The issue was raised and discussed in the UN General Assembly in 1988 and international meetings such as the 1988 Toronto Conference, the 1989 Hague and Noordwijk Conferences, and the 1990 Second World Climate Conference that attracted numerous ministers and even some heads of government (Bodansky 1994).

The development of the climate change issue initially took place in the scientific arena, as understanding of the climate change problem improved. The so-called Keeling curve, which shows the rise of atmospheric concentrations of CO_2, is one of the few undisputed facts in the climate change controversy and led to the initial growth of scientific concern in the late 1960s and early 1970s (Keeling 1960). During the 1970s and 1980s, improvements in computing power allowed scientists to develop much more sophisticated computer models of the atmosphere, which, while still subject to considerable uncertainty, led to increased confidence in global warming predictions. Moreover, in the mid-1980s, scientists recognized that emissions by humans of other trace gases such as methane and nitrous oxide also contribute to the greenhouse effect, rendering the problem more serious than previously believed. Finally, careful reassessments of the historical temperature record in the 1980s indicated that global average temperature had indeed been increasing since the middle of the twentieth century.

2.2.2 Agenda-Setting Phase, 1985–1988

Although the growth of scientific knowledge was significant in laying a foundation for the development of public and political interest, two additional factors acted as the direct catalysts for governmental action. First, a small group of Western scientists worked to promote the climate change issue on the international agenda. These scientists acted as "knowledge-brokers" and entrepreneurs, helping to translate and publicize the emerging scientific knowledge about the greenhouse effect through workshops and conferences, articles in nonspecialist journals, and personal contacts with policy makers. The 1985 and 1987 Villach meetings, the establishment of the Advisory Group on Greenhouse Gases under the joint auspices of World Meteorological Organization (WMO) and the United Nations Environment Program (UNEP), the report of the Enquete Commission in Germany, the testimony of climate modelers before US Congressional committees—all these developments helped familiarize policy makers with climate change and convert it from a speculative theory into a real-world possibility.

Second, as noted above, the latter half of the 1980s was a period of increased concern about global environmental issues generally. The discovery of the so-called Antarctic ozone hole, followed by the confirmation that it resulted from emissions of chlorofluorocarbons (CFCs), demonstrated that human activities can affect the global atmosphere and raised the prominence of atmospheric issues. Initially, public concern about global warming rode on the coat tails of the ozone issue.

A conference organized by the Canadian government in June 1988 called for global emissions of CO_2 to be reduced by 20 percent by the year 2005; the development of a global framework convention to protect the atmosphere; and establishment of a world atmosphere fund financed in part by a tax on fossil fuels (WMO 1989).

2.2.3 Prenegotiation Phase: Early International Responses, 1988–1990

1988 marked a watershed, with the emergence of the climate change regime as an intergovernmental issue. During the agenda-setting stage, the climate change issue had been dominated essentially by nongovernmental actors—primarily environmentally oriented scientists. Their actions were influential in communicating an ostensible scientific consensus about climate change and articulating a set of initial policy responses—but these were *non*governmental rather than *inter*governmental in character.

The period from 1988 to 1990 was transitional. Governments began to play a greater role, but non-governmental actors still exerted considerable influence. The Intergovernmental Panel on Climate Change (IPCC) reflected this ambivalence. Established by WMO and UNEP in 1988 at the instigation of governments, in part as a means of reasserting governmental control over the issue, the IPCC's most influential outputs have been their scientific assessment of global warming—products more of the international scientific community than of governments.

Among the landmarks of the pre-negotiation phase of the climate change issue were the following:

• The 1988 General Assembly resolution on climate change, characterizing the climate as the "common concern of mankind" (UN General Assembly 1988)

• The 1989 Hague Summit, attended by seventeen heads of state, which called for the development of a "new institutional authority" to preserve the earth's atmosphere and combat global warming (Hague Declaration on the Environment 1989)

• The 1989 Noordwijk ministerial meeting, the first high-level intergovernmental meeting focusing specifically on the climate change issue (Vellinga, Kendall, and Gupta 1989)

• The November 1990 Second World Climate Conference (SWCC), a major political event, held at the ministerial level (Jäger and Ferguson 1991)

By the end of 1990 three basic dynamics in the climate change negotiations, virtually unchanged today, had begun to emerge:

• First, a division among industrialized countries between supporters and opponents of binding, quantitative limits on greenhouse gas emissions

• Second, a division between industrialized and developing countries over their respective responsibilities for addressing climate change

• Finally, a division among developing countries between those concerned more about climate change and those concerned more about development and poverty eradication

Table 2.1

Milestones in the climate regime.

1988	*Toronto Conference* calls for a 20% cut in global CO_2 by 2005, and for a comprehensive framework convention on the law of the atmosphere.
1988	*UN General Assembly* characterizes climate change as a "common concern of mankind."
1989	*Hague Summit* calls for new institutional authority to combat global warming, involving nonunanimous decision making.
1990	*IPCC* issues first assessment report, estimating that global mean temperature likely to increase by about 0.3°C per decade, under business-as-usual emissions scenario.
1990	*Second World Climate Conference* concludes that countries need to stabilize GHG emissions and that developed countries should establish emissions targets and/or national programs or strategies.
1990	*UN General Assembly* establishes the INC to negotiate a climate change convention.
1992	INC adopts UNFCCC, which is opened for signature at Rio Summit.
1994	UNFCCC enters into force.
1995	COP 1 adopts Berlin Mandate authorizing negotiations to strengthen UNFCCC commitments.
1997	COP 3 adopts Kyoto Protocol, establishing quantitative limits on greenhouse gas emissions by industrialized countries.
2001	COP 7 adopts Marrakesh Accords, spelling out the detailed rules for the Kyoto Protocol.
2004	Kyoto Protocol enters into force.
2005	CMP 1 launches negotiations toward a second commitment period for Kyoto.
2007	COP 13 adopts the Bali Action Plan, initiating a new round of negotiations under the UNFCCC.
2009	COP 15 takes note of the Copenhagen Accord, establishing a new architecture, based on voluntary mitigation pledges and transparency.
2010	COP 16 adopts the Cancun Agreements, incorporating elements of the Copenhagen Accord into the UNFCCC process.
2011	COP 17 adopts the Durban Platform, launching negotiation toward a post-2020 agreement, with a scheduled end in 2015.
2012	CMP 8 extends the Kyoto Protocol for a second commitment period.
2013	COP 19 invites parties to prepare and submit "intended nationally determined contributions" in 2015.
2014	COP 20, Lima Call to Climate Action, sets the stage for the 2015 agreement, assuring parties balanced treatment across all elements of the Durban Platform.
2015	COP 21 adopts the Paris Agreement, setting forth a hybrid architecture for addressing climate change from 2020 onward, combining bottom-up nationally determined contributions to promote participation and top-down rules to promote transparency and ambition.

The division among industrialized countries was the first dynamic to emerge. At the 1989 Noordwijk meeting, the divergence became apparent. Most European countries supported adopting the approach that had been used to address the acid rain and stratosphere ozone depletion problems, namely, establishing quantitative limitations on national emissions of greenhouse gases ("targets and timetables"). The United States—supported at Noordwijk by Japan and the Soviet Union—challenged this approach, on the grounds that targets and timetables were too rigid, did not take account of differing national circumstances, and would be largely symbolic. Instead, the United States argued that emphasis should be placed on further scientific research and on developing national rather than international strategies and programs.

The Second World Climate Conference in 1990 saw the emergence of a second fault line in the climate change negotiations: the divide between developed and developing countries.[5] Earlier that year, at the London Ozone Conference, developing countries had successfully pressed for the establishment of a special fund to help them implement the Montreal Protocol on Substances that Deplete the Ozone Layer, and, in the UN General Assembly, had insisted that the environmental conference scheduled to be held in Rio de Janeiro in 1992 give equal weight to environment and development. In the climate change context, they sought greater representation and argued for climate change to be viewed as a development issue as well. For both reasons, they sought to move the negotiations from the comparatively technical, narrow confines of the IPCC to the UN General Assembly. Their efforts proved successful, and the December 1990 resolution authorizing the initiation of negotiations placed the negotiations under the auspices of the General Assembly (UN General Assembly 1990).

As early as 1990, however, the division among developing countries had also become apparent. Developing countries agreed on the need for financial assistance and technology transfer, but on little else. At one extreme, the small island countries, fearing inundation from sea level rise, supported strong commitments to limit emissions. At the Second World Climate Conference, they organized themselves into the Alliance of Small Island States (AOSIS), which played a major role in the subsequent UNFCCC negotiations in pushing for CO_2 emissions reductions. At the other pole, the oil-producing countries questioned the science of climate change and argued for a "go slow" approach. In the middle, the large developing countries such as Brazil, China, and India insisted that measures to combat climate change not infringe on their sovereignty, in particular, their right to develop economically. They argued that developed countries were historically responsible for creating the climate change problem and should therefore be responsible for solving it.

2.2.4 Constitutional Phase: Negotiation and Entry into Force of the UNFCCC

Although international environmental law underwent impressive growth in the 1970s and 1980s, when the climate change issue emerged in the late 1980s, international environmental law had little to contribute (Zelke and Cameron 1990). The existing air pollution conventions addressed transboundary air pollution in Europe (Convention on Long-Range Transboundary Air Pollution 1979) and depletion of the stratospheric ozone layer (UNEP 1985, 1987). While customary international law articulates general principles relevant to atmospheric pollution (see, e.g., UN Conference on the Human Environment 1972, principle 21), these principles do not have the specificity and certainty needed to address the climate change problem effectively (Magraw 1990). Therefore, it became evident that a new treaty would need to be negotiated. The process began in December 1990, when the UN General Assembly established the Intergovernmental Negotiating Committee (INC) for a United Nations Framework Convention on Climate Change (UNFCCC), with the mandate to negotiate a convention containing "appropriate commitments," in time for signature in June 1992 at UNCED (UN General Assembly 1990). Between February 1991 and May 1992, the INC held five sessions. It adopted the UNFCCC on May 9, 1992, shortly before UNCED, and the Convention entered into force less than two years later on March 21, 1994, as a result of its ratification by fifty countries.

The initial baseline for the UNFCCC negotiations was the "framework agreement" model. Framework conventions are largely procedural in nature. Their main purpose is to establish a legal and institutional framework for future work through regular meetings of the parties and the possible adoption of more substantive protocols (Bodansky 1999).

Most countries agreed that the UNFCCC should include, at a minimum, the basic elements of a framework convention. The main question was whether to include additional provisions. As a whole, the UNFCCC reflects the US preference for what might be called a "framework convention plus." It does not contain legally binding emission targets, as the EU and AOSIS advocated. But it extends beyond previous framework conventions by establishing a financial mechanism and comparatively strong implementation machinery, including detailed reporting requirements and international review.

However, the provisions of the UNFCCC did not resolve differences so much as paper them over, either through formulations that preserved the positions of all sides (see, e.g., UNFCCC 1992, art. 11), that were deliberately ambiguous (see, e.g., UNFCCC 1992, art. 4.2), or that deferred issues until later (see, e.g., UNFCCC 1992, art. 13). The Convention, therefore, represented not an end point but rather a punctuation mark in an ongoing process of negotiation that continues to this day.

2.2.5 Regulatory Phase: Negotiation and Elaboration of the Kyoto Protocol

The UNFCCC entered into force on March 21, 1994, less than two years after its adoption. Most countries agreed, however, that its commitments were inadequate and needed to be supplemented by more specific emissions limitation objectives. In 1995 the first Conference of the Parties (COP 1) adopted the "Berlin Mandate," which established the Ad Hoc Group on the Berlin Mandate (AGBM) charged with negotiating a new agreement that would specify additional commitments for industrialized countries for the post-2000 period, but would contain "no new commitments for developing countries."

The negotiations concluded with the adoption of the Kyoto Protocol in December 1997. Following the pattern of the UNFCCC negotiations, little progress was made initially, as some countries questioned the need for legally binding emission targets. Until the end, negotiations remained deadlocked over three issues: first, the emissions limitation targets for developed countries; second, the inclusion of "flexibility mechanisms," such as emissions trading, to allow countries to meet their targets in a cost-effective manner; and third, the inclusion of emissions limitation objectives for developing countries. With regard to the first issue, the EU initially proposed a 15 percent and then a 10 percent cut in GHG emissions below 1990 levels by the year 2010, while other industrialized countries such as the United States and Australia proposed much weaker targets, with Japan in the middle.

The debate about flexibility was similarly divisive. The United States sought mechanisms to allow developed countries to achieve their emissions targets in the most flexible, cost-effective manner possible, through mechanisms that would, among other things, allow countries to receive credit for emissions reductions in other countries as well as for forest and agricultural activities ("sink activities") that remove CO_2 from the atmosphere. The EU (generally supported by developing countries) wanted to limit these flexibility mechanisms to ensure that industrialized countries met their emissions targets primarily through emissions reductions at home. Finally, on the third issue, the United States pressed for the inclusion of a mechanism to allow developing countries to "voluntarily" assume emissions limitation objectives. Most developing countries strongly opposed this approach.

In essence, the Kyoto Protocol was the product of mutual concessions—the United States conceded on the stringency of the emission targets, the EU conceded on the flexibility mechanisms, and developing countries were exempted from mitigation targets. The United States accepted a much stronger target (minus 7 percent from 1990 levels) than it had wanted, but succeeded in incorporating significant flexibility into the Protocol. Most important, the Protocol provided for the development of an international emissions trading system; created the Clean Development Mechanism (CDM), by which industrialized countries can receive credit for emission reduction projects in developing countries; and allowed for the possibility of credits for certain sink activities. The Protocol also permitted countries to undertake mitigation commitments jointly, thereby allowing the EU the internal flexibility it had sought in fulfilling its commitments. Developing countries, however, successfully resisted strong pressure from the United States to establish a process by which they could assume quantitative emissions limitation goals. In essence, the Protocol reflected US architecture, EU targets, and developing country scope.[6]

While a tremendous achievement, the Kyoto Protocol deferred most of the detailed issues about how it would work to future negotiations, allowing states to attempt to renegotiate the Protocol in the context of elaborating its rules. The EU, for example, attempted to place quantitative limits ("concrete ceilings") on the extent to which developed countries could meet their targets through emissions trading, while the United States sought to weaken its own emission target through the inclusion of expansive credits for sink activities, as well as to persuade at least some developing countries to accept emissions targets of their own. The scope of these negotiations was agreed upon at COP 4 in the "Buenos Aires Plan of Action." Initially, the negotiations were scheduled to conclude in November 2000 at COP 6 in The Hague, but negotiations broke down at the eleventh hour, principally over the issue of credits for sink activities, and parties agreed to reconvene the following summer. The rejection of the Kyoto Protocol by the newly elected Bush administration in March 2001 led many to predict the Protocol's demise. But, the peremptory nature of the Bush administration's action galvanized other parties into action—in particular, the EU—and led them to make the necessary compromises for adoption in November 2001 of the Marrakesh Accords (UNFCCC 2002a, 2002b).[7] These Accords set forth detailed rules fleshing out the Kyoto Protocol's skeletal provisions. Ironically, the Marrakesh Accords largely reflected the US positions during these negotiations. In particular, they did not impose any quantitative limits on the use of the flexibility mechanisms, and they allowed significant credits for sink activities. As a result of Russia's ratification, the Protocol entered into force on February 16, 2005.

2.2.6   The Second Constitutional Phase: The Copenhagen Accord, Cancun Agreements, and Paris Agreement

In December 2005, at COP 11, which also served as the first Meeting of Parties to the Kyoto Protocol (CMP 1), discussions commenced on how the climate regime might be structured after 2012, when the Kyoto Protocol's first commitment period was scheduled to end. Although the Kyoto Protocol had entered into force earlier that year, many believed the climate regime to be inadequate in terms of coverage since both the United States and developing countries were not subject to targets and timetables, and in terms of stringency since the Protocol's first commitment period targets were set based on politics not science, and fell short of what science said was needed to prevent dangerous climate change. Two separate processes were therefore initiated: an ad hoc open-ended working group to consider further commitments for developed countries beyond 2012 under the Kyoto Protocol (AWG-KP) and a "Dialogue on Long-Term Cooperative Action" under the UNFCCC. The AWG-KP had no specific deadline, but was supposed to conclude its work "in time to ensure that there [was] no gap between the first and second commitment periods" (UNFCCC 2006, decision 1/CMP.1). The Dialogue, which stressed development and poverty eradication, as well as the role of technology, covered actions by *all* parties, but was neither binding nor authorized to open negotiations leading to new commitments.

In 2007 the Bali Action Plan (UNFCCC 2008, decision 1/CP.13) succeeded the Dialogue by launching a process to reach "an agreed outcome" to advance the climate regime with a scheduled end at COP 15 in 2009 at Copenhagen. The term *an agreed outcome* reflected a lack of agreement on both the legal form that the outcome should take, and the level of ambition that it should reflect. Despite intense negotiations at the highest levels in the two years leading to Copenhagen, COP 15 could not reach an "agreed outcome." A subset of parties to the UNFCCC did, however, arrive at the Copenhagen Accord (UNFCCC 2010, decision 2/CP.15).

The Copenhagen Accord was reached among twenty-eight parties to the UNFCCC, including all major emitters and economies, as well as those representing the most vulnerable and least developed countries. As deliberations remained deadlocked well into the second week of COP 15, the Danish Prime Minister, Lars Løkke Rasmussen, in a bid to salvage the floundering conference, organized a high-level negotiation, in parallel with the official negotiations, to agree on the elements of a political deal. On the final night of the conference, this small negotiating group reached agreement on the Copenhagen Accord. However, when the Accord was presented to the COP for adoption, it was categorically rejected on both procedural and substantive grounds by members of the Bolivarian Alliance for the Peoples of our America (ALBA)—Bolivia, Cuba, Ecuador, Nicaragua, Venezuela—as well as Sudan and Tuvalu. As COP decisions require consensus for adoption, the COP could resolve only to "take[s] note" of the Copenhagen Accord.[8]

The Copenhagen Accord was a political rather than a legal agreement. Nevertheless, it included a number of important substantive elements that significantly shaped the future evolution of the regime. It recognized "the scientific view that the increase in global temperature should be below 2 degree Celsius" (UNFCCC 2010, para. 2) but did not prescribe aggregate or individual emission reduction targets, either mid-term or long-term. Rather, it required Annex I Parties to commit to targets, and developing countries to undertake mitigation actions, which were to be inscribed in its appendices I and II, respectively, as well as compiled in information documents (UNFCCC 2010, paras. 4 and 5). The Accord addressed the related issue of transparency of mitigation actions, of interest to the United States, by significantly increasing the quantity and quality of mitigation-related information flowing through the system. It also created a Green Climate Fund (GCF), incorporated financial promises from the developed to the developing world, and launched a technology mechanism. The Accord, however, having merely been taken note of by the COP, had no formal legal standing in the UNFCCC process. At COP 16 in Cancun, a year later, parties agreed to incorporate the core compromises contained in the Copenhagen Accord into the UNFCCC process. In so doing, the Cancun Agreements fleshed out the cryptic outline of the Copenhagen Accord and ironed out the creases that are an inevitable part of any last-minute deal negotiated by heads of states.[9]

At COP 17 in Durban in 2011, parties operationalized many of the promises of the Copenhagen Accord and Cancun Agreements, and also launched a new process, the Ad Hoc Working Group on the Durban Platform (ADP) to negotiate a post-2020 climate agreement, which could take the form of "a Protocol, another legal instrument or agreed outcome with legal force under the Convention applicable to all" (UNFCCC 2012, decision 1/CP.17). This instrument was to be adopted in 2015 and implemented from 2020. It is significant that it was deemed necessary to launch a new process. The Bali Action Plan, 2007, which launched a process to reach an "agreed outcome" on long-term cooperative action on climate change could have offered the basis for a new climate regime. The Bali Action Plan, however, was interpreted by developing countries as creating a firewall between developed country commitments and developing country actions. In a bid to move away from the Bali "firewall," the United States, among others, insisted on a new process, and on terminating the Bali process in 2012. Durban delivered the new process and with it a clean slate on differentiation.[10]

In this context it is also significant that there was no reference in the Durban Platform decision to equity or the principle of common but differentiated responsibility and respective capabilities (CBDRRC). Most developed countries believe that economic and political realities have evolved since the UNFCCC was negotiated in 1992, and common but differentiated responsibilities must be interpreted as a dynamic concept that evolves in tandem with changing economic and other realities. Today, some non-Annex I Parties have higher per capita income than the poorest Annex I Party, leading some developed countries to argue that the Annex I / non-Annex I distinction should not be the basis of the climate change regime going forward. Many developing countries, in particular India and China, were not willing to countenance such an interpretation of the CBDRRC principle. As a compromise, the Durban Platform decision did not mention differentiation, but stated that the new instrument would be "under the Convention," thereby implicitly engaging the Convention's principles, including the principle of CBDRRC. Developing countries felt that this reference to the Convention would hold efforts to reinterpret and qualify this principle at bay, or at least leave the issue of "differentiation" to be resolved in the future.

COP 17 also proved momentous for the Kyoto Protocol. After years of uncertainty about the future of the Kyoto Protocol, in Durban, parties finally agreed to extend the Kyoto Protocol for a second commitment period. Although negotiations on a second commitment period had been ongoing since 2005, in the wake of the US rejection of the Kyoto Protocol and the gradual disenchantment of the rest of the developed world with a regime that included neither the United States nor emerging economies, the prospects for a renewal of the Kyoto Protocol appeared dim. The EU, Australia, New Zealand, Norway, and Switzerland, alone among Kyoto Annex B Parties, were willing to accept a second commitment period under the Kyoto Protocol. Their willingness was conditional, however, on the adoption of a road map toward a legally binding agreement applicable to all. Since the Durban Platform delivered such a road map, it was possible then to agree to a Kyoto second commitment period in Durban, which was formally adopted the following year at COP 18 in Doha.

Notwithstanding the adoption of a second commitment period, the future of the Kyoto Protocol beyond the second commitment period remains dim. Canada has withdrawn from the Kyoto Protocol, and Japan and Russia did not take on targets under the second commitment period. Although the text of the decisions emerging from COP 17 and CMP 7 are agnostic about the future of the Kyoto Protocol, the political understanding underlying the Durban deal was that there would be no further commitment periods of the Kyoto Protocol.

Following Durban, the international community engaged in intense negotiations, both in the context of the Durban Platform process and in other complementary plurilateral and multilateral fora, to design an agreement that addresses the climate change issue from 2020 onward. At Warsaw,

2013, a year after Doha, parties began to construct the building blocks of the 2015 climate agreement. Parties were invited to initiate or intensify their preparations for their "intended nationally determined contributions" (INDCs) to be submitted in 2015 (UNFCCC 2014, decision 1/CP.19). The term *contributions* encapsulated many ambiguities. First, it left open the scope of the contributions—that is, whether contributions would be limited to mitigation, as many developed countries preferred, or could also include adaptation, finance, technology transfer or capacity-building contributions, as most developing countries favored. Second, the term *contribution* was explicitly without prejudice to the legal nature of the contributions. It thus left open whether parties' nationally determined contributions would be legally binding.

After protracted negotiations, parties adopted the Paris Agreement on December 12, 2015. The Paris Agreement sets an ambitious direction for the climate regime, and complements this direction with a set of common core obligations for all countries, including legally binding obligations of conduct in relation to parties' NDCs, and an expectation of progression over time. It also establishes a common transparency and accountability framework and an iterative process, in which parties take stock, every five years, of their collective progress and put forward emission reduction contributions for the next five-year period.

The Paris Agreement, moreover, commands universal or near universal acceptance, and is applicable to all. As of October 27, 2016, countries representing roughly 99 percent of global emissions had put forward INDCs.[11] The Paris Agreement represents the culmination of three shifts in the climate change regime in relation to (1) the architecture of the regime, (2) differentiation between developed and developing countries, and (3) the legal character of commitments.

The architecture of the Paris Agreement: The Copenhagen Accord and the Cancun Agreements initiated the climate regime's experiments with the "bottom-up" approach. The commitments and actions required by the Copenhagen Accord were communicated by parties and enshrined in the climate regime through the Cancun Agreements. The Cancun Agreements merely took note of commitments and actions by developed and developing countries, respectively. They neither prescribed the nature, type and stringency of commitments or actions to be taken by countries nor imposed any informational requirements or rules in relation to these commitments and actions. In this regard, the Cancun Agreements adopted a truly bottom-up approach that deferred to national autonomy in arriving at commitments/actions in the face of diverse national circumstances and constraints (Bodansky 2011). It rapidly became evident, however, that such a bottom-up approach has its limits. It led to qualified and conditional pre-2020 GHG mitigation pledges of breathtaking diversity, dubious rigor, and inadequate climate impact, which did not add up to what is required to reach the 2°C global temperature goal. As a result of this experience, the 2015 Paris Agreement sought to discipline or circumscribe the discretion available to countries. The Warsaw decision inviting parties to initiate/intensify domestic preparations for nationally determined contributions firmly posited the bottom-up approach as the starting point (Rajamani 2014). The Lima Call to Climate Action laid out indicative information for parties to provide with their contributions, in order to promote clarity, transparency, and understanding, thus beginning to circumscribe the discretion available to parties. And the Paris Agreement crystallized this emerging hybrid architecture, in which bottom-up substance to promote participation (contained in parties' contributions) is combined with a top-down process to promote ambition and accountability. The bottom-up component of the Paris Agreement's hybrid architecture was nearly complete by the time the Paris conference began. Over the course of 2015, virtually every state submitted an INDC. The Paris Conference focused on the other half of the hybrid equation: the development of strong international rules to promote ambition and accountability. The Paris Agreement did not include a number of important proposals, such as that NDCs be quantified or quantifiable and include an unconditional element, and that proposed NDCs be subject to a formal process of ex ante review to consider their ambition, comparability, and fairness. Nevertheless, the Paris Agreement contains comparatively strong rules on transparency, accounting, and updating. In addition, the Agreement contains internationally determined provisions requiring parties' successive contributions to represent a progression on the last, and also reflect that parties' highest possible ambition. There are also provisions for collective assessment of progress toward the goals of the Agreement (global stocktake) and for a compliance system, the details of which are yet to be worked out (Bodansky, Brunnée, and Rajamani 2017).

Differentiation in the Paris Agreement: The Copenhagen Accord and the Cancun Agreements also initiated the move away from existing models of differentiation, in particular that of the Kyoto Protocol, which contains mitigation targets and timetables for Annex I Parties (usually equated with developed countries), but none for non-Annex I Parties (usually equated with developing countries). The Copenhagen Accord and the Cancun Agreements allowed parties, developed and developing alike, to self-select and list mitigation commitments and actions, effectively substituting a flexible regime of self-differentiation for all countries, in place of the bifurcated approach of the Kyoto Protocol. The Durban platform decision, with its emphasis that the 2015 agreement be "applicable to all," and the Warsaw decision that posited the starting point of the 2015 agreement as "nationally determined contributions" for all, further reinforced this trend, and the Paris Agreement cemented it. It neither creates explicit categories of parties nor tailors commitments to categories of parties as the UNFCCC and the Kyoto Protocol do. Rather, it tailors differentiation to the specificities of each issue area it addresses—mitigation, adaptation, finance, technology, capacity building, and transparency. In effect, this approach has resulted in different forms of differentiation in different issue areas. In the article on mitigation, for instance, the Paris Agreement combines self-differentiation with normative expectations for all countries of "progression" and "highest possible ambition," and for developed countries of leadership. In contrast, in the area of transparency, differentiation is tailored to capacities, by providing flexibility to those developing countries "that need it in the light of their capacities" (Bodansky, Brunnée, and Rajamani 2017).

Legal Form and Character in the Paris Agreement: The Durban Platform decision, in the absence of agreement on the legal form of the outcome, agreed to launch work toward a "protocol, another legal instrument or an agreed outcome with legal force under the Convention applicable to all Parties" (UNFCCC 2012, para. 2). This left the legal form of the 2015 agreement open. Parties chose not to decide the legal form of the 2015 agreement and the legal character of its constituent provisions until the end of the four-year negotiating process. Nevertheless, by the time parties arrived in Paris, there was emerging consensus that the 2015 agreement would take the form of a legally binding instrument. The United States was willing to accept a legally binding instrument, despite significant domestic political constraints, so long as developed and developing countries were equally bound by the agreement. India, despite its historical reluctance to accept a legally binding instrument, had softened its stance. Other developing countries were more concerned with particular provisions of the agreement than its legal form. The softening of positions in relation to legal form can be traced to at least three developments. First, a powerful political momentum had built up over time, due to the efforts of the EU and many vulnerable countries, toward adoption of a legally binding instrument. Second, the reluctance of many countries across the developed-developing country divide to take on internationally negotiated commitments had led to the emergence and gathering traction of the notion of "nationally determined contributions" (NDCs)—an approach that, by privileging sovereign autonomy, respecting national circumstances, and permitting self-differentiation, significantly reduced the sovereignty costs of a legally binding instrument. Third, due to the efforts of the United States and others, there was increasing recognition and acceptance by states of the distinction between the legal form of the instrument (i.e., could be binding) and the legal character of nationally determined contributions (i.e., could be nonbinding) (Bodansky, Brunnée, and Rajamani 2017).

Two key points are worth noting about the Paris Agreement. First, it is a treaty, as defined in the Vienna Convention on the Law of Treaties. It is titled the Paris Agreement rather than the Paris Protocol, in deference to US political sensitivities, and was not explicitly adopted under UNFCCC article 17, which governs the adoption of "Protocols." However, the nomenclature of an instrument is legally irrelevant.

Second, the Paris Agreement is an agreement "under the United Nations Framework Convention on Climate Change." As such, the provisions of the UNFCCC that apply to "related legal instruments" apply to the Paris Agreement, including the UNFCCC's ultimate objective (Bodansky, Brunnée, and Rajamani 2017).

The Paris Agreement contains a range of provisions, some with greater legal force and authority than others. The legal character of a provision depends on a range of factors including—location (where the provision occurs), subjects (whom the provision addresses), normative content (what requirements, obligations or standards the provision contains), language (whether the provision uses mandatory, hortatory, or advisory language), precision (whether the provision uses contextual, qualifying or discretionary clauses), and what institutional mechanisms exist for transparency, accountability and compliance. Taking these factors into account, the Paris Agreement contains provisions that span the spectrum of legal character, including some hard law provisions in relation to mitigation and transparency and soft law provisions in relation to adaptation (Bodansky, Brunnée, and Rajamani 2017).

2.3   Principal Elements of the International Climate Change Regime

Legal scholarship on the climate change problem reflects two contrasting approaches to international law—what might be called a "hard" and a "soft" approach. The hard approach views international law as a command backed by the threat of sanctions, while the soft approach views international law in facilitative terms, as a means of fostering greater cooperation among countries. At the risk of oversimplification, the UNFCCC reflects a soft approach to the climate change problem, the Kyoto Protocol reflects a much harder approach, and the Paris Agreement reflects a mixed approach with hard and soft elements.

The UNFCCC does not impose strong substantive commitments on countries, rather it puts in place a long-term, evolutionary process to address the climate change problem. Table 2.2 provides a snapshopt of its key provisions and table 2.3 lists Annex I Parties. In brief, the UNFCCC:

1. Enunciates the regime's ultimate objective and guiding principles
2. Establishes an infrastructure of institutions and decision-making mechanisms
3. Promotes the systematic collection and review of data
4. Encourages national action

By contrast, the Kyoto Protocol represents a much harder, more prescriptive approach, including legally binding, quantified emissions limitation targets (Bodansky 2011). Table 2.4 provides a snapshot of the key provisions of the Kyoto Protocol, and table 2.5 lists Annex B Parties. Its provisions include:

1. Specific emissions targets for each developed country party, which are legally binding, economy-wide, and absolute. The first commitment period addressed emissions from 2008 to 2012, and aimed at reducing overall developed country emissions by 5 percent from 1990 levels. The second commitment period addresses emissions from 2013 to 2020.
2. Mechanisms to allow countries to achieve these targets in a flexible manner, including international emissions trading, the CDM, Joint Implementation (JI), and the joint fulfillment of commitments ("bubbles").

Table 2.2
Key provisions of the UNFCCC.

Objective	Stabilize atmospheric greenhouse gas concentrations at a level that would prevent dangerous anthropogenic interference with the climate system, within a time frame sufficient to: (a) allow ecosystems to adapt naturally, (b) protect food production, and (c) allow sustainable economic development (art. 2).
Principles	Intra- and intergenerational equity; common but differentiated responsibilities and respective capabilities; special needs of developing country parties; right to sustainable development; precaution; cost-effectiveness; comprehensiveness; and a supportive and open economic system (art. 3).
Commitments	*All countries*—General commitments to: develop national GHG inventories; formulate national mitigation and adaptation programs; promote and cooperate in scientific research, education, training and public awareness (arts. 4.1, 5, 6).
	Developed countries (listed in Annex I)—Nonbinding aim to return emissions to 1990 levels by end of the decade (art. 4.2).
	OECD countries (listed in Annex II)—Commitments to fully fund developing country inventories and reports; to fund the incremental costs of agreed mitigation measures; to provide assistance for adaptation; and to facilitate, promote and finance technology transfer (arts. 4.3–5).
Bodies	Conference of the Parties (art. 7), secretariat (art. 8), Subsidiary Body for Scientific and Technological Advice (SBSTA) (art. 9), Subsidiary Body for Implementation (SBI) (art. 10), financial mechanism (art. 11).
Reporting ("communication of information")	*All countries*—National GHG inventories; steps taken to implement the Convention (art. 12.1).
	Developed countries (Annex I)—Detailed description of policies and measures to limit GHG emissions and enhance sinks, and a specific estimate of their effects on emissions (art. 12.2).
	OECD countries (Annex II)—Details of financial and technological assistance measures (art. 12.3).

Table 2.3
List of UNFCCC Annex-I Parties.

Australia	Greece	Poland
Austria	Hungary	Portugal
Belarus	Iceland	Romania
Belgium	Ireland	Russian
Bulgaria	Italy	Federation
Canada	Japan	Slovakia
Croatia	Latvia	Slovenia
Cyprus	Liechtenstein	Spain
Czech Republic	Lithuania	Sweden
Denmark	Luxembourg	Switzerland
Estonia	Malta	Turkey
European Union	Monaco	Ukraine
Finland	Netherlands	United Kingdom of Great
France	New Zealand	Britain and Northern Ireland
Germany	Norway	United States of America

3. Strong reporting, review, and compliance mechanisms, including requiring states to establish national systems for the estimation of anthropogenic emissions, submit annual inventories, and subject these to the scrutiny of expert review teams.

The Paris Agreement reflects a mix of hard and soft or prescriptive and facilitative approaches. Table 2.6 provides a snapshot of the key provisions of the Paris Agreement.

2.3.1 Basic Goals and Principles

The UNFCCC defines the regime's ultimate objective as the stabilization of atmospheric concentrations of greenhouse gases at safe levels (i.e., levels that would "prevent dangerous anthropogenic interference with the climate system") (UNFCCC 1992, art. 2). Stabilization should be achieved within a time frame that allows ecosystems to adapt naturally; ensures that food production is not threatened; and enables sustainable economic development (UNFCCC 1992, art. 2).

Three features of this objective are noteworthy. First, it focuses on atmospheric *concentrations* of GHG emissions rather than *emissions*, thereby emphasizing a buildup of emissions rather than current emissions alone. Second, it addresses not only concentration *levels* but also *rates of change*.

Table 2.4
Key provisions of the Kyoto Protocol.

Aim	Reduce Annex I country emissions by 5% from 1990 levels during the 2008–2012 commitment period (art. 3.1).
Commitments	Specific emissions target for each country listed in Kyoto Protocol Annex B for the 2008–2012 commitment period, generally defined relative to 1990 emissions.
	Applies to CO_2-equivalent emissions of basket of six GHG emissions (CO_2, methane, nitrous oxide, HFCs, PFCs and SF_6).
Institutions	Same as UNFCCC, except decision making by Meeting of the Parties, which meets as part of UNFCCC Conference of the Parties (art. 13).
Flexibility Mechanisms	*Bubbles* (art. 4)—Any group of Annex I Parties may, when ratifying, agree to pool their assigned amounts and fulfill their emissions commitments jointly.
	Joint implementation (art. 6)—Annex I Parties may earn emission reduction units (ERUs) for investments in mitigation projects in other Annex I Parties. ERUs are supplemental to domestic action.
	Clean Development Mechanism (CDM) (art. 12)—Annex I Parties may earn certified emission reductions (CERs) for emission reduction projects in non-Annex I Parties.
	Emissions Trading (art. 17) Annex B countries may engage in emissions trading supplemental to domestic action.
Transparency	Extensive target-related reporting requirements for Annex I parties, combined with expert review.
Compliance	COP/MOP to consider the question of compliance. Legally-binding consequences for noncompliance would require amendment of Kyoto Protocol (art. 18).

Thus far, states have not been able to agree on what concentration levels and rates of change the climate change regime should aim for. Although science can provide guidance on these questions, in the final analysis they involve value choices and will require political answers. Third, the reference to sustainable economic development requires that as states make the political choice of an objective, attention be paid to the impact this could have on sustainable development (Bodansky 1993).

States began to provide greater specificity to the objective in the Cancun Agreements by agreeing to hold global average temperature increase (some increase being inevitable) to below 2°C above preindustrial levels, and to review this 2°C goal in relation to a goal of 1.5°C (UNFCCC 2011, para. 4; 2010, para. 2). In the Paris Agreement parties agreed to hold the increase

Table 2.5
List of Kyoto Protocol Annex B parties.

Australia	Hungary*	Portugal
Austria	Iceland	Romania*
Belgium	Ireland	Russian Federation*
Bulgaria*	Italy	Slovakia*
Canada	Japan	Slovenia*
Croatia*	Latvia*	Spain
Czech Republic*	Liechtenstein	Sweden
Denmark	Lithuania*	Switzerland
Estonia*	Luxembourg	Ukraine*
European Community	Monaco	United Kingdom of Great
Finland	Netherlands	Britain and Northern Ireland
France	New Zealand	United States of America
Germany	Norway	
Greece	Poland*	

*Countries that are undergoing the process of transition to a market economy.

in the global average temperature to "well below 2°C above pre-industrial levels" and to pursue efforts toward 1.5°C. This goal is to be "implemented to reflect equity and the principle of common but differentiated responsibilities and respective capabilities, in the light of different national circumstances" (art. 2). The Paris Agreement also sets emissions goals, including a peaking of global emissions as soon as possible and net zero emissions in the second half of the century.

In addition to defining the regime's ultimate objective, the UNFCCC enunciates several guiding principles (UNFCCC 2011, art. 3). These include the following:

• *Equity and Common but Differentiated Responsibilities and Respective Capabilities (CBDRRC):* The UNFCCC is the first international environmental agreement to articulate the principle of equity and common but differentiated responsibilities and respective capabilities in an operational provision. Developing countries have used this principle to argue for leadership from developed countries and against proposals that require them to accept quantitative emission targets on par with developed countries. Developed countries argue, however, that economic and political realities have evolved since the UNFCCC was negotiated in 1992, and common but differentiated responsibilities must be interpreted as a dynamic concept that evolves in

Table 2.6
Key provisions of the Paris Agreement.

Purpose and Context	To hold the increase in the global average temperature to "well below 2°C above pre-industrial levels" and pursue efforts toward 1.5°C.
	Agreement to be "implemented to reflect equity and the principle of common but differentiated responsibilities and respective capabilities, in the light of different national circumstances" (art. 2).
Contributions	Each party to prepare, communicate, and maintain successive nationally determined contributions that they intend to achieve (art. 4.2).
	Each party to engage in adaptation planning processes and implement adaptation actions (art. 7.9).
	Each party should submit and update periodically adaptation communications (art. 7.10).
Ambition Cycle	Each party to submit a nationally determined contribution every five years (art. 4.9).
	Successive contributions to represent a progression on the current contribution, and to reflect the parties' highest possible ambition (art. 4.3).
	Global stocktake to assess collective progress toward long-term goals, and nationally determined contributions to be informed by the outcomes of the global stocktake (art. 14).
Market Approaches	Parties may engage in "cooperative approaches" to achieve their NDCs, involving the use of "internationally transferred mitigation outcomes" (art. 6.2).
	Sustainable Development Mechanism: new mechanism to "promote the mitigation of GHG emissions while fostering sustainable development" (art. 6.4).
Transparency	Enhanced transparency framework with common modalities, procedures, and guidelines, but with built-in flexibility for those developing countries that need it.
	Technical expert reviews, as well as a facilitative, multilateral consideration of progress.
Implementation and Compliance	A "transparent, non-adversarial and non-punitive" mechanism to facilitate implementation of and promote compliance with provisions of the Paris Agreement (art. 15).
Institutions	Same as UNFCCC, except decision making by Meeting of the Parties to the Paris Agreement (CMA), which meets as part of UNFCCC Conference of the Parties (art. 16).
Support	Developed countries to provide financial resources to assist developing countries with adaptation and mitigation, "in continuation of their existing obligations under the Convention" (art. 9).
	"Other Parties" encouraged to provide or continue to provide support voluntarily.

tandem with changing economic and other realities. Given interpretative differences over this principle, the Durban Platform that launched negotiations toward a 2015 agreement did not contain a reference to it. The principle was reintroduced into the 2015 negotiations in the Lima Call for Climate Action (para. 3) pursuant to a US-China bilateral statement that brokered an agreement on this principle with the inclusion of a qualification "in light of different national circumstances." This qualification arguably bolsters the dynamic character of the principle. The Paris Agreement contains references to the CBDRRC principle in a preambular recital, and in the provisions relating to the purpose of the agreement, progression and long-term low GHG development strategies, but always with the qualification, "in light of different national circumstances" (UNFCCC 2015, arts. 2, 4.3, and 4.11). The most significant of these references appears in article 2, which sets the regime's long-term temperature goal and frames the implementation of the entire agreement (Bodansky, Brunnée, and Rajamani 2017).

• *Precaution:* Given the significant uncertainties concerning climate change, the UNFCCC recognizes that lack of full scientific certainty should not be used as a reason for postponing action. This principle is often invoked by small island states in urging states to adopt ambitious and urgent action to address climate change.

• *Cost-effectiveness and comprehensiveness:* At the insistence of the United States, the UNFCCC explicitly articulates the principles of cost-effectiveness and comprehensiveness. Climate measures should provide global benefits at the lowest cost; cover all relevant sources, sinks, and reservoirs of GHG emissions; and comprise all economic sectors.

• *Sustainable development:* The UNFCCC recognizes that countries have a right to, and should, promote sustainable development, and that policies and measures to protect the climate system should be appropriate for the specific conditions of each party and should be integrated into national development programs. In this regard, the UNFCCC specifically acknowledges that the GHG emissions of developing countries will need to grow. The Cancun Agreements add further gloss to the principle of sustainable development. Developing countries, in particular BASIC (Brazil, South Africa, India, and China), sought and received recognition for "equitable access to sustainable development" (UNFCCC 2011, para. 6). The Paris Agreement contains several references to sustainable development (UNFCCC 2015, arts. 2.1, 4.1, 6, 7.1, 8.1, and 10.5), most noticeably in the chapeau of the provision that contains the long-term goals of the agreement, thus providing a context or frame of reference for the achievement of these goals.

• *International economic system:* The UNFCCC provides that countries should promote a supportive and open international economic system, and should not take measures that constitute arbitrary, unjustifiable or disguised barriers to trade. This provision was at the center of efforts by some developing countries, including China and India, to reject unilateral climate change measures taken by the EU in relation to aviation emissions.

The principles in the UNFCCC contribute to the conceptual architecture of the climate change regime. They provide benchmarks against which proposals such as targets and timetables may be evaluated. Most reflect more general principles of international law—for example, the principles of common but differentiated responsibilities, intra- and intergenerational equity, and precaution. But while these principles guide interpretations of current commitments, and set the terms of debate for future discussions and negotiations, they guide rather than determine what measures should or should not be taken. The precautionary principle, for example, does not specify the appropriate level of precaution or how much certainty is needed before taking action. Nor does the principle of CBDRRC specify the basis or extent of differentiation. Indeed, in the negotiation of the Paris Agreement, there were many divergent interpretations as well as applications of this principle proposed by parties, and the final resolution operationalizes the principle very differently than the Kyoto Protocol. Thus, in practice, resolution of issues generally depends on negotiation rather than on abstract principles (Bodansky, Brunnée, and Rajamani 2017).

2.3.2 Commitments
The UNFCCC and the Kyoto Protocol contain different categories of commitments applicable to different categories of countries. The Paris Agreement, in contrast, does not categorize parties or commitments and, with respect to mitigation, establishes common commitments for all parties.

General commitments: The UNFCCC's general commitments apply to all parties, both developed and developing, and are intended to promote long-term national planning and international review (UNFCCC 1992, art. 4.1). The most significant general commitment is to develop a national inventory of emissions by sources and removals by sinks of GHG emissions. These national inventories provide better information about countries' contribution to the climate change problem, and help promote an internal process of learning. Other general commitments include provisions to formulate and implement national programs to mitigate and adapt to climate change, and to promote and cooperate in scientific research, exchange of information, education, training, and public awareness related to climate change (FCCC, arts. 4.1, 5, 6). These commitments are general in their applicability to all countries and in their content. They do not compel particular actions; rather, they reflect a bottom-up approach, encouraging countries to undertake a comprehensive and systematic review of existing policies, to better coordinate the activities of different national agencies, and to implement their national programs to address climate change. The Kyoto Protocol reiterates the general commitments of the UNFCCC applicable to all parties (UNFCCC 1998, art. 10).

The vast majority of the Paris Agreement's provisions apply to all parties, albeit with contextual and discretionary elements that provide for some differentiation in practice for different countries. All parties are required to communicate and update nationally determined contributions every five years (UNFCCC 2015, art. 4). All parties are subject to transparency requirements, to the global stocktake and to the compliance mechanism (UNFCCC 2015, arts. 13, 14, and 15). The universality in application of many core provisions of the Paris Agreement proved possible in part both because these provisions, albeit binding, are what international lawyers refer to as "obligations of conduct" rather than result, and because the fundamental building blocks of the Paris Agreement are "nationally determined" contributions, rather than collectively negotiated targets.

Mitigation: Targets and timetables have thus far been the preferred international method for controlling atmospheric pollution. They are obligations of result rather than obligations of conduct. As such, while they constrain countries, they give each country the flexibility to choose how it will meet its national target, whether by means of direct regulation, market mechanisms, or taxes.

Emission targets can be specified in a variety of ways: they can set a fixed limit on emissions for a given time frame or they can be indexed to a variable such as gross domestic product or weather; they can apply on an economy-wide basis or to a particular sector; they can apply absolutely or be made conditional on, say, a state's economic wealth or on compliance costs remaining below a specified level (in order to prevent targets from imposing unacceptable economic costs). The emission targets specified in the Kyoto Protocol are fixed, absolute, economy-wide targets (UNFCCC 1998, art. 3).

From the outset of the UNFCCC negotiations, it was generally accepted that any quantitative limitations on greenhouse gas emissions would apply, at least initially, only to industrialized countries (listed in Annex I of the UNFCCC and generally referred to as Annex I Parties[12]). Despite strong efforts by the EU and the AOSIS to include a binding emission target, the UNFCCC includes only a nebulous, non-binding aim for industrialized countries to return, individually or jointly, to their 1990 level of emissions by the year 2000 (UNFCCC 1992, art. 4.2). Although the Annex I countries did jointly meet this aim, this was primarily due to the collapsing economies and corresponding emissions decreases in the economies in transition. Many OECD countries individually recorded significant increases. The principal exceptions were the United Kingdom and Germany, both of which had lower emissions in part due to nonclimate factors (in the case of the UK, the shift from coal to natural gas as a fuel source and, in Germany, reunification of the country).

The principal purpose of the Kyoto Protocol negotiations was to adopt binding emission targets for the post-2000 period. By the terms of the Berlin Mandate, these emission targets were to apply only to industrialized countries. Nevertheless, during the negotiations, the United States continued to press for "meaningful participation" by key developing countries, for example, in the form of "voluntary commitments" to limit GHG emissions. In the end, developing countries succeeded in resisting any new mitigation commitments and the Kyoto Protocol specifies emission targets only for industrialized countries. Rather than establish a single uniform target for all developed countries, the Protocol specifies individualized targets for each participating country, listed in Annex B, ranging from an 8 percent reduction from 1990 levels for the EU and a 7 percent reduction for the United States, to an 8 percent increase from 1990 levels for Australia and a 10 percent increase for Iceland.[13] Since emissions in most Annex I countries were expected to increase in the absence of the Kyoto Protocol, as a result of economic growth, the targets for most Kyoto countries required a bigger deviation from business as usual, and hence were more ambitious than the targets themselves would suggest.[14] The Russian target was a notable exception. Since it was considerably higher than Russia's expected emissions, Russia had a large supply of surplus credits (popularly known as "hot air") that it could sell to other countries through the emissions trading mechanism.

The thirty-eight industrialized countries with emissions targets accounted for 39 percent of 2010 global GHG emissions. Excluding the United States (which rejected the Protocol) and Canada (which withdrew from it), the remaining thirty-six countries accounted for 24 percent of 2010 global GHG emissions. These thirty-six Kyoto parties were in full compliance with their first commitment period targets (Shishlov, Morel, and Bellassen 2016).

Parties agreed in Durban, COP 17, to extend the Kyoto Protocol for a second commitment period, albeit with a reduced set of parties. Beyond that, however, there was much parties could not agree on, including the length of the commitment period (whether it would be five or eight years to coincide with the end date of the Copenhagen/Cancun pledges) and the scale or ambition of individual quantified emissions limitation and reduction objectives. These issues were addressed at COP 18 in Doha. Parties agreed to extend the second commitment period to 2020, that is, eight years. They accepted a collective target of 18 percent below 1990 levels, and individual targets consistent with the ones Annex B Parties had agreed to under the Cancun Agreements, but translated into quantified emissions limitation and reduction objectives for the entire commitment period, 2013–2020. Parties also agreed to revisit their quantified emission limitation and reduction commitment for the second commitment period by 2014, in line with a reduction of 25 percent to 40 percent below 1990 levels by 2020.

The Doha Amendment will enter into force when 144 parties have deposited their instruments of acceptance (arts. 21 and 20). To date, only seventy have done so, including only a handful of Annex B Parties. Parties provided for provisional application of the Doha Amendment, pending entry into force. Neither the Doha Amendment nor the 2015 Paris Agreement offers any clarity on the survival (or termination) of the Kyoto Protocol beyond 2020. However, the near-universal support for the Paris Agreement—its scope, coverage, and breadth; its hybrid architecture; and its distinctive approach to differentiation—is a strong signal that the political commitment underpinning the Kyoto Protocol has long since dissipated.

The political appetite among developed countries for extending the Kyoto Protocol beyond 2020 does not exist. Indeed, the eight-year duration of the second commitment period was chosen so as to end when the Paris Agreement's NDCs were expected to take effect, and thus to avoid a commitment gap (Bodansky, Brunnée, and Rajamani 2017).

Flexibility mechanisms: Kyoto's architecture reflects the flexible approach promoted by the United States from the beginning of the climate change negotiations. The nebulous emission target in the UNFCCC already incorporated this flexible approach by leaving open the possibility of trade-offs in emission controls both between different greenhouse gases (the "comprehensive approach") (Stewart and Wiener 1992), and between different countries (Kuik, Peters, and Schrijver 1994). The incorporation of various flexibility mechanisms into the Kyoto Protocol and their elaboration in the Marrakesh Accords also represented the triumph of what traditionally was perceived as the US approach to climate change mitigation. Central to this approach is flexibility in terms of what, when, and where emissions reductions will occur.

The Kyoto Protocol incorporates "what flexibility" in two ways. First, the Kyoto targets apply to the CO_2-equivalent emissions of a basket of six greenhouse gases (carbon dioxide, methane, nitrous oxide, and three trace gases), rather than to each gas individually, thereby giving parties flexibility in choosing the lowest-cost mix of gases to reduce (Kyoto Protocol Annex A). Second, parties may receive credit, up to specified limits, for the removal of carbon dioxide from the atmosphere through certain sink activities such as afforestation, reforestation, forest management, and agricultural lands management (arts. 3.3 and 3.4).

The Kyoto Protocol reflects "when flexibility" by defining targets not on a year-by-basis but for a five-year or eight-year commitment period. In addition, it allows countries to "bank" surplus emission reductions for application in subsequent commitment periods (art. 3.13). For the second commitment period, the Doha Amendment allows banking but restricts the extent to which banked units can be traded. Several Annex I Parties, including the EU, Australia, Norway, Japan, and Switzerland, recorded political declarations that they would not use surplus assigned amounts carried over from the first commitment period to meet their targets under the second commitment period (Bodansky, Brunnée, and Rajamani 2017).

The most important, and most innovative, type of flexibility in the Kyoto Protocol is "where flexibility." During the negotiations both before and after Kyoto, the EU and developing countries attempted to limit this type of flexibility, arguing that industrialized countries should achieve the bulk of their emission reductions at home, rather than pay for reductions elsewhere. At their insistence, the Kyoto Protocol includes language providing that emissions trading and JI should be "supplemental" to domestic action (UNFCCC 1998, art. 6). But during the negotiations leading to the Marrakesh Accords, efforts by the EU to define this supplementarity requirement in quantitative terms (by setting a "concrete ceiling" on use of the flexibility mechanisms) proved unsuccessful. The Marrakesh Accords do not impose any quantitative requirement about how much a country must do at home to achieve its target.

The Kyoto Protocol includes four mechanisms to enable countries to achieve their targets wherever emission reductions can be made most cheaply.

• *Emissions trading* (UNFCCC 1998, art. 17): Parties listed in Annex B of the Kyoto Protocol may trade parts of their "assigned amounts" with each other. The Kyoto Protocol represents the first significant application of a market-based approach to environmental regulation internationally. The Protocol authorized parties to develop rules for emissions trading, which were finalized in the 2001 Marrakesh Accords. The Kyoto emissions trading system provided the necessary impetus for the creation of regional and national emissions trading systems, including in particular in the EU. The EU Emissions Trading Scheme (EU-ETS), launched in 2005, now covers 11,000 installations in 31 countries accounting for 45 percent of the EU's GHG emissions (European Commission 2016).

• *Joint implementation among Annex I countries* (UNFCCC 1998, art. 6): In addition to emissions trading, developed country parties may receive "emission reduction units" (ERUs) through investments in projects in other developed country parties that result in emission reductions that are "additional" to any that would otherwise occur. These ERUs are added to the emissions target of the acquiring state and subtracted from the target of the transferring state. Like emissions trading, the acquisition of ERUs must be "supplemental to domestic actions," but, as noted above, this condition is not quantitatively defined in the Marrakesh Accords.

• *Clean Development Mechanism* (UNFCCC 1998, art. 12): The Kyoto Protocol establishes the CDM, which allows private and public entities to fund projects in developing countries, in order to generate "certified emission reductions" (CERs) that Annex I Parties may use to meet their emissions targets. In essence, the CDM allows joint implementation between developed and developing country parties. The CDM is under the control of the Meeting of the Parties and supervised by an executive board. Part of the proceeds from CDM projects are used to cover the CDM's administrative costs, as well as to assist developing country parties that are particularly vulnerable to climate change. As with emissions trading and JI, the modalities and procedures of the CDM were elaborated in the Marrakesh Accords. The CDM executive board has registered projects generating an estimated 8.4 billion CERs; the vast majority of these from projects located in China (nearly 50 percent), followed by India (20 percent).[15] This has led to calls from African countries in particular for "equitable geographical distribution of CDM projects."

• *Bubbles* (UNFCCC 1998, art. 4): Finally, the Kyoto Protocol allows any group of developed country parties, prior to ratifying the Protocol, to agree to pool their emissions targets. The EU used this provision to establish a collective target with a burden-sharing agreement that reallocates the Kyoto targets among EU member states.

Today, there is a vast institutional architecture to support the implementation of these mechanisms, and considerable public and private investment in them. However, there is uncertainty about the future of the Kyoto mechanisms. The demand for ERUs and CERs has dried up in recent years. The price of credits has dropped dramatically, attributed by scholars to the oversupply of credits, quantitative limits on their use in the EU ETS, and reduced demand due in part to the post-2007 economic crisis (Koch et al. 2014). In addition, parties have not strengthened the 2020 targets (which would have increased demand for Kyoto credits) and it is unclear whether and how the CDM and the JI will be used beyond 2020. The Paris Agreement and its accompanying decision are silent on the future of the JI and CDM. The Paris Agreement establishes a new mechanism, dubbed by some the sustainable development mechanism (SDM), which merges the functionality of the CDM and JI by encompassing emission reductions in both developed and developing countries, modalities for which have yet to be developed (UNFCCC 2015, art. 6). Although the Kyoto Protocol is not explicitly mentioned, due to sensitivities among non-Kyoto parties, the Kyoto Protocol is a "related legal instrument," so lessons learned from the Kyoto mechanisms are clearly relevant to the design of the new market mechanism. It is possible that the SDM will build on elements of JI and CDM but it is unclear, at this stage, how and in what ways this will occur (Bodansky, Brunnée, and Rajamani 2017).

Developing countries: In relation to developing countries, the UNFCCC seeks to enhance compliance with its obligations primarily through the provision of assistance. UNFCCC article 4.7 connects developing countries' participation and implementation with developed countries' implementation of their commitments. In so doing, article 4.7 underpins and reinforces the understanding that developing country action to protect the global environment will depend on assistance from developed countries. The precise contours of this understanding, however, are unclear. Do developing countries have a responsibility to contain climate change even if financial assistance and technology transfer are not forthcoming? Or is the provision of financial assistance and technology transfer a precondition to the implementation of their commitments? If assistance is critical to the implementation of the agreement, what is the content of the obligation to assist, what is its legal character, and to what extent is the UNFCCC regime designed to ensure compliance with this obligation?

Financial assistance: Apart from emissions targets, perhaps the most contentious issue in the climate change regime has been that of financial transfers from developed to developing countries. Financial assistance is important for both mitigation and adaptation purposes. Unlike ordinary development assistance, the financial and technological assistance required by the UNFCCC for mitigation purposes could be viewed as a form of partnership or solidarity. Its fundamental purpose is to benefit the global environment by averting climate change, not to benefit developing countries themselves. Nonetheless, the UNFCCC's provisions regarding financial assistance are weak. The UNFCCC requires certain developed countries (listed in Annex II) to provide financial assistance to developing countries, but neither specifies the amount of that assistance nor provides for mandatory assessments (UNFCCC 1992, arts. 4.3 and 4.4). The UNFCCC requires Annex II countries to provide full funding only for the costs of developing country inventories and reports. And even with respect to these costs, the UNFCCC does not require any particular country to contribute any specified amount. Financial assistance for other mitigation measures depends on approval by the Global Environment Facility (GEF) and covers only a project's "incremental" costs (i.e., the additional costs relating to climate change mitigation). Meanwhile, assistance for adaptation was limited initially to capacity building and demonstration projects.

The amount of assistance provided pursuant to the UNFCCC's provisions has been quite modest—particularly compared to the expectations of developing countries. During the negotiations leading to the Marrakesh Accords, developing countries renewed their efforts to obtain greater financial assistance. But, although the Marrakesh Accords established three new climate-related funds, these did not lead to significant increases in the funding provided.

The Copenhagen Accord, however, provided a fillip to efforts to obtain greater funding for climate change. The Accord decided to establish the Green Climate Fund (GCF) as an operating entity of the financial mechanism of the Convention. The GCF was subsequently incorporated into the UNFCCC process through the Cancun Agreements and operationalized in Durban at COP 17. Developed countries agreed to provide US$30 billion in the 2010–2012 time frame and to mobilize US$100 billion per year by 2020 (UNFCCC 2010, paras. 8 and 10). These are not direct transfers to developing countries, however. Such funding will come from a "wide variety of sources, public and private, bilateral and multilateral, including alternative sources of finance." A significant portion of such funding is intended to flow through the GCF which currently (as of June 2017) contains contributions of about US$10.3 billion (Green Climate Fund 2017).

The Paris Agreement obliges developed countries to provide financial resources to assist developing countries with adaptation and mitigation, "in continuation of their existing obligations under the Convention" (art. 9.1). Article 9 also creates a number of new reporting requirements relating to finance (including biennial reports that include projected levels of public finance), and introduces a new substantive norm, albeit soft, recommending that the mobilization of climate finance "should represent a progression beyond previous efforts" (art. 9.3). The Paris Agreement also expands the donor base to "other" parties on a voluntary basis (art. 9.2). It contains no quantitative finance goal, but the COP decision accompanying the Paris Agreement extends developed countries' existing US$100 billion mobilization goal through 2025 and provides that the parties shall set a new collective quantified goal prior to 2025 (not explicitly limited to developed countries), using the 100 billion US dollars per year figure as a floor (UNFCCC 2016b, para. 53).

Technical assistance: The UNFCCC's provisions on technology, like the provisions on financing, are relatively weak (UNFCCC 1992, art. 4.5). The UNFCCC requires developed countries to take "all practicable steps" to promote, facilitate, and finance, "as appropriate," the transfer of, or access to, environmentally sound technologies and know-how to developing countries. To discharge this obligation, industrial countries would need to show only that they have taken practicable steps to transfer technology, not that they have actually transferred technology. Although on the agenda of successive COPs, efforts to enhance technology transfer have only recently taken concrete shape. The Cancun Agreements created a Technology Mechanism to implement the UNFCCC's provision on technology. In particular the Technology Mechanism is required to recommend actions to promote environmentally sound technology transfer, provide guidance on policy and program priorities, facilitate collaboration between state and nonstate actors, recommend actions to address barriers to technology transfer, and catalyze development and use of technology road maps or action plans. The Paris Agreement creates a technology framework to provide overarching guidance to the work of the convention's Technology Mechanism (art. 10.4). It also makes support available to accelerate, encourage and enable innovation through collaborative approaches to research and development and by facilitating access to technology (art. 10.5).

Adaptation: Although adaptation is central to the UNFCCC, it suffered years of relative neglect as parties focused on the development of mitigation obligations. This neglect has been remedied in the recent past, most notably in the Paris Agreement. The Bali Action Plan identified adaptation as one of the pillars on which the future climate regime must be built. In furtherance of this mandate in Cancun, parties launched a "Cancun Adaptation Framework" as well as a "Work Programme on Loss and Damage" (UNFCCC 2011, paras. 13 and 26). The "Cancun Adaptation Framework" aims to enhance action on adaptation, including through international cooperation, and the "Work Programme on Loss and Damage" aims to strengthen international cooperation and expertise so as to understand and reduce loss and damage associated with the adverse effects of climate change in developing countries particularly vulnerable to climate change. The Paris Agreement requires parties to engage in adaptation planning and implementation of adaptation actions, and urges parties to submit and update adaptation communications (possibly as part of their NDCs) identifying priorities and needs, for listing on a public registry, and to strengthen cooperation on adaptation (arts. 7.9 and 7.10).

Adequacy of commitments and adjustment procedure: The UNFCCC acknowledges that its limited obligations may be inadequate, and that the regime will need to evolve in response to new scientific information. Accordingly, both the UNFCCC and the Kyoto Protocol call for periodic reviews, modeled on those of the ozone regime, which have led to progressively stricter international regulation of ozone-depleting substances. Thus far, however, the only review of commitments took place in 1995, initiating the Kyoto Protocol negotiations.

The Paris Agreement addresses the issue of adequacy of parties' contributions in relation to the long-term temperature goal by establishing a five-year "cycle of ambition," involving a "global stocktake" to assess the parties' collective progress toward the Agreement's long-term goals (art. 14), as well as the communication by each party of an NDC (art. 4.9). The global stocktake performs a crucial function in the context of NDCs. It allows a collective assessment of whether national efforts add up to what is necessary to limit temperature increase to well below 2°C (Bodansky, Brunnée, and Rajamani 2017). The outcomes of these global stocktakes are to "inform" parties in enhancing and updating their NDCs. The global stocktakes will begin in 2023 and will be comprehensive and facilitative, assessing all aspects of the Paris Agreement, including mitigation, adaptation, and finance (art. 14).

2.3.3   Implementation and Compliance

The development of a strong reporting and review procedure for industrialized countries has been one of the principal achievements of the climate change regime. Reporting and review serve several functions. First, they place pressure on countries by holding them up to domestic and

international scrutiny. Second, by improving transparency, review processes help build confidence among parties that others cannot free ride
without being caught. Third, reporting and review serve an educational
function. By sharing information, countries can benefit from one another's
experiences. Finally, reporting and review produce useful information for
assessing the effectiveness of the UNFCCC, the Kyoto Protocol and the Paris
Agreement, and the need for further commitments.

Reporting: Under the UNFCCC and the Kyoto Protocol, Annex I Parties are
required to submit annual greenhouse gas inventories and periodic national
communications containing detailed information on their climate change
policies (UNFCCC 1992, art. 12; 1998, art. 7). Developing countries are also
required to submit national reports or communications, but these are set to
longer time frames. The annual greenhouse gas inventories are the backbone
of the national communications process. They help improve understanding
of the sources and sinks of GHG emissions, provide a baseline for evaluating
the UNFCCC's implementation and effectiveness, and provide the basic data
needed to evaluate the compliance of Annex I Parties with their Kyoto targets. In order to be eligible to use the Kyoto flexibility mechanisms, Annex I
countries must show that their national systems to produce emission inventories meet detailed requirements designed to ensure reliability.

The Cancun Agreements enhance the rigor of national communications and inventory requirements for developed and developing countries
(UNFCCC 2011, paras. 40 and 60), as well as enhance the frequency of
reporting by developing countries. They require non-Annex I Parties to submit national communications every four years as well as biennial update
reports (UNFCCC 2011, para. 60 [b]). Previously non-Annex I Parties had
been required to submit their national communications every four to five
years, and Annex I Parties every four years. The Cancun Agreements render
national communication requirements symmetrical across developed and
developing countries. The requirement to produce biennial update reports
may prove particularly onerous for many developing countries. However,
the Cancun Agreements do recognize "flexibility" for least developed countries and small island developing countries (UNFCCC 2011, para. 60, chapeau), and condition the production of these reports on "capabilities and
the level of support provided" (UNFCCC 2011, para. 60 [c]). Parties agreed
in Durban to reporting guidelines for the enhanced and more frequent

reporting required of developing and developed countries, respectively, under the Cancun Agreements.

The Paris Agreement's transparency framework (art. 13) for action and support is comparatively robust, particularly given that it applies to developing as well as developed countries. It places extensive informational demands on all parties, and creates several review mechanisms. The purpose of the transparency framework is to ensure clarity and tracking of progress toward achieving parties' NDCs and adaptation actions, as well as to provide clarity on support provided and received by parties. Toward this end, parties are required biennially to provide a national inventory report of GHG emissions and removals and information necessary to track progress in implementing and achieving mitigation contributions (art. 13.7). Further, developed countries are required to provide information on financial, technology and capacity building support they provide to developing countries (art. 13.9).

International review: Under both the UNFCCC and the Kyoto Protocol, national communications by industrialized countries are subject to international review by teams of experts nominated by the parties (and certain international organizations) and selected by the UNFCCC secretariat. The expert review mechanism is intended to be nonconfrontational and facilitative in nature, and has two components:

1. In-depth reviews of each national communication to promote individual accountability and enhance comparability. These in-depth reviews are like outside audits; they examine the reliability, consistency, accuracy, and relevance of national communications by reviewing key data points, verifying methodologies, and comparing assumptions across countries and with international sources. Because objective international reviews are critical for assessing countries' compliance with their Kyoto targets, the Kyoto Protocol provides a considerably strengthened review process (UNFCCC 1998, art. 8).
2. A synthesis report pursuant to the UNFCCC, which compiles and aggregates the data in the various Annex I country reports, to determine their overall progress in implementing the Convention.

The Cancun Agreements added to the existing review processes for developed country communications a process of "international assessment and review" (IAR) (UNFCCC 2011, para. 44). For developing countries, the Cancun Agreements for the first time created a review process, although deliberately not titled as such. The biennial update reports that developing countries are required to produce are subject to a process of "international consultation and analysis" (ICA) (UNFCCC 2011, para. 63). The ICA process is to be conducted in a manner that is "non-intrusive, non-punitive and respectful of national sovereignty." In Durban, parties fleshed out the modalities for IAR and ICA—for developed and developing countries targets and actions, respectively. Both IAR and ICA are a judicious mix of technical and political components. These processes have been designed to be robust and to generate credible information on and confidence in mitigation targets and actions, but they are not authorized or tailored to address the issue of "adequacy" or "ambition" of these targets and actions in relation to the long-term temperature goal.

The Paris Agreement's enhanced transparency framework, details of which are to be worked out in the post-Paris negotiations, is intended to build on this system. The information submitted by all parties in relation to mitigation and by developed country parties on the provision of support will be subject to a technical expert review. This review will consider the support provided to parties, the implementation of their NDCs, and the consistency of the information they provide with guidelines parties will develop. In addition each party is expected to participate in a "facilitative, multilateral consideration of progress" with respect to the implementation and achievement of its NDC, as well as its efforts in relation to finance (arts. 13.11 and 13.12) (Bodansky, Brunnée, and Rajamani 2017). The enhanced transparency framework does not explicitly differentiate between developed and developing countries, but will provide "built-in flexibility" for those developing countries that need it.

Compliance system: As a cooperative, forward-looking instrument that attempts to encourage and facilitate rather than coerce national action, the UNFCCC does not include a robust dispute settlement mechanism. It includes a dispute settlement provision, calling for the settlement of disputes by negotiation, conciliation, and, if both sides agree, arbitration or the International Court of Justice (UNFCCC 1992, art. 14). But this type of procedure, found in most international environmental agreements, is seldom used in part because global environmental disputes do not have the bilateral character of traditional international disputes (Bodansky, Brunnée, and Rajamani 2017).

The UNFCCC also provided for the establishment of a multilateral consultative process (UNFCCC 1992, art. 13; 1999, decision 10/CP.4) for the resolution of questions regarding the implementation of the Convention. The rules for the multilateral consultative process were largely negotiated in the 1990s, but were never adopted. As a result, the multilateral consultative process has yet to be established. It was intended to provide advice on procuring technical and financial resources to address difficulties in implementation, and to clarify and resolve questions relating to implementation.

The Kyoto Protocol established a much more robust compliance system (UNFCCC 1998, art. 18), including a standing compliance body with two branches, one focused on facilitation and the other on enforcement. Of the two branches of the compliance committee, only the facilitative branch applies to developing countries (UNFCCC 2006, decision 27/CMP.1). And, the facilitative branch, which is empowered to provide financial and technical assistance, and/or advice, is required to do so "taking into account the principle of common but differentiated responsibilities and respective capabilities." The enforcement branch applies exclusively to developed countries. In the event that the enforcement branch determines that a country has not complied with its emission target, the Kyoto compliance system provides for the excess tons to be subtracted (at a 1.3:1 rate) from the country's emission target in the next commitment period. The Kyoto compliance system in its years of operation has successfully addressed several cases of noncompliance with national system requirements.

The Paris Agreement establishes a mechanism to facilitate implementation of and promote compliance with its provisions, but the skeletal provision establishing this new mechanism provides only minimal guidance on how it will work. Article 15 indicates that the mechanism is to be "transparent, non-adversarial and non-punitive," but it does not describe the relationship, if any, between the transparency framework and the new mechanism, and leaves the mechanism's modalities and procedures to be negotiated in the years to follow (Bodansky, Brunnée, and Rajamani 2017).

2.3.4 Governance Architecture

When the climate change issue first emerged as a policy issue, some leaders felt that it required the development of supranational bodies, with authority to adopt and enforce regulatory standards (Palmer 1992). At the 1989 Hague Conference, seventeen heads of state called for the establishment of "new institutional authority" to address climate change, with nonunanimous decision-making powers. This proposal was never pursued in the UNFCCC

Table 2.7

Climate change bodies.

Name	Acronym	Description
Intergovernmental Negotiating Committee	INC	Established December 1990 by UN General Assembly. Negotiated the UNFCCC. Now replaced by the UNFCCC Conference of the Parties (COP).
Conference of the Parties / Meeting of the Kyoto Protocol Parties / Meeting of the Paris Agreement Parties	COP/ CMP/ CMA	Established by UNFCCC art. 7. "Supreme body" of UNFCCC. Meeting of the Parties (CMP) of Kyoto Protocol held in conjunction with COP (Kyoto art. 13). Meeting of the Parties to the Paris Agreement (CMA) held in conjunction with the COP (Paris Agreement, art. 16). Functions: regular review of implementation; decisions necessary to promote effective implementation; adoption of amendments and protocols. Meets yearly.
Secretariat		Established by UNFCCC art. 8. Administrative functions in support of COP, CMP, CMA, and other Convention and Protocol institutions. Located in Bonn.
Subsidiary Body for Scientific and Technological Advice	SBSTA	Established by UNFCCC art. 9. Composed of government experts. Provides assessments of scientific knowledge, reviews scientific / technical aspects of national reports and effects of implementation measures. Also serves the Kyoto Protocol and Paris Agreement.
Subsidiary Body for Implementation	SBI	Established by UNFCCC art. 10. Composed of government experts. Reviews policy aspects of national reports; assists COP in assessing aggregated effect of implementation measures. Also serves the Kyoto Protocol and Paris Agreement.
Financial Mechanism		"Defined" by UNFCCC art. 11. Operation entrusted to GEF and GCF.
Inter-Governmental Panel on Climate Change	IPCC	Established in 1988 by WMO and UNEP to provide assessments of the science, impacts and policy aspects of climate change. First Assessment Report in 1990; Second Assessment Report in 1995; Third Assessment Report in 2000; Fourth Assessment Report in 2007; Fifth Assessment Report in 2013–2014.

Table 2.7 (continued)

Name	Acronym	Description
Global Environment Facility	GEF	Established by World Bank, UNDP, and UNEP in 1991. Restructured in 1994.
Clean Development Mechanism	CDM	Defined by Kyoto art. 12. Under the control of the COP, and supervised by an executive board.
Compliance Committee		Established by Marrakesh Accords pursuant to Kyoto art. 18. Facilitative and enforcement branches, each with ten members. Decisions by enforcement branch require double-majority of developed and developing country members.
Green Climate Fund	GCF	Established by the Cancun Agreements. The World Bank is its interim trustee, and the UNFCCC secretariat and the GEF its interim secretariat.
Technology Mechanism		Established by the Cancun Agreements. Comprises the Technology Executive Committee and the Climate Technology Centre and Network.

negotiations. Instead, the UNFCCC relies on more traditional types of international bodies, which are essentially intergovernmental rather than supranational in nature, and play a primarily coordinating and facilitative role. Table 2.7 provides an overview of key climate bodies.

Conference of the Parties: The annual COP serves as the UNFCCC's "supreme body," with authority to examine the Convention's obligations and institutional arrangements, to supervise its implementation, and to develop amendments and protocols (UNFCCC 1992, art. 7). Among its functions, it provides a permanent forum for discussion and negotiation and helps build a sense of community. Moreover, by permitting environmental and industry groups to attend as observers, it provides them a forum for offering inputs and exerting pressure. Although the COP has no explicit regulatory powers (unlike its analogue in the ozone regime, which can tighten regulatory measures on ozone-depleting substances by a two-thirds vote), its decision-making authority is broad. COP 1, for example, initiated the new round of negotiations that led to the Kyoto Protocol, established a

pilot phase of joint implementation, adopted reporting and review procedures, designated a permanent secretariat, and defined the roles of its subsidiary bodies. Similarly, COP 7 adopted the Marrakech Accords, which set
forth detailed operational rules for the Kyoto Protocol. COP 13 and COP 17,
respectively, launched the Bali Process that led to the Cancun Agreements
and the Durban Platform process that led to the 2015 Paris Agreement. The
COP's decision-making authority makes its voting rules vital, but because
countries have yet to reach agreement on a voting rule, the default has been
consensus, allowing small groups of countries to block adoption of decisions. The notion of consensus, however, was severely tested at COP 2 in
Geneva in the context of the Geneva Ministerial Declaration, at COP 16 in
Cancun, where the COP president declared consensus despite repeated,
explicit and vocal objections from Bolivia, and at COP 18 in Doha, where
the Doha Amendment was adopted over the protests of Russia and Ukraine.

Because membership in the Kyoto Protocol is different from the
UNFCCC, Kyoto provides for a Meeting of the Parties (CMP) to decide on
Kyoto Protocol issues (art. 13).[16] Although not authorized to adopt new
commitments, the CMP has significant powers, including the authority to
revise the rules governing emissions trading, the CDM, and credit for carbon
sinks. Similarly the Paris Agreement provides for a Meeting of Parties to the
Paris Agreement (CMA) (art. 16) with significant decision-making powers,
in particular in relation to the rule-making exercise parties have embarked
on post-Paris to flesh out the skeletal framework of the Paris Agreement's
oversight system.

Secretariat: The UNFCCC secretariat provides general administrative and policy support to the COP and its subsidiary bodies. The secretariat has grown
substantially in size since 1992. During the UNFCCC negotiations, it served
a primarily administrative function. But since the UNFCCC's adoption, it
has played an increasingly important role in organizing the UNFCCC's and
Kyoto Protocol's review processes and serving as an information clearing-
house. Under recent executive secretaries, the secretariat has also attempted
to inject itself more forcefully in the policy development process.

Financial mechanism: During the UNFCCC negotiations, the financial mechanism was one of the most contentious issues. Large donor countries insisted

on using the GEF to provide climate assistance, an institution created in 1991 at their instigation and which, through the World Bank, they dominated. Developing countries favored the creation of a new institution under the control of the COP. Article 11 of the UNFCCC represents a compromise between these positions. Rather than create a new fund, it entrusts the GEF with the operation of its financial mechanism on an interim basis and gives the GEF authority over individual funding decisions. But it gives the COP authority over the financial mechanism's policies, program priorities and eligibility criteria.

In 1994, in response to demands by developing countries and environmental groups for greater transparency and democracy, representatives of seventy-three countries participating in the GEF agreed to restructure it. The restructured GEF is functionally autonomous from the World Bank and is governed by a thirty-two-member council, evenly split between developing and developed country representatives. The decision-making rules require the concurrence of both developing and donor countries for all substantive decisions.

The GEF's mandate permits it to fund only those "incremental" costs of a project that produce global environmental benefits (and hence are ineligible for ordinary World Bank lending, which focuses on the local benefits of projects). Hence it is important to determine which costs are "incremental" and which benefits are global. The World Bank has favored limiting GEF assistance to "net incremental costs," that is, the difference between the total costs of a project and its local benefits. Developing countries and environmental NGOs, in contrast, have argued that the GEF should provide assistance for the full costs of projects to implement the UNFCCC. This would permit funding of "no regrets" strategies, which have a negative net cost. Since determining which costs produce local as opposed to global benefits is nearly impossible, in practice this issue is worked out flexibly and pragmatically, on a project-by-project basis, through negotiations between the GEF and the country concerned.

The Cancun Agreements established the GCF as an operating entity of the Convention's financial mechanism. The fund is accountable to and will function under the guidance of the COP. The assets of the fund are being managed by the World Bank on an interim basis, until a permanent trustee is selected, and the secretariat as well as GEF function as the fund's interim secretariat.

The Paris Agreement designates the financial mechanism of the UNFCCC as the mechanism for the Agreement (art 9.8).

IPCC: The IPCC has thus far served the crucial function of providing collective appraisals of scientific knowledge. Although questions have been raised about the IPCC's role, the IPCC has, in general, successfully walked the tightrope between governmental ownership and professional autonomy, thereby maintaining both political and scientific legitimacy. On the one hand, its intergovernmental character has given governments a sense of ownership and stake in its work, leading them to accept its assessments as authoritative. On the other hand, it has managed to maintain its autonomy as a scientific body and thereby its scientific credibility—a point substantiated by its receipt of the Nobel Peace Prize in 2007. The image of the IPCC did take a beating in 2007. Evidence emerged suggesting that some of the claims in the IPCC's 2007 report, for instance, in relation to the Himalayan glaciers, were inaccurate, and could be attributed to the IPCC's reliance on non-peer-reviewed sources. The IPCC issued a retraction in relation to these claims, and for its fifth assessment report (2014) tightened its literature review process.

2.4   Conclusion

This chapter sought to provide an overview of both the evolution of the climate change regime, as well as its architecture, from the initiation of the regime in the UNFCCC, through the legally binding targets and timetables approach of the Kyoto Protocol, to the more flexible, nationally determined approach of the Paris Agreement.

The UNFCCC serves as the foundation of the UN climate regime, and is the principal multilateral forum for negotiations among governments, as well as discussions among business and nongovernmental groups. It contains guiding principles and commitments that have framed climate action in the last two decades. Its system for reporting and review, augmented by the Cancun Agreements, provides a solid base of information on which credible climate actions have been built and can be scaled up.

The Kyoto Protocol establishes comparatively ambitious, internationally negotiated emission targets for most developed countries. Its flexibility mechanisms are remarkable in their novelty and complexity, and have catalyzed the emergence of a multi-billion-dollar carbon market. Yet Kyoto's targets, in particular for its second commitment period, cover only a fraction of global emissions. Even before Kyoto's first commitment period was underway, attention shifted first to the post-2012 period, when the first commitment period was to end, and then to the post-2020 period, when it became clear at the 2009 Copenhagen Conference that the political conditions for the adoption of a new legally binding instrument were not yet ripe. The negotiations since 2007 revealed that Kyoto, with its prescriptive, legally binding targets and timetables approach, had lost favor as a politically viable model. Although the Kyoto Protocol parties agreed in Durban and later in Doha to a second commitment period, it was clear that the end of the second commitment period would also mark the end of Kyoto. In its place, parties began exploring a more flexible design, reflected in the Paris Agreement. Nevertheless, Kyoto's mere existence changed the political and economic landscape. It spurred significant activity not only by parties but by subnational levels of governments such as cities and regions, as well as by the private sector. And its market-based approach, albeit in a new avatar, forms a part of the Paris Agreement.

Finally, this chapter outlined the key elements of the Paris Agreement, and documented the key shifts in the negotiations in the last decade. First, the Paris Agreement captures a hybrid approach. In contrast to the Kyoto Protocol, it involves different types of targets, commitments and actions, defined through a decentralized, bottom-up process, rather than through a global international negotiation. But it combines these bottom-up elements with top-down oversight elements such as robust transparency, stocktake, and compliance provisions. Second, it embodies a more nuanced form of differentiation—a model of differentiation and flexibility for all tailored to national circumstances—rather than binary differentiation between developed and developing countries, in particular the Kyoto variant of it. And the Paris Agreement is a legally binding instrument with soft and hard elements within it. The Paris Agreement has in several respects launched a new era in international climate change regulation. It remains to be seen how effective it will be in meeting the climate regime's long-term temperature goals.

Notes

This chapter draws from the authors' previously published work, including Bodansky, Brunnée, and Rajamani (2017); Bodansky (1993, 1994, 1995, 2005, and 2016); and Rajamani (2008, 2009, 2011, 2012, 2014, and 2016).

1. This chapter focuses on the United Nations climate change legal regime. This forms part of a larger "regime complex" on climate change, which includes activities in other multilateral institutions such as the World Bank, the International Maritime Organization (IMO), and the International Civil Aviation Organization (ICAO), as well as activities under multilateral environmental agreements such as the Montreal Protocol (Keohane and Victor 2010).

2. As of November 2016, 196 states (and the European Community) were party to the UNFCCC and 192 were party to the Kyoto Protocol.

3. CO_2 emissions from Annex I countries from 1850 to 2012 were 937,952 $MtCO_2$ and from non-Annex I were 388,623 $MtCO_2$. Data for Cumulative Total CO_2 Emissions Excluding Land-Use Change and Forestry from 1850 to 2012 from the World Resources Institute "Climate Analysis Indicator Tools" (WRI 2016).

4. Based on data from WRI 2016.

5. "Developed countries" are often considered to be those listed in Annex I of the UNFCCC, including the United States, Western European states, members of the former Soviet bloc, Japan, Canada, Australia, and New Zealand while "developing countries" are often equated with non-Annex I parties. But neither term is defined in international law, and whether comparatively poor countries such as Turkey should be considered "developed," or rich countries such as South Korea and Singapore should still be considered "developing," is not agreed.

6. On the Kyoto Protocol, see generally Oberthur and Ott (1999).

7. Among other things, the Marrakesh Accords laid down operating rules for the mechanisms and accounting procedures for emissions reduction credits (UNFCCC 2002a, 2002b). They also established a compliance system and set out the consequences for noncompliance.

8. On the Copenhagen Accord, see generally Bodansky (2010) and Rajamani (2010).

9. The Cancun Agreements, 2010, comprise UNFCCC, Decision 1/CP.16 2011 (hereinafter "Cancun Agreements LCA") and UNFCCC, Decision 1/CMP.6 2011.

10. On the Durban Platform, see generally Bodansky (2012) and Rajamani (2012).

11. On the Paris Agreement, see generally Bodansky (2016) and Rajamani (2016).

12. Annex I (see table 2.3) lists thirty-six states (or groupings) including all members of the OECD except Mexico, Korea, and Chile (which had not yet joined the OECD when the UNFCCC was adopted); countries with "economies in transition" (i.e., the former members of the Soviet bloc); and the European Economic Community. Six countries were added to this list, and one deleted in 1998, bringing the total to forty-one.

13. The targets in Annex B of the Protocol are defined in terms of an assigned amount of emissions for each country listed in Annex B.

14. For example, if the United States had joined the Protocol, it would have needed to reduce its emissions by about a third from business-as-usual scenarios for the 2008–2012 period.

15. As of July 31, 2016 (UNFCCC 2016a).

16. The CMP meets in conjunction with the COP and is referred to as the COP/CMP.

References

Arrhenius, Svante. 1896. "On the Influence of Carbonic Acid in the Air upon the Temperature of the Ground." *Philosophical Magazine* 5 (April): 237–276.

Bodansky, Daniel. 1993. "The United Nations Framework Convention on Climate Change: A Commentary." *Yale Journal of International Law* 18 (2): 451–558.

———. 1994. "Prologue to the Climate Change Convention." In *Negotiating Climate Change: The inside Story of the Rio Convention*, edited by Irving M. Mintzer and J. Amber Leonard, 45–74. Cambridge: Cambridge University Press.

———. 1995. "The Emerging Climate Change Regime." *Annual Review of Energy and Environment*, 20:425–461.

———. 1999. *The Framework Convention/Protocol Approach, WHO Technical Briefing Series.*: WHO/NCD/TFI/99.1.

———. 2005. "The International Climate Change Regime." In *Perspectives on Climate Change: Science, Economics, Politics, Ethics,* edited by Walter Sinnott-Armstrong and Richard B. Howarth, 147–180. Amsterdam: Elsevier.

———. 2010. "The Copenhagen Climate Change Conference: A Postmortem." *American Journal of International Law* 104 (2): 230–240.

———. 2011. "A Tale of Two Architectures: The Once and Future UN Climate Regime." *Arizona State Law Journal* 43:697–712.

———. 2012. "The Durban Platform Negotiations: Goals and Options." *Harvard Project on Climate Agreements Viewpoint*, July.

———. 2016. "The Paris Climate Change Agreement: A New Hope?" *American Journal of International Law* 110 (2): 288–319.

Bodansky, Daniel, Jutta Brunnée, and Lavanya Rajamani. 2017. *International Climate Change Law*. Oxford: Oxford University Press.

Brundtland, Gro Harlem. 1987. *Our Common Future*. Brussels: World Commission on Environment and Development.

Clark, William C. 1989. "Managing Planet Earth." *Scientific American* 261 (3): 47–54.

Convention on Long-Range Transboundary Air Pollution. 1979. Geneva: UN Economic Commission for Europe.

EIA. 2013. *International Energy Outlook 2013 with Projections to 2040*. Washington, DC: US Energy Information Administration.

European Commission. 2016. *The EU Emissions Trading System*. Brussels: European Commission, DG Climate Action.

Green Climate Fund. 2017. Status of Pledges and Contributions Made to the Green Climate Fund. Pledge Tracker, Green Climate Fund.

Hague Declaration on the Environment. 1989. UN Doc. A/44/340-E/1989/120, Annex 5.

IPCC. 2001. *Climate Change 2001: Synthesis Report, Contribution of Working Groups I, II, and III to the Third Assessment Report of the Intergovernmental Panel on Climate Change*. Cambridge: Cambridge University Press.

———. 2014. *Mitigation of Climate Change. Contribution of Working Group III to the Fifth Assessment Report of the Intergovernmental Panel on Climate Change*. Cambridge: Cambridge University Press.

Jäger, Jill, and Howard Ferguson, eds. 1991. *Climate Change: Science Impacts and Policy. Proceedings of the Second World Climate Conference*. Cambridge: Cambridge University Press.

Keeling, Charles. 1960. "The Concentrations and Isotopic Abundances of Carbon Dioxide in the Atmosphere." *Tellus* 12 (2): 200–203.

Keohane, Robert O., and David G. Victor. 2010. "The Regime Complex for Climate Change." *Perspectives on Politics* 9 (1): 7–23.

Koch, Nicolas, Sabine Fuss, Godefroy Grosjean, and Ottmar Edenhofer. 2014. "Causes of the EU ETS Price Drop: Recession, CDM, Renewable Policies or a Bit of Everything? New Evidence." *Energy Policy* 73 (6): 676–685.

Kuik, Onno J., Paul Peters, and Nico Schrijver. 1994. *Joint Implementation to Curb Climate Change: Legal and Economic Aspects*. Dordrecht, Netherlands: Kluwer Academic.

Magraw, Daniel B. 1990. "Global Change and International Law." *Colorado Journal of International Environmental Law and Policy* 1 (1): 1–10.

Oberthur, Sebastian, and Hermann Ott. 1999. *The Kyoto Protocol: International Climate Policy for the 21st Century*. Berlin: Springer.

Palmer, Geoffrey. 1992. "An International Regime for Environmental Protection." *Journal of Urban and Contemporary Law* 42 (3): 5–19.

Rajamani, Lavanya. 2008. "From Berlin to Bali and Beyond: Killing Kyoto Softly?" *International and Comparative Law Quarterly* 57 (3): 909.

———. 2009. "Addressing the Post-Kyoto Stress Disorder: Reflections on the Emerging Legal Architecture of the Climate Regime." *International and Comparative Law Quarterly* 58 (4): 803–834.

———. 2010. "The Making and Unmaking of the Copenhagen Accord." *International and Comparative Law Quarterly* 59 (3): 824–843.

———. 2011. "The Cancun Climate Change Agreements: Reading the Text, Subtext and Tea Leaves." *International and Comparative Law Quarterly* 60 (2): 499.

———. 2012. "The Durban Platform for Enhanced Actions and the Future of the Climate Regime." *International and Comparative Law Quarterly* 61 (2): 501–518.

———. 2014. "The Warsaw Climate Negotiations: Emerging Actions and the Future of the Climate Regime." *International and Comparative Law Quarterly* 63 (3): 721–740.

———. 2016. "Ambition and Differentiation in the 2015 Paris Agreement: Interpretative Possibilities and Underlying Politics." *International and Comparative Law Quarterly* 65 (2): 493–514.

Shishlov, Igor, Romain Morel, and Valentin Bellassen. 2016. "Compliance of the Parties to the Kyoto Protocol in the First Commitment Period." *Climate Policy* 16 (6): 768–782.

Stern, Nicholas. 2006. *Review on the Economics of Climate Change*. London: HM Treasury.

Stewart, Richard B., and Jonathan B. Wiener. 1992. "The Comprehensive Approach to Global Climate Policy: Issues of Design and Practicality." *Arizona Journal of International and Comparative Law* 9 (1): 83–112.

UN Conference on the Human Environment. 1972. *Declaration of the United Nations Conference on the Human Environment, UN Doc. A/Conf.48/14/Rev.1*. Stockholm: United Nations Conference on the Human Environment.

UN General Assembly. 1988. *Protection of Global Climate for Present and Future Generations of Mankind, UN General Assembly Res. 43/53, UN Doc. A/43/49. 70th Plenary Meeting*. New York: UN General Assembly.

———. 1990. *Protection of Global Climate for Present and Future Generations of Mankind, UN General Assembly Res. 45/212, UN Doc. A/45/49*. New York: UN General Assembly.

UNDP. 2008. *Fighting Climate Change: Human Solidarity in a Divided World - Human Development Report 2007–8*. New York: United Nations Development Program.

UNEP. 1985. *Vienna Convention for the Protection of the Ozone Layer*. Vienna: United Nations Environment Program/Ozone Secretariat.

UNEP. 1987. Montreal Protocol on Substances that Deplete the Ozone Layer.

UNFCCC. 1992. *United Nations Framework Convention on Climate Change*. New York: United Nations.

———. 1997. *Kyoto Protocol to the United Nations Framework Convention on Climate Change*. Kyoto: United Nations.

———. 1999. Decision 10/CP.4, Multilateral Consultative Process, in CP/1998/16/Add.1 (25 January 1999).

———. 2002a. Decision 1/CP.7, Marrakesh MInisterial Declaration, in FCCC/CP/2001/13/Add.1 (21 January 2002).

———. 2002b. Decisions 2-24/CP.7, Marrakesh Accords, in FCCC/CP/2001/13/Add.1-3 (21 January 2002).

———. 2006. Decision 1/CMP.1, Consideration of Commitments for Subsequent Periods for Parties Included in Annex I to the Convention under Article 3, Paragraph 9 of the Kyoto Protocol, in FCCC/KP/CMP/2005/8/Add.1 (30 March 2006).

———. 2008. Decision 1/CP.13, Bali Action Plan, in FCCC/CP/2007/6/Add.1 (14 March 2008).

———. 2010. Decision 2/CP.15, Copenhagen Accord, in FCCC/CP/2009/11/Add.1 (30 March 2010).

———. 2011. Decision 1/CP.16, Cancun Agreements: Outcome of the Work of the Ad Hoc Working Group on Long-Term Cooperative Action under the Convention, in FCCC/CP/2010/7/Add.1 (15 March 2011).

———. 2012. Decision 1/CP.17, Establishing of an Ad Hoc Working Group on a Durban Platform for Enhanced Action, 2011, in FCCC/CP/2011/9/Add.1 (15 March 2012).

———. 2014. Decision 1/CP.19, Further Advancing the Durban Platform, in FCCC/CP/2013/10/Add.1 (31 January 2014).

———. 2015. *Paris Agreement*. Paris: United Nations.

———. 2016a. Distribution of Registered Projects by Host Party. Edited by UNFCCC.

———. 2016b. Decision 1/CP.21, Adoption of the Paris Agreement, in FCCC/CP/10/Add.1 (29 January 2016).

Vellinga, Pier, Peter Kendall, and Joyeeta Gupta. 1989. *Noordwijk Conference Report.* Netherlands: Netherlands Ministry of Housing, Physical Planning and Environment.

WMO. 1989. "The Changing Atmosphere Implications for Global Security." Paper read at the World Conference on the Changing Atmosphere: Implications for Global Security, June 27–30, 1988, Toronto, Canada.

WRI. 2016. *Climate Analysis Indicators Tool.* Available from http://cait.wri.org/.

Zelke, Durwood, and James Cameron. 1990. "Global Warming and Climate Change: An Overview of the International Legal Process." *American University Journal of International Law and Policy* 5 (2): 249–290.

3 International Relations Theories and Climate Change Politics

Michaël Aklin

3.1 Introduction

Paraphrasing Michael Taylor (1987), the study of politics is the study of collective action problems. International relations, as a whole, and the issue of climate change, in particular, fit this definition. Climate change is the consequence of the collective behavior of billions of individuals, who, by emitting greenhouse gases (GHG) emissions, impose the costs of their deeds on each other. Another way to say this is that people impose negative externalities on each other. When these externalities are powerful enough to trigger climate change, then one may truly talk about a "tragedy of the commons" (Hardin 1968).

Collective action failures occur all the time. Generally, when they are localized in a small geographic area, mechanisms exist to ensure that people behave in a socially optimal way. For instance, if your neighbor plays music too loudly, there are rules to ensure that he will reduce the volume to an acceptable level. If he fails to comply with these rules, he may receive the visit of the police. If he still refuses to obey, then he may have to pay a fine. Thus, within a country, laws and enforcement mechanisms are designed to ensure that negative externalities remain limited and collective action failures hopefully confined to areas of lesser importance. More generally, we may think of the state as the institution responsible to reduce negative externalities and provide public goods.

Of course, there is no state or government at the international level. Thus, when entire countries impose negative externalities on each other, there is no readily available mechanism to make them stop. Even when states come to an agreement about how to behave, there is not always a police-like institution that can verify and enforce compliance. International relations are therefore fraught with situations in which the collective action of states (and their people) is not optimal. Climate change is a clear example: every country is free to keep the benefits of emitting GHG (such as a vibrant economy, the pleasure of driving polluting cars, and so forth) for itself while imposing the cost (global warming and its impacts) on the entire planet. Whether the Paris Agreement of 2015 will solve this remains to be seen. Its predecessor, the Kyoto Protocol, attempted to provide a legal framework to reduce GHG emissions. Its success, as indicated in chapter 1 in this volume, has remained limited. Why?

To answer this question, we need to understand why global collective action sometimes fails. International Relations (IR) theories provide us with tools to analyze and predict the reasons for international collective action failure. They offer us a blueprint of the international architecture, pointing at its weaknesses and kinks. They may also suggest ways to overcome existing issues. Just like a physician tries to establish a diagnostic from observing a patient's symptoms, the IR scholar will have in her mind a theory of how international relations function. She will identify the obstacle to fruitful cooperation, and then prescribe the appropriate medicine—if there is any.

To make a useful contribution to our understanding of the international politics of climate change, the IR scholar has to provide an explanation for two empirical facts. First, she will have to explain the successes and failures of the existing climate regime. The hopes generated by the Kyoto Protocol in 1997 faded soon after, despite occasional signs of progress. Overall, the success of the climate regime has been at best mixed. The degree to which countries achieved international cooperation is discussed in the next section. I draw on the major IR theories (realism, institutionalism, and constructivism) to explain the partial regulation of GHG emissions. Each theory points at different sources of collective action failures and prescribes a different medicine to solve these problems.

Second, an IR theorist must also contend with a more recent phenomenon: Even though international negotiations stalled between Kyoto and Paris, a number of countries engaged in unilateral climate policy making. For instance, the EU enacted a carbon emissions trading market, which caps emissions in a number of industrial sectors. Why the EU would do so if the rest of the world does not follow is not immediately evident. Similarly, many industrialized and developing countries implemented policies to promote clean energy, such as wind or solar power. By shifting energy generation from fossil fuels such as coal to renewable energy, these countries seek to slow down the growth of their GHG emissions. Again, why would they do that if other countries do not reciprocate?

For traditional IR theories, this is an unexpected turn of events. In the absence of a global agreement on GHG emissions, it is not clear why these countries would do this. Most IR theories focus on international cooperation; how can we make sense of these unilateral actions? This question is tackled in the third section. To understand these recent developments, we focus on theories that emphasize domestic and international linkages. Specifically, we examine how international shocks can affect domestic policy making, and how local policies can then reverberate to change the international system. These feedback loops may help us understand why climate politics dramatically shifted from the international to the national level.

3.2   International Theories and Climate Change

Social science theories generally consist of a "reasoned and precise speculation about the answer to a research question" (King, Keohane, and Verba 1994, 19). More often than not, the research topic in international politics revolves around a situation in which undesirable events occurred because important stakeholders failed to coordinate or to cooperate.[1] In IR, these stakeholders may be states, but this is not always the case (Lake 2008, 42). The English School, under the impulse of scholar such as Hedley Bull or John Burton, paid close attention to the role of transnational organizations such as corporations, religious institutions, and international political movements (Bull 2002; Burton 1972). In the United States, studies on transnational politics dealt with similar issues (Keohane and Nye 1977). In the context of climate politics, scholars have been particularly attentive to the role of NGOs and international firms (see chapters 8 and 9 in this volume). At any rate, to study climate change from an IR perspective is to analyze why governments and other relevant actors failed to come up with a solution to the central problem of GHG emissions. From a global perspective, it would be beneficial to reduce GHG emissions, but no country has an evident incentive to do so on its own. We next discuss the main schools and what they have to say about climate cooperation or the lack thereof.

3.2.1 Realism and Neorealism

A natural starting point to study international climate politics is the realist paradigm. One reason for this is chronological: realism was particularly important in the development of IR as a modern academic field after the Second World War, at least in the United States (for a history of IR, see Waever [1998]). Another reason is that realism has a high degree of abstraction, which places it at one extreme of IR scholarship.

Modern realism claims to have deep historical roots. Some interpretations have not been shy to trace realism all the way back to Thucydides (Keohane and Nye 1977, 42).[2] His account of the Peloponnesian War suggests that there is little order outside the *polis* (Forde 1995). Unchecked, human ambition unavoidably leads to conflicts and wars. In the absence of a powerful ruler, anarchy dominates. In an era characterized by widespread violence, such views were not uncommon and shared by observers in other parts of the world, such as Kautilya in India or Ibn-Khaldun in North Africa (Keohane and Martin 1995; Morgenthau 1952, 963).

Contemporary realism emerged in the first half of the twentieth century (although its modern roots can be traced back to the nineteenth century). The breakdown of the League of Nations system and the emerging Cold War motivated the development of a positive theory of IR that accounted for these two events (Carr 1940; Morgenthau 1948). The basic tenets of realism are that states seek power, because it is in their leaders' very nature (Morgenthau 1948, 36). Clearly inspired by the dramatic events of the World War II, Morgenthau and his like-minded fellows insist on the difficulty of taming mankind's natural instincts. This line of thought draws heavily on thinkers like Reinhold Niebuhr, who developed a similarly pessimistic view of human nature (Forde 1995).

This rationale was systematized under Kenneth Waltz's *neorealist* paradigm. Neorealism rests on a fairly simple set of claims (Waltz 1979). States are unitary actors. They are all alike in most respects, except for their power, meaning that their domestic characteristics matter little. States, like human beings, seek to prosper and possibly to expand. Given that this applies to all states, the international system is characterized by a state of anarchy, which implies that there are no rules to restrain the primary instincts of states. There is not much states can do about this: just like nature determines how animals have to behave to stay alive, states are forced by anarchy into focusing on survival. Prospects for meaningful cooperation are dire, because states cannot risk being taken advantage of. This diminishes the scope for long-term planning; instead, states have to focus on the short run. The world is best described by a prisoner's dilemma, whereby even though cooperation between states is appealing, defection remains invariably the best strategy for countries (see chapter 4 in this volume). International institutions are then either empty shells or simply the expression of the powerful (Mearsheimer 1995).

What, then, can neorealism teach us about climate change politics? First, neorealists may contend that it is not even clear whether states truly wish to reduce GHG emissions. Since power is partly drawn from a solid economy, anything that might curb growth in the short run should be viewed with suspicion (Waltz 2000). To the extent that a climate treaty requires the reduction of industrial activities, realists would be skeptical about whether states could credibly commit to it. In fact, when then-president George W. Bush announced his unwillingness to ratify the Kyoto Protocol, he motivated this decision by underscoring the economic cost of the treaty: "Kyoto would have wrecked our economy" (as quoted in Stevenson and Cowell 2005).

Second, even if states value cuts in GHG emissions, finding an agreement is expected to be extremely difficult. This has two reasons. The first is that states are unlikely to value the future enough to strike a deal with each other. Immediate survival outweighs potentially beneficial long-term gains. Short-termism is a problem because of the timeline of climate change, whose effect is expected to materialize over several decades. The second reason is that even if states do care about the future, then they may worry about the distributional consequences of a treaty. For instance, if the United States were asked to make concessions that could jeopardize its economic might, it would then be unlikely to agree to a deal, even if its leaders value the future (Walt 1998). The issue, from a neorealist perspective, is that a meaningful climate agreement requires very asymmetric efforts.

Third, even if the world's leaders manage to reach an agreement (like they did in Kyoto and Paris), they may still find the obstacles to the implementation of such an agreement overwhelming. States cannot help but be suspicious about each other. This, according to realism, has two reasons. To begin with, even if an international agreement to cut GHG emissions were agreed on (like the Kyoto Protocol), there is no enforcer to ensure compliance—there is no policeman, so to speak. If a country were to renege on its obligations—and some did so under Kyoto—then it would not have to suffer any consequence.

International treaties, in the realist perspective, are mostly toothless. In addition to this, it is difficult to monitor a country's behavior. How can the United States know what China's CO_2 emissions are? Statistics are typically collected by local officials and can be unreliable. International agreements generally make provisions for this. The Paris Agreement uses the word "transparency" seventeen times (for a total of twenty-nine articles!). But governments may lie and there is little their foreign counterparts can do about it. To the extent that monitoring is really difficult, states may be taken advantage of without even realizing it; clearly, this is highly undesirable from a policy maker's perspective and may discourage her from participating in an agreement in the first place. If the United States were to cut emissions under the assumption that China was doing so, too, but the latter in fact only pretended to reduce its emissions, then the United States would have hurt itself with little results to show for it.

These three issues—a short-time horizon as well as enforcement and monitoring problems—worsen the already difficult prospects for cooperation under anarchy. Neorealists would thus generally feel comforted by the failures of the Copenhagen, Cancun, and Durban meetings. Reducing GHG emissions is a threat to a country's power; there are no ways to monitor and enforce compliance with any prospective treaty, and international cooperation is hard anyway. If a regime were to emerge, it would be a weak one.

Does this mean that public goods are never provided at the global level? Some analysts (some of whom are realists, others who are not but accept some of its views) think that the situation is not completely hopeless. A *hegemon* may emerge and be willing to impose cooperation across the world (Gilpin 1988; Kindleberger 1973). In a sense, a hegemon solves the issue of enforcement: if the hegemon wants an international agreement to operate, it can use its resources to threaten recalcitrant partners.

IR scholarship has generally identified the United States as being the most recent international hegemon (Keohane 1984). In the aftermath of the Second World War, the United States has had the military and economic capabilities to enforce international contracts. There are, however, two issues with the United States as the hegemon in the case of climate change. First, its interest in this topic has been ambivalent at best. Despite initial support by the Clinton administration, President George W. Bush rapidly made it clear that he had little interest in a comprehensive climate treaty.

Second, the ability of the United States to provide hegemonic leadership declined over the past decades. It is nowadays difficult to imagine the United States having the means to coerce and cajole countries such as China or India into agreeing to cut their GHG emissions. Incidentally, the decline of American power coincides with the beginning of the climate negotiations. Hegemony theorists may thus be empowered to conclude that what the climate needs is the reemergence of a powerful hegemon that would provide order in an anarchic system.

3.2.2 Neoliberal Institutionalism

The emergence of neoliberal institutionalism in the 1980s coincides with two changes. The first is the belief mentioned above that the United States was abating and thus unable to provide hegemonic order in the international system (Keohane 1984). The second is the sense that international agreements and institutions may have been more effective than what realists were predicting. Success stories such as the trade regime under the General Agreement on Tariffs and Trade (GATT) and later under the World Trade Organization (WTO) were hard to square with the main predictions of realism. Together, these paved the way for the neoliberal institutionalist research agenda: Can international institutions solve global collective action problems, and have they actually done so?

Realists claim that most international interactions can be conceptualized as a prisoner's dilemma: they may agree that global cooperation would be desirable, but they point at the fact that the equilibrium of such a game is widespread defection. Neoliberal institutionalists generally accept that these are the rules of the game, but argue that there are ways in which states may be able to move from a noncooperative to a cooperative outcome. States are still selfish actors, but they may find a way to overcome their inability to secure international agreements. International institutions are then the tools that make this transition possible and long lasting.

The neoliberal institutionalist argument generally rests on bargaining theory. Ronald Coase (1960), a British economist, tried to understand how people and firms could efficiently deal with negative externalities such as pollution. Coase claimed that under certain precise conditions, firms could simply bargain with those who suffer from it. For instance, a firm could buy the right to pollute from the people who are hit by its factory's emissions. Or reversely, the victims could pay the firm to stop polluting. Regardless of its exact form, such an agreement could be socially optimal. The key for this argument to hold is that three conditions have to be met. First, information must be perfect (it must be clear who is polluting, who is the victim, and how much each side benefits and suffers from any agreement). Second, transaction costs must be nil (bargaining an agreement is quick and painless). Third, property rights must be well-defined (somebody has to be in a position to sell her right to pollute or her right to be protected from pollution). Keohane's (1984) key insight is that international institutions, by providing the groundwork for these three conditions to be fulfilled, could enable meaningful international cooperation (see chapter 1 in this volume for the strengths and limitations of this approach). Institutions can impartially collect data, provide a forum for negotiations, and provide a legal framework for the bargaining process.

To be certain, the prospects for cooperation are not always equally bright. Oran Young (1989) suggested that some problems are just harder to solve than others. Furthermore, some actors are more likely to be willing to cooperate than others. Arild Underdal (1980) and his followers note that international agreements tend to match the preferences of the least ambitious country that is part of it. David Victor (2006) notes that climate negotiations have been particularly prone to lack of ambition among key participants. Features that affect a bargaining process, such as an actor's patience, her outside options, and so forth, all determine the prospects for an international regime to emerge and be effective. Nonetheless, to the extent that a common interest and a solution exist, cooperation should be feasible.

The question, then, is to find the optimal design for international institutions (Koremenos, Lipson, and Snidal 2001; Mitchell 1994). Institutions vary in terms of the members they have, the degree of institutionalization, the presence of flexibility mechanisms, their enforcement rules, and so forth. A good example of a successful institution is the GATT/WTO, which allows states to opt out of their obligations if an emergency occurs (Rosendorff, Milner, and Milner 2001). This reassures states ex ante, and increases compliance. These parameters allow the architects of an institution to adapt it to the particular needs of an issue area. In turn, this enables them to improve the effectiveness of this institution.

Neoliberal institutionalism thus sees collective action failure in a different light than realism. Realism predicts that cooperation will be lacking because of the structure of the international system, and the inability of states to credibly comply with any agreement. Neoliberal institutional-ists see failure in collective action arising not from the intrinsic anarchy of international politics, but from the states' failure in creating adequate insti-tutions. Specifically, three problems may arise. First, the problem at stake may be too complex to enable a solution that satisfies all players. Clearly, climate change raises numerous issues. How much do emissions need to be reduced? This is a complex problem. In fact, climate change has been referred to as a "super wicked" problem (Levin et al. 2012). Super wicked problems are highly difficult to solve, because they are time sensitive (time is running out), there is no room for trial and error, and our understanding of the problem changes as scientists make new discoveries. By contrast, if one wants to increase, say, the buffalo population in the United States, one can experiment different repopulation strategies with different herds and pick the most successful one. Because of its long-term nature, there are no such opportunities to stop climate change.

Second, states may be unable to find a satisfactory agreement because of their own preferences. This is not because they worry about defection, but because states may differ in their priorities. For instance, states may have wildly different time horizons. An issue such as climate change is much more urgent for Pacific Islands than for, say, the United Kingdom. Some countries can afford to wait, and even if they value the future highly, they may be willing to hold out for a better deal (Fearon 1998). Another obstacle is that developing countries may value growth over mitigation more than industrialized countries (Aklin et al. 2013).

Actors' incentives certainly played a role in the obstacles faced by the climate regime. Dieter Helm succinctly summarized the problem:

the allocation of responsibility for the existing stock of carbon in the atmosphere (…) is complex; carbon emissions per head are low in those countries most rapidly increasing their emissions; some countries (…) may actually benefit from climate change, and generally the effects vary greatly between countries; there are powerful—multidimensional—free-rider incentives; the measurement of emissions (…) is at best weak; and there are, at present, no serious enforcement mechanisms. (2008, 219)

This leads him to conclude that "it is hard to think of an international problem which lends itself less to a coherent, credible, and sufficiently robust and comprehensive general agreement."

Third, collective action may be suboptimal because the relevant interna-tional institutions are poorly designed. Indeed, issues of institutional design certainly affected the Kyoto Protocol and its subsequent fortunes. This happened in two ways: (1) the allocation of duties and rights; and (2) the rules and procedures in case of noncompliance. The first issue is the distribution of responsibilities. GHG emissions need to be cut to reduce the pace of climate change. This, however, does not say *who* should be cutting their emissions. The fact that developing countries such as China were not required to reduce their GHG emissions became a source of contention and one of the reasons why the United States eventually decided to leave the Kyoto Protocol. On this front, the Paris Agreement appears to take a more flexible approach by letting countries decide themselves what their "nationally determined contribution" (i.e., emissions reductions) should be (UNFCCC 2015, art. 3).

The second issue pertains to the institutional mechanisms used to reduce GHG emissions. A key feature of the Kyoto regime was the so-called flexibility mechanisms. The idea was that the reduction of emissions should be done efficiently; instead of a fixed cap on emissions, countries should be able to buy and sell permits. This was an ambitious plan, not least because there were few past examples to learn from. It did not work, because it is really difficult to allocate these permits in a climate-friendly way (Victor 2004). Politicians are under tremendous pressure to create too many permits and pass them on to friendly business interests. The problem of monitoring worsens this issue.

3.2.3 Constructivism

Realism and neoliberal institutionalism seek to derive predictions from a number of well-established premises. States and their leaders possess well-defined preferences; the origins of these preferences are rooted in some variant of the will to survive. What "survival" exactly means in turn varies for each theory. However, these perspectives share the view that the interests of stakeholders are given by nature, and their interactions are defined by their material reality (Wendt 1999). What remains to be done, for realists and neoliberal institutionalists, is to understand what the implications of this setup are.

Constructivism challenges this worldview. Constructivists contend that preferences are shaped by beliefs, and these beliefs have societal sources. Material interests do thus not directly define preferences; rather, their effect is mediated by ideas and beliefs (Kratochwil 1989). Therefore, perceptions can change even in the absence of a change of the underlying material reality. For instance, Alexander Wendt famously and provocatively argued that "anarchy is what states make of it" (1992, 424). In other words, the existence of anarchy is a belief, a worldview that is socially constructed and does not necessarily correspond to a real phenomenon. By contrast, realists assume that preferences are exogenously determined and constrained by the harsh reality of the international system. Initially at least, neoliberal institutionalists shared similar beliefs.

The next step, then, is to understand what determines a state's preferences and ultimately its actions. This, according to Peter Haas, is "distributions of power, knowledge, and formal institutional properties" (2004, 585). Ideas (and the identity of those defending them) set the stage for state action in domestic and international politics. Constructivism therefore offers considerable room for nonstate actors, given that they could nudge the state in one direction or another (see chapters 8 and 9 in this volume on nonstate actors and firms).

What are the implications of the constructivist perspective for international relations and for climate politics in particular? They are twofold. The first is that cooperation is possible, but for different reasons than those argued by neoliberal institutionalists and realists. In the latter two approaches, states (or their leaders) have well-defined preferences; the obstacle to cooperation rests on issues such as monitoring or enforcement. For constructivists, preferences evolve through new ideas and learning, which happens through social mechanisms (Finnemore and Sikkink 2001, 406).

Therefore, cooperation may not necessarily be hard; what is required is that states understand each other and talk the same language (Hopf 1998). The "Special Relationship" between the United Kingdom and the United States, for instance, cannot readily be explained by traditional IR theories. Cultural affinity may facilitate interstate relations, which is consistent with a constructivist perspective. The question then is whether enough countries speak the same language with respect to climate change. Most certainly, profound disagreements about the origins and consequences of climate change, which may be affected by social beliefs, impeded past progress on the climate question. The deep divisions between the North (Annex I countries) and the South reflect not only material considerations, but also perceptions of what climate change entails and the responsibility of each in causing it.

The second implication is that the (social) roots of preferences and the way climate change is perceived must both be carefully studied. Preferences are complex and cannot easily be narrowed down to, say, power or wealth. Rather, they are the product of an evolutionary process that is rooted in both domestic and international experiences. In the case of climate change, one particularly relevant source of preferences comes from scientists and the so-called epistemic communities (Haas 1992). By raising the alarm about a topic such as climate change, they may be in a position to influence the policy debate. Haas (2004, 577) argues that in some cases, "the substance of regimes reflects scientific consensus about the most important environmental threats, and negotiated standards reflect consensus about the degree of environmental stress the target environment can sustain." Since few decision makers are in a position to understand the science underlying climate change directly, they rely on the beliefs that they have based on what the epistemic community may communicate to them. This point is discussed in greater detail in chapter 7.

At the same time, political agents with their own agenda often intercept knowledge for their personal benefit. For instance, David Demeritt (2006) documents the politicization of the climate question in the United States since the late 1980s. The transformation of the climate change question has been remarkable. The very perception of the reality of climate change has evolved from a bipartisan issue on which George H. W. Bush and Al Gore could agree to a deeply contentious problem (Boykoff and Boykoff 2004). Internationally, too, the way climate change is understood varies considerably. Haas (2004, 582) notices the underrepresentation of scientists from developing countries at the IPCC and suggests that it may impede cooperation. This, however, only further underscores the importance of understanding the roots of decision makers' preferences and how these evolve over time. This important insight reshaped the way many IR theorists model international politics (Wendt 1999).

3.2.4   The Limits of International Relations Theories

Any (probabilistic) theory, by definition, will at some point fail to account for some observable event. Since a theory simplifies reality, and there is an element of randomness in most events in which human beings are involved, a theory will inevitably make wrong predictions. What is important is whether (1) a theory *systematically* makes wrong empirical claims and (2) we can leverage this theory to shed light on a critical aspect of international politics. In other words, is this theory useful and unbiased (in the sense of not making repeatedly the same errors)?

Despite their partial successes, the theories mentioned so far struggle to deal with the current state of climate politics. To varying degrees, these theories shed light on the issues that prevent successful international cooperation. However, they are unable to explain an important puzzle in current climate politics: in the past decade, many climate-related policies have been enacted throughout the world even though international negotiations have made little progress. Countries are unilaterally implementing regulations that would not have existed if climate change had not become a major policy issue. To give just two examples, the EU implemented a large carbon emissions trading market (Ellerman and Buchner 2007), and vast amounts of money are invested in renewable energy around the world, even though there is little risk of fossil fuel shortages in the middle run (Aklin and Urpelain 2013). European efforts to curb carbon by putting a price on it, is puzzling from an IR perspective: Why would European countries agree to it, knowing that it will not solve the issue at the international level while being costly? And this puzzle is not limited to Europe. Renewable energy policies, for instance, have spread to many countries, both rich and poor. Figure 3.1 shows that numerous countries across the world adopted pro-renewable energy policies, even in the absence of a robust international climate treaty.[3]

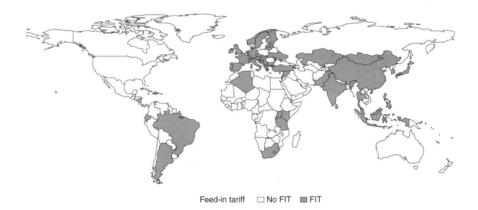

Feed-in tariff   □ No FIT   ■ FIT

Figure 3.1
Feed-in tariffs across the world.
Source: Data from REN21 (2013) and Bayer and Urpelainen (2016).

In most cases, these policies are sold to people as a tool to combat climate change. In the absence of international agreements, it is unclear why countries would unilaterally proceed this way. In fact, it goes against some of the basic tenets of the theories we mentioned above, namely, the selfish pursuit of self-interest. Why do countries behave this way? And what are the implications for international climate negotiations? To answer these questions, we need to dig deeper in the interactions between domestic and international politics.

3.3 Domestic-International Linkages

The study of the interactions between domestic and international politics in climate politics is a more recent development of the scholarship in environmental politics (with exceptions, such as Sprinz and Vaahtoranta 1994). Realism and, to a lesser extent, neoliberal institutionalism spend scant attention on domestic politics. Constructivists do study them, but often provide few ways to operationalize the way social forces shape state preferences.

There are two reasons why we should pay close attention to what happens inside countries. First, foreign policy making is partly determined and constrained by domestic audiences (Fearon 1994). Voters and lobbies observe what their officials do, and this may in turn affect the latter's policy preferences. For instance, if German voters want to see cuts in carbon emissions, their chancellor is more likely to act than if they do not care. More generally, if voters and interest groups want something, then it is unclear whether states are still trapped in a prisoner's dilemma (Urpelainen 2009).

Second, climate change is strongly affected by technology. In fact, climate change as a policy issue would promptly be solved if a new technology that could cheaply prevent GHG emissions were developed. Technology, in turn, is a function of domestic politics and the support research and development obtains from policy makers. The extent to which states are able to spread technologies is a topic of international politics, but the original impetus stems from mostly domestic considerations.

3.3.1 International Relations and Domestic Politics

It is, of course, inaccurate to claim that IR theorists have been blind to domestic politics. There are entire streams of research, presented below, which have studied the interactions between the domestic and international levels.

Classical realists knew from experience that domestic politics could interfere with sound foreign policy. Even neorealists, to some degree, agreed. Kenneth Waltz himself argued that "states are not and never have been the only international actors (…). The importance of nonstate actors and the extent of transnational activities are obvious" (1979, 93). However, it is natural that the emphasis of IR scholarship has focused on the *international* sources of failure and success rather than the *domestic* obstacles to sound climate policies.

As previously mentioned, many political scientists have readily conceded that domestic politics matters in international politics. This point was made forcefully by Putnam (1988), who modeled international negotiations as a situation in which a government has to take into account both domestic and international considerations (see chapter 7 in this volume). Some schools such as the "new liberal" approach have pointed at the role of domestic interests in shaping foreign policy (Bueno de Mesquita et al. 2003; Moravcsik 2003). For instance, democracies have been found more willing to cooperate and promote peace, at least among each other. These scholars generally belong to one of two traditions. First are those who examine how domestic political factors shape IR. Second are those who examine the reverse, namely how IR defines domestic outcomes. We next examine both cases.

3.3.2   From Domestic to International Politics: The Second Image

The basic idea that what happens within the state may have an effect on international politics is as old as politics itself. Kenneth Waltz refers to this view as the "second image" (Waltz 1979). In fact, that is the very object of IR as a field of study. Underneath this, however, is a subtler idea: two states placed in an identical situation may behave very differently depending on their domestic conditions. Realists consider this to be nonsense: states are forced by the nature of the international system to behave in a way that maximizes their survival chances. Neoliberal institutionalists similarly focus more on interstate relations than on intrastate politics. This, however, ignores the wealth of differences that exist across countries and that may shape a government's foreign policy.

The basic premise of second-image approaches is that there is something in the domestic arena that incentivizes or constrains decision makers to behave in a certain way. There are four main sources for this. First, *citizens* may have particular preferences for a certain type of action. Local values and culture may shape the way a country responds to a challenge.

Second, decision makers may also be nudged by *interest groups*. An interest group is a collection of agents who have agreed to pool their resources to influence policy makers. Interest groups may include business communities, trade unions, religious entities, and so forth. A coal-mining firm, for instance, is particularly likely to have preferences that differ from an environmentally minded citizen.

Third, *political parties* may have very different views about what the right policy is. A green party is obviously likely to care more about the environment than its competitors. In response, traditional parties may develop their own environmental policies (Dalton 1994). It is particularly leftist parties that have typically been more likely to exhibit pro-environmental stances than their rightist counterparts (Neumayer 2003). To some degree, their views are certainly shaped by their supporters; however, it is doubtlessly true that politicians in different political parties have profound ideological differences, and these may shape the way they prioritize climate policies.

This leads us to the last element, namely, *domestic institutions*. By institutions, we refer to the set of rules that determine how collective decisions are made at the national level. Institutions vary tremendously across countries. Some have democratic rules, some are heavily gangrened by corruption, and some are highly efficient. And this is not an exhaustive list. Some democracies have adopted a federal system (e.g., the United States), whereas others have a centralized government (e.g., France) (Lijphart 1999).

Why does this matter? The way institutions adjudicate conflicts and aggregate the preferences of a society's main stakeholders (citizens, interest groups, and parties) affects the kind of policies that will be enacted in this particular country. Regardless of what the British prime minister does, the German chancellor has to carefully examine demands by voters, industrial interests, green NGOs, and the parliament. She also has to take into account the electoral rules of her country: What do farmers in Bavaria want? Are their votes more important than coal miners from the Ruhr's votes? Similarly, a dictator may face very different constraints on her power than a democratically elected official does (Bueno de Mesquita et al. 2003).

How does this help us in our quest to understand current climate policies? Scholarship has shown that all factors mentioned—citizens, interest groups, parties, and institutions—have had some effect on climate policy making. Beginning with individuals, studies have shown that people's views on environmental issues vary greatly depending on who they are. For instance, wealthier individuals seem in some cases to be more likely to be pro-environment (Franzen and Meyer 2010).[4] The same goes with more educated people (Aklin et al. 2013).

Similarly, the role of interests such as firms has often been mentioned. Of course, firms that emit large amounts of GHG may have an incentive to torpedo international climate agreements. However, business interests sometimes also work to improve environmental regulations. David Vogel (1997) argues that international trade plays here a key role: firms that want to sell their goods in countries with high environmental standards may push their domestic governments to enact tougher environmental regulations. The reason is that they do not want to be excluded from these lucrative markets. Vogel labeled it the "California effect."

Parties may play a key role too (Bernauer and Koubi 2009). A typical example is the case of renewable energy policy. Since the 1980s, leftist parties have tended to provide a more favorable environment for renewable energy generation (Aklin and Urpelain 2013). For instance, the role of the red-green coalition in Germany in expanding public support for renewable energy in 1998 and 2000 was instrumental in making the country a worldwide powerhouse. And the election in the 2001 Danish elections of Anders Fogh Rasmussen and his Venstre party (center right) marked a period of decline for its wind industry (Ryland 2010).

Finally, the institutional setting in which parties, interest groups, and citizens exist is central in the formulation of environmental and climate policies. Democratic institutions have attracted a lot of attention. There are two reasons for this. First, democracies are more likely to generate high levels of public goods (Bueno de Mesquita et al. 2003). Second, they are more likely to be able to overcome the obstacles to international cooperation. There are various explanations for this, one of which is that democratic leaders have to respond more closely to their electors' demands and it is harder for them to renege on past commitments. Michèle Bättig and Thomas Bernauer (2009) find that democracies tend to make stronger commitments to implement climate policies than nondemocracies do. Dai (2005, 2006) models patterns of compliance among democracies and shows that it varies with the relative strength of interest groups and how well informed these are. Her findings further underscore the critical role played by domestic factors in environmental politics.

Therefore, for IR scholars sympathetic to the second image approach, the roots of unilateral climate activism are to be found in the domestic structure of a country (DeSombre 2000). Countries behave differently because they have different voters, different interest groups, different political parties, and different institutions. This is not to say that these scholars think that international collective action issues do not exist. However, these issues per se do not yet prevent countries that want to implement climate and climate-related policies from doing so. A head of state will not care about being the only one to enact a carbon tax as long as her supporters want her to do so. In other words, the German chancellor will continue to support renewable energy as long as it generates political rewards, regardless of whether Washington or Beijing agree on a global climate agreement or not.

3.3.3 From International to Domestic Politics: The Second Image Reversed

What are the consequences of these unilateral environmental policies? Do the actions of a few countries that wish to promote climate policies have any external effects? If the answer is no, then we are back to square one: long-term climate policies can then come only from international agreements and cannot be sustained by ephemeral benign domestic conditions. Pro-climate parties can lose power and citizens may lose patience. However, if the answer is yes, then these local initiatives possibly have important implications. What leading countries do for their own climate may have global consequences.

The school that studies how the international system shapes domestic politics is generally referred to as the "second image reversed" (Gourevitch 1978). Peter Gourevitch inverses the perspective of Waltz: instead of considering how individual countries affect international politics, Gourevitch examines how international forces determine what happens in a country. In recent years, the notion of "diffusion" has examined a similar question (Dobbin, Simmons, and Garrett 2007). Events in one country seem sometimes to spread to other countries, a bit like a disease. This suggests that countries are not isolated islands, but tributary to what happens elsewhere.

This, of course, is particularly relevant for the climate issue. There are two main reasons for this. To begin with, since climate change is due to excessive GHG emissions, and since these emissions are the product of economic activity, the role of technology is key. How much GHG emissions a country emits will depend on the cleanliness of its technologies and production. Technologies, in turn, are another kind of public good. They can be shared and benefit whoever learns how to use them.

It then becomes clear why climate policies in Berlin, Copenhagen, and elsewhere may be relevant for the entire world. To the extent that these local initiatives lead to the development of new technologies, they affect the entire climate change issue. In a perfect world, a scientist may discover a way to make GHG emissions disappear and share her discovery with the rest of the world; this would magically solve the climate change problem. And in fact, scientists have long been trying to develop carbon capture technologies, whereby carbon is prevented from entering our atmosphere (Haszeldine 2009). Of course, these mechanisms may be limited to countries that have the resources and the capacity to implement new technologies. Take renewable energy: a country needs a decent amount of insolation for this technology to be effective. Moreover, for a long time, the cost of solar photovoltaic panels may have deterred poorer countries from using them.

Technologies are not the only climate-related item that can spread across countries. Many social scientists insist that domestic policies and even institutions can follow such a process. There are various reasons why this may happen (Gilardi 2010). A political leader may observe a successful policy somewhere else and decide that it would be a good fit for her own country. Or she might have strategic reasons to do so. A typical example is taxation: If France cuts its tax rates, Germany has an incentive to follow to avoid seeing its richest inhabitants leave for Paris. Of course, not all countries are equally likely to be responsive to these external shocks.[5] These analyses have their climate counterparts. Aklin (2016) shows that wealthy countries tend to outsource their CO_2 emissions to poorer countries. This could imply a race to the bottom, although Vogel's "California effect," mentioned earlier, might counterbalance this problem.

IR scholars have shown that these diffusion processes are certainly at work in the realm of environmental policies as well. Hugh Ward and Xun Cao (2012) argue that this occurred in the case of green taxation. Aklin and Urpelain (2014) contend that even environmental ministries are a recent innovation that has spread across the world over the past three decades. Therefore, local innovations (whether in the realm of technology or policy making) can have international consequences by changing the costs of tackling climate change across countries.

There is still a great deal of research required to understand how the domestic and international levels interact. Many examples above refer to broader environmental policies, without a clear reference to policies that directly relate to the climate issue. Furthermore, it is unclear how these unilateral decisions affect international climate negotiations. Perhaps they will have a beneficial effect. For instance, Europe's willingness to push for a new climate deal before the Paris Agreement is likely to be related to economic opportunities for its clean technology industry (Torney 2015). Beyond this, understanding the ties between the obstacles to international policy making (section 3.2) and the determinants of domestic policy making (section 3.3) is critical. Will countries that have invested in renewable energy behave differently at the bargaining table? Will it increase or will it reduce their appetite for a grand bargain? How will it affect the views of emerging countries? These are still open questions.

3.4   Conclusion

This chapter has reviewed the contributions of IR theories to our understanding of international climate politics in two ways. First, IR theorists, not unlike physicians, attempt to understand what may or may not cause international collective action failures. In other words, they seek to understand why states fail to cooperate and behave in a socially optimal way. Different schools predict different reasons why cooperation may fail. Realists underscore the anarchy of the international system, institutionalists focus on the obstacles to international bargaining, and constructivists argue that the study of the social origins of state preferences is key to understanding why cooperation occurs or fails to do so. At the same time, there is also considerable overlap between institutionalism and both realism and constructivism. Like realism, it is embedded in a rationalistic framework. Like constructivism, it devotes considerable attention to the role of domestic audiences and common knowledge, as noted in chapter 1 in this volume. Ultimately, the value of these very general theories may not lie in their validity (as we saw that they all fail to account for important facts), but rather in their ability to generate useful hypotheses as to why our efforts to solve environmental issues such as climate change often come up short. From a policy and a research perspective, the interesting questions then are: How can we improve the design of agreements? How can useful knowledge be shared with decision makers? How can better policies be spread around the world?

Second, we noticed that despite the failures of international policy making, a number of countries undertook in the past few years unilateral programs that are relevant to climate change. These recent developments are hard to square with the IR perspectives discussed above. However, they are understandable if one accounts for the many (bidirectional) linkages between international and domestic politics. Domestically, politicians may be incentivized to be proactive by public opinion and interest groups. This, in turn, feeds into the policy-making process in other countries. From both a normative and positive perspective, the most pressing needs are to understand the mechanisms that lead some countries to experiment with new ideas and those that allow these ideas to travel. Ultimately, this suggests that we need to improve our theoretical understanding of (1) the microfoundations of international politics (especially with respect to the interactions between citizens' preferences and institutions) and (2) the feedback loops that tie people across countries. Climate policy making is particularly complex and requires thinking in terms of the numerous layers that constitute the international system. It would therefore be particularly valuable to learn from countries that have demonstrated the ability to learn and become robust to shocks similar to climate change.

Notes

1. In some cases, undesirable events occurred because players cooperated *too well*. For instance, security alliances between states may lead to war.

2. For a skeptical take on this view, see Bagby (1994).

3. The policy reported here are feed-in tariffs, which are a widely used type of regulation favoring the deployment of renewable energy.

4. There is a considerable debate around the effect of income on environmental views. For more details, see Franzen and Meyer (2010).

5. Of course, there are frictions that prevent these forms of competition from spiraling out of control (Plümper, Troeger, and Winner 2009).

References

Aklin, Michaël. 2016. "Re-exploring the Trade and Environment Nexus through the Diffusion of Pollution." *Environmental and Resource Economics* 64 (4): 663–682.

Aklin, Michaël, and Johannes Urpelain. 2014. "The Global Spread of Environmental Ministries: Domestic-International Interactions." *International Studies Quarterly* 58 (4): 764–780.

———. 2013. "Political Competition, Path Dependence, and the Strategy of Sustainable Energy Transitions." *American Journal of Political Science* 57 (3): 643–658.

Aklin, Michaël, Patrick Bayer, S. P. Harish, and Johannes Urpelain. 2013. "Understanding Environmental Policy Preferences: New Evidence from Brazil." *Ecological Economics* 94:28–36.

Bagby, Laurie M. Johnson. 1994. "The Use and Abuse of Thucydides in International Relations." *International Organization* 48 (1): 131–153.

Bättig, Michèle, and Thomas Bernauer. 2009. "National Institutions and Global Public Goods: Are Democracies More Cooperative in Climate Change Policy?" *International Organization* 63 (2): 281–308.

Bayer, Patrick, and Johannes Urpelainen. 2016. "It Is All about Political Incentives: Democracy and the Renewable Feed-In Tariff." *Journal of Politics* 78 (2): 603–619.

Bernauer, Thomas, and Vally Koubi. 2009. "Effects of Political Institutions on Air Quality." *Ecological Economics* 68 (5): 1355–1365.

Boykoff, Maxwell T., and Jules M. Boykoff. 2004. "Balance as Bias: Global Warming and the US Prestige Press." *Global Environmental Change* 14 (2): 125–136.

Bueno de Mesquita, Bruce, Alastair Smith, Randolph M. Siverson, and James D. Morrow. 2003. *The Logic of Political Survival*. Cambridge, MA: MIT Press.

Bull, Hedley. 2002. *The Anarchical Society: A Study of Order in World Politics*. 3rd ed. Basingstoke: Palgrave.

Burton, John W. 1972. *World Society*. New York: Cambridge University Press.

Carr, Edward H. 1940. *The Twenty Years' Crisis*. London: Macmillan.

Coase, Ronald H. 1960. "The Problem of Social Cost." *Journal of Law and Economics* 3 (1): 1–44.

Dai, Xinyuan. 2006. "The Conditional Nature of Democratic Compliance." *Journal of Conflict Resolution* 50 (5): 609–713.

———. 2005. "Why Comply? The Domestic Constituency Mechanism." *International Organization* 59 (2): 363–398.

Dalton, Russell J. 1994. *The Green Rainbow. Environmental Groups in Western Europe*. New Haven, CT: Yale University Press.

Demeritt, David. 2006. "Science Studies, Climate Change, and the Prospects for Constructivist Critique." *Economy and Society* 35 (3): 453–479.

DeSombre, Elizabeth R. 2000. *Domestic Sources of International Environmental Policy: Industry, Environmentalists, and US Power*. Cambridge, MA: MIT Press.

Dobbin, Frank, Beth A. Simmons, and Geoffrey Garrett. 2007. "The Global Diffusion of Public Policies: Social Construction, Coercion, Competition, or Learning." *Annual Review of Sociology* 33:449–472.

Ellerman, A. Denny, and Barbara Buchner. 2007. "The European Union Emissions Trading Scheme: Origins, Allocation, and Early Results." *Review of Environmental Economics and Policy* 1 (1): 66–87.

Fearon, James. 1998. "Bargaining, Enforcement, and International Cooperation." *International Organization* 52 (2): 269–305.

———. 1994. "Domestic Political Audiences and the Escalation of International Disputes." *American Political Science Review* 88 (3): 577–592.

Finnemore, Martha, and Kathryn Sikkink. 2001. "Taking Stock: The Constructivist Research Program in International Relations and Comparative Politics." *Annual Review of Political Science* 4 (1): 391–416.

Forde, Steven. 1995. "International Realism and the Science of Politics: Thucydides, Machiavelli, and Neorealism." *International Studies Quarterly* 39 (2): 141–160.

Franzen, Axel, and Retor Meyer. 2010. "Environmental Attitudes in Cross-National Perspective: A Multilevel Analysis of the ISSP 1993 and 2000." *European Sociological Review* 26 (2): 219–234.

Gilardi, Fabrizio. 2010. "Who Learns from What in Policy Diffusion Processes?" *American Journal of Political Science* 54 (3): 650–666.

Gilpin, Robert. 1988. "The Origin and Prevention of Major Wars." *Journal of Interdisciplinary History* 18 (4): 591–613.

Gourevitch, Peter. 1978. "The Second Image Reversed: The International Sources of Domestic Politics." *International Organization* 32 (4): 881–912.

Haas, Peter. 1992. "Introduction: Epistemic Communities and International Policy Coordination." *International Organization* 46 (1): 1–35.

———. 2004. "When Does Power Listen to Truth? A Constructivist Approach to the Policy Process." *Journal of European Public Policy* 11 (4): 569–592.

Hardin, Garrett. 1968. "The Tragedy of the Commons." *Science* 162 (3859): 1243–1248.

Haszeldine, R. Stuart. 2009. "Carbon Capture and Storage: How Green Can Black Be?" *Science* 325 (5948): 1647–1652.

Helm, Dieter. 2008. "Climate-Change Policy: Why Has So Little Been Achieved." *Oxford Review of Economic Policy* 24 (2): 211–238.

Hopf, Ted. 1998. "The Promise of Constructivism in International Relations Theory." *International Security* 23 (1): 171–200.

Keohane, Robert O. 1984. *After Hegemony: Cooperation and Discord in the World Political Economy*. Princeton, NJ: Princeton University Press.

Keohane, Robert O., and Joseph S. Nye. 1977. *Power and Interdependence: World Politics in Transition*. Boston: Little, Brown.

Keohane, Robert O., and Lisa L. Martin. 1995. "The Promise of Institutionalist Theory." *International Security* 20 (1): 39–51.

Kindleberger, Charles P. 1973. *The World in Depression, 1929–1939*. Berkeley: University of California Press.

King, Gary, Robert O. Keohane, and Sidney Verba. 1994. *Designing Social Inquiry*. Princeton, NJ: Princeton University Press.

Koremenos, Barbara, Charles Lipson, and Duncan Snidal. 2001. "The Rational Design of International Institutions." *International Organization* 55 (4): 761–799.

Kratochwil, Friedrich V. 1989. *Rules, Norms, and Decisions: On the Conditions of Practical and Legal Reasoning in International Relations and Domestic Affairs*. Cambridge: Cambridge University Press.

Lake, David. 2008. "The State and International Relations." In *The Oxford Handbook of International Relations*, edited by Duncan Snidal and Christian Reus-Smit, 41–61. Oxford: Oxford University Press.

Levin, Kelly, Benjamin William Cashore, Steven Bernstein, and Graeme Auld. 2012. "Overcoming the Tragedy of Super Wicked Problems: Constraining Our Future Selves to Ameliorate Global Climate Change." *Policy Science* 45:123–152.

Lijphart, Arend. 1999. *Patterns of Democracy*. New Haven, CT: Yale University Press.

Mearsheimer, John J. 1995. "The False Promise of International Institutions." *International Security* 19 (3): 5–49.

Mitchell, Ronald B. 1994. "Regime Design Matters: Intentional Oil Pollution and Treaty Compliance." *International Organization* 48 (3): 425–458.

Moravcsik, Andrew. 2003. "Liberal International Relations Theory: A Scientific Assessment." In *Progress in International Relations Theory: Appraising the Field*, edited by Colin Elman and Miriam F. Elman, 159–204. Cambridge, MA: MIT Press.

Morgenthau, Hans J. 1952. "Another "Great Debate": The National Interest of the United States." *American Political Science Review* 46 (4): 961–988.

———. 1948. *Politics among Nations*. New York: Albert Knopf.

Neumayer, Eric. 2003. "Are Left-Wing Party Strength and Corporatism Good for the Environment? Evidence from Panel Analysis of Air Pollution in OECD Countries." *Ecological Economics* 45 (2): 203–220.

Plümper, Thomas, Vera E. Troeger, and Hannes Winner. 2009. "Why Is There No Race to the Bottom in Capital Taxation?" *International Studies Quarterly* 53 (3): 761–786.

Putnam, Robert D. 1988. "Diplomacy and Domestic Politics: The Logic of Two-Level Games." *International Organization* 42 (3): 427–460.

REN21. 2013. *Renewables Global Futures Report: 2013.* Paris: Renewable Energy Policy Network for the 21st Century.

Rosendorff, B., Peter Milner, and Helen V. Milner. 2001. "The Optimal Design of International Trade Institutions: Uncertainty and Escape." *International Organization* 55 (4): 829–857.

Ryland, Elisabeth. 2010. "Danish Wind Power Policy: Domestic and International Forces." *Environmental Politics* 19 (1): 80–85.

Sprinz, Detlef, and Tapani Vaahtoranta. 1994. "The Interest-Based Explanation of International Environmental Policy." *International Organization* 48 (1): 77–105.

Stevenson, Richard W., and Alan Cowell. 2005. "Bush Arrives at Summit Session, Ready to Stand Alone." *New York Times,* July 7.

Taylor, Michael. 1987. *The Possibility of Cooperation.* Cambridge: Cambridge University Press.

Torney, Diarmuid. 2015. *European Climate Leadership in Question: Policies toward China and India.* Cambridge, MA: MIT Press.

Underdal, Arild. 1980. *The Politics of International Fisheries Management. The Case of the Northeast Atlantic.* Oslo: Universiteitsforlaget.

UNFCCC. 2015. *Paris Agreement.* Paris: United Nations.

Urpelainen, Johannes. 2009. "Explaining the Schwarzenegger Phenomenon: Local Frontrunners in Climate Policy." *Global Environmental Politics* 9 (3): 82–105.

Victor, David G. 2004. *The Collapse of the Kyoto Protocol and the Struggle to Slow Global Warming.* Princeton, NJ: Princeton University Press.

———. 2006. "Toward Effective International Cooperation on Climate Change: Numbers, Interests and Institutions." *Global Environmental Politics* 6 (3): 90–103.

Vogel, David. 1997. "Trading up and Governing Across: Transnational Governance and Environmental Protection." *Journal of European Public Policy* 4 (4): 556–571.

Waever, Ole. 1998. "The Sociology of a Not So International Discipline: American and European Developments in International Relations." *International Organization* 52 (4): 687–727.

Walt, Stephen M. 1998. "International Relations: One World, Many Theories." *Foreign policy* 110: 29–46.

Waltz, Kenneth N. 2000. "Structural: Realism after the Cold War." *International Security* 25 (1): 5–41.

———. 1979. *Theory of International Politics*. Reading, MA: Addison-Wesley.

Ward, Hugh, and Xun Cao. 2012. "Domestic and International Influences on Green Taxation." *Comparative Political Studies* 45:1075–1103.

Wendt, Alexander. 1992. "Anarchy Is What States Make of It: The Social Construction of Power Politics." *International Organization* 46 (2): 391–425.

———. 1999. *Social Theory of International Politics*. Cambridge: Cambridge University Press.

Young, Oran R. 1989. "The Politics of International Regime Formation: Managing Natural Resources and the Environment." *International Organization* 43 (3): 349–375.

4   Cooperation on Climate Change: Insights from Game Theory

Frank Grundig, Jon Hovi, and Hugh Ward

4.1   Introduction

In the aftermath of the Copenhagen, Cancun, Durban, and Paris meetings, it is difficult to be optimistic about our chances of avoiding increases in global average temperature and associated changes to the climate that will not only damage many communities and nations but also destroy species and ecosystems. In particular, current attempts to construct a regime to deal with climate change hardly seem capable of averting potentially tragic collective action failure. All Annex B countries met their commitments to reduce emissions under the Kyoto Protocol, but the reductions in their emissions compared to business as usual were generally small, and they were offset by increases in emissions from some developing countries; so the overall impact of the process on climate change was trivial (Rosen 2015). Although the 2015 Paris Agreement was widely greeted with enthusiasm and scores reasonably highly on depth and ambition of commitments, its Achilles' heel is likely to be compliance, and it does little to restructure states' incentives so as to avoid free riding (Bang, Hovi, and Skodvin 2016).

It is widely accepted that the main factor causing such collective action failure is states' calculations about the degree to which it is rational for them to reduce their emissions of greenhouse gases or take other measures that might slow down climate change. Such calculations are understood to be based on economic factors such as perceived loss of competitiveness and opportunities foregone for economic growth, political factors such as degree of support among the electorate and the power of the carbon lobby, and institutional factors governing the degree to which pressure from the electorate and organized groups translates into policy. Such factors seem to explain some of the variance in the willingness of a state to make commitments on climate change (Harrison and McIntosh-Sundstrom 2010) and levels of cooperation (Bernauer and Böhmelt 2013). From the perspective of collective action theory, the basic problems are that states (1) do not factor in the spillover effects their actions have on other states and (2) heavily discount future benefits. As a result, they tend to underinvest in reducing emissions and, because controlling climate change in terms of mitigation is a nonexcludable public good, to free-ride on the actions taken by others (Barrett 1999; Sandler 1997; Ward 1996). The efficient Coasian solution (Coase 1960), based on informal bargaining from a preexisting distribution of enforceable property rights, is inapplicable, because no enforceable rights over climate stability exist in international law.

Two widely applicable ideas make rational choice models relevant for understanding climate change cooperation: The first is that we are witnessing a collective action failure over climate change. The second is that states choose efficient means to attain economic and political goals that are largely uninfluenced by the domestic and international political processes and institutions built around climate change. The rational choice approach has received considerable criticism, though. Green and Shapiro (1994) famously argue that rational choice is prone to making itself unfalsifiable by carrying out ad hoc adjustments to fit inconvenient facts, but no such amendments seem necessary to us in relation to climate change, where (national) self-interest clearly has led to collective action failure. Some liberal institutionalists argue that rational choice ignores the way that political processes, institutions and ideas frame the possibilities of efficient contracting but, perhaps more significantly, also alter the way that states perceive problems and their underlying preferences (Young 1999). We recognize that the fact that climate change is on the international agenda is a clear indication that ideas matter and that rational choice has little distinctive to say about belief and preference change. For good or quite possibly for ill (Victor 2011), the institutional architecture of the Kyoto Protocol has influenced developments. For some states and, notably, for the EU, the influence of international processes on voters and corporate interests has mattered to their willingness to go further than some (see chapter 9 in this volume). Nevertheless, climate change illustrates the power of the rational choice approach.

Although the idea of collective action failure seems a powerful one, an important issue is whether we need to develop more sophisticated models.

The basic understanding of collective action failure in public goods games goes right back to the work of Olson (1965). However, we do need to press further; and the essential reason is that, even if their underlying goals are fixed, the best policies to attain those goals will often depend on what other states do. At least for the largest emitters (see chapter 7 in this volume), their best course of action depends on that chosen by other states, and vice versa. The importance of such strategic interdependence and the use of game-theoretic tools to model it was introduced into the literature on collective action in international relations in the 1980s (Axelrod 1984; Axelrod and Keohane 1985; Keohane 1984). Where interactions can be characterized as a game, states' underlying preferences cannot be read off directly from their actions, as often seems to be assumed in accounts of climate change in the policy studies and comparative literatures. In a single-shot Prisoner's Dilemma, it is obvious what a rational player will do because each has a dominant strategy of noncooperation; but it is unlikely that such dominant strategies exist in climate change politics (Dasgupta and Heal 1979, 21). Dominant strategies do not exist in many of the models we survey (for example, there are no dominant strategies in the infinitely repeated Prisoners' Dilemma). Game theory helps us to understand how states will behave in strategically complex environments.

In section 4.2 we describe some rather discouraging results about the prospects for effective climate cooperation that are offered by the formal modeling literature. The models we consider highlight the importance of incentives, while downplaying the role of other factors, such as social norms. It is therefore pertinent to say that we agree with Barrett (2007, 21), who insists that norms can sometimes "move mountains." However, our view is that in relation to climate change, some key nations such as the United States see such overwhelming economic costs to rigorous action that norms of appropriate behavior in relation to the global commons are unlikely to affect what they do, though we do consider some relevant evidence from laboratory games that norms matter. In section 4.3 we go on to consider some ideas suggesting there might be light at the end of the tunnel after all, *even if norms* are of little consequence.

Given the large number of models we consider, space does not permit us to describe and analyze each model in detail. Instead we offer a fairly compact sketch of each model and outline the main results. We hope readers will get the main message from each model and encourage them to consult the referenced literature for more details on models they find particularly interesting.

4.2   Some Discouraging Results on Climate Change Cooperation

A climate agreement will be effective to the extent that it successfully mitigates anthropogenic climate change. Thus, effectiveness requires broad participation, deep commitments by the participating countries, and high compliance rates. Importantly, *all* of these three requirements must be met; meeting only one or two of them is of little or no help (Barrett and Stavins 2003).

Because the avoidance of climate change is a global public good, countries have an incentive to free ride on other countries' mitigation efforts. This will generally cause suboptimal global abatement levels (Finus and Rundshagen 2003). In the case of the Kyoto Protocol, at least four different forms of free riding may be distinguished. First, a few countries—most importantly the United States—never ratified it. Second, Canada ratified the agreement (December 2002) and thus participated initially but exited shortly before the Kyoto Protocol 1st commitment period expired in December 2012. Third, the non-Annex I countries (i.e., developing countries) ratified without a legally binding emissions limitation target. Finally, several countries such as Russia and Ukraine ratified with a legally binding but very lax commitment (the so-called hot air problem).

The problem of suboptimal global abatement has been addressed by a significant amount of formal work (notable examples include Barrett 1994, 1999, 2002, 2003; Carraro and Siniscalco 1992, 1993; Hoel 1992; Tulkens 1979). This formal work has aimed at identifying conditions for the formation of multilateral agreements (or coalitions) that are self-enforcing or stable (Grundig et al. 2012). The need for self-enforcement (or stability) originates from the anarchic character of the international system, meaning that no supranational authority can be relied on for enforcement, a point agreed on by both liberal institutionalists and realists (see chapter 3 in this volume).

4.2.1   Coalition Models

Models of international climate cooperation differ both with respect to which stability concept they use and in the way they specify countries' payoff functions. However, they can largely be categorized into two major types—coalition models and repeated-game models. Coalition models aim to analyze the conditions for the formation of coalitions that are both internally and externally stable. A coalition is said to be internally stable if no member can benefit by exiting and externally stable if no nonmember can benefit by joining.

Carraro and Marchiori (2003) distinguish three main coalition formation rules. The open membership rule specifies that each country is free to decide whether it will join or leave the coalition; hence, the coalition accepts any country that wishes to join as a member (e.g., Carraro and Siniscalco 1993). The exclusive membership rule means that a consensus among the existing members is required for a country to join; however, each country is free to exit the coalition (e.g., Yi and Shin 2000). Finally, under the coalition unanimity rule the formation of a coalition requires a consensus among its members, meaning (1) that players are not free to join the coalition, and (2) that if a country leaves, the coalition will cease to exist (e.g., Chander and Tulkens 1992).

These three rules entail different incentives for countries. In the setting of a global public good, the open membership rule entails strong incentives for free riding that resemble those found in the Kyoto process. In contrast, the exclusive membership rule resembles the requirements for accession to the EU or the WTO, and may relate to Victor's (2011) vision of a carbon club. Finally, the coalition unanimity rule can have a disciplining effect on countries, because it makes certain types of free riding (e.g., free riding by withdrawal) difficult.

Coalition models depict international cooperation as a two-stage game. At stage 1, countries choose whether to participate (i.e., whether to be a signatory or a nonsignatory). At stage 2, they choose their abatement level (Carraro and Siniscalco 1993; Chander and Tulkens 1992; Hoel 1992).[1] Different models make different assumptions about behavior at each stage (Finus 2008). We here outline what is perhaps the most basic coalition model, while we consider some extensions in section 4.3.1.

At stage 1 countries choose simultaneously (i.e., without knowing other countries' choices) whether they will become a coalition member or not. The model assumes that only a single coalition (agreement) can be formed, so countries that do not join have no option but to act individually. Finally, the model assumes open membership, meaning that no country can be barred from joining the coalition if it wants to.

At stage 2 countries simultaneously choose their abatement levels jointly, aiming to maximize the combined payoff of all coalition members.

Thus, the coalition internalizes the external effects across members but not the external effects caused by members on nonmembers. In contrast, each country *not* in the coalition chooses the abatement level that maximizes its individual payoff. The model assumes that no side payments or issue linkages occur, and that decisions are made exclusively on the basis of material costs and benefits. Finally, these costs and benefits are assumed to be known with certainty (Finus 2008, 36).

Coalition models are analyzed by backward induction, meaning that the analyst considers stage 2 before turning to stage 1. Thus, to decide what to do in stage 1, countries must map the implications that each stage 1 option will have at stage 2.

The basic model provides very pessimistic predictions for climate change cooperation. The reason is that stable coalitions are typically (very) small. Barrett (2005) provides a simple illustration, based on a linear benefit function and a quadratic cost function. Stability then requires that the coalition has exactly three members. This equilibrium is unique with regard to the number of member countries, but obviously not with regard to their identities; as countries are assumed to be *identical*, any coalition consisting of exactly three countries will be stable. In a world with nearly two hundred countries, a coalition of only three countries obviously cannot achieve very much.

Although models reviewed in this section might lead us to be pessimistic about the chances of a climate treaty with a coalition including all significant emitters, some argue that such an agreement is not necessarily required for effective action. A regime complex (Raustiala and Victor 2004) consists of a set of fragmented, loosely coupled regimes that, nevertheless, converge to some extent around a specific issue (on definitional problems, see Orsini, Morin, and Young 2013). In relation to climate change, such a complex arguably already exists, generated by divergence in interests, uncertainty, and the complexity and range of policy questions involved (Keohane and Victor 2011). Complexes can be effective because they provide flexibility, allow "coalitions of the willing" to come together, and are adaptable. However, among other things effectiveness requires a degree of coordination between the regimes in the complex, which is difficult when relations between individual regimes in the complex are conflictual, not synergistic, and where there is dysfunctional fragmentation (Orsini, Morin, and Young 2013).

Emergent regime complexes are partly the result of accident and unanticipated consequences, but there is also a process of selection on what serves states' interests (Orsini, Morin, and Young 2013). At first sight game theory seems ill adapted to model such a process. In such a complex context some would argue that it demands too much of the rational capacity of players (Hastie and Dawes 2001; Simon 1985), although others argue that realism of assumptions is not necessary in formal models (Friedman 1953). The "heuristics and biases" research program in psychology and behavioral economics (Gilovich, Griffin, and Kahneman 2002; Kahneman, Slovic, and Tversky 1982) presents a serious challenge to mainstream rational choice in emphasizing that individuals' use of shorthand guides to try to bring about desirable outcomes in the face of cognitive limitations may lead to suboptimal decisions and that, moreover, individuals do not behave as subjective expected utility maximizers would in the face of uncertainty. Individual regimes within a complex may align with particular ministries within a state's government, raising issues about whether states can be treated as unitary actors here (Allison and Zelikow 1999). Models of regime complexes need to provide microfoundations for systemic effects (Gehring and Faude 2013). Agent-based modeling (Epstein and Axtell 1996) starting from the assumption that agents adopt simple heuristic rules to cope with complexity might help us understand how regime complexes evolve as a result of competition between components of regime complexes—states, NGOs, etc.—(Gehring and Faude 2013), and whether what emerges is functional. One starting point for such a model might be whether states would initially join "climate clubs" (Keohane and Victor 2011) where some private-good benefits are confined to club members. Where adaptation and learning are possible, as long as states' underlying preferences are fixed, we should eventually observe patterns corresponding to a subclass of Nash-equilibria according to evolutionary game theory (Gintis 2009); however, agent-based modeling can help us understand how the starting point of the process conditions which of several equilibria will emerge.

4.2.2 Repeated-Game Models

Whereas coalition models typically focus on participation, repeated-game models typically focus on compliance; they aim to analyze the conditions under which countries that participate in a climate agreement will meet their commitments.

A game is repeated if it can be reduced to a series of iterations of some smaller game. Applications of repeated-game models to climate change cooperation typically center on the infinitely repeated N-player Prisoners' Dilemma (e.g., Asheim et al. 2006; Barrett 1999, 2003; Finus and Rundshagen 1998; Froyn and Hovi 2008) or some other set up that closely resembles the Prisoners' Dilemma (e.g., Asheim and Holtsmark 2009; Heitzig, Lessmann, and Zou 2011; Kratzsch and Sieg 2012).

Before the game begins, countries are assumed to enter into an agreement that the parties must enforce throughout the game using credible threats (e.g., Barrett 1999, 2003). The structure of the game enables a country to obtain (at least short-term) net gains by free riding; hence, the agreement must specify a strategy that can enforce compliance.

In most repeated-game models the only leverage available to a country is to threaten retaliation in kind, that is, to respond to noncompliance by either terminating (permanently) or suspending (temporarily) its own commitment. Most older and some more recent repeated-game literature assumes that cooperation is based on the so-called Grim Trigger strategy, by which even a single case of noncompliance will cause termination of the agreement. However, terminating an agreement will entail that the future gains from cooperation will be lost, thereby harming noncompliant countries and compliant countries alike. Thus, compliant countries will be better off if they abstain from implementing the punishment prescribed by the agreement and simply resume cooperation as if nothing had happened. A country contemplating noncompliance will rationally foresee this possibility of renegotiation, meaning that the agreement's stability will be undermined.

To deter noncompliance an agreement must therefore be based on a strategy that can sustain the agreement as a renegotiation-proof equilibrium. While several notions of renegotiation proofness exist, most applications to climate change cooperation use Farrell and Maskin's (1989) notion of a weakly renegotiation-proof equilibrium, which requires that not all players be strictly worse off by carrying out the punishment than by renegotiating. In other words, it must be in each party's best interest to conform to the specified strategy and it must be in at least some country's best interest to decline an invitation to renegotiate should a deviation from the strategy occur (Barrett 1999, 2003; Finus and Rundshagen 2003).

Most of the recent repeated-game literature ensures (weak) renegotiation proofness by replacing the Grim Trigger strategy with some other strategy, typically one that prescribes less severe punishment for noncompliance. For example, Barrett (1999) uses a strategy he calls Getting Even, and Asheim et al.

(2006) use a strategy they call Penance. These two strategies resemble each other in that they both prescribe that a noncompliant country must endure punishment (pay penance) in one period of the repeated game before cooperation can be resumed. Assuming that countries do not discount future payoffs too heavily, these strategies ensure (1) that it is in the noncompliant country's best interest to accept the punishment (because accepting the punishment will cause cooperation to be resumed after one period of punishment and will then last indefinitely unless another case of noncompliance arises) and (2) that it is in some other country's (or countries') best interest to insist that the punishment be carried out before cooperation can be resumed.

Repeated-game models teach us that a climate treaty with broad participation and deep commitments is unlikely to be self-enforcing (in the sense of being weakly renegotiation proof). The reason is that renegotiation becomes more attractive the larger the number of parties. Suppose that each country faces only two options in each period, abate and not abate. Suppose furthermore that if member country j fails to abate in a given period, then the agreement requires country j to pay penance in the next period by playing abate while *all* other member countries are allowed to play not abate. If the member countries do as the agreement requires, the punishing countries will obtain the payoff resulting from just one country playing abate. In contrast, by renegotiating they will obtain the payoff associated with the outcome where all member countries choose abate. The latter payoff is an increasing function of the number of member countries, so the larger the number of member countries, the less likely it is that the agreement will be renegotiation proof. In other words, the agreement can be weakly renegotiation proof only for a moderate number of participating countries.

Using a repeated-game model, Barrett (2002) demonstrates that it is possible to construct what he calls a consensus treaty, that is, a global agreement where all countries participate. However, he finds that a consensus treaty is possible only if commitments are unambitious ("shallow"). This finding suggests that a trade-off exists between the depth and the breadth of an agreement.

Infinitely repeated games generally have infinitely many equilibria if the rate at which players discount future benefits is low enough and the punishment for players breaking away from conditionally cooperative behavior is credible and great enough. Players' interests generally diverge among the set of efficient equilibria. By way of illustration one equilibrium may involve country A delaying the start of cooperation while B starts immediately, while another equilibrium may reverse this pattern. Games with divergent preferences over equilibria generate incentives for players to precommit to doing less, as in the paradigmatic examples of Chicken and Battle of the Sexes. Generally the literature has not dealt with the dangers that arise from multiple equilibria where credible commitments can be made, but this is a real danger in climate change politics where nations can use (and perhaps overstate) the strength of domestic vetoes to make credible commitments to do little so as to try to hijack others to do more, with the danger of a "collision" when too many precommit (Ward 1996).

Despite the attention on renegotiation-proofness in the literature, remarkably little has been said about how to theorize the actual process of climate change negotiations. Noting that multiple efficient ways of sharing the burden of dealing with climate change could be stable under conditional strategies in an infinitely repeated game, Grundig, Ward, and Zorick (2001) suggest the application of the Nash/Rubinstein bargaining solution to predict which of the efficient, enforceable patterns will eventuate. This approach highlights breakdown payoffs and rates of time discount as determinants of the size of burden a nation will have to take up; but it says little or nothing about negotiation dynamics. Putnam (1988) argues that international negotiation is deeply affected by the fact that negotiators have to get the agreement of domestic veto players before they can settle, which allows a negotiator who is weak domestically to get good deals by claiming that domestic players would not agree to anything worse—a role the US Congress often plays in climate negotiations. There is some talk of bilateral climate deals between the EU and developing countries. Mansfield, Milner, and Pevehouse (2007) show that the chances of bilateral deals generally go down with the number of domestic vetoes.

4.2.3   Other Approaches

The rather pessimistic conclusions reached by the coalition literature and the repeated-game literature sit well with inferences drawn from the literature studying the conditions for international cooperation more generally. For example, the so-called law of the least ambitious program states that what can be achieved through international cooperation is limited to the platform advocated by the least enthusiastic party (Underdal 1980, 1998).

The reason is that treaty formation usually requires unanimity (or consensus) among the participating countries, which enables the least enthusiastic party to veto any proposal that is more ambitious than its own. In principle, it might be possible to move beyond the least ambitious platform simply by accepting nonparticipation by the least ambitious country. Notice, however, that the resulting agreement will then still be limited to the platform preferred by the least ambitious *remaining* party. Moreover, in the case of global climate change cooperation it is likely to be difficult to move significantly beyond the least ambitious program by excluding the least ambitious party or parties. One reason is that the world's largest emitters, China and the United States, are among the least ambitious countries. Clearly, if these countries are omitted, the resulting agreement cannot be effective. Another reason is that the climate negotiations take place within the institutional structure of the UNFCCC, where decisions are made by consensus. China has repeatedly made it clear that it is unwilling to negotiate over climate change cooperation in any other forum.

Even more pessimistic concerning the potential for effective cooperation is the relative-gains literature, a branch of neorealist theory. This literature argues that states' concern with relative gains may further constrain or even completely eliminate the potential for international cooperation (Snidal 1991). Grundig (2006) argues that relative-gains concerns are particularly important in cases such as climate change, which involve both significant economic costs and a non-excludable good. This might help explain why cooperation to mitigate climate change (high costs and a nonexcludable good) has been far less successful than cooperation to avoid ozone depletion (nonexcludable good but only moderate costs) and cooperation on international trade (high costs but excludable good).

4.3   Light at the End of the Tunnel?

Our presentation thus far suggests that the prospects for solving the climate change problem through international cooperation are very bleak indeed. In this section we ask if there may be some light in the tunnel after all. Existing formal models offer several glimpses of hope. First, the coalition literature provides some ideas that might help enhance cooperation by making large(r) coalitions stable. Second, an emerging branch of the repeated-game literature suggests that it might in fact be possible to design a renegotiation-proof climate agreement with broad or even full participation. Third, while the law of the least ambitious program clearly pinpoints some severe constraints on the prospects for cooperation, some scholars have suggested that this law nevertheless has its limits. Fourth, nations may use cooperative probes to build trust. Fifth, some scholars argue that cooperation might emerge in a completely decentralized fashion. Finally, the results from game-theoretically oriented experiments indicate that the prospects for cooperation are better than the formal results mentioned in section 4.2 lead us to believe.

4.3.1 Making Larger Coalitions Stable

We noted in section 4.2.1 that stable coalitions are typically (very) small, at least within the framework provided by what we have termed the basic version of the coalition model. An obvious question is therefore whether modifying the assumptions of this model could somehow produce more optimistic predictions concerning participation. A number of such modifications have been explored, with varying degrees of success. We here focus on three: issue linkage, trade restrictions, and multiple coalitions.

Carraro and Siniscalco (1997) use a coalition model in which cooperation on climate change is linked to cooperation on technology R&D. The idea is that such linkage may increase participation, assuming that the fruits of technology R&D is a club good, so that countries that do not participate in climate-change cooperation may be excluded from sharing the fruits of technology R&D.[2] Carraro and Siniscalco show that, given this crucial assumption, full cooperation is possible even with a very large number of countries. However, noting that such linkage is rare in international environmental agreements, others have questioned whether restricting the fruits of technology R&D to countries that cooperate on climate change is possible or (if possible) in signatories' best interest (e.g., Barrett 2005).

A second popular suggestion for increasing participation is that signatories impose trade restrictions on nonsignatories. Consider a climate treaty that requires signatories to trade only with signatories. Barrett (1997) argues that this requirement would change the game into Assurance. If few other countries participate in the treaty, the free-rider incentive will dominate the cost of being excluded from trade with signatories, thereby making participation unattractive. However, if sufficiently many other countries participate, the cost from the trade restrictions will dominate the free-rider incentive; in particular, participation will be attractive for every country when all other countries are signatories. If this account were correct, all that would be needed to ensure a stable coalition with full participation would be a simple clause stating that the treaty will enter into force only after the critical number of countries have ratified. For such a clause to solve the problem, however, the threat to exclude nonsignatories from trade with signatories must be credible. As trade restrictions are costly for both sides, it is far from obvious that this requirement is actually met (Aakre 2016; Barrett 1999).

Finally, several coalition models have modified the basic model's assumption that only a single coalition is possible, thereby opening up for the possibility that more than one climate agreement may be negotiated (Bloch 1997; Carraro 1999, 2000; Carraro and Siniscalco 1998). Typically, this modification leads to more than one coalition in equilibrium and thus also to more cooperation than in the basic model. Global welfare is thus usually higher with multiple agreements than with a single global accord (Carraro 2000).

4.3.2 Making a Renegotiation-Proof Climate Agreement Consistent with Broad or Even Full Participation

A series of articles have questioned the claim that a weakly renegotiation-proof agreement must necessarily entail either moderate participation or shallow commitments. Asheim et al. (2006) show that multiple (e.g., regional) agreements can enhance participation even when the depth of cooperation is taken as a given. Their model builds on Barrett (1999), but admits the possibility not only of negotiating a single global agreement but also of negotiating two regional agreements. Identifying upper and lower bounds on the number of participating countries in each case, they show that two agreements can involve a greater number of countries than a single global agreement can. Moreover, they demonstrate that a climate regime based on two agreements Pareto dominates a regime based on a single global agreement. Thus, their results mirror those of Carraro and others, using a coalition model (see section 4.3.1).

Asheim et al.'s (2006) model follows Barrett's (1999) in that noncompliance must be punished by all other participating countries in the perpetrator's *own region*. Although this specification restricts the number of participating countries in each region, the existence of two agreements ensures that the total number of participating countries in the two agreements combined becomes larger than the number of participating countries in a single global agreement.

Froyn and Hovi (2008) extend Asheim et al.'s (2006) analysis by showing that full participation can be sustained as a weakly renegotiation-proof equilibrium also in a single global agreement. They demonstrate that even when abatement levels are held constant, participation can be increased by limiting the punishment for noncompliance. While Barrett's "Getting Even" strategy allows *all* other participating countries to punish a noncompliant country, the strategy used by Froyn and Hovi permits only a *subset* of the participating countries to punish. Using a strategy formulation that makes it possible to study how the number of participating countries in equilibrium varies with the number of countries allowed to punish noncompliance, they provide lower and upper bounds on the number of punishing countries that is consistent with full participation (in equilibrium).

The models studied by Barrett (1999), Asheim et al. (2006), and Froyn and Hovi (2008) assume that countries face a simple binary choice between cooperate (abate) and defect (not abate). Subsequent research has relaxed this assumption. Asheim and Holtsmark (2009) demonstrate that full participation is also possible when countries face a continuum of alternative emission levels. They show that in their model a Pareto-efficient climate agreement can always be implemented as a weakly renegotiation-proof equilibrium, provided that countries do not discount future payoffs too heavily. This result suggests that one need not choose between a narrow but deep agreement and a broad but shallow agreement. However, Asheim and Holtsmark's (2009) results also demonstrate that designing an enforcement system that makes a broad and deep agreement possible is no trivial matter.

Asheim and Holtsmark's (2009) results are supported by the findings of Heitzig, Lessmann, and Zou (2011), who propose an enforcement system based on a simple dynamic strategy of linear compensation. This strategy redistributes abatement obligations according to past compliance levels, while keeping the overall abatement level constant across periods. Heitzig, Lessmann, and Zou (2011) show that their strategy can be used to implement any given allocation of emissions reductions, thereby casting further doubt about the existence of a "narrow but deep" versus "broad but shallow" trade-off.

All models considered thus far in this section treat emissions as a flow variable. Thus, these models assume (usually implicitly) that emissions in a particular period have no lasting effect over time and that payoffs are identical across all stages of the repeated game. These assumptions are arguably implausible for applications to climate change cooperation. Kratzsch and Sieg (2012) invoke the more realistic assumption that greenhouse gas emissions build up a stock in the atmosphere over time and that it is the current stock that influences the climate. They show that broad or full participation is possible even when the model takes into account that emitted gases is a stock variable that is depreciated only slowly over time, an important generalization of results from previous studies. Their model also enables them to identify certain effects that are difficult to spot when emissions are modeled as a flow variable. For example, they show that treaties with broad participation are more easily achieved for long-lasting gases than for short-lived ones.

4.3.3   The Law of the Least Ambitious Program Does Not Always Apply

Around three-quarters of the regimes coded by Breitmeier, Young, and Zürn (2006) operate on the basis of unanimity or consensus. Moreover, the UN Framework Convention on Climate Change operates by consensus, too. The Law of the Least Ambitious Program thus seems quite widely applicable. While many regimes formally operate using some version of a qualified majority rule, at least on occasion (Hovi and Sprinz 2006), Underdal (1998) notes that the argument might still apply to the country most loath to see action among those vital to progress, for instance to the most loath member of a k-subgroup just large enough to make cooperation worthwhile if all members of the subgroup cooperate. This would seem a potentially important argument given that perhaps no more than twelve states are crucial to making progress on climate change, based on their percentage of global emissions (Victor 2006). Among these the most plausible to exercise unit vetoes are probably China, India, and the United States. However, there are reasons to doubt that the Law of the Least Ambitious Program *always* applies. First, if unanimity makes it difficult to ratchet up effectiveness beyond the level set by independent decision making when a regime is being built up, equally it makes it difficult to revert from an established policy to one with lower effectiveness (Hovi and Sprinz 2006). Moreover, the opposition of veto players under unanimity may be bought out by making side payments (Barrett 2003; Ward, Grundig, and Zorick 2001).

In collective action games side payments are (1) transfers of private goods between players interacting over provision of a public good or (2) concessions on dimensions of policy relevance to the provision of the public good. In relation to climate change, an example of the former are transfers between the North and South under the Global Environment Facility, while an example of the second kind are flexibility mechanisms under the Kyoto Protocol demanded by the United States and some other states (Barrett 2003; Ward, Grundig, and Zorick 2001; see also chapter 2 in this volume).

Side payments are usually seen as a trade between agents with different degrees of concern about an issue. Barrett (2003, 335–354) shows that asymmetries in the provision function can lead to stable arrangements where some countries are induced to cooperate by side payments. He considers an n-player Prisoner's Dilemma where each member of a subgroup of 1<k<n countries can benefit from cooperating so long as all the other members of the k-subgroup do so, but a group larger than k is unstable because for additional members marginal costs exceed marginal benefits from environmental improvement. In the symmetric version of the game (i.e., players are identical in all relevant respects), side payments cannot induce extra cooperation. Suppose that one extra country is induced to join by a side payment. Then any member of the original k-subgroup will have an incentive to defect, because there are now more than k cooperators and it can avoid the costs of making side payments. However, things may be different in an asymmetric game where countries' incentives and capabilities differ. Suppose there are two k-subgroups of cooperating countries and that the addition of an extra member of the second group brings less marginal public good benefits than the addition of an extra member to the first group. Then it may pay a member of the first group to continue to cooperate when an extra member is added to the second group, because defection would reduce provision of the public good more at the margin than it has been increased through inducing a member of the second group to join. Depending on the costs of making side payments and the degree of asymmetry between groups, equilibria in which k members of the first group cooperate and all members of the second group are induced to do so through side payments are possible.

Unlike Barrett's game, in Ward, Grundig, and Zorick's model (2001) side payments can also be used to block progress toward a more effective regime. It is assumed that there is a status quo point on the effectiveness dimension and any country can veto change. Countries can locate either on the progressive side of the status quo or on the opposite side. One subset of the countries is a progressive coalition and another is a laggard coalition. The progressive coalition can make side payments to compensate unattached countries that would otherwise be loath to see progress, so they no longer veto such progress, but the laggard coalition can attempt to counter this. The progressive coalition must be highly predominant in its ability to overcome the efforts of the laggard coalition if progress is to come about, because the laggard coalition need only focus its attention on one veto, whereas the progressive coalition has to bribe all unattached players who are initially opposed to progress. Even if the progressive coalition is predominant enough to get progress, the degree of progress will generally be limited. There is nearly always a member of the progressive coalition wanting less progress than any other that can limit its contributions to the fund of side payments so that its desired level of progress or something close to it is achieved.

Ward, Grundig, and Zorick (2001) re-instate a version of the Law of the Least Ambitious Program: Progress will likely be limited to what the least ambitious member of the progressive coalition wants—if it occurs at all. More work needs to be done in this area, though. While Barrett ignores the role of side payments from a laggard coalition, Ward, Grundig, and Zorick (2001) assume side payments are costless so as to highlight the most progressive equilibrium possible. The benefits generated by the use of side payments are nonexcludable, for example, a country wanting progress could do nothing and still benefit from others making side payments to bring it about. Neither contribution deals with the issue of collective action failure over who will pay for side payments to be made, though this seems to be empirically important to regime effectiveness (Grundig and Ward 2015).

4.3.4 Trust and Networks Can Make a Difference

In reality, nation a may be uncertain about whether nation b is the type that genuinely wishes to conditionally cooperate or whether it is the type whose statements to conditionally cooperate are a pretense (Kydd 2007). If b's actions significantly affect a's payoffs, a may take a considerable risk in shifting energy paths, because it may take a long time to be sure that b is not reciprocating and then a long time to switch its own strategy. So initiating unilateral cuts in emissions, such as those under the EU's 20 percent emissions cuts by 2020 (the "20:20:20" policy), is a gamble.[3] Why take such a gamble?

The nations' background of common knowledge of each other sets the a priori probability that a country is of the type that actually wishes conditionally to cooperate in a game of incomplete information about the others' types. As the game progresses a nation may choose to send a costly signal that indicates its type, because only countries of this type would make such a move in equilibrium. Others update their prior beliefs about the nation sending the signal, using what they can infer from the signal and the equilibrium; and these updated beliefs support the (perfect Bayesian) equilibrium (Fudenberg and Tirole 1992, 207–241; Kydd 2007, 183–205). Perhaps the EU's 20:20:20 policy is a signal of this sort. In international crises states may attempt to reverse a potential escalation toward war by starting with relatively small cooperative gestures which, if reciprocated, lead to further de-escalatory steps (Osgood 1962). By starting small, states may both signal something about their type and learn a lot about others. This may illuminate the institutional architecture of environmental regimes starting with a framework convention and gradually tightening through additional protocols.

In such a game, the nations' prior beliefs can be thought of as the degree of background trust they have in each other, and such trust is vital to whether they will risk conditional cooperation (Kydd 2007). Trust can arise during specific negotiations through "cheap talk" (Fudenberg and Tirole 1992, 361–362; Ostrom, Gardner, and Walker 1994) but it also arises through numerous interactions, including those in other issue domains than climate. When nations meet each other in the course of routine diplomacy, by direct contact they learn about each other's interests, capabilities and trustworthiness. They also create networks that enable them to learn about each other *indirectly* as information travels through the network. Nations that meet frequently, with many others and in many forums are central to the network, or highly embedded. They are in a position to learn most, but also to affect flows of information, giving them brokerage power (Hafner-Burton, Kahler, and Montgomery 2009; Maoz 2010). Interstate networks are supplemented by networks between nonstate actors such as NGOs, corporations, and scientific bodies such as those that have come to exist in climate governance (Andonova, Betsill, and Bulkeley 2009; see also chapter 8 in this volume).

Although networks should be conceptually confused with neither trust nor with social capital (cf. Dasgupta 2008; Ostrom and Ahn 2008), there is strong evidence at the individual level that dense networks are often associated with higher levels of trust. Beliefs about the trustworthiness of nations central to dense networks will have lower variance. Moreover, because a highly embedded nation is more involved in a range of international inter-actions it has more to lose if its reputation for trustworthiness is harmed by failure to reciprocate on a single issue such as climate change. They may also be more influenced by evolving patterns of international norms (Florini 1996) and information cascades resulting in perceptions of the costs of action falling. There is emerging empirical evidence from the environmental realm that highly embedded nations act more cooperatively (Bernauer et al. 2010; Ward 2006; cf. Grundig and Ward 2015; see also chapter 8 in this volume).

So far we have discussed the possibilities of cooperation between states, but some see promise in transnational climate governance (TCG)— networks created when governments, cities, corporations and NGOs enter joint arrangements to share information, set standards, make pledges, and to foster flows of investment (Andonova, Betsill, and Bulkeley 2009; Bulkeley et al. 2014; Hale and Roger 2014). The rational choice approach has proven extremely useful, alongside others, in constructing descriptive narratives about TCG (Bulkeley et al. 2014; Schäferhoff, Campe, and Kaan 2009). For instance, Green (2013) uses a rational choice supply/demand model to develop hypotheses about why states delegate authority to private actors in some instances while private organizations develop "entrepreneurial authority" in others. Cao and Ward (2017) use a simple microeconomic approach to show that the more legislative action there has been at the domestic level, the greater the participation of national actors in TCG. This is because if they can bank on the domestic legislative environment being favorable to their interest in climate change governance, organizations are less resource constrained in relation to participation in TCG.

4.3.5 Decentralized Cooperation

The general pessimism in the coalition and repeated-game literatures is shared by several studies considering whether unilateral emissions reduc-tions by one or a few countries may cause other countries to follow suit. For example, Hoel (1991) and Buchholz, Haslbeck, and Sandler (1998) find that unilateral emissions reductions are unlikely to cause other countries to follow suit and could even cause them to *increase* their own emissions. According to them, unilateral action is at best pointless and at worst counterproductive.

However, a few scholars have begun to question this pessimistic view of unilateral policies, arguing that unilateral action may be rational even for a government at the national, regional or local level (or even for an individual firm). Urpelainen (2009) suggests that ancillary benefits at the national, regional, or local level can motivate unilateral emissions reductions. Moreover, Luterbacher and Davis (2010) argue that, as an effective global climate agreement becomes more likely, the risks involved in holding on to carbon-intensive technologies will increase. Drawing on work by Milnor and Shapley (1978) on so-called oceanic games (i.e., games with an infinite number—an "ocean"—of players) and by Straffin Jr. (1977) on bandwagon effects in US presidential nominations, they find that abandoning investments in carbon-intensive technologies might entail significant first-mover advantages. If some countries, regions or municipalities begin to introduce regulation to limit the use of carbon-intensive technologies, the risks for other countries, regions or municipalities of continued use of such technologies will increase. Thus, their incentive to switch to low carbon technologies will also increase. If the size of the coalition of low carbon countries reaches a certain threshold, a bandwagon effect may set in, creating a very rapid increase in the number of countries switching to low carbon technologies. According to Luterbacher and Davis (2010), this bandwagon effect will be stimulated further if the coalition of low carbon countries is able to use sanctions to motivate other countries to join.

4.3.6   Some Lessons from the Experimental Literature on Cooperation

As very few climate agreements exist, the possibilities for using field data to test hypotheses about climate cooperation are limited. It is therefore interesting to explore other options. One such option is to use laboratory experiments. A significant number of such experiments have considered the conditions for public goods provision. What can these experiments teach us about the prospects for effective climate cooperation?

The experimental literature largely considers variations of the following game: N subjects endowed with z units of a numéraire good (usually money allocated to the subjects at the beginning of each period of the game) decide simultaneously how much of their endowment they will keep for themselves and how much they will contribute to a public good for the subject group. The aggregate contribution is multiplied by a factor between 1 and N and then divided equally among all subjects. Assuming subjects are rational actors that maximize their own monetary payoff, the unique Nash equilibrium in this game is that every subject keeps its entire endowment and thus contributes nothing to the public good. This equilibrium is inefficient; all subjects would be better off if every subject were to contribute its entire endowment to the public good.

Several experiments add an enforcement stage, allowing subjects to allocate punishment points to other subjects. One allocated punishment point normally detracts three units of the numéraire good from the punished player's payoff and one unit of the numéraire good from the punishing player's payoff. Thus, punishment is costly both for the punished subject and for the punishing subject.

Experimental studies of such public goods games with enforcement (e.g., Fehr and Gächter 2000; Kosfeld and Okada 2009) typically permit subjects to play the game a fixed number of times (usually ten). Given the above-mentioned assumptions, the subgame-perfect equilibrium in such a finitely repeated game is that every player keeps the entire endowment in every period, and that no punishment ever takes place.

Typically, the behavior observed in experiments deviates significantly from these equilibrium predictions. In experiments without an enforcement stage, average contributions typically begin at 40–50 percent of the endowment in the first period and then decreases to 10–15 percent of the endowment by the last period. In experiments with an enforcement stage, average contributions typically start higher (at 60–70 percent of the endowment), and increase even further (often to 90–100 percent of the endowment) by the last period. Thus, adding enforcement seems to influence behavior significantly.

The mechanisms producing these results are not very well understood; however, a popular hypothesis is that motivational heterogeneity plays a major role. Quite a few subjects seem to be "reciprocators" (Fehr and Gächter 2002) who increase their current contribution if the average contribution in the preceding period was below their own, and reduce their current contribution if the average contribution in the preceding period was above their own. Reciprocators' behavior could be thought of as, at least in part, norm led. The tendency of average contributions to decline over time is believed to stem from reciprocators' underestimating the portion of purely self-regarding players (existing data suggest that this portion constitutes around one-third of the subject pool in modern societies). Reciprocators' miscalculation concerning the subject pool causes them to make considerable contributions in the first period, and to reduce their contributions as they observe lower average contributions than they expected.

Experiments with enforcement permit subjects to discipline free riders. Subjects often allocate punishment points, even though such allocation is costly for the punishing subject. A common explanation is that "strong reciprocity" plays a role. A strong reciprocator is willing to forego monetary benefits to penalize subjects that do not cooperate. If a purely self-regarding player believes strong reciprocation is sufficiently widespread, and if allocation of punishment points is possible, contributing at a level that avoids punishment may well be a best response (see, e.g., Fehr and Fischbacher 2005; Gürerk, Irlenbusch, and Rockenbach 2006).

Assuming that lab experiments are relevant for international climate cooperation, these experimental results offer some hope by suggesting (1) that a potential for moderate levels of cooperation may exist even *without* enforcement and (2) that even very high cooperation levels may be sustainable *with* enforcement. Interestingly, enforcement seems to encourage cooperation even when it is based on threats that are not credible (in the narrow sense that they are costly to implement). The latter result could mean that the credibility requirements imposed in most formal models are excessively strict. However, recent experimental research also suggests that enforcement of both participation and compliance may be required to obtain high cooperation levels (Aakre, Helland, and Hovi 2016).

4.4 Conclusion

As this chapter has shown, the formal modeling literature is somewhat open-ended concerning the prospects for climate change cooperation. Many formal contributions offer a rather pessimistic view, suggesting that a self-enforcing climate treaty must necessarily display limited participation, shallow commitments, or low compliance rates. However, other contributions indicate that there may be some light at the end of the tunnel after all: effective climate cooperation may be difficult but not impossible.

We have discussed a number of what might be regarded as more hopeful suggestions from the rational choice literature for building international cooperation. It might be questioned why, by and large, these have not been tried by the international community. For instance, why has building climate clubs using trade sanctions to leverage cooperation not been tried? One answer may be the institutional path dependence of regime architecture initiated under the Framework Convention on Climate Change and proceeding through stages of development of the Kyoto Protocol. Such path dependence could have arisen because of increasing returns (Pierson 2000) to regime deepening, some of which did occur under Kyoto, generating increased incentives for pressing on further. Seen in this way, the Copenhagen meeting may have marked the point at which it became clear that the Kyoto architecture could not be pushed any further, leading to the break from it that occurred in the Paris Agreement. It is hard to forecast the way that things will develop, but the fact that a quite radical change in direction has occurred suggests to us that some of the ideas we have discussed for very different architectures should not be ruled out.

We follow Hovi, Ward, and Grundig's (2015) account of specific features that the literature suggests would be helpful in designing a new treaty, more effective than we suspect the Paris Agreement will be. First, a carefully chosen entry-into-force clause might help attract more signatories. A demanding clause is particularly likely to have this effect. Indeed, in a symmetric setting, an entry-into-force clause requiring *all* countries to participate may even be able to sustain full participation as an equilibrium. However, the real-world setting of climate negotiations is clearly *not* symmetric, so more research is needed on what type of entry-into-force clause may be expected to work best in *asymmetric* settings.

Second, limiting the targets for emissions reductions can induce more countries to participate with binding emissions reduction commitments. A broad but shallow agreement can—given certain conditions—be more effective than a narrow but deep agreement. This result suggests that negotiators might be well advised to choose a design with moderate targets—at least in the initial phases of a new climate treaty.

Third, if countries are asymmetric—either in terms of their capacity for contributing to climate change mitigation or in terms of how much they benefit from such mitigation—progressive countries might be able to offer side payments to unattached countries, thereby making larger coalitions stable.

Fourth, designing a potent enforcement system that is also politically feasible is a great challenge. Importantly, deterring only one type of free riding (e.g., noncompliance) may simply shift free riding to other types (such as non-ratification, ratification with no commitment, ratification with only a very shallow commitment, or withdrawal). To ensure a new climate agreement's effectiveness, the enforcement system must therefore be able to deter all types of free riding.

Fifth, formal models provide insights into the strengths and weaknesses of specific proposals for enforcement systems. For example, they have been used to study the possible merits of trade sanctions. One major conclusion is that effective enforcement through issue-specific reciprocity is possible and consistent with broad participation but requires rather intricate designs and probably presupposes too much flexibility to be politically attractive.

Finally, an emerging branch of formal modeling studies the effect of replacing the standard assumption that all countries are fully rational and purely self-interested with an assumption that at least some countries are reciprocators or have a preference for equity. Such models entail far more optimistic results concerning the potential for cooperation than standard models do. In particular, they offer some encouragement to environmental NGOs and other green pressure groups: If such NGOs and pressure groups could convince the governments in sufficiently many countries that climate change is better seen in terms of equity or reciprocity than in terms of national interests, they would also significantly enhance the likelihood of effective climate cooperation.

Notes

1. In some models, nonparticipating countries independently choose their abatement levels in stage three (e.g., Barrett 2005).

2. This idea resembles Victor's (2011) idea of a "carbon club."

3. The European Commission claims significant short-term economic benefits for the EU.

References

Aakre, Stine. 2016. "The Political Feasibility of Potent Enforcement in a Post-Kyoto Climate Agreement." *International Environmental Agreements: Politics, Law and Economics* 16 (1): 145–159.

Aakre, Stine, Leif Helland, and Jon Hovi. 2016. "When Does Informal Enforcement Work?" *Journal of Conflict Resolution* 60 (7): 1312–1340.

Allison, Graham T., and Philip Zelikow. 1999. *Essence of Decision: Explaining the Cuban Missile Crisis*. London: Pearson.

Andonova, Liliana B., Michele M. Betsill, and Harriet Bulkeley. 2009. "Transnational Climate Governance." *Global Environmental Politics* 9 (2): 52–73.

Asheim, Geir B., Camilla Bretteville Froyn, Jon Hovi, and Fredric C. Menz. 2006. "Regional versus Global Cooperation for Climate Control." *Journal of Environmental Economics and Management* 51 (1): 93–109.

Asheim, Geir B., and Bjart Holtsmark. 2009. "Renegotiation-Proof Climate Agreements with Full Participation: Conditions for Pareto-Efficiency." *Environmental and Resource Economics* 43 (4): 519–533.

Axelrod, Robert. 1984. *The Evolution of Cooperation.* New York: Basic Books.

Axelrod, Robert, and Robert O. Keohane. 1985. "Achieving Cooperation under Anarchy: Strategies and Institutions." *International Organization* 25 (4): 866–874.

Bang, Guri, Jon Hovi, and Tora Skodvin. 2016. "The Paris Agreement: Short-Term and Long-Term Effectiveness." *Politics and Governance* 4 (3): 209–218.

Barrett, Scott. 1994. "Self-Enforcing International Environmental Agreements." *Oxford Economic Papers* 46 (4): 878–894.

———. 1997. "The Strategy of Trade Sanctions in International Environmental Agreements." *Resource and Energy Economics* 19 (4): 345–361.

———. 1999. "A Theory of Full International Cooperation." *Journal of Theoretical Politics* 11 (4): 519–541.

———. 2002. "Consensus Treaties." *Journal of Institutional and Theoretical Economics* 158 (4): 529–547.

———. 2003. *Environment and Statecraft: The Strategy of Environmental Treaty-Making.* Oxford: Oxford University Press.

———. 2005. "The Theory of International Environmental Agreements." *Handbook of Environmental Economics* 3:1457–1516.

———. 2007. *Why Cooperate? The Incentive to Supply Global Public Goods.* Oxford: Oxford University Press.

Barrett, Scott, and Robert Stavins. 2003. "Increasing Participation and Compliance in International Climate Change Agreements." *International Environmental Agreements* 3 (4): 349–376.

Bernauer, Thomas, and Tobias Böhmelt. 2013. "National Climate Policies in International Comparison: The Climate Change Cooperation Index." *Environmental Science & Policy* 25:196–206.

Bernauer, Thomas, Anna Kalbhenn, Vally Koubi, and Gabriele Spilker. 2010. "A Comparison of International and Domestic Sources of Global Governance Dynamics." *British Journal of Political Science* 40 (3): 509–538.

Bloch, Francis. 1997. "Non-Cooperative Models of Coalition Formation in Games with Spillovers." In *New Directions in the Economic Theory of the Environment*, edited by Carlo Carraro and Domenico Siniscalco, 311–352. Cambridge: Cambridge University Press.

Breitmeier, Helmut, Oran R. Young, and Michael Zürn. 2006. *Analyzing International Environmental Regimes*. Cambridge, MA: MIT Press.

Buchholz, Wolfgang, Christian Haslbeck, and Todd Sandler. 1998. "When Does Partial Cooperation Pay?" *Finanzarchiv* 55:1–20.

Bulkeley, Harriet, Liliana B. Andonova, Michele M. Betsill, Daniel Compagnon, Thomas Hale, Matthew J. Hoffmann, Peter Newell, Matthew Paterson, Stacy D. VanDeveer, and Charles X. Roger. 2014. *Transnational Climate Change Governance*. New York: Cambridge University Press.

Cao, Xun, and Hugh Ward. 2017. "Transnational Climate Governance Networks and Domestic Regulatory Action." *International Interactions* 43 (1): 76–102.

Carraro, Carlo. 1999. "The Structure of International Agreements on Climate Change." In *International Environmental Agreements on Climate Change*, edited by Carlo Carraro, 9–25. Dordrecht: Kluwer.

———. 2000. "The Economics of Coalition Formation." In *Climate Change and European Leadership*, edited by Joyeeta Gupta and Michael Grubb, 135–156. Dordrecht: Kluwer.

Carraro, Carlo, and Carmen Marchiori. 2003. "Stable Coalitions." In *The Endogenous Formation of Economic Coalitions*, edited by Carlo Carraro, 156–198. Cheltenham: Edward Elgar.

Carraro, Carlo, and Domenico Siniscalco. 1992. "The International Dimension of Environmental Policy." *European Economic Review* 36 (2): 379–387.

———. 1993. "Strategies for the International Protection of the Environment." *Journal of Public Economics* 52 (3): 309–328.

———. 1997. "R&D Cooperation and the Stability of International Environmental Agreements." In *International Environmental Agreements: Strategic Policy Issues*, edited by Carlo Carraro, 156–198. Cheltenham: Edward Elgar.

———. 1998. "International Environmental Agreements: Incentives and Political Economy." *European Economic Review* 42 (3): 561–572.

Chander, Parkash, and Henry Tulkens. 1992. "Strategically Stable Cost-Sharing in an Economic-Ecological Negotiation Process." CORE Discussion Paper, no. 9135, revised 1992, Louvain, 1–19.

Coase, Ronald H. 1960. "The Problem of Social Cost." *Journal of Law and Economics* 3 (1): 1–44.

Dasgupta, Partha. 2008. "Economic Progress and the Idea of Social Capita." In *Social Capital: A Multifaceted Perspective*, edited by Partha Dasgupta and Ishmail Serageldin, 120–147. Washington, DC: World Bank.

Dasgupta, Partha S., and Geoffrey M. Heal. 1979. *Economic Theory and Exhaustible Resources*. Cambridge: Cambridge University Press.

Epstein, Joshua M., and Robert Axtell. 1996. *Growing Artificial Societies: Social Science from the Bottom Up*. Cambridge, MA: MIT Press.

Farrell, Joseph, and Eric Maskin. 1989. "Renegotiation in Repeated Games." *Games and Economic Behavior* 1 (4): 327–360.

Fehr, Ernst, and Urs Fischbacher. 2005. "The Economics of Strong Reciprocity." In *Moral Sentiments and Material Interests. The Foundations of Cooperation in Economic Life*, edited by Herbert Gintis, Samuel Bowles, Robert T. Boyd, and Ernst Fehr, 151–214. Cambridge, MA: MIT Press.

Fehr, Ernst, and Simon Gächter. 2000. "Cooperation and Punishment in Public Goods Experiments." *American Economic Review* 90 (4): 980–994.

———. 2002. "Altruistic Punishment in Humans." *Nature* 415 (6868): 137–140.

Finus, Michael. 2008. "Game Theoretic Research on the Design of International Environmental Agreements: Insights, Critical Remarks, and Future Challenges." *International Review of Environmental and Resource Economics* 2 (1): 29–67.

Finus, Michael, and Bianca Rundshagen. 1998. "Renegotiation–Proof Equilibria in a Global Emission Game When Players Are Impatient." *Environmental and Resource Economics* 12 (3): 275–306.

———. 2003. "Endogenous Coalition Formation in Global Pollution Control: A Partition Function Approach." In *Endogenous Formation of Economic Coalitions*, edited by Carlo Carraro, 199–241. Cheltenham: Edward Elgar.

Florini, Ann. 1996. "The Evolution of International Norms." *International Studies Quarterly* 40 (3): 363–389.

Friedman, Milton. 1953. *Essays in Positive Economics*. Chicago: University of Chicago Press.

Froyn, Camilla Bretteville, and Jon Hovi. 2008. "A Climate Agreement with Full Participation." *Economics Letters* 99 (2): 317–319.

Fudenberg, Drew, and Jean Tirole. 1992. *Game Theory*. Cambridge, MA: MIT Press.

Gehring, Thomas, and Benjamin Faude. 2013. "The Dynamics of Regime Complexes: Microfoundations and Systemic Effects." *Global Governance* 19 (1): 119–130.

Gilovich, Thomas, Dale Griffin, and Daniel Kahneman. 2002. *Heuristics and Biases: The Psychology of Intuitive Judgment*. Cambridge: Cambridge University Press.

Gintis, Herbert. 2009. *Game Theory Evolving: A Problem-Centered Introduction to Modelling Strategic Interaction*. Princeton, NJ: Princeton University Press.

Green, Donald P., and Ian Shapiro. 1994. *Pathologies of Rational Choice Theory: A Critique of Applications in Political Science*. Cambridge: Cambridge University Press.

Green, Jessica F. 2013. *Rethinking Private Authority: Agents and Entrepreneurs in Global Environmental Governance*. Princeton, NJ: Princeton University Press.

Grundig, Frank. 2006. "Patterns of International Cooperation and the Explanatory Power of Relative Gains: An Analysis of Cooperation on Global Climate Change, Ozone Depletion, and International Trade." *International Studies Quarterly* 50 (4): 781–801.

Grundig, Frank, Jon Hovi, Arild Underdal, and Stine Aakre. 2012. "Self-Enforcing Peace and Environmental Agreements: Toward Scholarly Cross-Fertilization?" *International Studies Review* 14 (4): 522–540.

Grundig, Frank, and Hugh Ward. 2015. "Structural Group Leadership and Regime Effectiveness." *Political Studies* 63 (1): 221–239.

Grundig, Frank, Hugh Ward, and Ethan Zorick. 2001. "Modeling Global Climate-Change Negotiations." In *International Relations and Global Climate Change*, edited by Urs Luterbacher and Detlef F. Sprinz, 153–182. Cambridge, MA: MIT Press.

Gürerk, Özgür, Bernd Irlenbusch, and Bettina Rockenbach. 2006. "The Competitive Advantage of Sanctioning Institutions." *Science* 312 (5770): 108–111.

Hafner-Burton, Emilie M., Miles Kahler, and Alexander H. Montgomery. 2009. "Network Analysis for International Relations." *International Organization* 63 (3): 559–592.

Hale, Thomas, and Charles Roger. 2014. "Orchestration and Transnational Climate Governance." *Review of International Organizations* 9 (1): 59–82.

Harrison, Kathryn, and Lisa McIntosh-Sundstrom. 2010. "Conclusion: The Comparative Politics of Climate Change." In *Global Commons, Domestic Decisions. The Comparative Politics of Climate Change*, edited by Kathryn Harrison and Lisa McIntosh-Sundstrom, 261–290. Cambridge, MA: MIT Press.

Hastie, Reid, and Robyn Mason Dawes. 2001. *Rational Choice in an Uncertain World*. Thousand Oaks, CA: Sage.

Heitzig, Jobst, Kai Lessmann, and Yong Zou. 2011. "Self-Enforcing Strategies to Deter Free-Riding in the Climate Change Mitigation Game and Other Repeated Public Good Games." *Proceedings of the National Academy of Sciences of the United States of America* 108 (38): 15739–15744.

Hoel, Michael. 1991. "Global Environmental Problems: The Effects of Unilateral Actions Taken by One Country." *Journal of Environmental Economics and Management* 20 (1): 55–70.

Hoel, Michael. 1992. "International Environment Conventions: The Case of Uniform Reductions of Emissions." *Environmental and Resource Economics* 2 (2): 141–159.

Hovi, Jon, and Detlef F. Sprinz. 2006. "The Limits of the Law of the Least Ambitious Program." *Global Environmental Politics* 6 (3): 28–42.

Hovi, Jon, Hugh Ward, and Frank Grundig. 2015. "Hope or Despair? Formal Models of Climate Cooperation." *Environmental and Resource Economics* 62 (4): 665–688.

Kahneman, Daniel, Paul Slovic, and Amos Tversky. 1982. *Judgment under Uncertainty: Heuristics and Biases*. Cambridge: Cambridge University Press.

Keohane, Robert O. 1984. *After Hegemony: Cooperation and Discord in the World Political Economy*. Princeton, NJ: Princeton University Press.

Keohane, Robert O., and David G. Victor. 2011. "The Regime Complex for Climate Change." *Perspectives on Politics* 9 (1): 7–23.

Kosfeld, Michael, and Akira Okada. 2009. "Institution Formation in Public Goods Games." *American Economic Review* 99 (4): 1335–1355.

Kratzsch, Uwe, and Gernot Sieg. 2012. "An International Agreement with Full Participation to Tackle the Stock of Greenhouse Gases." *Economics Letters* 115 (3): 473–476.

Kydd, Andrew H. 2007. *Trust and Mistrust in International Relations*. Princeton, NJ: Princeton University Press.

Luterbacher, Urs, and Peter Davis. 2010. "Explaining Unilateral Cooperative Actions: The Case of Greenhouse Gas Regulations." *Monash University Law Review* 36:121.

Mansfield, Edward D., Helen V. Milner, and Jon C. Pevehouse. 2007. "Vetoing Co-Operation: The Impact of Veto Players on Preferential Trading Arrangements." *British Journal of Political Science* 37 (3): 403.

Maoz, Zeev. 2011. *Networks of Nations: The Evolution, Structure, and Impact of International Networks, 1816–2001*. New York: Cambridge University Press.

Milnor, John Willard, and Lloyd S. Shapley. 1978. "Values of Large Games II: Oceanic Games." *Mathematics of Operations Research* 3 (4): 290–307.

Olson, Mancur. 1965. *The Logic of Collective Action: Public Goods and the Theory of Groups*. Cambridge, MA: Harvard University Press.

Orsini, Amandine, Jean-Frédéric Morin, and Oran Young. 2013. "Regime Complexes: A Buzz, a Boom, or a Boost for Global Governance?" *Global Governance* 19 (1): 27–39.

Osgood, Charles Egerton. 1962. *An Alternative to War or Surrender*. Urbana-Champaign: University of Illinois Press.

Ostrom, Elinor, and Toh-Kyeong Ahn. 2008. "The Meaning of Social Capital and Its Link to Collective Action." In *Handbook on Social Capital: The Troika of Sociology, Political Science and Economics*, edited by Gert T. Svendsen and Gunnar L. Svendsen, 17–35. Northampton, MA: Edward Elgar.

Ostrom, Elinor, Roy Gardner, and James Walker. 1994. *Rules, Games and Common-Pool Resources*. Ann Arbor: University of Michigan Press.

Pierson, Paul. 2000. "Increasing Returns, Path Dependence, and the Study of Politics." *American Political Science Review* 94 (2): 251–267.

Putnam, Robert D. 1988. "Diplomacy and Domestic Politics: The Logic of Two-Level Games." *International Organization* 42 (3): 427–460.

Raustiala, Kal, and David G. Victor. 2004. "The Regime Complex for Plant Genetic Resources." *International Organization* 58 (3): 277–309.

Rosen, Amanda M. 2015. "The Wrong Solution at the Right Time: The Failure of the Kyoto Protocol on Climate Change." *Politics & Policy* 43 (1): 30–58.

Sandler, Todd. 1997. *Global Challenges: An Approach to Environmental, Political, and Economic Problems*. Cambridge: Cambridge University Press.

Schäferhoff, Marco, Sabine Campe, and Christopher Kaan. 2009. "Transnational Public-Private Partnerships in International Relations: Making Sense of Concepts, Research Frameworks, and Results." *International Studies Review* 11 (3): 451–474.

Simon, Herbert A. 1985. "Human Nature in Politics: The Dialogue of Psychology with Political Science." *American Political Science Review* 79 (2): 293–304.

Snidal, Duncan. 1991. "Relative Gains and the Pattern of International Cooperation." *American Political Science Review* 85 (3): 701–726.

Straffin, Philip D. Jr. 1977. "The Bandwagon Curve." *American Journal of Political Science* 21 (4): 695–709.

Tulkens, Henry. 1979. "An Economic Model of International Negotiations Relating to Transfrontier Pollution." In *Communication and Control in Society*, edited by Klaus Krippendorff, 199–212. New York: Gordon and Breach.

Underdal, Arild. 1980. *The Politics of International Fisheries Management. The Case of the Northeast Atlantic*. New York: Columbia University Press.

———. 1998. "Introduction." In *The Politics of International Environmental Management*, edited by Arild Underdal, 1–11. Dordrecht: Kluwer.

Urpelainen, Johannes. 2009. "Explaining the Schwarzenegger Phenomenon: Local Frontrunners in Climate Policy." *Global Environmental Politics* 9 (3): 82–105.

Victor, David G. 2006. "Toward Effective International Cooperation on Climate Change: Numbers, Interests and Institutions." *Global Environmental Politics* 6 (3): 90–103.

———. 2011. *Global Warming Gridlock: Creating More Effective Strategies for Protecting the Planet*. Cambridge: Cambridge University Press.

Ward, Hugh. 1996. "Game Theory and the Politics of Global Warming: The State of Play and Beyond." *Political Studies* 44 (5): 850–871.

———. 2006. "International Linkages and Environmental Sustainability: The Effectiveness of the Regime Network." *Journal of Peace Research* 43 (2): 149–166.

Ward, Hugh, Frank Grundig, and Ethan R. Zorick. 2001. "Marching at the Pace of the Slowest: A Model of International Climate-Change Negotiations." *Political Studies* 49 (3): 438–461.

Yi, Sang-Seung, and Hyukseung Shin. 2000. "Endogenous Formation of Research Coalitions with Spillovers." *International Journal of Industrial Organization* 18 (2): 229–256.

Young, Oran. 1999. *Governance in World Affairs*. Ithaca, NY: Cornell University Press.

5   Computational Models, Global Climate Change, and Policy

Thierry Bréchet and Urs Luterbacher

5.1   Introduction

This chapter is about computational and simulation approaches based on computer-based modeling. Modeling has long been used in the climate change analysis to calculate temperature increase, sea level rise, and ocean acidification. What is different with the computational models we discuss here are the linkages made with policy questions. This necessitates a representation of at least the economic and demographic sectors of either the world economy as a whole or better yet of the different countries or regional groupings that matter in the climate change debate. If the latter formal representation is achieved, it will also permit investigation of the various "national interests" sometimes aligned or sometimes opposed within the potential climate negotiations. The structures of emerging coalitions could then be assessed—an aspect that links the questions presented in this chapter to the game and coalition analyses of chapter 4.

The discussions and negotiations for a post–Kyoto Protocol within the UNFCCC have shown that considerable and to some extent irreconcilable differences exist among several important countries or regional groupings. The fact that the United States did not ratify the Kyoto Protocol was greatly related to the attitudes of some of the major developing countries such as India and China. The ratification of the Kyoto Protocol by the United States is now a moot question since it has lost all significance. The United States will probably always be reluctant to accept constraining arrangements like the Kyoto Protocol unless emerging countries express a willingness to accept some form of more stringent commitments to climate policies, which was not obvious during the 2015 Conference of the

Parties in Paris. Moreover, emerging countries themselves will in all likelihood not enter into any commitments if the United States does not show any willingness to do so, something that may probably not happen any time soon. The elaboration of the Paris Agreement in December 2015 does not really fundamentally change this issue. The Paris Agreement rests on purely voluntary country fulfillments of greenhouse gas reduction efforts that are nationally determined. Even if those are indeed supposed to be reviewed periodically by the Conference of the Parties to the UNFCCC, they are not subject to any effective internationally organized enforcement mechanism.[1] The Paris Agreement from that point of view thus leaves a lot to be desired.[2]

The analytic frameworks available so far suggest that such opposition to an agreement is not accidental and usually rests on the formulation of too narrow a win set in specific countries by the executive or international bodies.[3] In other words, powerful domestic interests exist that do not see any gain for themselves in the ratification of an agreement and thus use all their influence to derail the confirmation process. Yet political positions may change depending on global economic evolutions and on the way the political processes, either internal or external, evolve.

This situation leaves a lot of room for analysis: all new regulations, especially if they stem from international agreements, usually produce winners and losers whether at the domestic or at the international level. It is important to be able to anticipate such distributions of costs and benefits. As we show here, modeling and simulation are important tools for such an assessment. The use of these tools should also lead negotiators to anticipate the kinds of coalitions that are likely to form or that would be desirable to arise around specific issues. Here computational models and simulations might help.

The role of computational models within the policy process must be clearly defined. One may not expect mathematical models to do the whole job. Put differently, the policy process by itself is part of the climate problem. Computational models might help decision makers (whoever they are—we shall come back to that) better understand the potential implications of their choices. What policy makers do need is a better understanding of what is at stake (a bit more light on climate and economic sciences), but they certainly do not want to be told what they should do. This has to do with the normative versus positive dimensions of applied modeling (see the following discussion on cost-benefit versus cost-efficiency).

Climate policies need to be scientifically underpinned by adequate supporting tools and methodologies. When focusing on climate issues, the problems to be dealt with become particularly intricate, given their global context, the complexity of the systems considered and their different space and time scales (global *versus* local, short-term *versus* long-term). There are risks and uncertainties, conflicting values, high stakes, and an urgent need to make decisions. Politically, it is necessary to ensure more transparency, to promote stakeholder participation in both policy making and research, to apply the precautionary principle, and to integrate simultaneously economic efficiency, ecological integrity, and social equity. In this respect, climate has a lot to do with sustainable development with regard to policy making (see Boulanger and Bréchet 2002, 2005). All these challenges require adequate scientific tools and decision-making practices. On climate issues, in contrast to many other policy issues, computational models have been used, and the Energy Modeling Forum (EMF) experience represents a good illustration of that kind of process.[4] But one may question to what extent these models integrate the policy dimension. It appears that most models put the purely economic-efficiency dimension forward and neglect the policy dimension, which refers to the cost-benefit perspective outlined above concerning gains and losses.

5.2   Simulation Models of Social Systems and Global Climate Change

Climate itself is the outcome of highly complex and nonlinear relations linking the atmosphere, oceans, sea and land ice, snow, land and its features, and hydrology. To understand the system as a whole and to predict its evolution, it is necessary to account for feedback and interaction among its components.

The complexities of the system and the uncertainties about many of the key processes and interactions preclude the use of very empirical or statistical models. Climate must therefore be studied with numerical models based on physical principles. Social systems can also be defined in terms of relations and feedback among economic, political, sociocultural, and demographic processes. To capture the most important features of social systems, social scientists have constructed various types of models. The ones considered here are *quantitative simulation models*—that is, those that use mathematical formulations to express key relationships within the system. Theories about the function of physical and social systems are the basis on which these models are developed. They are elaborated in quantitative terms so that it is possible to test hypotheses about the importance of changes in key variables for the evolution of other aspects of the system and to explore different trajectories they may take in the future. Such an approach can provide important insights for decision making about global environmental change because it permits an analysis of impacts of physical change for social processes and vice versa. Modeling policy alternatives also allows for the assessment of consequences of political and economic measures for the physical system and for society. Therefore, in contrast to simple empirical or statistical testing procedures such as regression or factor analysis, simulation has the advantage of providing the decision maker with a tool that can be adapted to answer specific questions about the effectiveness or consequences of policy choices.

Simulations are a set of instruments that can be used many times. They can and should be improved and modified according to new insights or new questions. The fact that simulation models can be adapted to different research questions and assumptions is one of their strengths, along

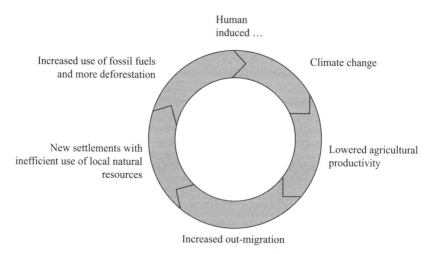

Figure 5.1
Amplifying climate change feedback effects through socioeconomic processes.

with the computational accuracy and (true) representation of the referent world that they offer. These features are particularly important when looking at the interactions between social systems and global environmental change. Many predictions concerning global environmental change, such as climate change, cannot be based entirely on extrapolation from empirical observations.

Modeling plays an important role in the prediction process itself, which is highly contingent on assumptions about some physical aspects but especially about social trends. Such social trends are often considered exogenously within the natural science model of global environmental change but are best analyzed in terms of their feedback structures with natural processes. For instance, simulation of socioeconomic processes can show the sequence that occurs in figure 5.1.

5.3 Resource Use, Climate Change, and Policy

5.3.1 Preliminary Considerations

As the previous brief discussion shows, the external environment poses complex challenges to policy making. Pressure comes from different arenas, and its form and stringency will depend as much on existing rules as on external actors' use of these rules. Actors, both domestic and international, can thus be considered as strategic players under specific decision-making rules and procedures. Within this perspective, external pressure can be envisioned as a process of eliminating domestic options that fall outside the range of feasible outcomes at the international level. In other words, it is important to determine a kind of external "win set"[5]—that is, a set of domestic options that can accommodate external developments and thus be viable. If external pressure reduces the range of viable options, domestic actors can choose; it still leaves open a significant range of choices. Accordingly, the analysis should focus on bargaining at the national level inside the externally restricted space. Major actors have to be identified and their interests determined. Assessing interests is difficult; however, simulation methods allow one to do it in a novel and rigorous way. Based on the premise that key determinants of actors' preferences are the costs associated with various policy changes, one can follow an *aggregate quantitative path*. This way of proceeding is justified because a macro-approach should not only reveal the costs but also the benefits of different types of policies for a country as a whole. Simulation approaches will yield a measure of the utility that domestic and international actors assign to various options. On that basis, simulation analysis of decision making is similar to the analysis of spatial voting (see Enelow and Hinich 1990; Hinich and Munger 1997) to determine the set of policy options that can be accepted at the domestic level. It should be noted here that this "domestic politics" emphasis encompasses the much debated notion of the "relative gains" perspective (Grieco 1988) since in this case what matters is the issue of relative competitiveness between domestic and foreign firms. The underlying argument claims that a selective application of emission restriction rules in favor of some countries, such as developing and emerging ones, would actually put firms of developed nations at a competitive disadvantage over those of all other ones. The goal would be here to protect or to further a relative advantage of domestic firms over foreign ones.

The size and location of this set will reflect the interests of actors and their power, as well as the agenda-setting effect of various institutional structures (for a use of spatial preference analysis in the framework of macro simulation model, see Luterbacher, Schellnhuber, and Wiegandt 1998; Nordhaus and Yang 1996). Simulation approaches of this kind usually base their results on the analysis of decision making within the framework of resource use. In particular, they try to tie together the evolution of a resource base influenced by various partially exogenous processes (such as climate change) and the resulting preference analysis and decision-making scenarios. Simulation models represent one of the approaches being used to capture the interaction between natural processes such as climate change and human activities. In this chapter, we describe some of the essential features of this type of simulation, briefly review some characteristic formulations, and discuss their strengths and weaknesses. As we point out, there are numerous simulation approaches that offer a great variety of conceptions. Since we are focusing here on the international aspects of global climate change we, after a brief discussion of various simulation concepts, mostly discuss models that include policy processes explicitly within their framework. In other words, our purpose here is not to thoroughly review "classical" descriptive simulation models of climate or climate-induced ecosystem and socioeconomic changes, or classical costs of climate change, or climate change mitigation models.[6] We focus instead on models that may employ some of these features to explain the evolution of either policy making or the negotiation process surrounding the climate change agreements.

In our conception, global environmental change as presented in figure 5.1 may generate unstable socioeconomic amplifying feedback processes, which in turn produce instabilities in the "natural" components of environmental processes. Policy processes may either mitigate or enhance such feedback mechanisms. To produce such results, simulation models of social processes interacting with global environmental change usually have the following characteristics:

• A *theoretically well-articulated representation* of a "real" or at least paradigmatic social system.[7] This representation might be based on an idealized view of some aspects of that reality, which assumes, for example, that all markets are in equilibrium or population rates are stable.

• The theoretically well-articulated representation is embedded in a *formal language, preferably a well-defined mathematical structure*. This permits computational analyses of the simulation models through calculation of logical consequences of the model formulation using appropriate computer programs.

• Particular assumptions about relationships among variables are expressed through *parameters* that measure their size and direction.

These computations, also referred to as *simulation output*, can be displayed in the form of graphs or other visual representations to allow a *comparison of simulation output* under several types of parameter configurations, and a possible *comparison of simulation output with different kinds of empirical observations*. In this latter case, the procedures permitting the comparisons are usually made explicit. They are generally statistical analyses based on comparisons between observed and computed data. Such statistical analysis is often in the form of an optimization process by which the parameters of the simulation model are slowly adjusted to minimize a discrepancy between observed and calculated values. Such optimization processes can also be used to implement the consequences of a scenario. They adjust the parameters of a simulation model to an outcome that appears desirable either from the point of view of the experimenter or from the point of view of various actors or agents represented in the model. This feature is particularly important for global change analysis. It allows for the evaluation of the extent to which behavior must change in order to make a certain policy effective. It also links simulation models explicitly with decision-making models such as the ones represented within game theory (see chapter 4 in this volume). This combined methodology facilitates the analysis of strategic implications (in the sense of the rational execution of planned political actions) of various policies. The basic characteristics of simulation models illustrate their advantages for the analysis of complex situations in which policy choices will influence the evolution of the system. Simulations clarify feedback relations and allow for a comparison of impacts of different policy options.

A note of caution about simulation is nevertheless warranted. Simulation output represents only a *particular solution* of the formal model on which it is based. Therefore, its results do not have general validity in terms of its formal consistency. Only a pure formal analysis leading to the establishment of theorems provides analytically consistent results. Nevertheless, simulation is useful in visualizing consequences of formal models, especially if the complexity it describes renders purely analytic representations difficult or impossible. Robustness of a particular model is of key importance here. It should be always tested, either by simple sensitivity analyses (rerunning the model by changing a single parameter value) or with more complex stochastic simulations procedures.

5.3.2 Types of Simulation Models

Many types of simulation models have been developed. They can be distinguished by their different conceptualizations of time, level of analysis, or degree of empirical representation. Each has its strengths and weaknesses that will be discussed in the context of descriptions of particular formulations. Usually researchers who study the relations between global environmental change and societies insist on looking at these interactions through time. Such approaches can be *truly dynamic* in the sense that the models generate their own time evolution or take a *comparative static perspective* where several runs of a model computed for different moments are put together and compared. The models that generate their own time evolution can rely on events or on an explicit, continuous, or discrete time reference.

Event-driven dynamic simulation models change their evolution when a particular event, such as a decision, takes place within them. A decision tree is a good example of such types of models. Models that rely on either a discrete or a continuous time referent change in step with the evolution of that referent. A model may thus evolve over time because budgetary decisions are taken once a year by a government, which would make it a discrete-time simulation. If a model changes at all moments or at random moments sufficiently close to each other, continuous time is then usually the preferred mode of representation.

Demographic simulation models are expressed in continuous time because the discrete events that characterize them—births, deaths, or migrations—occur randomly but close to each other through time. Models can also be distinguished by the level of aggregation of the phenomena they describe. Families of models exist that emphasize *aggregate behavior*; others describe the *micro-level* and thus will focus on the individual or on a sector of society. They can also be either essentially *theoretical* or *empirically based*, *dynamic*, or *equilibrium formulations*. Models in all these categories have been constructed to deal with social aspects of environmental change, and it is useful to examine various types to assess their effectiveness. At present, few models fully include both physical and social processes. Ultimately, this will be essential for exploring the feedback between climate and society. Indeed, policy choices must be made with knowledge about the impacts on both the physical environment and on social organization and behavior of measures devised to adapt to or mitigate climate changes. A review of existing formulations will nevertheless provide insights about particularly fruitful directions for future research.

5.3.3   Simulation Models: Methodological and Conceptual Aspects

Simulation models differ from each other both conceptually and methodologically. We have already mentioned the conceptual difference between descriptive and cost models on the one hand and the policy-interest-based models that help us understand the dynamics of a negotiation process on the other hand. We first briefly review the methodological differences and then examine the policy models in greater depth. Methodologically, simulation models can be envisaged either at the micro-level or at the macro-level.

Micro-level simulations present their object of research from the "bottom up," looking at particular individuals, groups, and institutions such as firms or sectors of an industry. For environmental questions, such approaches have tended to investigate how individuals influence each other on environmental matters (Gutscher and Mosler 1995) or how particular technologies work themselves out in terms of their impact on energy consumption (and thus emissions) through land use and specific industrial scenarios (Alcamo 1994).

So-called agent-based models are constructed on similar principles: the representation of individual actors based on some characteristic stylized behavioral aspects. The major specificity of agent-based models is the following. While the structure of the population is taken as given (and constant) in other models, this structure becomes endogenous with agent-based models as it emerges from the interaction between individual's decisions, like in evolutionary systems modeled in biology. The size and the structure of the population are not given beforehand by some law of motion just depending on time, but they are truly endogenous as they depend on agents' behavior (see, e.g., Bousquet and Le Page 2004).[8] As interesting as these micro-approaches are, they are usually limited to sectorial representations because a full description of a social system at the micro-level would lead to vastly complex formulations. Therefore, macro-level simulations are sometimes more adequate to examine problems related to global environmental change.

Macro-level simulations focus on particular aggregates such as various types of demand and supply of goods (in particular, natural resources or fuels) or productive capacities, government expenditures, or averages, such as public opinion data. Macro-level models are formulated either as dynamic (sometimes called econometric) or general equilibrium approaches. These two types of modeling are quite different in their scope and methodologies. *General equilibrium models* contain an explicit representation of economic agents at the aggregate level and of their linkages. Price mechanisms lead to price-clearing equilibria in all markets. These equilibria are conceived a priori as perfect and complete. Models are designed in such a way that they are realized at a given moment. This conceptualization ignores the adjustment path to equilibrium and ignores suboptimalities, such as imperfect labor or capital markets. General equilibrium models thus lead to comparative-static type evaluations. Time evolutions are in principle represented via crucial parameter changes (such as taxation rates). The new general equilibria are then recalculated and lead to a new model solution, which is then compared with the old one. Such models have the advantage of always leading to precise analytic solutions since these are, by the logic of general equilibrium modeling, defined at each relevant moment in time. Their strength lies in their ability to be simulated far into the future because they will not collapse under the influence of inherent instabilities.

It is therefore not surprising that most macro models dealing with global environmental change have been formulated as general equilibrium models. These models include the following:

- International Energy Agency (IEA) model
- Manne and Richels (1992) model
- Edmonds and Reilly model or ERM (Edmonds and Reilly 1983)
- OECD General Equilibrium Environmental model (GREEN) (OECD 1993)
- Whalley and Wigle (1991) model
- Nordhaus DICE (Nordhaus 1994) and RICE (Nordhaus and Yang 1996) models

Most of these focus on energy production and consumption and on the production of greenhouse gases (usually exclusively CO_2) to assess the impact of the economy on the earth's climate system as well as the cost to the economy or the trade system of various abatement and mitigation policies.

Dynamic formulations are primarily designed to reproduce the underlying "reality" of a social system and its time evolution. They do not say—in contrast to general equilibrium models, which have a prescriptive dimension in their representations—what this reality ought to look like given certain equilibrium constraints introduced extraneously. Once this "reality" is reproduced correctly, the researcher can raise general questions of the choice of strategies to reach certain goals. A dynamic perspective is not incompatible with optimization questions addressed by general equilibrium models. To date, however, most dynamic models have not focused on optimization questions and have concentrated on more or less sophisticated descriptions of the evolving reality. At best, different paths of adjustment are evaluated in terms of different possible scenarios, but not in terms of finding a best possible policy either from a national or a world perspective. Moreover, as a result of computational difficulties, these types of models have incorporated either short time horizons or relatively crude formulations that minimize feedback loops within the social structure. The study of various impacts of global change, such as the studies undertaken by Rosenzweig and Parry (1994) on the effects of global climate change on agriculture, use similar combinations of dynamic modeling extrapolated into the future under various scenario assumptions. The accuracy and usefulness of dynamic modeling can be increased by incorporating optimization procedures into the model structure, thereby improving the closeness of fit between model results and empirical observations. This in turn enhances the reliability of projections into the future and comparisons of impacts of different policy options.

The combination of dynamic modeling with optimization procedures that adopt either global optimum calculations or best-reply strategies of decision makers with respect to each other is very useful. A first application of such optimization procedures uses statistical analysis to calibrate a simulation model to data series (usually time series, but spatial calibration can also be envisaged). A second application consists of calculating best reply strategies through the maximization of utility functions that are attributed to the various actors. Because of their emphasis on the policy and negotiation process, only models of this latter type are examined in more detail here.

5.3.4 Policy Models

Policy models provide useful tools to assess various countries' positions in a negotiation process as well as their evolution under different proposals. A systematic use of simulation techniques can thus greatly benefit the student and the negotiator of climate change and other environmental agreements. Game theory can usefully provide the framework within which the decision-making process is simulated. The "game" amounts to two or several actors maximizing their particular value or utility function with the strategic consequences that derive from this optimizing behavior. These utility functions can be defined as resulting from some economic benefit calculations, such as maximizing consumption or income or some other more strategic variable. Two broad categories of game-theoretic approaches provide the basis for the particular decision models integrated into the simulation:

Differential game approaches investigate attempts by one or several decision makers to follow what they consider to be an optimal trajectory through time but subjected to certain constraints. Optimal trajectories can be described in terms of several objective functions that are to be reached during a given period of interaction between decision makers (here, simulation period). Calculations of objective functions can proceed along the lines outlined above for the statistical estimation of parameters. The dynamic equations of the simulation model act as constraints on the object of opti-mization. An objective function can often be expressed in terms of revenue maximization over time (global consumption minus costs due to environ-mental degradation and to mitigation policies, for example). Several scenarios can be envisaged. Decision makers can try to reach their optimal trajectories separately or cooperatively. Different game theoretical equilibria will emerge accordingly. As shown by Nordhaus and Yang (1996), an analysis of the appli-cation of such differential game techniques demonstrates that often, but not always, separate approaches lead either to unequal or to suboptimal results for the individual countries or regions represented by the decision makers.

Backward-induction techniques can also be used within the context of dynamic simulation procedures to explore, for instance, effects of the imple-mentation of particular mitigation policies. Take, as an example, two coun-tries A and B who have the choice of implementing either separately or jointly a tax to limit emissions of a given pollutant. The simulation model allows for the calculation of costs and benefits of taxation policies. If, for each country individually, the cost of taxation exceeds the benefits of pol-lution reduction, a tax-alone policy might not succeed, and a joint taxation policy for the two countries might be necessary. However, there is, in this case, an incentive not to cooperate because an individual country could be better off letting the other one deal alone with pollution abatement.

Backward-induction techniques (see also the chapter 4 in this volume) will indicate whether the countries do or do not have an advantage in implementing taxation policies jointly or in letting a country tax itself. Moreover, a simulation approach can also determine if a country has suf-ficient retaliatory means at its disposal to induce the other country to adopt pollution-abating taxation policies. Country A could force country B to join a taxation policy rather than pollute, because of retaliation by A toward B. If A figures out that by threatening strong retaliation—whose effects can be calculated with the simulation model at the end of this decision sequence—B would have an incentive to tax jointly with A rather than to continue pol-luting. A (that by assumption prefers taxation) will initiate a taxation pol-icy. Such a decision will appear to be best because calculations of policy choices carried out from the end of the above decision tree (hence *backward induction*) will determine the optimal policy sequence from the beginning for an actor (see figure 5.2). Game theory, however, shows that backward

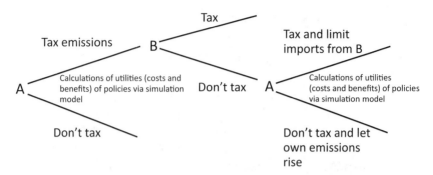

Figure 5.2
Calculation of best decision path with backward induction.

induction type analysis breaks down when incomplete and imperfect information situations between international actors occur. More subtle investigation types are then required which involve the explicit introduction of uncertainty in the form of expected utility calculations. Here also, computational models can be used to deal with these issues. Bueno de Mesquita (2009) develops a general model of collective decision making at the international level based on an expected utility perspective, which he then applies to climate change issues. He predicts thus a general failure of institutional settings such as the Kyoto Protocol especially after 2050. His approach depends heavily on evaluating subjective elements such as influence of an international actor and the salience of the issue to him. He also mostly neglects domestic influences. The evaluation procedure for determining such dimensions in quantitative form seems rather opaque and thus difficult to assess. Moreover, Bueno de Mesquita's games rest on very classical expected utility formulations that have been questioned for a long time especially when they touch on extreme situations such as floods or drought, which are precisely important for policy makers within the context of climate change (cf. Allais 1953; Quiggin 1982).

Hence, when dealing with climate coalitions, one must take into consideration both the abatement costs and the benefits (avoided damages) for each individual country or group of countries. In a climate game the payoff function of a country or a coalition depends on both effects, and countries or coalitions differ from each other with respect to these two aspects. To make it clear, the benefit of a country to join a coalition and to accept some abatement effort is given by the comparison between the abatement cost and the benefit from lower damages, taking as given what the other countries or coalitions are doing. The optimal solution of a coalition of countries is such that, as a whole, its marginal abatement cost equals the marginal avoided damages, taking as given what the other countries or coalitions do. Thus, comparing the payoff of different structures of coalition boils down to comparing the outcome of different cost-benefit analyses. As will be explained below, this is exactly what the so-called *integrated assessment models* do: they just compare costs and benefits of any policy resulting from an international agreement. And thus the related question: Is a country better off or worse off by choosing one type of international agreement, as opposed to another one?[9] Coalition theory does answer this question with the help of computational integrated assessment models. Yet the whole story is not told, simply because many political dimensions of the problem remain unanswered, which leaves room for policy or diplomacy. Typically, the equity (or distributional) issues still need to be handled. Although as we point out below, efficient policies can also solve the equity question (Chichilnisky and Luterbacher 2012).

The Nordhaus DICE and especially the Nordhaus-Yang RICE model constitute good examples of such a focus on policy processes because they try to assess the economic costs of climate change in interaction with the production part of the economy. Thus, abatement and mitigation policies are evaluated in terms of their impact on reducing the economic costs of climate change. In other words, Nordhaus introduces a cost-benefit analysis that leads to what could be called an optimal pollution level in terms of all greenhouse gases (not just CO_2). Moreover, the Nordhaus-Yang RICE model represents a *regionalized* version of the DICE model with the same general approach. The regionalization perspective leads Nordhaus and Yang (1996) to an interesting comparison of more local effects of abatement policies. They can then assess possible divergences in interests between regions that are hit differentially by abatement policies. These differences in interests between the various regions and relevant actors in the climate change debate are calculated by using backward-induction techniques specially adapted to simulation models. We already referred to these techniques previously and have pointed out some of their weaknesses such as the problems raised by incomplete information where they break down. However, through their use Nordhaus and Yang can show the possible impact of particular dispositions of global environmental accords, such as the FCCC, which can be evaluated, as can the likelihood of compliance and noncompliance. The dynamic feedback characteristics of the Nordhaus-Yang perspective make it useful for the evaluation of international policies. With respect to the negotiation process connected to the evolution of the UNFCCC and the Kyoto Protocol, the Nordhaus-Yang perspective can thus shed some light on the evolution of national or regional interests with respect to the climate change policy debate.

If a particular actor gains little from the realization of a worldwide climate policy such as the one included in the Kyoto Protocol, problems in the ratification of the agreement have to be expected. As we point out again later, the Nordhaus-Yang analysis stresses that the United States would obtain a smaller gain with respect to its long-term economic interests (even if the effects of climate change are included in the model) by cooperating with the international community in this matter than by implementing its own noncooperative policies. Their simulation predicts in some way the expected difficulties in the ratification process. These results are obtained, however, under specific assumptions about the dynamics of climate change for the United States and about the use of particular instruments to implement mitigation policies, such as carbon taxes. Other instruments, such as tradable permits, technology transfers, or an emphasis on carbon sinks, might change the incentive structure inside the United States and alter the politics of ratification. The win set for the Kyoto Protocol could thus be completely changed and could lead to a change in the attitude of the US Senate.

The importance of the simulation technique lies in the fact that such elements can be analyzed precisely through changes in the relevant variables or parameters included in the model. The results obtained by simulation models demonstrate the usefulness of the methodology. Based on their data and initial parameter values—which include cost estimates of reducing CO_2 emissions, climate damage estimates for each major climate actor, and emissions from land use and industrial production—Nordhaus and Yang (1996) conclude that the win set for the United States in the climate negotiation is not adequate, and that it is better off not joining the rest of the world in a cooperative policy to solve the climate problem. This can explain why the United States sought the inclusion of more greenhouse target gases and more instruments such as tradable permits, joint implementation, and the consideration of carbon sinks in the drafting of the Kyoto Protocol.

However, by using a modified version of the same model with different initial conditions and parameters,[10] Eyckmans and Tulkens (2003) come to a totally different conclusion: China's win set is unsatisfactory, given that country's development goals and growth targets, elements that are not taken into account by Nordhaus and Yang. China would thus be the nation that does not benefit from a cooperative solution and has the biggest incentive to free-ride (see also chapter 7 in this volume). An update proposed by Bréchet, Gerard, and Tulkens (2011) shows, using both cooperative and noncooperative game theory concepts, that some of these outcomes may change when considering the most recent economic evolutions. It reveals how growth or population patterns (along with technological progress) may influence the cost-benefit analysis underpinning climate negotiations among countries. Another contribution to this field (with the WITCH model) is provided by Bosetti et al. (2013).

Another vexing question is the influence of discount rates on future cost-benefit calculations, and so on coalitions formation. For instance, the Stern Review (Stern 2006) released by the British government emphasizes the dramatic consequences of climate change in terms of loss of welfare if nothing is done to mitigate and prevent it soon. This goes against previously held convictions held mostly by economists that the best policies on climate change should entail small mitigation efforts now and then increase much more in the future. As emphasized by Nordhaus (2006) and Dasgupta (2006), the dramatic character of the conclusions of the report is heavily dependent on the assumptions of a relatively low discount rate. Admittedly, discounting is one of the more contentious issues in the climate debate. The discount rate is related to the *when-flexibility* (while heterogeneity among countries in each period of time yields the *where-flexibility*). In that sense, discounting makes the link between efficiency (optimal intertemporal abatement profile) and intergenerational equity (distributional impacts of costs and benefits among generations). What should be the discount rate in a model? One may distinguish a *descriptive* or a *prescriptive* approach, and decide to whom this rate is applied (individual consumer, a firm, or a government). With a descriptive approach, one relies on market-oriented criteria such as the long-run rate of return on capital, and not on subjective criteria such as the utility discount rate (which represents the pure time preference at the individual's level). This is what is used in the MERGE model developed at Stanford by Manne (2005). It is clearly necessary to be able to understand the consequences of the assumptions about different discount rates in order to get a clear picture of future costs and possible benefits of climate change.

Here also computational models are useful especially because discount rates may not only differ in time but also in space: different regions of the globe can have different discount rates because some are more concerned with present issues than with the future. The Eyckmans and Tulkens (2003) paper mentioned previously assumes different discount rates in different regions, higher ones for emerging and developing countries, lower ones for industrialized countries. They show that this assumption has two important consequences: First, emerging countries such as India and China do not have an interest as great as developed countries and even as the United States in cooperative arrangements for climate change. This means that these countries will have to be induced to cooperate by incentive methods rather than by binding commitments to engage in climate change abatements—perhaps for many years into the future (see also chapter 4 in this volume). Second, the Nordhaus contention that it is better to abate little now and more so in the future does not apply to developed countries but to developing and emerging ones only. In that sense, the structure of the Kyoto Protocol, which has put the initial effort squarely into the hands of developed countries, seems to be justified by this simulation finding. It may be expected that differences in discount rates may also completely reshape the composition of climate coalitions by leading to different intertemporal cost and benefit sharing across regions or countries. It is also possible that climate damages could have important international and interregional feedback effects. On the one hand, damages do not take legal national frontiers into account. On the other hand, spillovers effects between nations can occur (dissemination, migration, etc.). This means that losses due to climate change in one region/country may yield significant losses in other parts of the world.

A last discussion that deserves attention is about how uncertainties on future climate change (e.g., on climate sensitivity) influence climate policies when policy makers are risk adverse. A first analysis is provided by Bréchet et al. (2012) with an eighteen-region IAM model. The authors show that international cooperation not only leads to a reduction in the *expected* global warming (a lower mean temperature increase) but also to a drastic reduction of the *risk* of facing very high climate damages in the future. This is because climate change has many different dimensions, such as extreme meteorological events and sea level rise, that are not linearly related to the mean temperature increase. Admittedly, all these points deserve more attention in future research.

These elements illustrate the usefulness of combining computational models and game theory. If we assume that both analyses could be right, we can conclude that simulation techniques have the potential to show why and under which conditions inadequate win sets for particular nations or groups of nations might emerge. Moreover, the precise values of the variables involved can be pinpointed and eventual corrective measures analyzed. Simulation techniques can thus show why China is so reluctant to take on obligations in terms of climate change policies. Further calculations and elaborations of the model should allow researchers and possibly also policy makers to determine the conditions under which developing nations such as India and China could join the Kyoto process more actively and take on some commitments similar to the ones taken by Annex I countries. In a more sectorial context, Luterbacher, Schellnhuber, and Wiegandt (1998) show that cooperation on the use of water resources in the Middle East benefits all parties unless an extreme asymmetry between the countries exists, such as a difference in their position in a river basin. The upstream nation in particular—if it also enjoys demographic and economic predominance—has a big advantage in terms of bargaining power and can thus mostly impose its own views to the detriment of the others. These results point to what can happen in a particular sector of production, which may entail an important role for the economy and the polity as a whole. Unfortunately, computational modeling with decision-making analysis by state actors has so far been conducted at the country level and has ignored subnational issues. This might be deplored in view of the results achieved by the political economy approach in this regard. Several studies within the trade literature show how protectionist barriers that benefit small groups but harm society as a whole are established (e.g., Grossman and Helpman 1994). The story that emerges is one of companies that are threatened by liberalization or regulations, preferring to invest in the political process to extract protective measures from legislation rather than improve their own competitiveness or conform to rules. While trade agreements differ fundamentally from environmental agreements, in the sense that in the latter case first mover advantage in the form of refusal to cooperate presents immediate benefits for individual states,[11] the consequences are similar. In both cases, some industries or some segments of the population are more affected by the obligations stemming from the treaty than others. Thus similar incentives exist to fight the ratification of particular agreements. So even though the costs of implementing an environmental agreement might be low for the society at large (as they seem to be for the United States, for instance) and offer tangible long-term advantages, the immediate impact on some segments of society and industries might be extremely large. In such cases, the national interest, which in a computational country-based model is defined in terms of the welfare of the national society as a whole, is inadequate to represent its utility profile at the international level. A definition that takes into account the successful lobbying efforts of particular groups would be much more adequate. Nevertheless this does not mean that the methodology suggested by the computational approach is not useful. It just means that it has not been applied yet.

In a general equilibrium setting, productivity of capital may have a major influence on both prices and quantities, notably on greenhouse gas abatement efforts. But, under full emission trading, emission rights have only a minor effect on the total value of each region's endowments. Thus, by comparing numerically two rules for allowances of emission rights, egalitarian—emission rights are allocated in proportion to each region's initial population—or pragmatic, emission rights are allocated in proportion to year 2000 emissions with a gradual transition (by 2050) to shares based on each region's initial population, Manne (2005) shows that changing the allocation rule has less impact on a region's welfare than changing the discount rate if the market for emission rights works. This result illustrates the fact that, contrary to what is often pointed out in the literature as an advantage of tradable permits, separation of equity from efficiency can only happen in a static partial equilibrium such as the one evoked by Montgomery (1972). Efficiency and equity are actually not separable issues, a point of view reaffirmed by Chichilnisky and Luterbacher (2012).

5.4 Conclusion

In this chapter we have tried to point out why computational and simulation models of climate change are useful tools to not only understand and illuminate the current debate but also to assist negotiators of agreements of how to envisage alternative future possibilities. We have shown how these models can help evaluate future costs and benefits of climate change even when broken down into different countries and regions and help with the assessment of the use of various kind of discount rates. These models are still in need of further developments. At the economic level, they usually do not represent trade and capital relations adequately. At the political level, the important question of proper win set representation in each country or region evoked in the beginning of the chapter is not touched on. Nevertheless, the models show us paths that could be followed to tackle a variety of questions, including the ones we just alluded to.

Notes

1. The insistence by the former American secretary of state John Kerry to change a passage of the Paris Agreement text that could hint at internationally imposed obligations at the last minute is quite revealing.

2. This point is well emphasized Tulkens (2016).

3. This was emphasized in chapter 4 of this volume.

4. The EMF at Stanford University is an international forum for sharing and facilitating discussions on energy policy and global climate issues among experts. The EMF seeks to improve the understanding of the energy/environment problem by harnessing the collective capabilities of participating experts, and to explain the strengths, limitations and caveats of alternative analytical approaches (see Stanford University 2013).

5. The original formulation of this concept in the context of the interface between domestic and international politics is presented in Putnam (1988).

6. For a good review of these, see Mabey et al. (1997).

7. By *paradigmatic* we mean an artificial but exemplary and generic representation of a social system, such as a market, or a partially controlled economy or an authoritarian or democratic system, without reference to a precise empirical case.

8. For a survey, see Janssen (2005); for application to climate change, see also Janssen and De Vries (1998) or Davidson and Moss (2001).

9. It is striking that policy makers usually focus on the costs of a policy and not on its benefits. They look unfavorably on the cost-benefit principle. For a discussion and a numerical illustration of this issue, see Bréchet and Tulkens (2015).

10. Their estimate of climate damage and costs of CO_2 reductions are different.

11. In this way somebody else is either taking care of the problem or can be blamed for it. The now defunct Global Climate Change Coalition's main argument was that supposedly large polluters, such as China and India, would be exempt of obligations.

References

Alcamo, Joseph. 1994. *Image 2.0: Integrated Modeling of Global Climate Change.* Dordrecht: Kluwer.

Allais, Maurice. 1953. "Le Comportement De L'homme Rationnel Devant Le Risque: Critique Des Postulats Et Axiomes De L'école Américaine." *Econometrica: Journal of the Econometric Society* 21:503–546.

Bosetti, Valentina, Carlo Carraro, Enrica De Cian, Emanuele Massetti, and Massimo Tavoni. 2013. "Incentives and Stability of International Climate Coalitions: An Integrated Assessment." *Energy Policy* 55:44–56.

Boulanger, Paul-Marie, and Thierry Bréchet. 2002. *Setting Concepts into Motion. Improving Scientific Tools in Support of Sustainable Development Decision-Making.* Brussels: European Commission, Directorate General Research—Environment and Sustainable Development Programme and Belgian Science Policy.

———. 2005. "Models for Policy-Making in Sustainable Development: The State of the Art and Perspectives for Research." *Ecological Economics* 55 (3): 337–350.

Bousquet, François, and Christophe Le Page. 2004. "Multi-Agent Simulations and Ecosystem Management: A Review." *Ecological Modelling* 176 (3): 313–332.

Bréchet, Thierry, François Gerard, and Henry Tulkens. 2011. "Efficiency vs. Stability in Climate Coalitions: A Conceptual and Computational Appraisal." *Energy Journal* 32 (1): 49.

Bréchet, Thierry, Julien Thénié, Thibaut Zeimes, and Stéphane Zuber. 2012. "The Benefits of Cooperation under Uncertainty: The Case of Climate Change." *Environmental Modeling & Assessment* 17 (1–2): 149–162.

Bréchet, Thierry, and Henry Tulkens. 2015. "Climate Policies: A Burden, or a Gain?" *Energy Journal* 36 (3): 155–170.

Bueno de Mesquita, Bruce. 2009. *The Predictioneer's Game: Using the Logic of Brazen Self-Interest to See and Shape the Future.* New York: Random House.

Chichilnisky, Graciela, and Urs Luterbacher. 2012. "Climate Change, Security, and Redistribution: How Can Political Dilemmas Linked to the Global Environment Be Solved." *Brown Journal of World Affairs* 18 (2): 227–260.

Dasgupta, Partha. 2006. "Comments on the Stern Review's Economics of Climate Change." Prepared for a seminar on the Stern Review's Economics of Climate Change organized by the Foundation for Science and Technology at the Royal Society, London, November 8.

Davidson, Paul, and Scott Moss. 2001. *Multi-Agent-Based Simulation, Lecuture Notes in Computer Science.* Berlin: Springer.

Edmonds, Jae, and John Reilly. 1983. "A Long-Term Global Energy-Economic Model of Carbon Dioxide Release from Fossil Fuel Use." *Energy Economics* 5 (2): 74–88.

Enelow, James M., and Melvin J. Hinich. 1990. *Advances in the Spatial Theory of Voting.* Cambridge: Cambridge University Press.

Eyckmans, Johan, and Henry Tulkens. 2003. "Simulating Coalitionally Stable Burden Sharing Agreements for the Climate Change Problem." *Resource and Energy Economics* 25 (4): 299–327.

Grieco, Joseph. (1988). Anarchy and the Limits of Cooperation: A Realist Critique of the Newest Liberal Institutionalism. *International Organization* 42 (3): 485–507.

Grossman, Gene M., and Elhanan Helpman. 1994. "Protection for Sale." *American Economic Review* 84 (4): 833–850.

Gutscher, Heinz, and Hans-Joachim Mosler. 1995. "Why Analyze 10,000 Rather Than One? Simulating Interactions in Populations." In *Paper Presented at the First Open Meeting of the Human Dimensions of Global Environmental Change Community.* Durham, NC: Duke University.

Hinich, Melvin J., and Michael C. Munger. 1997. *Analytical Politics.* New York: Cambridge University Press.

Janssen, Marco. 2005. "Agent-Based Modeling." In *Modeling in Ecological Economics,* edited by John Proops and Paul Safonov, 155–172. Cheltenham, UK: Edward Elgar.

Janssen, Marco, and Bert De Vries. 1998. "The Battle of Perspectives: A Multi-Agent Model with Adaptive Responses to Climate Change." *Ecological Economics* 26 (1): 43–65.

Luterbacher, Urs, Hans-Joachim Schellnhuber, and Ellen Wiegandt. 1998. *Water Resource Conflicts: The Use of Formal Approaches, Working Paper.* Potsdam: Potsdam Institute for Climate Impact Research.

Mabey, Nick, Stephen Hall, Clare Smith, and Sujata Gupta. 1997. *Argument in the Greenhouse.* London: Routledge.

Manne, Alan. 2005. "General Equilibrium Modeling for Global Climate Change." In *Frontiers in Applied General Equilibrium Modeling,* edited by Timothy J. Kehoe, Thirukodikaval Nilakanta Srinivasan, and John Whalley, 255–276. Cambridge: Cambridge University Press.

Manne, Alan, and Richard Richels. 1992. *Buying Greenhouse Insurance: The Economic Costs of CO_2 Emission Limits.* Cambridge, MA: MIT Press.

Montgomery, David W. 1972. "Markets in Licenses and Efficient Pollution Control Programs." *Journal of Economic Theory* 5 (3): 395–418.

Nordhaus, William. 1994. *Managing the Global Commons*. Cambridge, MA: MIT Press.

———. 2017. A Review of the Stern Review on the Economics of climate Change" *Journal of Economic Literature* XLV: 686–702.

Nordhaus, William, and Zili Yang. 1996. "A Regional Dynamic General-Equilibrium Model of Alternative Climate-Change Strategies." *American Economic Review* 86 (4): 741–765.

OECD. 1993. *Green: The User Manual*. Paris: Organisation for Economic Cooperation and Development.

Putnam, Robert D. 1988. "Diplomacy and Domestic Politics: The Logic of Two-Level Games." *International Organization* 42 (3): 427–460.

Quiggin, John. 1982. "A Theory of Anticipated Utility." *Journal of Economic Behavior & Organization* 3 (4): 323–343.

Rosenzweig, Cynthia, and Martin L. Parry. 1994. "Potential Impact of Climate Change on World Food Supply." *Nature* 367 (6459): 133–138.

Stanford University. 2013. *Energy Modeling Forum*. Available from emf.stanford.edu.

Stern, Nicholas. 2006. *Stern Review on the Economics of Climate Change*. London: HM Treasury.

Tulkens, Henry. 2016. "Cop 21 and Economic Theory: Taking Stock." *Revue d'économie politique* 126 (4): 471–486.

Whalley, John, and Randall Wigle. 1991. "The International Incidence of Carbon Taxes." In *Global Warming: Economic Policy Responses*, edited by Rudiger Dornbusch and James Poterba, 233–262. Cambridge, MA: MIT Press.

6 Environmental Protection, Differentiated Responsibility, and World Trade: Making Room for Climate Action

Urs Luterbacher, Carla Norrlof, and Jorge E. Viñuales

6.1 Introduction

Trade and the environment are closely linked. The capacity of economies to produce goods and services is an important prerequisite for international commerce. Viewed from the environmental perspective, resources are vital inputs for economic activity, and waste is a by-product of any economy's output, at least at present. In policy terms, the adoption of international environmental agreements such as the UNFCCC, the Kyoto Protocol, and the Paris Agreement all raise the problem of their consistency with other types of international cooperative arrangements. Consistency problems might also appear as a result of the special status of developing countries recognized by these global environmental agreements under the label of common but differentiated responsibilities of countries with respect to climate change, which is affirmed in the preamble to the UNFCCC. In this chapter we show how trade and environmental protection interact and point to the specific ways in which the climate regime may come into conflict with the trade regime. Focusing on the interplay between environmental regimes and the trade regime is important because the trade regime is the most highly institutionalized regime in the world, and one that has an automatically binding enforcement mechanism (as a result of the Dispute Settlement Panel's negative consensus rule). The prospect of successfully enforcing environmentally friendly policies through the trade regime (more on this below) creates opportunities that are fundamentally different than incentives to strategically link the climate change regime to human rights, security, or biodiversity (cf. Jinnah 2011). The coherence between environmental regimes and the trade regime matters in the opposite way, as well. The elaborate rules and disciplines enshrined in the General Agreement on Trade and Tariffs/World Trade Organization (GATT/WTO) framework can severely limit countries' ability to achieve environmental objectives, establishing a de facto policy hierarchy, prioritizing trade objectives.

The UNFCCC includes a "GATT-compatible clause" (UNFCCC 1992, art. 3 [5]) stipulating that efforts to mitigate climate change "should" not "constitute a means of arbitrary or unjustifiable discrimination or a disguised restriction on international trade." For many years, trade provisions of multilateral environmental agreements were not at the heart of interstate disputes (Gonzalez 2000). The only direct conflict so far arose from the EU's ban on imports of genetically modified products.[1] The dispute was brought before the WTO dispute settlement body and the EU referred, unsuccessfully, to its obligations under the 2000 Cartagena Biosafety Protocol.

But despite the evidence suggesting that the risk of conflict is relatively low, there are three reasons why disputes about such cases have become more frequent and carry more fundamental implications. First, the international trade regime includes a powerful quasi-judiciary dispute-settlement mechanism that was strengthened by the Uruguay Round. States may therefore bring trade disputes with environmental components before the WTO, even though the organization has repeatedly stated that, as a matter of principle, it does not want to get involved in environmental disputes. Moreover, the WTO provides members with powerful retaliation and compliance mechanisms. A set of strong rules and institutional mechanisms provides the trade regime with greater enforcement power than other organizations. Under certain conditions, if rules are violated, states may retaliate against others by establishing discriminatory measures by closing their domestic markets to a range of foreign products (Bown and Pauwelyn 2010). Second, by targeting fossil fuel emissions (carbon dioxide and nitrous oxide) and methane, among others, the UNFCCC, the Kyoto Protocol, and the Paris Agreement cover the great majority of current industrial and agricultural products. They also encompass such activities as transportation and aviation. Third, and crucially, the types of domestic mitigation policies brought under the umbrella of the Paris Agreement involve the massive reallocation of investment toward greener forms of energy. This move has a variety of trade implications, ranging from the effects of green industrial policies (particularly those favoring the emergence of a domestic renewable energy sector) on foreign competitors to carbon equalization measures (to reflect the environmental externalities of using carbon-intensive inputs in the production of goods abroad).

Thus, the relevance of trade disciplines for climate change policy must not be underestimated. This issue is being reflected in the difficult negotiations within the Forum on the impact of implementation on response measures established in 2011 under the UNFCCC and it has transpired in parts of the Paris Agreement, including its preamble and article 4 (15) (Viñuales 2017). A major concern of developing countries is precisely the competitive disadvantage that their products may face as a result of climate change policies (response measures) adopted in developed countries. The need to make such measures trade-compatible hides a fundamental tension between the internalization of negative externalities (greenhouse gas emissions) called for by climate policies and the nondiscrimination standards as currently envisaged in international trade law.

In this chapter, after a brief discussion of the most relevant aspects of trade rules, we examine their implications for areas where environmental considerations could be raised at both the production and consumption levels. We then provide theoretical background for the importance of proper regulation and definition of property rights for standard mechanisms of domestic and international commercial exchange to work without exacerbating environmental degradation. We subsequently proceed to review how environmental agreements, including the global climate change regime, may be at variance with WTO trade provisions. We conclude our chapter by discussing policy implications.

6.2   Trade Rules

The WTO regime is an upgraded and extended version of the GATT, which was adopted in 1947. The trade rules envisioned by the GATT, which serve to promote trade liberalization through reciprocity and nondiscrimination, essentially remain the same under the WTO. But the added institutional dimension has strengthened the system by means of mechanisms such as the enhanced compliance mechanism for dispute settlement (DSB), the new system for trade policy review (TPRM), and the greater prominence of Ministerial Meetings (which replace GATT bargaining rounds). The scope of the regime has also been extended substantively to include services and intellectual property rights, as well as numerous refinements regarding trade in goods.

The core idea is to promote free trade through a generalized nondiscrimination principle, as well as through a preference for tariffs (that are to be reduced over time by means of negotiations) over quantitative trade restrictions—such as quotas—which are banned by Article XI. This generalized nondiscrimination principle includes the most-favored-nation (MFN) obligation to not discriminate among the goods of GATT/WTO member countries (Article I). In addition, provisions under Article III require national treatment of like products; in other words, the same national treatment has to be accorded to both foreign and domestic goods.

The greater emphasis of the WTO on enforcing trade disciplines continues to be balanced with institutional mechanisms for flexibility in trade policy through various derogations, exemptions, exceptions, and other mechanisms. The general-exception clause (Article XX) is of particular importance. It is structured in terms of an introductory part called the "chapeau" and a list of specific exceptions. A measure in breach of GATT disciplines (e.g., Articles I, III, or XI) may be justified if it meets the conditions of one specific exception and is also consistent with the general requirements of the chapeau of Article XX. Significantly, however, GATT/WTO-inconsistent trade policies have been the exception rather than the rule because justifying alternative policies carries a number of legal and practical implications (burden of proof, interpretation, non-self-judging character, interactions with other norms/treaties) when determining the extent to which trade rules allow countries to pursue genuine environmental regulation. In order to understand this point, the interactions between trade rules and environmental policy require further elaboration.

6.3   Consumption, Production, and Differential Responsibilities

6.3.1   Consumption

As a general matter, international trade law does not hamper the right of states to regulate consumption for health or environmental purposes as long as they remain within certain bounds. The very existence of "bounds" placed by trade regulation may appear illegitimate, as health and environmental considerations are at least as (and perhaps more) important than trade. According to existing rules, states must have scientific grounds for their action and/or must act consistently with international standards, and they cannot arbitrarily or unjustifiably discriminate between two like products. Norms on gasoline composition and phytosanitary measures illustrate this point. A country is free to impose an environmental norm such as particular standards for the composition of gasoline if the norm is universally applied. The same is true for a phytosanitary measure, such as the fixing of a minimum level of a pesticide or other reputedly dangerous products in food.

For example, in a case brought by the United States against the EU over the presence of growth hormones in beef products, the WTO panel and Appellate Body sided with the United States (and other beef exporters using growth hormones) largely because of the lack of evidence concerning the health effects of that particular substance. In a subsequent case, a WTO panel ruled against certain restrictions on GMOs by the EU and some of its member states, despite the fact that the 2000 Cartagena Biosafety Protocol required exporters to label products that could contain GMOs and allowed countries to invoke the precautionary principle to ban imports of such products until it was established that GMOs did not pose health or environmental risks. Even when the health effects are well known, a trade restriction may be construed as a breach of trade rules. Such was the case when the government of Thailand wanted to ban cigarettes for health reasons. The GATT panel found that raising import barriers could not be justified under Article XX(b). Although a measure may be justified when "necessary to protect human or animal life," the panel did not find that import restrictions were in this case "necessary" because alternative measures consistent with Article XX(d) and III(4) were available. The regulation of consumption may also relate to the processes and production methods (PPMs) used to produce a good. This is particularly the case with respect to labeling but the PPM issue is better framed from the perspective of production, to which we now turn.

6.3.2 Production

From a production perspective, there are two main questions raised by the interactions between trade disciplines and environmental policy. As noted above, the first one relates to the so-called *processes and production methods* (PPMs). The key issue is whether a country can treat two goods differently when they are similar in composition but are produced using processes that have a different environmental footprint. Perhaps more fundamentally, this issue goes to whether a country is entitled, through its trade policies (and "market power"), to influence the way in which production is organized abroad. This is particularly important in the case of climate change where the carbon intensity of traded goods is a major concern. It seems unrealistic to design mitigation policies that do not address carbon intensiveness in production processes and methods.

The second production-related question concerns *green industrial policies* (Wu and Salzman 2014). Shifting investment and industrial practices toward greener products and solutions (e.g., electricity from renewable energy or efficiency-related equipment) may take time and, through the transitional process, a domestic industry that is less competitive than similar foreign industries may lose market shares. Thus, countries may be tempted to protect their nascent industries against foreign competitors. From an environmental perspective, it is good to push industries to move from brown to green, but from a trade perspective giving an advantage to domestic (over foreign) products can seem unfair. Yet creating an environmental market that undermines the local industry and favors foreigners may be politically unrealistic unless some advantage (e.g., local content requirements [LCRs]) is given to local producers, an advantage that may be inconsistent with trade rules. A good illustration of this problem is provided by the *India–Solar cells* case, where the local content requirements imposed by India as a condition to benefit from renewable energy subsidies were found to be in breach of WTO rules by the Panel and the Appellate Body.

There are several examples of these production-related issues. However, because of space constraints, this chapter focuses on the question of PPMs. It is nonetheless worth mentioning that there are an increasing number of trade disputes in connection with green industrial policy (Lewis 2014).

6.3.3   Processes and Production Methods

A key aspect of the PPM question is the extent to which a difference in the environmental footprint of a production process or method makes two otherwise similar products dissimilar (unlike) for purposes of Articles I (MFN clause) and III (national treatment clause) of the GATT. In the last several years, there has been much discussion about measures that would treat two similar products (e.g., electricity, cement, aluminum) differently on the basis of their carbon footprint. Depending on the specific context, such measures have been called carbon equalization measures or border measures.

From a legal perspective, they can be framed in at least four ways. One is to say that such products are not "alike," and that a condition for the breach of Articles I or III is therefore missing. Another way is to consider such products as alike but that differential treatment is fully justified under one exception (meeting both the conditions of an exception and the requirements of the chapeau). In the latter case, the respondent State would carry the burden of proving that PPM-based differentiation—despite constituting a breach—is justified, something so difficult that it has never been successful. The third way, which reflects current practice, is to view PPM-based differentiation as potentially justified (i.e., that it fits under one or more of the letters of Article XX, which are being increasingly tested in litigation) but falling short of the requirements of the chapeau as regards the way the relevant measures were applied (and hence not justified). The fourth and lowest watermark is that PPM-based differentiation simply is not justified under Article XX (a view reflected in pre-WTO practice as well as in the 2016 *India–Solar cells* case).

The lowest watermark is epitomized by the early *Tuna-Dolphin* saga. In this case, Mexico argued before a GATT panel that a US ban on the import of tuna caught with nets harmful to dolphins was in breach of GATT nondiscrimination disciplines. The United States had imposed dolphin-protecting nets on their own fishermen, who then clamored for equal treatment with foreign imports. The United States argued that tuna caught with different methods amounted to different kinds of products, an argument that was finally rejected by the panel deciding the case. According to the panel, tuna is tuna, no matter how it is caught. Tuna captured using a particular method could not be subjected to different treatment. The case set a precedent for the treatment of like products and the rejection of environmental norms as a constraint on free trade. These principles were initially reaffirmed in a WTO panel ruling in a similar case, concerning the impact on turtles of certain shrimp-harvesting techniques. In this case, the United States had banned imports of shrimp caught with nets detrimental to sea turtles, an internationally protected species under CITES (Biggs 2000, 17).[2] One of the objectives of the measure was to force foreign fishermen exporting shrimp to the United States to use special turtle-escape-nets. The WTO Panel ruled against the United States on grounds similar to those of the *Tuna-Dolphin* case.

However, the Appellate Body partially reversed the panel's findings introducing what, after more than fifteen years, still remains the high watermark of PPM-based environmental differentiation, namely, the possibility of justification under Article XX (without actual justification *in casu*). Indeed, the Appellate Body did not criticize the intention behind US policy but the way it had been implemented, thereby paving the way for the future justification of trade restrictions for purely environmental purposes. This is where the trade/environment legal connection still stands with regard to PPM-based differentiation. Environmental differentiation on the basis of PPMs has to evolve within then narrow bounds of an exception that has never been fully granted. No case so far has moved environmental differentiation up the ladder toward either actual justification or unlikeness (Dupuy and Viñuales 2015, 401). Clearly, such a position gives pre-eminence to trade rules over environmental protection, with the attendant (il)legitimacy implications.

One can ask whether some alternative avenues exist to accommodate environmental differentiation. A possibility currently being explored is the conclusion of an agreement (whether applicable to all WTO Members or to some of them) reducing the tariffs applicable to "environmental goods" (the so-called Environmental Goods Agreement). But such goods are likely to be defined on the basis of their specific features (or composition) rather than their PPMs. Two major exceptions for which WTO rules admit PPM-based differentiation constitute another avenue, namely, goods produced by child, forced, prisoner, and slave labor (the exchange of which is generally banned), or goods produced on the basis of a violation of intellectual property rights (as protected by the agreement on Trade-Related Aspects of Intellectual Property Rights [TRIPS]). According to the latter, goods such as fake-brand-name watches or pirated compact discs can not only be stopped at the border but can even be seized and destroyed. The TRIPs agreement has in this sense accomplished much more for producers of technology-intensive goods than several previous intellectual property agreements under the supervision of the World Intellectual Property Organization (WIPO). Differential production standards, in the form of different property rights regimes, create a biased playing field in another way. When countries trade, the lack of well-defined and enforceable property rights for environmental resources places countries with ill-defined property rights at an economic disadvantage (Chichilnisky 1994; Luterbacher and Norrlof 2008). And as we have argued before, in addition to experiencing unfavorable economic outcomes, countries lacking strong property rights definitions and/or poor resource management can experience a loss in political bargaining power (Luterbacher and Norrlof 2001). We suggested that this explains why the WTO enforces mostly intellectual property rights and does not regulate how the production and international exchange of goods is affected by property rights protection of environmental assets. Intellectual property rights protection is in the interest of advanced economies that have strong property rights definitions and protection. Regulating how goods are produced, specifically requiring enforceable property rights, is in developing countries' (long-term) interest. In the following section, we briefly review the commercial and environmental consequences of property rights definitions for effective environmental protection, including climate change.

6.4 Theoretical Considerations[3]

We start with the observation that resources that are not regulated through enforceable property rights will tend to be overextracted, contributing to environmental degradation and resource depletion (Dasgupta and Heal 1979). However, we place no a priori judgment on whether the property rights regime is a private property rights regime or a common property rights regime.[4]

Trade has consequences for resource use because trade generates greater external demand, increasing production of resource-intensive (tradable) goods. Poor resource management owing to a poor legal framework further increases overextraction to the point where countries with ill-defined property rights engaging in commercial exchange develop a superficial comparative advantage in the good (Chichilnisky 1994). Trade creates additional pressure to extract the resource, making it seem more abundant in the country with ill-defined property rights, even though the resource would not be abundant if properly regulated and even though other countries (regulating the resource) have greater abundance. In this case, the higher demand generated through trade raises production of the resource-intensive good beyond sustainable levels (Chichilnisky 1994). As Chichilnisky (1994) explains, the country with ill-defined property rights experiences not only environmental damage in the form of deforestation or excessive land use for agriculture but actual losses from trade. Environmental degradation and commercial impoverishment coincide and become mutually reinforcing.

The only way to break this negative cycle is to regulate production methods. If the country is already poor, a tax on the resource will not promote sustainable resource use since workers receiving subsistence wages must extract more and more of the resource to compensate for the tax (Chichilnisky 1994). Rich-country protection, which represents a tax on developing country exports, also magnifies negative economic and environmental repercussions from trade.

This analysis has implications for climate change. Committing to reduce carbon emissions will be less costly for countries with well-defined property rights. By contrast, countries experiencing a negative dynamic between environmental assets and trade will, in the absence of positive incentives (such as carbon credits), find it prohibitively costly to switch to environmentally friendly technology to reduce carbon emissions, as required by climate change agreements. They are only likely to participate voluntarily. This can be seen as a justification for the Berlin Mandate established at the first Conference of the Parties in Berlin 1995 which primarily put the onus of greenhouse gas emission reductions on developed countries. More generally, this argument underpins the resilience of the common but differentiated responsibilities (CBDR) principle (article 3[1] UNFCCC and article 2[2] of the Paris Agreement), which has structured the climate negotiations under both the Ad Hoc Working Group for Long-Term Cooperative Action, or AWG-LCA (launched in 2007), and the Durban Platform on Enhanced Action leading to the Paris Agreement. Of note is that the latter does not mention the CBDR principle but the principle nonetheless lives on in the Paris Agreement (see chapter 2 in this volume).

Before looking at how trade and environmental provisions could come into conflict in this context, the trade principles included in the GATT/WTO can be summarized as follows:

• Countries are mostly free to establish and enforce their own environmental or safety standards, provided that sufficient scientific evidence is available to support these standards and that measures are nondiscriminatory.
• The enforcement of national environmentally justified production standards cannot be extended abroad (extraterritorially) through trade restrictions except under very specific circumstances.
• Goods produced in violation of TRIPS can be subject to trade restrictions and prohibition. Other property rights considerations remain non-actionable.

6.5   Types of Conflict

In what ways could trade rules interfere with global environmental agreements? Environmental agreements can either call explicitly for the adoption of trade-restrictive measures (WTO/CTE 2007) or simply contemplate a broad obligation for states to adopt measures, which may include trade-restrictive ones (Dupuy and Viñuales 2015).

An illustration of the first approach is given by the Montreal Protocol, which explicitly prohibits trade in ozone-depleting substances (including substances with global warming effects) with nonparties. This particular trade measure (article 4) was introduced at the request of the chemical industries producing substitutes for ozone-depleting substances, so they would not be undercut in price by cheap imports coming from nonparties to the Protocol. This trade measure has never been challenged as a breach of WTO disciplines, but it is not only relevant from the perspective of ozone-depleting substances. In fact, some ozone-depleting substances are also powerful global warmers and the Montreal Protocol has had a more significant impact in reducing greenhouse gas emissions than the Kyoto Protocol (Velders et al. 2007). Moreover, a number of countries have presented amendment proposals (including one from Canada, Mexico, and the United States) to bring certain greenhouse gases used for refrigeration processes, hydrofluorocarbons (HFCs), that are not ozone-depleting substances, under the Montreal Protocol. The environmental rationale is twofold. First, the Montreal Protocol is widely perceived to be a more sophisticated regulatory framework than any instrument of the climate change regime, not least because of its trade measures.[5] Second, the rise in the production and consumption of HFCs is a direct result of the Montreal Protocol's phasing out of powerful ozone-depleting substances, namely, hydrochlorofluorocarbons (HCFCs). HFCs are indeed a substitute for HCFCs. Although emissions of HFCs were already regulated by the Kyoto Protocol (see Annex A), the projects undertaken in this connection led to important distortions in the operation of the Clean Development Mechanism (Wara 2008).

The second approach can be illustrated by existing climate agreements. Neither the UNFCCC nor the Kyoto Protocol, nor the Paris Agreement, explicitly calls for restrictions on trade. In fact, article 3(5) of the UNFCCC seeks to minimize tensions between environmental protection and trade. Yet, among the broad range of measures that states can adopt to fight climate change, some may be trade restrictive. Indeed, mechanisms enumerated in the Kyoto Protocol are just one way of reducing greenhouse gases and the Paris Agreement, even more than the Kyoto Protocol, leaves the choice of the specific mitigation/adaptation measures to states. Abatement can thus take place through all kinds of other means, be they voluntary measures on the part of industries, so-called carbon taxes, cap-and-trade systems (linked and unlinked), some form of command and control, or through the enhancement of carbon sinks. Quite clearly, depending on the selected policy, environmental agreements will impact a state's trade relations. As illustrated by the *India–Solar cells* case as well as by the earlier *Canada–Renewables* case, supporting the domestic production of renewable energy equipment through the use of LCR is in breach of trade disciplines, irrespective of the fact that it may be politically indispensable in order to secure new legislation (or regulatory measures) to expand renewable energy and thereby reduce emissions. Similarly, the requirement not to treat products differently even if they have different carbon footprints creates significant competitive disadvantages for companies using cleaner and more expensive production processes, discouraging the transition to the low carbon economy envisioned in the UNFCCC, the Kyoto Protocol, and the Paris Agreement.

6.6   Green Protectionism?

Clearly, the important efforts required from governments to transition to a low-carbon economy are likely to be accompanied by protectionist pressures, as suggested by the cases of China and India concerning solar panels.[6] Linking climate discipline to trade discipline may otherwise amount to "de facto" discrimination, insofar that unprepared countries with uncompetitive industries are required to buy foreign low-carbon products and technologies to meet their mitigation obligations while meeting climate change discipline. Politically, this is unlikely to happen without friction, particularly as trade discipline purporting to prevent de jure or de facto discrimination at the country level would actually be used to enforce de facto discrimination among prepared and unprepared countries at the global level. Moreover, developed countries may also be led to adopt protectionist measures to account for the higher environmental/carbon footprint (reflecting lower environmental standards) of goods produced in certain developing countries at a lower cost.

Import policies based on production methods would thus flourish in both developing and developed countries. Examples abound. We have already referred to LCRs, which are frequent in the design of feed-in-tariff schemes. As for protection from the cost advantages of low environmental standards, this was precisely what was behind the French initiative to introduce a "green" (carbon) tax on countries not party to the Kyoto Protocol. The proposal, which dates back to November 13, 2006, smacked of green protectionism and was subsequently shot down by the former European Union's trade commissioner, Peter Mandelson. "Food miles" is another protectionist device that is gaining ground. Under the pretext of reducing carbon emissions, proponents suggest taxing goods that travel long distances (and incidentally have a higher probability of being foreign as a consequence). Yet keeping food miles at a strict minimum does not necessarily alleviate environmental damage. Buying local will not reduce emissions if products travel more frequently in smaller vehicles as opposed to the larger trucks used for longer distances. This is precisely what will happen if many producers cater to customers in different locations and if many customers seek out different producers in different locations. To respect the environment, the number of vehicles in circulation and the quantity transported by each vehicle must be taken into account. Other, often neglected, considerations must also be weighed for an accurate assessment of environmental damage under these two scenarios. For instance, more carbon dioxide is released when Northern countries insist on growing vegetables out of season in artificially heated greenhouses than is emitted when importing such farm products from the South.

Climate-related trade policies could also take the form of Border Tax Adjustments (BTAs). Under such a scheme, imported goods would be taxed at a country's border with an amount equal to what they would have been subject to had they been produced domestically. Once exported, domestically produced goods would receive a tax refund through a procedure that bears some analogy with value-added tax refunds. Depending on their specific features, such BTAs could be seen as an actionable subsidy that can be challenged before the WTO Dispute Settlement Board (Maruyama 2011) or as a breach of Articles I or III of the GATT (unless they strictly impose

the same burden on all imports as well as on domestic products). Although
there are precedents for such border taxes in the case of toxic waste or especially dangerous chemicals, their application to a wide array of products
could create a significant backlog of trade cases at the WTO. According
to current GATT/WTO trade rules, it is not permissible to favor domestic
products by imposing higher border taxes than the corresponding taxes
on domestic like products (Sampson 1999, 37). This also applies to BTAs
introduced to adjust for environmentally motivated taxes (Petersmann
1996, 176). However, if BTAs are not allowed to correct for environmentally related taxes and other such fees, domestic products could be rendered
less competitive than their foreign counterparts. Since it is not possible
to impose BTAs to offset environmentally motivated taxes for production
inputs when such input taxes discriminate between like products, measures
to adjust for environmental taxes may prove incompatible with GATT/
WTO trade rules (Petersmann 1996, 176). BTAs could, in any case, only be
permitted for direct taxes on any given product. Indirect taxation, such as
social security and other transfer schemes, could not be accounted for. The
taxation problem could be particularly acute with regard to the current
liberalization policies in the electricity domain. Under existing climate
agreements, non-fossil-fuel means of producing electricity should clearly
be favored. However, both hydroelectric power, especially if produced from
accumulation dams, or nuclear installations, require heavy investments
that have to be amortized over a long period. A major shift of electricity
production could occur toward countries that are only subject (or have committed) to minor mitigation targets and that generate electricity with coal,
natural gas, or diesel fuel. Such a shift is also happening within the EU where
Eastern European countries because of their inherited "hot air" do not have
as many restrictions on their fossil fuel use as Western ones. BTAs could
be challenged within the GATT/WTO system as discriminatory, therefore
undermining the effectiveness of climate agreements.

6.7 Market Mechanisms

In addition to these general problems, the market mechanisms contained in the Kyoto Protocol (articles 6, 12, and 17) and envisioned in the
Paris Agreement (articles 5 and 6) raise some problems of their own. The

discussion about flexibility mechanisms and trade continues to be relevant as the Paris Agreement maintains the possibility of international emissions trading implemented by the Kyoto Protocol (through linking of subnational, domestic, and regional emissions trading systems and exchanges of Internationally Transferred Mitigation Outcomes, or ITMOs), as well as project-based mechanisms (whether in connection with land use change, including the so-called REDD-plus mechanism, or for other types of projects, as suggested by the new sustainable development mechanism which combines elements of Kyoto's Joint Implementation mechanism and Clean Development Mechanism [CDM]). Emissions trading does not affect trade directly since there seems to be a consensus that emissions certificates would not be considered merchandise but financial instruments like securities or stocks (see Cosbey 1999). According to Chichilnisky (1996, 326), emissions trading could also alleviate some of the trade policy problems generated by other climate change instruments such as taxes. This is because emissions trading minimizes distortions and could in principle be carried out by firms buying and selling certificates with each other across borders. Financial instruments are not presently covered by any of the multilateral GATT/WTO rules. The same would apply to project-based mechanisms that result in the issuance and transfer of emission credits. However, a General Agreement of Trade in Services that includes financial services will be elaborated in subsequent WTO negotiations. Under such an agreement, providers of financial services from all countries (even those not party to a climate agreement) would be allowed to broker trades in emission reductions. Other investment rules might also be included in such an agreement. This part does not, however, represent a major obstacle to emissions trading.

Another more serious problem lies in the way emissions-reduction rights are allocated by governments. Initial allocations in cap-and-trade systems were largely based on former use. This is, in effect, what several European governments did under earlier phases of the Emission Trading Scheme (ETS), amounting to what is called "grandfathering." Subsequently the system evolved toward a more auction-based allocation (ETS II and III). Depending on how the allocation is made, it may amount to an actionable subsidy to a local industry in breach of the WTO's Agreement on Subsidies and Countervailing Measures (SCM). Since the EU is a single actor in the WTO context, EU members cannot raise subsidy complaints against each other at the WTO. But as soon as emission-trading systems are coordinated between the EU and other countries, which is currently envisioned in article 6 of the Paris Agreement, there is a risk of such complaints before the WTO. Of course, subsidies of this kind are not necessarily illegal under WTO rules, and cannot automatically be challenged by another country before a panel. Another state must show that the subsidies are export promoting, local content dependent, or actionable in another way (because of their industry specificity and trade-distorting effects). The three grounds for challenging a subsidy are possible in the context of climate change policies, although the latter is more likely. When the United States and the EU were at odds over the offshore tax havens used by American firms to promote exports, a WTO panel ruled against the United States. If that case is any indication, one should expect the WTO to clamp down on practices that could be construed as implicit subsidies. Rights-allocation procedures are thus very important in promoting or preventing trade-environment regime conflicts.

Another aspect of the future General Agreement on Trade in Services (GATS) system concerns aviation and airline services. However, since this particular agreement has not made much progress so far, it is unlikely to affect particular policies of national or subnational entities concerning environmental matters. For instance, it seems difficult to contest the decision of the EU to subject all airlines landing in the EU to ETS before WTO panels (cf. Bartels 2012). At present, this question is latent, as the implementation of the extension has been suspended until 2016 while an agreement is reached under the aegis of the International Civil Aviation Organization. This move is subject to a strong challenge by emerging nations such as China and India but has not yet been evoked within the WTO, probably because of the implementation delay. Similar issues are raised with regard to shipping services. Both the aviation and maritime industries emit GHG emissions whereas neither are regulated by the multilateral climate regime or the world trade regime (Hepburn and Müller 2010; Brewer 2010).

Project-based mechanisms (particularly the CDM under Kyoto and perhaps the Sustainable Development Mechanism [SDM] under the Paris Agreement) are the most interesting but also the most problematic of the global climate change regime. Since it was dedicated to promoting clean technology transfers between Annex I and also non-Annex I countries as a means of reducing GHG emissions, its proper operation is important for the relations between developed and developing countries. A CDM or

SDM project that provides above-market advantages to a company could potentially breach nondiscrimination disciplines or the SCM Agreement. For example, if a state only channels CDM/SDM-related inward foreign investment into local companies (specifically to convert its own production matrix into a low-carbon one) that could give an advantage to the products of such companies in breach of the national treatment clause (in regard to foreign products sold in the country) or the SCM Agreement (if the products are exported to other countries). In some cases, CDM/SDM projects could also entail local content requirements. For example, a foreign company may only have access to certain markets (e.g., the provision of renewable energy–based electricity at a guaranteed rate for a given period of time) if, among others, it conducts a CDM/SDM project in the country. Depending on the modalities of such a project, this could amount to a local content requirement in breach of trade disciplines.

Beyond these market mechanisms, some other aspects of the climate agreements could be problematic. These include the possible adoption of environmental standards (a form of command and control), or the use of government procurement or direct subsidies to achieve mitigation goals. As emphasized in the discussion of consumption/production aspects of trade and their environmental consequences, the GATT/WTO framework does not impose particular norms on specific countries. Under GATT/WTO rules, the ability of countries to change other countries' policies through the use of trade sanctions (relying on their own market power) is highly constrained. Such unilateral attempts would likely be contrary to the chapeau of Article XX even when justified under one of its letters. States could also be inclined to use government procurement (directly through government purchases or indirectly through LCRs as a condition for such purchases) to achieve some mitigation goals. A significant share of the gross domestic product in OECD countries is due to government purchases. Such purchases are not subject to the same rules as ordinary purchases and can therefore in principle discriminate on the basis of the way a product is manufactured. However, even here, the Agreement on Government Procurement in the WTO has attempted to open national-government buying procedures in such a way that some extreme measures might be actionable. Specific subsidies to promote a particular greenhouse gas technology tilted in favor of certain procedures could also come into conflict with the Agreement on Subsidies and Countervailing Measures.

6.8   The Future of the Trade and Environment Regimes and the UNFCCC

The traditional institutional constructions to promote international trade, GATT, and GATT's successor organization—the WTO—have sought to promote international trade liberalization and fight domestic special interests through a broad system of both global and increasingly bilateral and regional rules. Despite the disenchantment with multilateral trade negotiations in recent years, overall efforts to liberalize trade flows have been largely successful. Of particular note is the frequent resort and great influence of the WTO Dispute Settlement Body. Indeed, the chief purpose behind the transformation of GATT into the WTO was to enhance the institutional foundations, especially the enforcement of negotiated agreements, to promote "free trade."

However, such a system developed in a context where the importance of environmental protection was not fully perceived. Even during the last phase of the Uruguay Round, which was influenced by the 1992 Rio Conference on Environment and Development, environmental concerns played an ambiguous role in the minds of negotiators as both an important objective (sustainable development was introduced in the preamble of the Marrakesh Accord setting up the WTO) and a potential excuse for protectionist practices. In hindsight, the latter concern has clearly prevailed in the actual application of trade discipline, as suggested by our analysis of the PPM question. But the pressure to pursue environmental goals is increasing, particularly as a result of climate change, a high-profile global problem. Transitioning massively to a low-carbon economy will be extremely challenging from a political perspective, and trade rules may, in fact, hinder rather than facilitate such a transition. The *India–Solar cells* case epitomizes this tension. There is little doubt that LCRs amount to a breach of GATT discipline (and likely of similar disciplines in Regional Trade Agreements, unless an exemption/derogation/exception is added), but there is equally little doubt that a country like India (or other developing countries) can hardly make such a transition if it amounts to a massive transfer of resources toward foreign companies selling renewable energy equipment.

A fundamental question arises, namely, the extent to which preserving a narrow vision of "free trade" should prevail, over effectively transitioning to a low-carbon economy.[7] This is something of a Gordian knot, and it is unclear how exactly it can be cut. Stating that politically important LCRs are in breach of free trade rules, although legally correct, may be politically and environmentally shortsighted. But the opposite may also be true, as a blank acceptance of environmental considerations to justify trade barriers would push the world into protectionism. Many options may be explored between these two extremes. But as suggested in this chapter, it seems unlikely that environmental differentiation in the age of climate change can be accommodated through a single narrow exception, such as Article XX of the GATT or other similar legal devices. Much more will be needed, and if the WTO proves to be unable to offer such room, it may be side-tracked either legally (through the increasing conclusion of Regional Trade Agreements) or in practice, through overt noncompliance by at least some major countries.

Notes

1. The 1973 Convention on International Trade of Endangered Species of Fauna and Flora (CITES) has featured in the decisions of the WTO Dispute Settlement Body (see the Shrimp-Turtle case) but not with specific reference to its trade restricting permit system.

2. In 1989, Section 609 was laid down in order for the US government to negotiate international agreements to promote fishing methods compatible with the protection of sea turtles. The initiative was extended on a global basis in 1996 in the sense that the exporting country had to attest that the shrimps exported to the United States had been caught by using sea turtle–friendly methods (Biggs 2000, 16).

3. Details about these issues and their formalization can be found in Luterbacher and Norrlof (2006).

4. We simply note that common property rights regimes may complicate enforcement. For a more complete discussion, see Luterbacher (1994) on enforceability, as well as Luterbacher and Norrlof (2008) on how ill-defined property rights affect resource use and political conflict.

5. The argument according to which the Montreal Protocol's design would make it effective to fight climate change may be accurate for some greenhouse gases (and ozone-depleting substances) but not necessarily for carbon dioxide, which is the main global warmer. The Montreal Protocol, despite its trade measures and noncompliance procedure, would very likely encounter the same difficulties as the

Kyoto Protocol (and perhaps more—given its top-down approach—than the Paris Agreement) if it attempted to regulate carbon dioxide. This is because, unlike the other regulated substances, carbon dioxide emissions result from the foundational features of our fossil fuel–based civilization (electricity and heat production, transportation, conventional agriculture).

6. We already mentioned the WTO Indian solar cell case. There is a dispute between the EU and China that has flared up recently concerning allegation of Chinese dumping of solar panels. This latter case has not made it to the WTO.

7. One could argue that in a larger sense there should be no contradiction between efficiency as enhanced by free trade and environmental goals. As shown by Chichilnisky (1994), free trade between regions with different property rights system can be detrimental to the environment.

References

Bartels, Lorand. 2012. "The Inclusion of Aviation in the EU ETS: WTO Law Considerations." In *Trade and Sustainable Energy Series*. Geneva: International Centre for Trade and Sustainable Development.

Biggs, Gonzalo. 2000. "Reflections on the WTO and Sustainable Development." In *Trade, Environment and Sustainable Development: Views from Sub-Saharan Africa and Latin America*, edited by Peider Könz, 3–21. Tokyo: United Nations University Institute of Advanced Studies and the International Centre for Trade and Sustainable Development.

Bown, Chad, and Joost Pauwelyn, eds. 2010. *The Law, Economics and Politics of Retaliation in WTO Dispute Settlement*. Cambridge: Cambridge University Press.

Brewer, Thomas L. 2010. "Trade Policies and Climate Change Policies: A Rapidly Expanding Joint Agenda." *World Economy* 33 (6): 799–809.

Chichilnisky, Graciela. 1994. "North-South Trade and the Global Environment." *American Economic Review* 84 (4): 851–874.

———. 1996. *Development and Global Finance: The Case for an International Bank for Environmental Settlements*. New York: United Nations Development Programme.

Cosbey, Aron. 1999. *The Kyoto Protocol and the International Trading System*, Urs. London: Royal Institute of International Affairs.

Dasgupta, Partha S., and Geoffrey M. Heal. 1979. *Economic Theory and Exhaustible Resources*. Cambridge: Cambridge University Press.

Dupuy, Pierre-Marie, and Jorge E. Viñuales. 2015. *International Environmental Law*. Cambridge: Cambridge University Press.

Gonzalez, Carmen G. 2000. "Beyond Eco-Imperialism: An Environmental Justice Critique of Free Trade." *Denver University Law Review* 78 (4): 979–1016.

Hepburn, Cameron, and Benito Müller. 2010. "International Air Travel and Greenhouse Gas Emissions: A Proposal for an Adaptation Levy." *World Economy* 33 (6): 830–849.

Jinnah, Sikina. 2011. "Climate Change Bandwagoning: The Impacts of Strategic Linkages on Regime Design, Maintenance, and Death." *Global Environmental Politics* 11 (3): 1–9.

Lewis, Joanna I. 2014. "The Rise of Renewable Energy Protectionism: Emerging Trade Conflicts and Implications for Low Carbon Development." *Global Environmental Politics* 14 (4): 12–35.

Luterbacher, Urs. 1994. "International Cooperation: The Problem of the Commons and the Special Case of the Antarctic Region." *Synthese* 100 (3): 413–440.

Luterbacher, Urs, and Carla Norrlof. 2001. "The Organization of World Trade and the Climate Regime." *International Relations and Global Climate Change*, edited by Urs Luterbacher and Detlef F. Sprinz, 279–295. Cambridge: MIT Press.

———. 2006. Production, Protection and Trade, Working Paper. Geneva: IUHEI.

———. 2008. "Securing the Environment and Securing States." *Contributions to Conflict Management, Peace Economics, and Development* 6:267–297.

Maruyama, Warren H. 2011. "Climate Change and the WTO: Cap and Trade versus Carbon Tax?" *Journal of World Trade* 45 (4): 679–726.

Petersmann, Ernst-Ulrich. 1996. "Trade and the Protection of the Environment after the Uruguay Round." In *Enforcing Environmental Standards: Economic Mechanisms as Viable Means?*, edited by Rüdiger Wolfrum. Berlin: Springer.

Sampson, Gary. 1999. "WTO Rules and Climate Change: The Need for Policy Coherence." In *Global Climate Governance: Inter-Linkages between the Kyoto Protocol and Other Multilateral Regimes*, edited by Bradnee Chambers, chapter 4, 29–38. Tokyo: United Nations University—Institute for Advanced Studies.

UNFCCC. 1992. *United Nations Framework Convention on Climate Change*. New York: United Nations.

Velders, Guus J. M., Stephen O. Anderson, John S. Daniel, David W. Fahey, and Mack McFarland. 2007. "The Importance of the Montreal Protocol in Protecting Climate." *Proceedings of the National Academy of Sciences* 104 (12): 4814–4819.

Viñuales, Jorge E. 2017. "The Paris Agreement on Climate Change: Less Is More." *German Yearbook of International Law*, 59. Berlin: Duncker & Humblot.

Wara, Michael. 2008. "Measuring the Clean Development Mechanism's Performance and Potential." *UCLA Law Review* 55 (6): 1759–1803.

WTO. 1986. *The General Agreement on Tariffs and Trade (GATT) and Amendments.* Geneva: World Trade Organization.

WTO/CTE. 2007. Matrix on Trade Measures Pursuant to Selected Multilateral Environmental Agreements, WT/CTE/W/160/Rev.4, TN/TE/S/5/Rev.2 (14 March 2007). Geneva: World Trade Organization / Committee on Trade and Environment.

Wu, Mark, and James Salzman. 2014. "The Next Generation of Trade and Environment Conflicts: The Rise of Green Industrial Policy." *Northwestern University Law Review* 108:401–474.

7 Major Countries

Detlef F. Sprinz, Guri Bang, Lars Brückner, and Yasuko Kameyama

7.1 Introduction

Global climate change is a long-term policy challenge created at the local and national levels by human activities producing greenhouse gas (GHG) emissions (Stocker et al. 2013). It is also a collective action challenge that ideally requires a joint policy response beyond the aggregation of uncoordinated domestic policies. While the Paris Agreement entered into force on November 4, 2016, the election of Donald Trump as president of the United States has cast some doubts about the future of global climate policy, especially his announcement on June 1, 2017, to leave the Paris Agreement. Nevertheless, the role of major actors will remain one enduring element of global climate policy over time.

This chapter builds and expands on the important roles of environmental non-governmental organizations, the business sector, and the role of equity covered in previous chapters (see chapters 2, 8, 9, and 10 in this volume). In particular, we look at the country-specific foundations of international climate policy.

Some countries play more crucial roles in international climate negotiations than others because of their economic importance, the size of their GHG emissions, and their position as leaders or laggards. As a qualifier for focusing on the most important countries in this context, based on the World Resources Institute's CAIT database (WRI 2014), we suggest that countries that emit 2 percent or more of worldwide GHG emissions (including land use change and forestry in both 1990 and 2010) qualify as *major countries* (see figure 7.1). In the long run, substantial GHG mitigation is the prerequisite for reducing climate-related impacts.

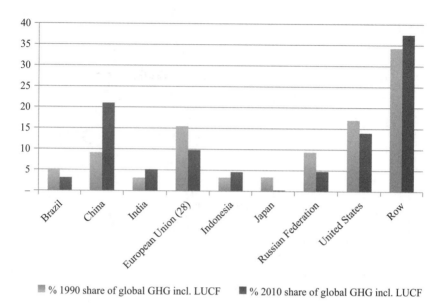

% 1990 share of global GHG incl. LUCF   % 2010 share of global GHG incl. LUCF

Figure 7.1
Shares of global GHG emissions by major countries.
Source: WRI (2014).
Note: ROW=rest of world
LUCF=land use change and forestry

Applying this criterion, eight countries qualify as major countries in both time periods: four emerging economies (Brazil, China, India, and Indonesia) as well as four developed countries or groups of countries (the EU-28, Japan, the Russian Federation, and the United States). While worldwide total GHG emissions grew by one-third between 1990 and 2010 (WRI 2014), the composition of the shares by country has shifted considerably: all developed countries have reduced their fraction of emissions, while China and India have significantly increased their share. This reflects the new realities in the world economy, with emerging economies like India, China, and Brazil gaining more prominent positions both as key economic players and as large GHG emitters. For the purposes of this chapter, we decided to select three countries from each group for further analysis. These include Brazil, China, the EU-28, India, Japan, and the United States, thereby covering all major continents with major emitters for each of the two groups.

Major countries also play a distinct role from a theoretical perspective related to the provision of (global) public goods. The general idea was already explored in Mancur Olson's (1971) "Logic of Collective Action" more than four decades ago. Olson differentiated privileged, intermediate, and latent groups.[1] Given the distribution of emissions of greenhouse gases around the world (see figure 7.1) as well as their impacts (see figure 7.2), it appears likely that we live in a "climate world" of intermediate groups if we solely focus on major countries—with many of the smaller countries (summarized as "rest of world" in figure 7.1) qualifying as a latent group (see chapter 3 in this volume).[2] For each of these six major economies and political systems, we will attend to their domestic politics vis-à-vis a potential low-GHG transition as such an ambition necessitates substantial domestic support (Putnam 1988).

In the following, we discuss two conceptual approaches to the study of the climate policy of major countries: the interest-based explanation of country positions in international negotiations, augmented by a domestic politics explanation of efforts in support of strong GHG mitigation.

7.2   Two Conceptual Approaches

7.2.1   The Interest-Based Explanation

In order to establish initial expectations about the positioning of countries in international climate negotiations, an approach similar to unitary cost-benefit analyses could be employed. One such candidate is the "interest-based explanation of international environmental policy" (Sprinz and Vaahtoranta 1994). This explanation posits that a country's enthusiasm for negotiating an international climate agreement to curb the effects of climate change is determined by (1) its (environmental) vulnerability to climate impacts and (2) the change in economic welfare associated with significant reductions of its GHG emissions.[3] If both dimensions can be assumed to be independent of each other, and each country can be put into a high versus low category on each of these two dimensions, generic predictions of the likely negotiation positions of countries in international climate negotiations become feasible.

Overall, the interest-based explanation distinguishes between four predicted roles of countries in international environmental negotiations: (1) "pushers," (2) "draggers," (3) "intermediates," and (4) "bystanders" (Sprinz and Vaahtoranta 1994, 80–81). Countries with high vulnerability and low welfare losses ("pushers") should argue for ambitious GHG emissions reductions as they can expect a favorable benefit-cost ratio. Conversely, countries

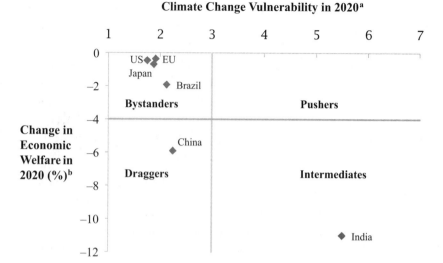

Figure 7.2
Major countries and the interest-based explanation.
Source: (a) DARA and Climate Vulnerable Forum (2012). Interpolated climate vulnerability index score for 2020; higher values indicate higher vulnerability to the impacts of climate change; (b) Computed by the EPPA model (see main text).

with low vulnerability and high welfare losses ("draggers") have little incentive to contribute. Predicting the negotiating behavior of countries that do not fall into either group (1) or (2) is more difficult as their enthusiasm for costly mitigation measures should be somewhere between both ends of the spectrum. Their high vulnerability to climate impacts gives "intermediates" incentives for ambitious emissions reductions, whereas their enthusiasm is dampened by high welfare losses associated with such reductions. In contrast, the welfare losses of emissions reductions for "bystanders" are comparatively low, but their benefits from mitigating climate change and thus their incentives for ambitious emissions reductions are also limited.

A broad range of data sources could be used to gauge a country's vulnerability to the impacts of climate change and the change in economic welfare associated with significant domestic emissions reductions. Our data on vulnerability to the impacts of climate change are derived from the second edition of the "Climate Vulnerability Monitor" by DARA and the Climate Vulnerable Forum (2012).[4] For 184 countries, the Monitor evaluates their vulnerability to climate change in 2010 and 2030 based on "22 indicators across four Impact Areas (Environmental Disasters, Habitat Change, Health Impact, Industry Stress) measuring the positive and negative effects of climate change" (DARA 2012, 4). Climate impacts are assessed in terms of mortality or share of GDP (DARA 2012, 6). Depending on its score on the aggregate climate index,[5] the overall climate vulnerability of a country or the EU as a whole is classified as "low" (index score <=2), "moderate" (>2 and <=3), "high" (>3 and <=4), "severe" (>4 and <=5), or "acute" (>5) (DARA 2012, 5, 11–12). To estimate the climate vulnerability in 2020, we calculated the arithmetic mean of the index scores for 2010 and 2030.

The MIT Emissions Prediction and Policy Analysis (EPPA) model[6] (Morris, Paltsev, and Reilly 2012) was used to estimate the relative change in economic welfare[7] in 2020 for each of the countries induced by a policy to cut GHG emissions by 20 percent by 2020 as compared with 2005. In the absence of policy interventions elsewhere, the policy is introduced relative to a business-as-usual (BAU) scenario for every country or the EU region.[8] The resulting relative loss in economic welfare in 2020 is then calculated as the ratio of the monetized welfare loss in 2020 (due to the emissions reductions policy) to the welfare expected for 2020 (under BAU conditions).

Combining both explanatory factors, figure 7.2 shows the relative change in economic welfare in 2020 as a result of the GHG reduction policy and the vulnerability to the impacts of climate change in 2020 for the five countries selected and the EU. To predict their position with the interest-based explanation, we introduced "low/high" thresholds on each of the two dimensions. Climate vulnerability is coded as "low" if a country originally falls under the "moderate" or "low" category of the DARA Monitor index. As the threshold for "low" versus "high" welfare losses, we selected a loss of 4 percent in view of the large gap between Brazil (1.9 percent) and China (5.9 percent), as well as the substantive magnitude of such a loss. Accordingly, the United States, Japan, the EU, and Brazil are expected to behave as "bystanders." China's low vulnerability and high welfare losses associated with the reduction policy predict it to be in the "draggers" category. Lastly, India is considered an "intermediate" with high climate vulnerability and high welfare losses.

7.2.2 Domestic Politics

An alternative to the interest-based explanation is the domestic politics explanation. This explanation relaxes the assumption that countries are unitary rational actors, and acknowledges that complex domestic decision-making processes form the basis for a country's climate policy and negotiation position at international negotiation tables. In this chapter, we are interested in the *nexus* of the international position of countries with their domestic policy configuration. Several key elements are important to conduct a comprehensive analysis of the decision-making processes that underpin domestic climate action (Bang, Underdal, and Andresen 2015; Milner 1997). First, the configuration of key domestic actors involved should be identified to assess which decisionmakers, interest groups, NGOs, and other stakeholders participated actively in—and potentially dominated—the process. Second, the domestic politics explanation emphasizes that domestic actors are rational, assuming that their interests and preferences (material, nonmaterial, or power related) guide their decisions and actions. And third, the decision-making process takes place within an institutional context that enables or limits the access and voice of different actors. Some actors have better access and voice in the process than others.

Domestic decision making entails prioritizing among more or less urgent policy issues, including climate change action, and poses a core challenge for governments. We explore key domestic climate policy decisions, including the Nationally Determined Contributions (NDCs) pledged in the Paris Agreement for the six countries or groups of countries we study.

NDCs and related regulatory or legislative decisions inform us about politically feasible climate policy options (Skodvin 2010). For instance, it is difficult for policy makers to enact and implement policies without public support from key stakeholders. National climate policies and the configuration of domestic actors reflect the domestic configuration of preferences and problem perceptions, the institutional setting (e.g., decision-making rules in the legislature), and the distribution of political resources and power among the parties involved (DeSombre 2011; Harrison and Sundstrom 2010). Importantly, climate policy can seldom be adopted and implemented without critical levels of support from key interest groups and voters—at least in democracies like Brazil, the EU, India, Japan, and the United States. These domestic actors control public support that policy-makers need to implement their preferred policy (Jones et al. 2009; Skodvin, Gullberg, and Aakre 2010; Tsebelis 2002). Even in an autocracy, like China, domestic elite support for public policies is needed (Bueno de Mesquita et al. 2003), and autocrats and ruling party elites have good reasons to worry about widespread public dissatisfaction and possible disintegration of their power base. Hence, underlying demand from the public or stakeholders may be politically significant, particularly if found within the regime's principal constituency.

According to the domestic politics explanation, we should expect the following:

1. Actors with strong interests and clear preferences related to the policy issue will be active participants and try to dominate the domestic climate policy decision-making process.

2. The institutional context, that is, the division of power between political institutions involved, gives the more powerful institutions a stronger voice in the decision-making process.

3. Actors with strong interests and clear preferences are likely to have a powerful role in the decision-making process.

In the remainder of this chapter, the domestic politics explanation has two important functions. First, it helps us elucidate whether the predictions of the interest-based explanation correspond with domestic climate politics in the countries selected and seeks to explain the reasons for possible mispredictions of the interest-based explanation. Second, the domestic politics approach sheds light on the domestic political configuration of actors, interests, and institutions that also shaped the NDCs in the five countries and the EU that we cover in this chapter. This may serve as a proxy for the likely domestic political support for international policies on mitigation in the post-Paris 2015 period.

7.3   Country Perspectives

7.3.1   Brazil

Brazil is a key player in international climate politics, with a growing population currently at 210 million; an emerging economy that enjoyed high growth rates until recently, and a relatively large share of world total GHG emissions (see figure 7.1).[9] Importantly, Brazil holds the most crucial forest carbon stock on the planet (Aamodt 2015; Viola and Franchini 2014). Brazil's pledge in the Paris Agreement is to cut GHG emissions 37 percent below 2005 levels by 2025; 43 percent by 2030 (Government of Brazil 2015). Over the past decade, Brazil mitigated more emissions than most other countries; aggregate emissions in 2013 were 33 percent lower than the emissions in 2005. Emissions from land use change and deforestation, the main emissions source in Brazil, were 73 percent lower in 2013 compared to their peak year 2004. However, emissions from agriculture and, in particular, from energy are growing, and these sectors are each now responsible for around one-third of Brazil's aggregate emissions (Aamodt 2015; SEEG 2014). Brazil's energy matrix has traditionally been relatively clean, due to the world's most advanced bioethanol industry, a 31.5 percent share of energy from biomass, and more than 80 percent of electricity production from hydro power. With more access to domestic petroleum, the energy mix could change toward more fossil fuel dependence in the future (Viola and Franchini 2014).

The interest-based explanation   According to figure 7.2, the climate vulnerability of Brazil is relatively low in 2020 and at about the same level as in China, the United States, the EU, and Japan. The welfare losses associated with climate policy measures to reduce GHG emissions by 20 percent during 2005–2020 are estimated to be 1.92 percent by 2020, which is significantly higher than that of other countries in the "bystanders" category (see figure 7.2). The expected behavior of a bystander, with both low costs of emissions reductions and limited benefits from mitigating climate change, is a passive role in the negotiations. This prediction does not find much support empirically.

Brazil considers itself a crucial actor in the international climate negotiations. The country had an important role in introducing and supporting the Clean Development Mechanism (CDM) in the Kyoto Protocol negotiations, and the concept that all countries have a specific share of the historical responsibility for climate change and other global environmental problems. Brazil hosted the UN Conference on Environment and Development in Rio de Janeiro in 1992, and its main negotiation strategy since the Rio Summit has been to persuade other countries to utilize more renewable energy (Christensen 2010). Brazil is one of the leading countries in the G77 group of developing countries in the international climate negotiations. The country was central in forming the BASIC group (Brazil, South Africa, India, and China) that played a key role at the Conference of the Parties (COP) 15 in Copenhagen in 2009. BASIC has since become an important group voicing the concerns of emerging powers in international climate politics (Aamodt 2015; Rong 2010). At COP 15, Brazil made a voluntary commitment to reduce GHG emissions by 36–39 percent from a BAU trajectory by 2020 (UNFCCC 2009), a goal that Brazil is on track to meet.[10] At Paris in 2015, Brazil pledged to meet this commitment by 2030, making it the country's formal Nationally Determined Contribution.

Brazil is the country with the greatest biodiversity in the world. The Convention on Biological Diversity (CBD) Secretariat estimates that Brazil hosts between 15–20 percent of the entire world's biological diversity, and the greatest number of endemic species on a global scale (CBD 2013). Both the flora and fauna are vulnerable to changes in temperature and weather, in particular in rainforest areas where many species still unknown to humans might have important medical value. Floods and mudslides caused by heavy rain on the Atlantic coast have caused some of the highest losses of lives due to natural disasters in Brazilian history, especially among low-income groups living in poorly constructed houses (BBC 2011). Furthermore, the vast agricultural lands in Brazil are at risk of droughts, floods, and reduced harvests. In line with this knowledge, Brazilian decision makers perceive the country to be relatively vulnerable to global climate change, and Brazil has engaged in an active role in the international climate negotiation process (Rong 2010)—which puts the country closer to a pusher position, especially due to avoided deforestation.

The domestic politics explanation   Brazilian climate change policies are designed differently than in most industrialized countries, chiefly because Brazil's energy-related emissions are very low, at only 18.6 percent of Brazil's total GHG emissions in 2016 (SEEG 2018), and the country's historical contribution to the climate change problem has come largely through deforestation and agriculture (Aamodt 2015). In 2008 a National Climate Change Plan was launched. The plan was prepared jointly by seventeen ministries, and it committed Brazil to reduce deforestation in the Amazon by 70 percent until 2017 as compared with 2006 levels (Government of Brazil 2008). In 2009 the country adopted a climate law. In 2010 President Lula signed a decree detailing a policy framework to implement the climate law and to ensure that Brazil complies with the 36–39 percent emissions reduction target. The National Policy on Climate Change announced key sectorial plans with measures aimed at reducing emissions (Silva 2012). These plans cover the plan for deforestation-control in the Amazon; the plan for deforestation-control in the Cerrado; the energy plan; the low-carbon agriculture plan (the ABC-plan); and the steel industry plan. Four more mitigation plans were added later, for transport and urban mobility; mining; industry; and health. The most important plans from a mitigation perspective are the ones targeting the emissions from deforestation, agriculture, and energy (Aamodt 2015).

The central governmental agencies in Brazil responsible for developing domestic climate policies are the Ministry of the Environment (MMA), Ministry of Mines and Energy (MME), Ministry of Foreign Affairs (Itamaraty), and the president. The Brazilian Institute of Environment and Renewable Natural Resources (IBAMA) has a special role for implementation, supervision and education about climate policy programs (Roman and Carson 2010). Regional environmental agencies and national councils for areas such as water resources, geology, environmental issues, forests, and biodiversity are also important governmental actors.

Deforestation has been the crucial climate change issue for Brazil, both in domestic politics and through international pressure to preserve the Amazon rainforest. The Forest Code law plays an important role for limiting deforestation, which decreased markedly between 2002 and 2012. A reform of the Forest Code in 2011, allowing more "legal" deforestation, caused concern among environmentalists predicting reversal of the great achievements in the forest sector (Viola and Franchini 2014). The majority of Brazilian GHG emissions are derived from agriculture, land use change, and forest management. Agriculture, including cattle ranching, has a vital role in the national economy (Roman and Carson 2010). Forest clearing practices to expand agricultural activities are the major source of deforestation. Representing one of Brazil's strongest economic sectors, the landowners in the agricultural sector have robust political influence on domestic climate policy debates. The ethanol program established in the 1970s as a response to the oil crises created a large market for ethanol that provided direct economic benefits to landowners (Roman and Carson 2010). Ethanol fuel is produced from sugarcane, Brazil has the largest sugarcane crop in the world, and it is the largest exporter of ethanol in the world. As a result of its ethanol fuel production, Brazil has sometimes been described as a bioenergy superpower.

Since the 1980s, the role and importance of NGOs dedicated to environmental causes and sustainable development has increased. Numerous NGOs throughout the country participate in local, regional, and federal policy debates as information providers and government critics. Domestic NGOs working on the environment and climate change, for example, Fundação

SOS Mata Atlântica, and Instituto Socioambiental, are typically focused on the deforestation issue, given its importance for national emissions levels. Some international NGOs have quite large branches in Brazil, for instance, Greenpeace, Friends of the Earth, and WWF (Hochstetler and Viola 2012).

Public support for climate change policy, and especially reduced deforestation, is strong in Brazil. Numerous studies and assessment reports by research organizations and governmental agencies underpin public support, providing broad knowledge and advice on deforestation reduction measures, mitigation and adaptation policies (Aamodt 2015). Furthermore, as a Pew Research Center study (Stokes, Wike, and Carle 2015) shows, Brazilians are at the top of worldwide concern for fearing climate impacts and are at the top for taking action against climate impacts if compared with the other countries included in this chapter.

The National Confederation of Industry is chiefly concerned with trade issues, securing economic growth, and energy security for the industry. These positions most often fall in line with the government's concerns, and only limited lobbying takes place against environmental policies from industrial actors. The two major energy companies, Petrobras (oil and gas) and Electrobras (electricity), are state owned, and the government sees them as instruments rather than opponents in environmental politics. This picture might change as the Brazilian energy mix is becoming more carbonized in step with economic growth, increasing energy demand, and more access to domestically produced oil (Aamodt 2015). The country's oil reserves off the Atlantic coast are expected to turn Brazil into an oil and gas exporter when the fields become fully operational.

In summary, energy emissions have an increasing role for Brazil's GHG emissions, but the main focus for Brazilian mitigation policy is likely to remain on deforestation. Deforestation has increased since 2012, and the struggle between the environmental and the agribusiness coalitions will continue (Aamodt 2015). Deforestation rates are closely connected to Brazil's international image, and the country is likely to continue with efforts to control deforestation. Domestic policy action lays the foundation of Brazil's position in the international negotiations, and there seems to be little doubt that Brazil will reach its official emissions reduction target by 2020 with current policies. Whether the country is willing to take on stronger climate policies in future rounds of NDCs is more uncertain, especially given the already large reductions in deforestation.

7.3.2 China

China's position on climate change policy and the world's expectation vis-à-vis China has changed dramatically in the last twenty years. Rapid economic growth has been the main contributor toward increasing CO_2 emissions. China surpassed the United States and became the largest emitter of CO_2 in 2007 (IEA 2012). As of 2013, China's GHG emissions alone represent more than a quarter of the world's total emissions, and its per capita emissions exceed that of the world average.

In November 2014 Chinese president Xi Jinping made a joint statement with former US president Barack Obama regarding their commitments to reaching an ambitious 2015 agreement in Paris, and announced China's intention to achieve the peaking of CO_2 emissions around 2030, as well as to make best efforts to peak early. Furthermore, China plans to increase the share of non–fossil fuels in primary energy consumption to around 20 percent by 2030 (White House 2014). China continued showing strong support for the success of the Paris deal at COP 21 and thereafter. Together with the United States, China promised in March 2016 to ratify the Paris Agreement, and actually did so on September 3, 2016.

The interest-based explanation   China's position in figure 7.2 suggests that the country is facing relatively low vulnerability to the impacts of climate change in 2020 as well as serious welfare losses if it were to reduce its GHG emissions by 20 percent compared with 2005. The interest-based explanation predicts China to be a dragger in international negotiations. This explanation is consistent with positions China used to take until the mid-2000s, but China's position has changed dramatically since then, partially driven by other interests.

With respect to vulnerability, the Chinese government began acknowledging that there have already been indications of climate change as retreating glaciers and precipitation changes have been observed. In 2011 alone, natural disasters affected 430 million people and caused direct economic losses of 309.6 billion yuan (about USD 44.7 billion) (National Development and Reform Commission [NDRC] 2012). Another environmental concern in China has been the impact of serious air pollution on people's health (WHO 2016), particularly in mega cities such as Beijing and Shanghai. The major sources of pollutants are coal-burning power plants, heavy industry, and vehicle use. Policies to improve ambient air quality are easily combined with GHG reducing policies for co-benefits.

When it comes to welfare losses due to GHG reduction measures in China, there have been divergent views and arguments. The level of ambitiousness of China's emission intensity target has been widely debated already in 2009 when China announced its 2020 targets: it would reduce its emissions per GDP by 40–45 percent by 2020 compared with 2005, increase the share of non-fossil-fuel energy use to 15 percent of total energy use by 2020, and increase its forest cover by forty million hectares from 2005. On the one hand, some studies expected China's emissions to continue to grow in the next several decades under a BAU scenario; limiting or reducing its emissions was considered to hamper the country's economic growth (Zhang 2011). On the other hand, some other modeling exercises (Fan et al. 2011; Jiang 2011) showed that the change of GDP in emissions reduction scenarios can be either positive or negative compared with the BAU scenario, depending on the policy instruments chosen and the level of transformation from energy-intensive to less energy-consuming industries. China has benefited economically from industries related to renewable energy (Lewis 2010). In more recent years, the world has observed China's CO_2 emissions growth to stall since 2014, mostly due to the slowdown of the economy, and the replacement of old coal-burning power plants with renewable energy sources (IEA 2015). The country will be able to reach a certain absolute emission level less costly if the BAU case emissions were to shift downward anyway. Accumulation of these experiences in recent years may further alter China's perception on the cost of emissions reductions, which could ultimately change its position toward a bystander.

The domestic politics explanation   The central government and the Chinese Communist Party (CCP) play core roles in Chinese decision making. Nongovernmental actors have had little power to influence governmental decisions (Jeffreys and Sigley 2009). In earlier days of the UNFCCC, it was mainly the Ministry of Foreign Affairs that participated in international negotiations (Economy 1997; Hatch 2003). For China, global environmental affairs had long been a part of its diplomacy, emphasizing its concerns about equity between the North and the South, and about rights for economic development (Harris 2011). Since the "Leading Group on Climate

Change, Energy Conservation and Emission Reduction Projects," headed by then premier Wen Jiabao, was established in 2007, the NDRC has become the center of climate change policy making (Yu 2008). The role of the NDRC has been effective in mainstreaming climate change policies by incorporating them into China's Five-Year Plans (Chen 2012).

The business community in China is less involved in climate change policy making compared with business communities in the industrialized countries. Civil society organizations specialized in climate change started to develop in the late 2000s. Today, many Chinese environmental NGOs have included climate change in their portfolio and strive to influence the government (Stensdal 2012), although they are still not very influential compared with those in other countries. Coalitions of the central government, media, and citizens' groups have become effective in putting stronger pressure on polluting industries to take immediate actions on CO_2 emissions reductions than in past years, which also improves local air quality. There are twenty-three provinces in China, but the relationship between the central government, especially NDRC, and the provincial governments is not always smooth. Many provinces rely on coal and coal-related industries, leading to resistance to low-carbon policies.

The Pew Research Center (Stokes, Wike, and Carle 2015) found that climate change is not yet an issue of grave concern to the Chinese public and that the willingness of its citizens to take action is much lower as compared with the other countries included in this chapter.

Internal changes of decision-making process, starting with the establishment of the Leading Group in 2007, and deeper engagement of the NDRC into climate change policy making since then, have effectively influenced China's position on climate change. Meanwhile, there still seem to be meager pressures from domestic stakeholders, including industries, citizen groups, and local governments, which are important actors in the national decision making in many industrialized democracies.

China's new role in world politics   China's position in the international arena independent of climate change negotiations has fundamentally changed in the 2000s mostly as a result of its expansion of economic activity. China is now regarded as a major country that is expected to show "responsible" behavior. The world's attention to China during COP 15 in Copenhagen in 2009 swelled, and the failure of the meeting was partially tied to China's strong rejections of some key issues during COP 15 (Stensdal 2015). Since then, China's position at climate-related meetings has become more cooperative. Being responsible for more than a quarter of global GHG emissions, China is fully aware that it has veto power, a power that should not be overused if China wants to be seen as a "good" nation in climate-related meetings. In this sense, the positioning of China in climate change negotiations could be explained by hegemonic stability theory, developed in the late 1970s and 1980s, which suggests that a leading country is responsible for making contributions to the supply of global public goods (Kindleberger 1973).

Another dimension of foreign policy that affected China's positioning up to COP 21 in Paris was its bilateral relationship with the United States. Since the beginning of his administration in January 2009, former US president Barack Obama has made great efforts to strengthen bilateral ties between the two countries by establishing the US-China Strategic and Economic Dialogue. The dialogue covered economic activity, energy, technology, and many other issues, including climate change as one of the key pillars of bilateral cooperation. Most of China's key announcements related to climate change since 2014 have been conveyed jointly with the United States. As these two countries have many conflicting issues, such as security in marine areas, trade, and human rights, climate change is one of the few agenda items of mutual benefit.

Overall, the interest-based approach explains China's earlier positioning well while its new stature in global politics explains its current engagement on global climate policy. In response to President Trump's announcement to withdraw from the Paris Agreement, China has decided to adhere to it and signed agreements with the EU and California in June 2017 (European Commission 2017a; Reuters 2017; White House 2017).

7.3.3 The European Union

For more than two decades, the European Union has been a strong supporter of binding mitigation commitments in international climate negotiations and has introduced several measures to reduce GHG emissions, most notably the EU Emissions Trading System (EU ETS) in 2005.[11] In that year, the Kyoto Protocol entered into force after the EU secured the necessary ratifications (Groenleer and Van Schaik 2007, 985). In March 2007, the EU committed itself "to achieve at least a 20% reduction of greenhouse gas emissions by 2020 compared to 1990" (European Council 2007, 12). Moreover, the EU offered to take on a more ambitious 30 percent target under a post-2012 global climate agreement,

provided that other developed countries commit themselves to comparable emission reductions and economically more advanced developing countries to contributing adequately according to their responsibilities and respective capabilities. (European Council 2007, 12)

EU leadership on climate change,[12] however, did not produce the desired results at the 2009 COP in Copenhagen: no legally binding agreement was adopted, and the EU played a rather marginal role in the negotiations of the Copenhagen Accord (Dimitrov 2010; Oberthür 2011). One explanation for the EU's lack of influence on this accord is its decreasing share of global GHG emissions (see figure 7.1), which has reduced the EU's relative power at the negotiation table (Bäckstrand and Elgström 2013; Oberthür 2011). Despite this trend, the EU was instrumental in shaping the outcome of the Durban climate summit in 2011, which included a second commitment period under the Kyoto Protocol and the negotiation of what would become the Paris Agreement in 2015 (IISD 2011, 28–30). According to Bäckstrand and Elgström (2013, 1370), the contrast between Copenhagen and Durban can be explained by different strategies, with the EU in Durban acting as "a 'leadiator' (leader-cum-mediator) rather than a leader" who "combine[d] unilateral concessions with careful coalition-building and bridge-building activities." With a 20 percent GHG emissions reduction target relative to base-year levels for the second commitment period under the Kyoto Protocol from 2013 to 2020,[13] the EU is destined to become the last remaining major actor bound by specific emissions reductions under international law.

At the European Council meeting in October 2014, the heads of state or government of the member states agreed on "a binding EU target of at least 40% domestic reduction in greenhouse gas emissions by 2030 compared to 1990" (European Council 2014, 1). This target was also the intended NDC of the EU (Latvia and European Commission 2015). In the run-up to and at the Paris summit in 2015, the EU and its member states relied on the coalition- and bridge-building strategy from Durban, including identifying areas of agreement with Brazil, China, and the United States (Oberthür 2016, 122). As part of the "high-ambition coalition," the EU was a key player in the negotiations and many of the EU's positions were integrated into the Paris Agreement such as "mitigation commitments for all countries" (Oberthür 2016, 121–122). The EU ratified the Paris Agreement in October 2016.

The EU-15 (i.e., the fifteen member states before the EU enlargement in 2004) met their joint Kyoto target of reducing GHG emissions by 8 percent relative to base-year levels for the first commitment period from 2008 to 2012 (European Commission 2013). In 2016 the European Environment Agency (EEA) reported that total GHG emissions in the EU had declined by 23 percent between 1990 and 2014, implying the EU is likely to also deliver on its 2020 target (EEA 2016, 17).

The interest-based explanation   The EU's observed behavior in international climate negotiations corresponds to that of a pusher in the terminology of the interest-based explanation. Therefore, the EU should be characterized by low welfare losses induced by significant GHG emissions reductions and a high vulnerability to the impacts of climate change. Policy measures to reduce emissions by 20 percent between 2005 and 2020 are estimated to result in a welfare loss of only 0.36 percent in 2020—the lowest of all major emitters in this chapter and especially small compared with the estimated losses of China and India. According to the Monitor data, the EU's vulnerability to the impacts of climate change is projected to be relatively low in 2020. Thus, the interest-based explanation incorrectly classifies the EU as a bystander and fails to predict its actual pusher role (see figure 7.2).

EU politics   In addition to the EU's GHG emissions reduction target, its leaders also agreed in March 2007 that by 2020 renewable energy should account for 20 percent of the EU's energy consumption and energy efficiency should increase by 20 percent compared to a BAU scenario (European Council 2007). To this end, the Climate and Energy Package was adopted in 2009 (European Commission 2017b). The legislative measures in the package included a revision of the EU ETS and the "Effort Sharing Decision" (European Parliament and Council of the European Union 2009a; b). The latter decision contained binding national emissions targets for 2020 relative to 2005 for the approximately 55 percent of the EU's emissions not covered by the EU ETS (European Commission 2017b): member states with the highest GDP per capita, such as Denmark, have to reduce their emissions by 20 percent, whereas Bulgaria's target, on the other end of the spectrum, is to limit the *increase* in its emissions to 20 percent (European Parliament and Council of the European Union 2009b). Because the Climate and Energy Package succeeded in addressing the differences between the member states and their respective concerns across its various elements, the package was acceptable to all of them (Skjærseth, Bang, and Schreurs 2013).

Since October 2009, the EU has had the long-term goal "to reduce emissions by 80–95% by 2050 compared to 1990 levels" (European Council 2009, 3). Furthermore, moving to a higher target for 2020 had been debated but never garnered EU-wide support (Skovgaard 2014). Poland, where coal is by far the main source of electricity, has especially been a dragger and rejected, for example, the European Commission's (2011) *Roadmap for Moving to a Competitive Low Carbon Economy in 2050* with domestic reductions of 25 percent by 2020 on an emissions pathway to the EU's 2050 goal (European Commission 2011; Neslen and Simon 2012; Skovgaard 2014). To achieve domestic reductions of 80 percent in a cost-effective manner by that year, the roadmap also puts forward reduction milestones of 40 percent by 2030 and 60 percent by 2040 (European Commission 2011, 4). Thus, the EU's 2030 emissions target is consistent with the roadmap.

Similar to the "20-20-20" targets for 2020, the European Council agreed on three main targets in the EU's 2030 Climate and Energy Policy Framework during its October 2014 meeting: In addition to cutting European GHG emissions by at least 40 percent, the share of renewable energy should reach at least 27 percent, whereas energy efficiency should improve by at least 27 percent (European Council 2014). However, while the member states have binding national renewables targets for 2020 (European Parliament and Council of the European Union 2009c), this will not be the case for 2030 (European Council 2014, 5). The EU's energy efficiency target for 2030 is "indicative," that is, non-binding (European Council 2014, 5). Prior to the meeting, Germany and Denmark were among the countries that had favored higher EU targets for renewable energy and energy efficiency—both of which would have been binding (EurActiv 2014; Ydersbond 2016, 70–71). In contrast, the Visegrad Group—the Czech Republic, Hungary, Poland, and Slovakia—together with Bulgaria and Romania wanted nonbinding targets for renewable energy (27 percent) and energy efficiency (25 percent) as well as to avoid the inclusion of the phrase "at least" in the formulation of the emissions and renewables targets, which leaves the option to increase the targets in the future (EurActiv 2014; Ydersbond 2016, 70–71). Elements of the 2030 framework addressed their concerns regarding its associated costs and the interests of other member states such that Poland, for example, did not carry out its veto threat (Fischer 2014; Skjærseth 2015; Ydersbond 2016).

Other stakeholders called for both more and less ambitious targets in the process leading to the adoption of the 2030 framework.[14] The final targets for GHG emissions reductions and the share of renewables were almost identical to the European Commission's proposal from January 2014, which only lacked the "at least" formulation for the emissions target (European Commission 2014a). A 2030 target for energy efficiency (30 percent improvement) was put forward by the Commission in July later that year (European Commission 2014b). In February 2014, the European Parliament adopted a resolution that supported higher renewables (at least 30 percent) and energy efficiency (40 percent) targets as compared with the final framework (European Parliament 2014). Moreover, interest groups actively participated in the process, including lobbying for higher targets (e.g., environmental NGOs) or against renewables and energy efficiency targets (e.g., a group of major European energy companies) (Ydersbond 2016, 91–92).

Public opinion on climate change varies between France, Italy, Germany, Spain, the UK, and Poland, according to the study by the Pew Research Center (Stokes, Wike, and Carle 2015). In Poland only 19 percent of respondents see global climate change as "a very serious problem" compared with 41 percent in the UK and 53 percent to 56 percent in the other four EU countries included in the study (Stokes, Wike, and Carle 2015, 13). This result might point to differences in public demand for climate policies and is in line with the (climate) dragger role of Poland in the EU.

In conclusion, EU climate policy is better explained by EU politics than the interest-based explanation. The member states reached agreement on EU climate and energy targets for 2020 and 2030, despite different national circumstances (e.g., relative wealth, energy mix) and more general institutional challenges due to the financial and governance crisis in recent years. Negotiations were complex. However, in the end, the willingness to compromise and make concessions to veto players such as Poland prevailed. Still, it remains unclear whether this will also be the case for future ambitious EU climate and energy policies. These kind of ambitious policies will be necessary in light of the EU's 2050 goal, for which the EEA (2016, 30) underlined that "[s]uch a reduction can take place only in the context of a major transformation of the EU's socio-technical systems, such as the energy, food, mobility and urban systems." Thus, it will be interesting to see if the EU increases its targets for 2030 in the next years to accelerate this process and reduce the effort that is required in the following two decades. The outcome of the Brexit referendum may have an impact on future EU climate policy, since the UK was a pusher (emissions targets) as well as a dragger (renewables and energy efficiency targets) in internal EU debates (Rayner and Moore 2016, 16; Skovgaard 2014). In international climate negotiations, the EU will likely continue with the coalition- and bridge-building strategy that proved successful in Durban and Paris (Oberthür 2016, 128).

7.3.4 India

As a major developing country, India has seen a trajectory of increasing attention to climate change on the domestic agenda, a shift from an equity-oriented, principled bargainer on the international stage to a major global actor around the Copenhagen COP in 2009. It returned to an equity-based justification of its international position shortly thereafter and commensurate with its elevated power status on the global scale, India has become aware of the increasing demands placed on its climate policy. In line with this role, India announced in 2009 that it would reduce its GHG intensity by 20–25 percent until 2020, and it upgraded this position in the run-up to the Paris Agreement to 33–35 percent by 2030, both based on the reference year 2005 (Government of India 2015).

On the international stage, India has long seen itself as a spiritual co-leader of the postcolonial developing countries. Early work by Agarwal and Narain (2012) emphasized the historical responsibilities of countries and, subsequently, influenced the Indian position on emphasizing the UNFCCC's common but differentiated responsibilities. India elevated the issue of adaptation to a priority issue when hosting the 2002 COP in New Delhi, and it has switched from opposition to the CDM to become an eager participant (Nautiyal and Varun 2012; Sengupta 2012). Moreover, India joined a range of global fora which reflected its heightened standing, including the Asia-Pacific Partnership (2006),[15] the Major Economies Forum (2009), and became a member of the BASIC coalition of leading emerging economies. The BASIC group has had a pivotal effect on the future shape of global climate policies since the 2009 COP owing to its substantial increase in the share of global GHG emissions (Dasgupta 2012) (see figure 7.1), yet during the climate negotiations resulting in the 2015 Paris Agreement, India looked more like it was reacting to the positioning of other BASIC countries rather than being itself a leader in the global negotiations.

The interest-based explanation   Our previous exposition of the interest-based explanation showed that India is very vulnerable to climate impacts and would incur major welfare losses if it pursued a 20 percent GHG emissions reduction goal during 2005–2020. Unlike any other major country reviewed in this chapter, it displays, by far, the highest degree of vulnerability to climate change. As the agricultural sector of India is of major significance to the Indian economy, changes in precipitation and weather extremes have a marked effect on India's vulnerability to climate change. In addition, its welfare losses associated with a 20 percent emissions reduction from 2005 to 2020 would, in comparison with other major countries, be very substantial.

These macro-quantitative impressions are backed up by academic perspectives, the Government of India, as well as surveys of the mass public. Dubash and Joseph (2016, 45) suggest that India "is simultaneously a highly vulnerable country; a 'major emitter' when measured by annual emissions; and a very low contributor to the problem when measured by per capita or historical emissions." The Government of India (2015) concurs in its intended NDC that emissions will keep increasing for some time, and a study by the Asian Development Bank projects economic losses in India to be 1.8 percent of annual GDP in 2050 without deviation from a GHG-intensive pathway (Ahmed and Suphachalasai 2014). Given the cost of a transition to a low-GHG economy, India uses internal funding (such as a tax on coal) and expresses expectations about external funding, yet it takes optimism for external funding to materialize on a major scale (Sethi 2016). Therefore, the government of India makes some of its promises conditional on the realization of external funding (Government of India 2015, 29–30). This information should be seen against the backdrop of a mass public that sees climate change as a major challenge that might affect respondents. It places India among the top publics concerned about climate impacts in an international comparison (Stokes, Wike, and Carle 2015).

In combination, India appears to be correctly classified as an intermediate country: it has incentives to reduce its own emissions and asks others to reduce their emissions, yet is reluctant to commit itself to absolute emissions reductions due to the high welfare losses it would incur and the need to alleviate the situation of its sizeable poor segment of society by way of economic growth.

The domestic politics explanation   Over the past two decades, India has built a political and scientific institutional structure to respond to the challenge of climate change, including the 2008 National Action Plan on Climate Change which highlighted the co-benefits of climate policies. As a result thereof, eight National Climate Missions were created. India's international stance proliferated from an early insistence on equal per capita carbon emissions to a pledge at the 2007 Heiligendamm G20 meeting by then prime minister Singh of not surpassing the per capita emissions of developed countries. In 2008 the Prime Minister's Council of Climate Change released the National Action Plan on Climate Change with an array of domestic climate missions to be pursued. Subsequently, India's former minister of environment, Ramesh, announced in 2009 that India will reduce its GHG emissions intensity by 20–25 percent between 2005 and 2020, excluding the agricultural sector. This position was essentially unilateral, to be brought about by domestic action—comparable with announcements by other BASIC countries (Raghunandan 2012; Sengupta 2012). In late 2015, India upgraded its international position, in response to the positioning by other BASIC countries, to 33–35 percent by 2030, using 2005 as the reference year. In addition, the government of India has developed a comprehensive list of domestic environmental and climate policies (Government of India 2015)—which both represent its international and domestic commitment—yet also reveal the fragmentation of domestic climate policies.

On many policy issues, Indian politics follows party lines and can be divisive. For climate change, however, Prabhu (2012, 232) suggests:

[T]here are no party positions ... What one also sees in debates on climate change [in Parliament] is that there is a mixing of views across party positions ... Climate change as an issue is not a constituency mover.

In effect, policy formulation is strongly influenced by the federal or union level, whereas at the stage of implementation, the states become more strongly involved.[16] Furthermore, industry and environmental NGO lobbying is not yet as advanced as in industrialized countries, and together with research NGOs, these non-governmental actors exert influence mostly by way of the Prime Minister's Council on Climate Change or the Expert Panel on Low Carbon Strategies for Inclusive Growth. Only the Green India Mission resulted in broader participation of the mass public (Dubash and Joseph 2016, 48). Ministers are probed on their negotiation positions, criticized for potential policy reversals during international negotiations, and criticized if they appear to deviate from India's long-held, equity-oriented position in international negotiations:

"With respect to the international dimension of climate change debates, there is complete unanimity across party lines on the issue of equity. There is also complete agreement with regard to the Kyoto Protocol and in India's stand not to take on binding commitments. Indian MPs swear by the UNFCCC process" (Prabhu 2012, 233).

The election of the Modi government at the union level in 2014 upheld the long-established priority for poverty eradication combined with priority for economic development. Prime Minister Modi can build on his experience as former chief minister of the state of Gujarat where he oversaw substantial solar power development—a period when 70 percent of India's total solar energy supply originated from his state (Hope 2014). He then authored the book *Convenient Action—Gujarat's Response to Challenges of Climate Change* (Modi 2011). While Prime Minister Modi was originally less forthcoming than Chief Minister Modi on climate change, he wishes to replicate the renewables expansion at the union level. For example, a program to add 100 GW of solar energy by 2022 has been announced and embedded in a strategy to create 175 GW of installed renewables capacity by 2022. Furthermore, the federal government strengthened adaptation policies as well as policies to improve energy efficiency. The name of the lead ministry was changed to Ministry of Environment, Forest and Climate Change. In addition, after three years of inactivity, the PM's Council on Climate Change was reconstituted and revamped in late 2014 and held its inaugural meeting on January 19, 2015 (Goswami 2015; Government of India 2015; Hope 2014).

Although the policies are in the hands of a widening group of federal ministries, the cancellation of the position of the Special Envoy on Climate Change after only a few years led to diminished interdepartmental coordination. Dubash and Joseph (2016) suggested that the institutionalization of climate policies has led to only limited capacity to deal with climate change.

In conclusion, the domestic politics of India do depend to a considerable degree on the prime minister's priorities, do not afford fragmentation across party lines, and are mostly driven by economic, ethical, social, and financial considerations. The lack of enthusiasm for very strong emissions reductions is correctly predicted by the interest-based explanation, as other goals often take priority over climate change and secure energy supply. The three propositions of the domestic politics model appear to be supported, albeit reduced to mostly interdepartmental considerations at the federal government level. Moreover, India intends to stick to the Paris Agreement despite President Trump's intention to leave it (*Hindustan Times* 2017).

7.3.5 Japan

Japan has always taken an ambivalent position on emissions reductions during climate change negotiations over the last two decades. Japan agreed on the 6 percent emission reduction target for the years 2008–2012 under the Kyoto Protocol, mainly because Japan hosted COP 3 at Kyoto—where the Kyoto Protocol was adopted. However, after the United States withdrew from the Kyoto Protocol, Japan became less enthusiastic about supporting it (Tiberghien and Schreurs 2007). An ambitious 25 percent emissions reduction target by 2020 from 1990 was announced in September 2009 as the national target, but criticism was heard within Japan that the government did not thoroughly examine how the target was to be achieved. The Tohoku regional earthquake and the Fukushima Daiich nuclear plant accident in March 2011 totally scrapped Japan's climate mitigation plan, as much of the 25 percent reduction target owed to the use of nuclear power plants. In 2011, at COP 17, Japan announced that it would not participate in the second commitment period of the Kyoto Protocol as Japan wanted a new agreement in which all major emitting countries participated. At COP 19 in 2013, Japan announced a revised GHG emissions reduction target for the year 2020: a 3.8 percent GHG emission reductions from 2005. This target assumes no use of nuclear power. It further submitted its intended NDC in July 2015, which included a GHG emissions reduction target of 26 percent by 2030 from 2013.

The interest-based explanation   Based on figure 7.2, it was predicted that Japan takes a bystander position regarding emissions reduction targets. On the impact side of climate change, major reports estimate both positive and negative effects in Japan. Positive effects are represented by increasing yields of rice and other cereals and milder temperature in winter, while negative effects are projected for other agricultural products, extreme weather events such as typhoons, as well as health hazards due to summer heat. The potential damage due to intensive rainfall that may cause floods in megacities could reach 1 trillion yen (ca. 63 billion USD) per year by 2050 (Project Team for Comprehensive Projection of Climate Change Impacts 2008).

Regarding the cost of emission reductions, estimates are undertaken each time the government intends to make decisions on emissions targets. The 25 percent emissions reduction target announced in 2009 was calculated to change Japanese GDP between −5.6% and +1.2% compared with BAU (Central Environment Policy Council 2010). Emissions reduction policies will have a positive effect on the economy in terms of energy savings, while the additional costs of energy will put a high burden on the economy. Meanwhile, after the total phase-out of nuclear power plants, it was suggested that Japan would be able to reduce its GHG emissions by only 5 to 9 percent from 1990 levels until 2020 if the country wanted to maintain its positive economic growth without the use of nuclear power (Council of Energy and Environment Japan 2012). This implies that ambitious mitigation would be costly. Overall, Japan's actual position is broadly congruent with that of a bystander as it behaved rather passively during the Paris negotiations.

The domestic politics explanation   The nearly always ruling Liberal Democratic Party (LDP) has strong ties with the business sector, the latter being most prominently represented by Keidanren (Japan Business Federation). The Japanese industries and policy makers are basically aware of and publicly accept the urgency of climate change mitigation policies. However, they also consider Japan to be one of most energy efficient countries (Keidanren 2010). Being responsible for less than 4 percent of global GHG emissions, the business sector suggests that Japan should contribute to reducing emissions by way of undertaking emissions reductions abroad rather than at home. It will be less costly to reduce emissions in developing countries, and an ambitious long-term target cannot be achieved in any case without meaningful participation of major emitters such as the United States and China. This argument has received support by government officials and the business community alike. In Japan little attention is paid to its own responsibility for its historical or its per capita emissions.

This framing of the climate change problem heavily influenced Japan's decision making toward its 2020 emissions reduction target. Taro Aso of the LDP, then prime minister, announced in June 2009 that Japan's midterm emissions target for the year 2020 would be a 15 percent reduction from

2005, equivalent to an 8 percent reduction from 1990. This was a prudent ambition once compared with the 6 percent reduction between 2008 and 2012 that is enshrined in the Kyoto Protocol.

Japan's cautious position changed when the Democratic Party of Japan (DPJ) took office between 2009 and 2012. The DJP sought support from citizen groups that espoused environmental consciousness. Environmental NGOs in Japan used to have little power to influence national decisions (Fisher 2003), but the situation improved to some extent. The DPJ supported a 25 percent reduction target from 1990 by 2020, but the target was nullified after the complete phase-out of nuclear power plants following the earthquake in 2011. Civil society became more cautious of the risks related to nuclear power than the risks related to climate change. The nuclear power industry, supported by power companies, asserted that nuclear power plants were indispensable if Japan were to make contributions to climate change mitigation. This campaign and framing of the two issues—nuclear and climate change—affected people's (mis)understanding that pro-climate assertions equated pro-nuclear assertions.

The phase-out of nuclear power plants also led industry to perceive renewable energy as too expensive and too unstable to rely on, and industry pushed the government to reconsider the phase-out of nuclear power plants. In April 2014 Japan publicized the Basic Energy Plan, which included nuclear power as one important source of energy in the future. The plan was followed by the Long-Term Supply and Demand Perspective for Energy, released in July 2015. The perspective included a vision that nuclear power would supply around 20–22 percent of electricity in 2030. The perspective was designed to advance Japan's NDC submission; the two projections shared the same assumptions. In summary, industry groups were the actors with strong interests and clear preferences related to climate change policies that became active participants and dominated the domestic climate policy decision-making process. This is in line with the domestic politics approach. Given that polls of climate change sentiment show that Japan is nearly always in the top half of concern for climate change impacts and willingness to take action (Stokes, Wike, and Carle 2015), business exercised very strong influence on Japanese climate policy.

Japan as a medium-size power   For Japan, it has been more important not to stick its head out among other countries than to being regarded as an ambitious leader on climate change. For instance, Japanese business has always been concerned about the relative effort to reduce emissions by making comparisons with the emissions targets of the United States, the EU, and China (Hattori 2007). It was important for business to undertake efforts comparable to other countries—neither more nor less.

Japan did not want to be seen as a clear laggard, either. In June 2008 then prime minister Yasuo Fukuda announced the "Fukuda Vision" and set a voluntary long-term emission target of 60–80 percent reductions for Japan by 2050 as compared with "the present year"—indicating a base year somewhere around 2005 without clearly defining any specific year (Prime Minister's Office 2008). The aim was to show Japan's willingness to tackle global issues at the G8 Toyako Summit in July 2008. Japan has neither strongly supported nor opposed the insertion of wording such as "not to exceed 2°C" or "developed countries reducing GHG emissions by 80% or more by 2050" in any of the following G8(7) meetings (L'Aquila G8 Summit 2009), despite strong opposition to these long-term goals in Japan.

At the time of the development of Japan's NDC in 2015, Prime Minister Shinzo Abe is said to have given three instructions: (1) the total cost of energy should not be more expensive than before; (2) renewable energy as a share of total electricity supply should exceed that of nuclear power; (3) the GHG emissions reduction target should be as ambitious as those of other major industrialized economies (Nikkei Shimbun 2015). The base year of the NDC—2013—was selected to fulfill the third instruction, because Japan's emissions reduction percentage would be higher than that of the United States and the EU when the year 2013 was chosen as the base year for all countries. These instructions fit the two approaches used in this chapter. Overall, the attention to welfare losses in the interest-based explanation affected Japan's stakeholders' views on climate change mitigation policies, which ultimately determined the country's position explicated in more detail in the domestic politics approach.

7.3.6   The United States

The United States is the world's second-largest emitter of GHG emissions after China. The country has a population of 320 million, and heavily depends on fossil fuels for energy production. However, US energy-related CO_2 emissions dropped considerably over the past few years, chiefly because natural gas replaced coal use in the utility sector from 2009 onward as new technologies for hydraulic fracturing and horizontal drilling gave access to huge deposits of shale gas. The proven shale gas reserves are at least 199 trillion cubic feet according to 2015 estimates; only China has larger reserves of shale gas than the United States (EIA 2015). The increase of homegrown shale gas in the US market caused natural gas prices to fall dramatically, and many electricity producers switched from coal to natural gas as their fuel of choice.

The United States also holds the world's largest estimated recoverable reserves of coal and is a net exporter of coal. In 2012 US coal mines produced more than a billion short tons of coal, and more than 81 percent of this is used by domestic power plants to generate electricity (EIA 2013). In the short run, a continued transition from coal to natural gas will further reduce CO_2 emissions because of the lower carbon density of natural gas.

The United States has been committed to key positions in the international climate change negotiations that defined the country's role in the negotiations since the outset in Rio in 1992. Two issues are important for the United States: broad participation (commitments for all major emitters in the international regime to avoid carbon leakage) and flexibility in terms of domestic policy measures aimed at fulfilling pledges (to minimize economic losses for participants). These positions emerged as a result of domestic policy debates, defined by staunch opposition to costly climate policies that could hurt the US economy. The Byrd-Hagel Senate Resolution, passed in July 1997, and the decision to reject participation in the Kyoto Protocol in 2001 reflected a strong opposition to climate action in the US Congress. In 2009 President Obama took a leading role in developing the Copenhagen Accord—which was a step away from a "top-down"-oriented process requiring quantified emissions reductions targets. At COP 16 in Cancun, the United States strongly advocated and won support for a more "bottom-up" oriented international climate regime based on "pledge and review" of national commitments. This "bottom-up" approach formed the basis of the 2015 Paris Agreement, and the United States took a leading role in successfully negotiating the deal. In particular, the Obama Administration's active diplomacy vis-à-vis the Chinese leadership resulted in crucial bilateral declarations of common leadership by the two countries in the run-up to the Paris meeting (Goldenberg 2014). The two major emitters committed to reduce GHG emissions levels and phase in more renewable energy in their domestic energy mix (see above). The US pledge in the Paris Agreement amounted to a 26–28 percent cut in GHG emissions by 2030 as compared with 2005, while China committed to cap its emission level and to phase in at least 27 percent renewables in the energy mix by 2030 (Bang 2015). This bilateral cooperation is generally perceived to be a key factor for the successful outcome of the Paris negotiations.

However, President Trump inflicted a major blow to the Paris Agreement on June 1, 2017, when withdrawing US participation, citing the very same arguments used by President Bush in 2001: The deal would impose costs on the domestic economy that were too high and would give a competitive advantage to China and other international trade competitors. The enduring lack of bipartisan agreement regarding US federal climate policy, and resulting instability in policy approach and treaty participation, therefore remain a caveat for international climate cooperation.

The interest-based explanation   If compared with other countries (see figure 7.2), the climate vulnerability of the United States is relatively low, and the welfare losses associated with measures to reduce emissions by 20 percent by 2020 relative to 2005 are estimated at approximately 0.5 percent in 2020. Given the thresholds, the interest-based explanation predicts the United States to be a "bystander." The behavior of a bystander is expected to be a passive role in the mitigation negotiations because of both low welfare losses due to emissions reductions and limited benefits from mitigating climate change.

Until recently, policy makers in the United States were unalarmed by expected climate vulnerability. Expected climate impacts in the United States include increases in heavy rainfall, higher temperatures, more wildfires, and increasing sea levels, which can cause more extreme weather events similar to Hurricane Sandy that hit New York, New Jersey, and Connecticut especially hard in October 2012. Other expected changes are rapidly retreating glaciers, thawing permafrost, lengthening growing seasons, lengthening ice-free seasons in the ocean and on lakes and rivers, earlier snowmelt, and alterations in river flows. Furthermore, crop and livestock production will be increasingly challenged (US Global Change Research Program 2014). The Obama administration proposed more focus on adaptation measures in the Climate Action Plan announced in 2013, which was pursued in national budget processes during his tenure.

The prediction of the interest-based explanation that the United States will be a bystander in the international climate negotiations does not describe actual behavior very well. The United States has been a key actor in shaping the direction of the negotiations—especially in the Paris Agreement negotiations, and has taken on the role of laggard when discussions developed in undesirable directions.

The domestic politics explanation   During the eight years of the Obama administration (2009–2017), climate policy was on the domestic policy agenda in different ways. In his first term as president, Obama tried to move climate legislation through Congress, but he failed. In his second term, Obama applied his executive powers to develop federal climate policy.

Resistance to comprehensive federal climate policies has persisted in the US Congress for the past twenty years. Legislative proposals to introduce a price on carbon failed in the Senate in 2003, 2005, and 2008. In 2009 the House of Representatives passed the American Clean Energy and Security Act by a razor-thin margin (219–212)—the first time climate legislation won a vote in Congress. In 2010 this bill stalled and eventually died in the Senate. Since then Congress has not seriously debated climate legislation (Bang and Skodvin 2014). Staunch and constant opposition to federal climate policy is rooted in the perception that such policies would be too expensive and threaten jobs. Many US senators and members of the House of Representatives are elected in states that are economically dependent on fossil energy sources for electricity production, process industry, manufacturing, and agriculture. For carbon intensive industries, such as coal, oil, automobile, airline, agriculture, and manufacturing industries, policies designed to reduce CO_2 emissions represent a significant challenge to their conventional ways of doing business (Bang and Schreurs 2011).

Environmental NGOs concerned about the negative effects of global warming pursue a science-based strategy to reduce GHG emissions. Some NGOs function as legal watchdogs, for instance the Natural Resources Defense Council and the Environmental Defense Fund. For the insurance, renewable energy, and various high-technology industries, climate policies are also seen as business opportunities (Bang and Schreurs 2011).

US public opinion on climate policy action is very polarized. In 2014, 88 percent of Democrats stated they believe that global warming is happening, and 82 percent expressed their willingness to support strict CO_2 emission limits on power plants (Leiserowitz et al. 2014). The Obama administration's push for climate policy change clearly had support from a majority of Democrats. However, climate change is an increasingly partisan issue. With the growth of the Tea Party movement within the Republican Party since 2009, congressional Republicans increasingly tend to vote against any proposed climate policy programs (Skocpol 2013). The general public's attitude toward federal energy and climate policy is influenced by their levels of concern about energy security, energy prices, and environmental protection. While slightly more than half of Americans (56 percent) in 2016 believed that human actions are mostly to blame for climate change, their willingness to endure higher energy prices (for instance, as a result of carbon pricing) was much higher, with 70 percent of respondents supporting setting strict limits to carbon emissions from power plants (Leiserowitz et al. 2016). Nevertheless, if compared with other countries included in this chapter, the US public scores toward the lower end of concern with and action on climate change (Stokes, Wike, and Carle 2015).

Having failed with pushing a federal climate law through Congress, President Obama used his executive powers during his second term to introduce federal climate policy. After coining a Climate Action Plan in 2013, the president authorized the Environmental Protection Agency (EPA) to develop new regulations aimed at cutting CO_2 emissions through existing law. As a result, state-specific CO_2 regulations for power plants (the Clean Power Plan—CPP) were developed within the jurisdiction of the Clean Air Act. Furthermore, Obama authorized stricter emissions standards for vehicles and proposed policies to address the impacts of climate change (Bang and Schreurs 2017). The Obama administration's executive action proved to be highly controversial, especially since it intended to circumvent veto players in Congress and to implement climate policy regulations despite deep polarization and cleavages among federal legislators. This polarized situation resulted in two major turnarounds in US climate policy during the first year of the Trump administration, namely a decision to dismantle the CPP (Schlossberg 2017) and the announcement on June 1, 2017, to leave the Paris Agreement (see also chapter 12 in this volume). These decisions show clearly that a high level of instability in US climate policy still remains a crucial factor, and that the lack of bipartisan agreement on how to approach the climate change issue affects the country's ability to respond to this huge societal challenge.

In response to Trump's new turn in climate policy, many states have put on hold any efforts to develop state implementation plans for adhering to the CPP, while other states are pursuing climate action, despite the lack of climate action at the federal level (C2ES 2017). Clearly, deep polarization in US climate policy affects the United States' ability to participate as a reliable partner in international climate cooperation. With the Trump administration's approach, the United States does not have a credible domestic policy plan to achieve its 2030 emissions reduction target (Bang, Hovi, and Skodvin 2016). Given the long-term controversy and deep divisions in the United States on climate policy, the future of US climate policy is difficult to predict.

In sum, US domestic politics have a crucial impact on the scope for US commitments in future international climate change negotiations. Given the politics of the Trump administration, domestic policy instability will likely affect the dynamics of the international climate negotiations (see also Sprinz et al. 2017).

7.4 Comparison across Countries and Conceptual Approaches

The interest-based explanation offers us a prediction of the negotiation positions of countries (see figure 7.2). It is a static explanation, and its predictions of country behavior only change as a result of major changes in abatement costs or expected climate impacts. We expected Brazil, the EU, Japan, and the United States to behave as bystander countries, China as a dragger, and India as an intermediate. There is no obvious candidate for a pusher. These predictions appear to be only partially supported, with several countries behaving differently than predicted.

In particular, the climate policies of India, Japan, and partially China until the mid-2000s appear to be correctly predicted, while the vigor of policies and international negotiation positions of Brazil, the EU, and the United States appear to be mispredicted.

Abstract forces such as climate impacts and welfare losses of mitigation measures cannot, by themselves, exert political influence. It is domestic political actors and the coalitions among these actors that determine political outcomes at the national level and influence the international negotiation positions. In the cases where the interest-based explanation of international environmental politics leads to correct predictions, domestic political factors reinforce that explanation. In particular, China and India do not have fully fledged interest representation across business and environmental NGOs as compared with Brazil, the EU, and the United States. Furthermore, in the

Table 7.1
Comparison across countries and conceptual approaches.

Support for Explanation	Brazil	China	EU-28	India	Japan	USA
Interest Based	P: bystander A: pusher	P: dragger A: dragger until mid-2000s; pusher thereafter	P: bystander A: pusher	P: intermediate A: intermediate	P: bystander A: bystander (on balance)	P: bystander A: pusher during Obama administration
Domestic Politics	Fully differentiated political representation	Government led (esp. NDRC); not fully differentiated political representation	Fully differentiated political representation; disagreements among member states hamper EU at large	Mostly interdepartmental and government-led; in practice, not fully differentiated political representation	Strong role of industry that emphasizes costs of mitigation; political representation favors business	Fully differentiated political representation; strong internal divisions between Congress and the Obama administration; strong partisan divide; in June 2017, President Trump announced a plan to withdraw from the Paris Agreement
Additional Aspects	Aim to limit deforestation; well-established bioethanol industry	Rise to global power status overall as well as in terms of GHG emissions; strong coordination with United States during Obama administration	EU governance crisis since 2007/2008	Prioritization of economic and development agenda	Tohoku earthquake and Fukushima Daiichi nuclear plant accident; self-perception as a middling power that does not want to "stick out its head"	Strong coordination with China during Obama administration

P=predicted behavior, A=actual behavior

case of Japan, business exerts strong impact on the dominant, ruling party. It is in those cases where we have the most developed, broad-based interest representation on climate policy, namely in Brazil, the EU, and the United States, where the interest-based explanation fails.

Factors extraneous to climate policy factors are likely to play a major role in a range of countries. In Brazil, the successful management of its rainforest with respect to carbon releases as well as the long-established bioethanol industry provide pillars of support for climate policies, although both issues have been on the agenda since the 1970s—long before climate policy became an important agenda item. Moreover, the Chinese and US positions should be seen against the backdrop of a duopoly of world governance that makes these countries indispensable for global mitigation efforts as these countries are not only the main two emitters but are also among the largest economies in the world. While the countries are rivals, climate change has become one issue—under the Obama administration—where coordinated action among both countries paved the way for the successful completion of the 2015 Paris Agreement. Thus, additional factors can explain to some degree the mispredictions of the interest-based explanation.

Finally, there is no assurance that there will be continued leadership on global climate policy. The EU has entered a legitimacy crisis with the 2016 "Brexit referendum" in the UK, and the multifaceted challenges of the financial, political credibility, and refugee influx crises of the past decade absorb much of its political energy. Furthermore, some member states are challenging constitutive political elements of the European Union's order. While the EU may still be interested in free trade and has established itself as a global power in this policy area, the challenges posed by member states and statements by US President Trump may render this leadership role in world politics moot. While the EU has been successful in reducing its GHG emissions, its dwindling share thereof on the world stage also leads to a lower weight in the climate negotiations—except if the EU is successful in a low-GHG transition and others wish to emulate the potential frontrunner. Besides the EU, US leadership has relied on the Obama administration's political agenda rather than on strong congressional support. President Obama essentially ruled by executive order instead of legislative approval, which made his policies fragile and vulnerable to reversal. Both Bush administrations acted rather reluctantly on climate change mitigation, and the Clinton administration was unable to find congressional support for the Kyoto Protocol. While many of the reservations the US Congress held in the past were bypassed by the Obama administration, a continued partisan split in the United States may not augur well for continued US leadership on global climate change. If China, unlike its present response to President Trump's announcement to leave the Paris Agreement (Griffiths 2017), responds negatively to a US retreat, the world may run out of pushers with global clout.

In the absence of global government, global climate policy largely rests with national governments, especially in the major countries that are the purview of this chapter. Any single major country can influence negatively the vigor of future climate policy ambitions at the global level, either due to its emissions weight or the example it sets for other countries. We reviewed the policies of six major countries or groups of countries while employing two conceptual lenses, namely the interest-based explanation and the domestic politics approach. None of these lenses is able to provide a complete explanation of all country positions by itself, yet each adds important aspects to explain why politics has eschewed both negligence of the issue of climate change and, so far, also abstained from enthusiastic pursuit of domestic and global climate policies that would achieve the 1.5–2°C goal with high probability. While we highlighted the role of national governance in this chapter, nongovernmental actors play an important role not only in the domestic domain but also transnationally. Chapters 8 and 9, Skodvin on nongovernmental actors and Paterson on business, respectively, highlight these actors on their own merit in substantially more detail.

Notes

1. For privileged groups, it is profitable for a single country to supply a public good herself; in intermediate groups, provision of the public good is not assured as the lack of contribution by a member has a noticeable effect on the behavior of others; and for latent groups, the contribution (or absence thereof) has no impact on others and leads to the *nonprovision* of the public good (Olson 1971).

2. This should not be confused with the "intermediates" to be subsequently introduced in the interest-based explanation.

3. Sprinz and Vaahtoranta (1994) originally used the terms *ecological vulnerability* and *abatement cost*. See also Sprinz and Weiß (2001) for an earlier application of the interest-based explanation to the issue of climate change. This chapter solely focuses on climate mitigation. Alternatively, efforts could be directed at adaptation measures, yet this extension is beyond the confines of this chapter.

4. We are indebted to DARA for providing additional data, for example, for the EU-27 as a whole (Croatia became the twenty-eighth EU member state in July 2013 only after the publication of the Monitor).

5. For details, see DARA (2012).

6. On the EPPA model, see Paltsev et al. (2005) and the updates in Paltsev et al. (2009, 2011). Note that these articles describe version 4 of the model, whereas the results discussed in this chapter were obtained with version 5. Version 5 is documented in the supplementary material to Reilly et al. (2012). We are indebted to Sergey Paltsev for generating custom simulations in January 2013. They accounted for the surge in fracking in the United States, but did not include a potential nuclear phase-out in Japan after the Fukushima incident; the EU region in version 5 of the EPPA model comprises the EU-27, Norway, Switzerland, Iceland, and Liechtenstein (personal communication with Sergey Paltsev, January 2013). In the following, we use the results of the EU region as an estimate for the EU, since the other four countries are small in comparison.

7. "[A] measure, common in economic analysis, is the change in economic welfare measured as equivalent variation. Conceptually, this is the amount of income needed to compensate the representative agent for welfare losses suffered as a result of the policy. In most EPPA applications, this is measured by the change in aggregate consumption, (…)" (Paltsev et al. 2005, 9). In the version of the EPPA model used for this chapter, there is no representation of the labor-leisure trade-off (personal communication with Sergey Paltsev, November 2016). "If the model does not include non-market activities (like leisure, etc.), then the changes in consumption and in welfare are the same" (Paltsev and Capros 2013, 19).

8. BAU levels are based on projections of future emissions if no new or additional mitigation is undertaken.

9. We thank Solveig Aamodt for excellent research assistance for the Brazil case study.

10. In this new commitment the mitigation target is compared to 2005 and not BAU levels, hence making the commitment more stringent than the previous one described above.

11. For a detailed account of the history of EU climate policy, see, for example, Jordan and Rayner (2010) or Oberthür and Pallemaerts (2010).

12. See, for example, Schreurs and Tiberghien (2007), Oberthür and Roche Kelly (2008), and Wurzel and Connelly (2011).

13. This is a joint target with Iceland (European Commission 2015).

14. For a detailed description and analysis of the negotiation process and the positions of stakeholders, see Ydersbond (2016).

15. Closed in 2011.

16. Interview with former Union Minister of Environment and Forests Jairam Ramesh, December 16, 2014.

References

Aamodt, Solveig. 2015. "To Be—or Not to Be—a Low-Carbon Economy: A Decade of Climate Politics in Brazil." In *The Domestic Politics of Global Climate Change: Key Actors in International Climate Cooperation*, edited by Guri Bang, Steinar Andresen, and Arild Underdal, 25–48. Cheltenham: Edward Elgar.

Agarwal, Anil, and Sunita Narain. 2012. "Global Warming in an Unequal World: A Case of Environmental Colonialism." In *Handbook of Climate Change and India: Development, Politics and Governance*, edited by Navroz K. Dubash, 81–88. Abingdon: Earthscan.

Ahmed, Mahfuz, and Suphachol Suphachalasai. 2014. *Assessing the Costs of Climate Change and Adaptation in South Asia*. Mandaluyong City, Philippines: Asian Development Bank.

Bäckstrand, Karin, and Ole Elgström. 2013. "The EU's Role in Climate Change Negotiations: From Leader to 'Leadiator.'" *Journal of European Public Policy* 20 (10): 1369–1386.

Bang, Guri. 2015. "The United States: Obama's Push for Climate Policy Change." In *The Domestic Politics of Global Climate Change: Key Actors in International Climate Cooperation*, edited by Guri Bang, Arild Underdal, and Steinar Andresen, 160–181. Cheltenham: Edward Elgar.

Bang, Guri, Jon Hovi, and Tora Skodvin. 2016. "The Paris Agreement: Short-Term and Long-Term Effectiveness." *Politics and Governance* 4 (3): 209–218.

Bang, Guri, and Miranda A. Schreurs. 2011. "A Green New Deal: Framing US Climate Leadership." In *The European Union as a Leader in International Climate Change Politics*, edited by Rüdiger K. W. Wurzel and James Connelly, 235–251. London: Routledge.

———. 2017. "The United States: The Challenge of Global Climate Leadership in a Politically Divided State." In *The European Union in International Climate Change Politics. Still Taking a Lead?*, edited by Rüdiger K. W. Wurzel, James Connelly, and Duncan Liefferink, 239–254. London: Routledge.

Bang, Guri, and Tora Skodvin. 2014. "US Climate Policy and the Shale Gas Revolution." In *Toward a New Climate Agreement. Conflict, Resolution and Governance*, edited by Todd Cherry, Jon Hovi, and David M. McEvoy, 76–90. London: Routledge.

Bang, Guri, Arild Underdal, and Steinar Andresen, eds. 2015. *The Domestic Politics of Global Climate Change: Key Actors in International Climate Cooperation*. Cheltenham: Edward Elgar.

BBC. 2011. "Brazil Floods: 'Never Seen Anything Like It.'" *BBC*, January 14.

Bueno de Mesquita, Bruce, Alastair Smith, Randolph M. Siverson, and James D. Morrow. 2003. *The Logic of Political Survival*. Cambridge, MA: MIT Press.

C2ES. 2017. State Climate Policy. Center for Climate and Energy Solutions 2017. Available from https://www.c2es.org/content/state-climate-policy.

CBD. 2013. *Country Profiles—Brazil*. Convention on Biological Diversity 2013. Available from http://www.cbd.int/countries/?country=br.

Central Environment Policy Council. 2010. *Vision for Policies and Measures to Achieve the Mid- and Long-Term Emissions Reduction Targets (Mid- and Long-Term Roadmap: Interim Report)*. Tokyo: Government of Japan.

Chen, Ying. 2012. "Performance Evaluation for Energy Conservation Targets in the Eleventh Five-Year Plan." In *China's Climate Change Policies*, edited by Weiguang Wang and Guoguang Zheng, 21–42. Abingdon: Routledge.

Christensen, Steen Fryba. 2010. Brasiliens Take-Off Som Brik-Land. Conference Paper at the General Assembly of Dansk Selskab for Statskunskab 4–5 November 2010. Aalborg: Institut for kultur og globale studier, Aalborg Universitet.

Council of Energy and Environment Japan. 2012. *Innovative Energy and Environment Strategy*. Japan: Cabinet Office.

DARA. 2012. *Methodology Note: Methodological Documentation for the Climate Vulnerability Monitor 2nd Edition*. Madrid: Fundación DARA Internacional.

DARA and Climate Vulnerable Forum. 2012. *Climate Vulnerability Monitor 2nd Edition: A Guide to the Cold Calculus of a Hot Planet*. Madrid: Fundación DARA Internacional.

Dasgupta, Chandrashekhar. 2012. "Present at the Creation: The Making of the UN Framework Convention on Climate Change." In *Handbook of Climate Change and India: Development, Politics and Governance*, edited by Navroz K. Dubash, 89–97. Abingdon: Earthscan.

DeSombre, Elizabeth R. 2011. "The United States and Global Environmental Politics: Domestic Sources of U.S. Unilateralism." In *The Global Environment: Institutions, Law and Policy (3rd Edition)*, edited by Regina S. Axelrod, Stacy D. VanDeveer, and David Leonard Downie, 70–91. Washington, DC: CQ Press.

Dimitrov, Radoslav S. 2010. "Inside UN Climate Change Negotiations: The Copenhagen Conference." *Review of Policy Research* 27 (6): 795–821.

Dubash, Navroz K., and Neha B. Joseph. 2016. "Evolution of Institutions for Climate Policy in India." *Economic & Political Weekly* 51 (3): 44–54.

Economy, Elizabeth C. 1997. "Chinese Policy-Making and Global Climate Change: Two-Front Diplomacy and the International Community." In *The Internationalization of Environmental Protection,* edited by Miranda A. Schreurs and Elizabeth C. Economy, 19–41. Cambridge: Cambridge University Press.

EEA. 2016. *Trends and Projections in Europe 2016: Tracking Progress towards Europe's Climate and Energy Targets* [PDF version]. Copenhagen: European Environment Agency.

EIA. 2013. *International Energy Outlook 2013 with Projections to 2040.* Washington, DC: US Energy Information Administration.

———. 2015. *Shale Gas (in Billion Cubic Feet).* Washington, DC: US Energy Information Administration.

EurActiv. 2014. *Member States' Positions on EU 2030 Climate Targets.* Available from http://cf.datawrapper.de/kbpOX/4/.

European Commission. 2011. *A Roadmap for Moving to a Competitive Low Carbon Economy in 2050.* Brussels: European Commission.

———. 2013. *EU Over-Achieved First Kyoto Emissions Target, on Track to Meet 2020 Objective.* Available from https://ec.europa.eu/clima/news/articles/news_2013100901_en.

———. 2014a. *A Policy Framework for Climate and Energy in the Period from 2020 to 2030.* Brussels: European Commission.

———. 2014b. *Energy Efficiency and Its Contribution to Energy Security and the 2030 Framework for Climate and Energy Policy.* Brussels: European Commission.

———. 2015. *EU and Iceland Sign Agreement for Joint Fulfillment of Second Phase of Kyoto Protocol.* Available from https://ec.europa.eu/clima/news/articles/news _2015040101_en.

———. 2017a. *EU-China Summit: Moving Forward with Our Global Partnership.* Brussels: European Commission.

———. 2017b. *2020 Climate & Energy Package.* Available from https://ec.europa.eu/ clima/policies/strategies/2020_en.

European Council. 2007. *Brussels European Council 8/9 March 2007: Presidency Conclusions.* Brussels: European Council.

———. 2009. *Brussels European Council 29/30 October 2009: Presidency Conclusions.* Brussels: European Council.

———. 2014. *European Council (23 and 24 October 2014): Conclusions.* Brussels: European Council.

European Parliament. 2014. *European Parliament Resolution of 5 February 2014 on a 2030 Framework for Climate and Energy Policies (2013/2135(INI))*. European Parliament: Strasbourg.

European Parliament and Council of the European Union. 2009a. "Directive 2009 /29/EC of the European Parliament and of the Council of 23 April 2009 Amending Directive 2003/87/EC so as to Improve and Extend the Greenhouse Gas Emission Allowance Trading Scheme of the Community." *Official Journal of the European Union*. L 140/63-87.

———. 2009b. "Decision No. 406/2009/EC of the European Parliament and of the Council of 23 April 2009 on the Effort of Member States to Reduce Their Greenhouse Gas Emissions to Meet the Community's Greenhouse Gas Emission Reduction Commitments up to 2020." *Official Journal of the European Union* L 140/136-148.

———. 2009c. "Directive 2009/28/EC of the European Parliament and of the Council of 23 April 2009 on the Promotion of the Use of Energy from Renewable Sources and Amending and Subsequently Repealing Directives 2001/77/EC and 2003/30/EC." *Official Journal of the European Union*. L 140/16-62.

Fan, Gang, Nicholas Stern, Ottmar Edenhofer, Xu Shanda, Klas Eklund, Frank Ackerman, Li Lailai, and Karl Hallding, eds. 2011. *The Economics of Climate Change in China: Towards a Low-Carbon Economy*. Abingdon: Earthscan.

Fischer, Severin. 2014. "The EU's New Energy and Climate Policy Framework for 2030: Implications for the German Energy Transition." *SWP Comments 55 (December)*. Berlin: German Institute for International and Security Affairs.

Fisher, Dana R. 2003. "Beyond Kyoto: The Formation of a Japanese Climate Change Regime." In *Global Warming and East Asia: The Domestic and International Politics of Climate Change*, edited by Paul G. Harris, 187–205. London: Routledge.

Goldenberg, Suzanne. 2014. "Secret Talks and a Personal Letter: How the US-China Climate Deal Was Done." *Guardian*, November 12.

Goswami, Umi. 2015. "PM Narendra Modi to Meet Climate Experts' Council before US President Obama's Visit." *Economic Times*, January 15.

Government of Brazil. 2008. *National Plan on Climate Change*. Brasilia: Government of Brazil.

———. 2015. *Intended Nationally Determined Contribution towards Achieving the Objective of the United Nation's Framework Convention on Climate Change*. Brasilia: Government of Brazil.

Government of India. 2015. *India's Intended Nationally Determined Contribution*. Available from www4.unfccc.int/ndcregistry/PublishedDocuments/India%20First /INDIA%20INDC%20TO%20UNFCCC.pdf.

Griffiths, James 2017. "Can China Pick Up US Slack on Climate Change?" *CNN*, March 29.

Groenleer, Martijn L. P., and Louise G. van Schaik. 2007. "United We Stand? The European Union's International Actorness in the Cases of the International Criminal Court and the Kyoto Protocol." *Journal of Common Market Studies* 45 (5): 969–998.

Harris, Paul G. 2011. "Diplomacy, Responsibility and China's Climate Change Policy." In *China's Responsibility for Climate Change: Ethics, Fairness and Environmental Policy*, edited by Paul G. Harris, 1–21. Bristol: Policy Press.

Harrison, Kathryn, and Lisa MacIntosh Sundstrom, eds. 2010. *Global Commons, Domestic Decisions: The Comparative Politics of Climate Change*. Cambridge, MA: MIT Press.

Hatch, Michael T. 2003. "Chinese Politics, Energy Policy, and the International Climate Change Negotiations." In *Global Warming and East Asia*, edited by Paul G. Harris, 43–65. London: Routledge.

Hattori, Takashi. 2007. "The Rise of Japanese Climate Change Policy: Balancing the Norms of Economic Growth, Energy Efficiency, International Contribution, and Environmental Protection." In *The Social Construction of Climate Change: Power, Knowledge, Norms, Discourses*, edited by Mary E. Pattenger, 75–97. Aldershot: Ashgate.

Hindustan Times. 2017. "India Says Committed to Paris Climate Deal Despite Trump's Move to Withdraw US," June 2.

Hochstetler, Kathryn, and Eduardo Viola. 2012. "Brazil and the Politics of Climate Change: Beyond the Global Commons." *Environmental Politics* 21 (5): 753–771.

Hope, Mat. 2014. "Is India's Prime Minister, Narendra Modi, a Climate Leader?" *Carbon Brief*, November 25.

IEA. 2012. *CO_2 Emissions from Fuel Combustion: Highlights*. Paris: International Energy Agency.

———. 2015. *CO_2 Emissions from Fuel Combustion*. Paris: International Energy Agency.

IISD. 2011. "Summary of the Durban Climate Change Conference: 28 November–11 December 2011." *Earth Negotiations Bulletin* 12 (534). Available from http://www.iisd.ca/download/pdf/enb12534e.pdf.

Jeffreys, Elaine, and Gary Sigley. 2009. "Governmentality, Governance and China." In *China's Governmentalities*, edited by Elaine Jeffreys, 1–23. Abingdon: Routledge.

Jiang, Kejun. 2011. "Potential Secure, Low Carbon Growth Pathways for the Chinese Economy." CSIS Working Paper. Beijing: Energy Research Institute. Available from https://www.csis.org/analysis/potential-secure-low-carbon-growth-pathways-chinese-economy.

Jones, Bryan D., Frank R. Baumgartner, Christian Breunig, Christopher Wlezien, Stuart Soroka, Martial Foucault, Abel François, Christoffer Green-Pedersen, Chris Koski, and Peter John. 2009. "A General Empirical Law of Public Budgets: A Comparative Analysis." *American Journal of Political Science* 53 (4): 855–873.

Jordan, Andrew, and Tim Rayner. 2010. "The Evolution of Climate Policy in the European Union: An Historical Overview." In *Climate Change Policy in the European Union: Confronting the Dilemmas of Mitigation and Adaptation?*, edited by Andrew Jordan, Dave Huitema, Harro van Asselt, Tim Rayner, and Frans Berkhout, 52–80. Cambridge: Cambridge University Press.

Keidanren, Nippon. 2010. *Towards a Truly Effective International Framework to Combat Climate Change: Expectations for COP16*. Available from http://www.keidanren.or.jp /english/policy/2010/108.html.

Kindleberger, Charles P. 1973. *The World in Depression, 1929–1939*. Berkeley: University of California Press.

L'Aquila G8 Summit. 2009. *Responsible Leadership for a Sustainable Future, Declaration by Heads of the G8 Member States*. Available from www.mofa.go.jp/policy/economy /summit/2009/declaration.pdf.

Latvia and European Commission. 2015. *Intended Nationally Determined Contribution of the EU and Its Member States*. Riga: Latvian Presidency of the Council of the European Union.

Leiserowitz, Anthony, Edward Maibach, Connie Roser-Renouf, Geoff Feinberg, and Seth Rosenthal. 2014. *Climate Change in the American Mind: October 2014*. Edited by Yale University and George Mason University. New Haven, CT: Yale Project on Climate Change Communication.

———. 2016. *Politics and Global Warming, Spring 2016*. Edited by Yale University and George Mason University. New Haven, CT: Yale Program on Climate Change Communication.

Lewis, Joanna I. 2010. "The Evolving Role of Carbon Finance in Promoting Renewable Energy Development in China." *Energy Policy* 38 (6): 2875–2886.

Milner, Helen V. 1997. *Interests, Institutions, and Information: Domestic Politics and International Relations*. Princeton, NJ: Princeton University Press.

Modi, Narendra. 2011. *Convenient Action: Gujarat's Response to Challes of Climate Change*. Delhi: Macmillan Publishers India.

Morris, Jennifer, Sergey Paltsev, and John M. Reilly. 2012. "Marginal Abatement Costs and Marginal Welfare Costs for Greenhouse Gas Emissions Reductions: Results from the EPPA Model." *Environmental Modeling & Assessment* 17 (4): 325–336.

National Development and Reform Commission. 2012. *China's Policies and Actions for Addressing Climate Change*. Beijing: National Development and Reform Commission.

Nautiyal, Himanshu, and Varun. 2012. "Progress in Renewable Energy under Clean Development Mechanism in India." *Renewable and Sustainable Energy Reviews* 16 (5): 2913–2919.

Neslen, Arthur, and Frédéric Simon. 2012. "Poland Defies Europe over 2050 Low-Carbon Roadmap." *EurActiv*, December 14. Available from: http://www.euractiv.com/section/development-policy/news/poland-defies-europe-over-2050-low-carbon-roadmap/.

Nikkei Shimbun. 2015. "Ondanka-Gasu Sakugen No Shusho Shiji, Sanpo Ni Hairyo (Prime Minister's Instruction on GHG Gas Reduction, Considerations for Three Dimensions)," May 2.

Oberthür, Sebastian. 2011. "The European Union's Performance in the International Climate Change Regime." *Journal of European Integration* 33 (6): 667–682.

———. 2016. "Where to Go from Paris? The European Union in Climate Geopolitics." *Global Affairs* 2 (2): 119–130.

Oberthür, Sebastian, and Marc Pallemaerts. 2010. "The EU's Internal and External Climate Policies: An Historical Overview." In *The New Climate Policies of the European Union: Internal Legislation and Climate Diplomacy*, edited by Sebastian Oberthür and Marc Pallemaerts, 27–63. Brussels: VUB Press.

Oberthür, Sebastian, and Claire Roche Kelly. 2008. "EU Leadership in International Climate Policy: Achievements and Challenges." *International Spectator* 43 (3): 35–50.

Olson, Mancur. 1971. *The Logic of Collective Action: Public Goods and the Theory of Groups*. Cambridge, MA: Harvard University Press.

Paltsev, Sergey, and Pantelis Capros. 2013. "Cost Concepts for Climate Change Mitigation." *Climate Change Economics* 4 (Supplement 1): 1340003.

Paltsev, Sergey, Henry D. Jacoby, John M. Reilly, Qudsia J. Ejaz, Jennifer Morris, Francis O'Sullivan, Sebastian Rausch, Niven Winchester, and Oghenerume Kragha. 2011. "The Future of U.S. Natural Gas Production, Use, and Trade." *Energy Policy* 39 (9): 5309–5321.

Paltsev, Sergey, John M. Reilly, Henry D. Jacoby, Richard S. Eckaus, James McFarland, Marcus Sarofim, Malcolm O. Asadoorian, and Mustafa Babiker. 2005. The MIT Emissions Prediction and Policy Analysis (EPPA) Model: Version 4. In *MIT Joint Program on the Science and Policy of Global Change* Report 125. Available from https://globalchange.mit.edu/sites/default/files/MITJPSPGC_Rpt125.pdf.

Paltsev, Sergey, John M. Reilly, Henry D. Jacoby, and Jennifer Morris. 2009. "The Cost of Climate Policy in the United States." *Energy Economics* 31 (S2): 235–243.

Prabhu, Suresh. 2012. "Climate Change and Parliament." In *Handbook of Climate Change and India: Development, Politics and Governance*, edited by Navroz K. Dubash, 230–233. Abingdon: Earthscan.

Prime Minister's Office. 2008. *Low-Carbon Society and Japan (the Fukuda Vision)*. Tokyo: Government of Japan.

Project Team for Comprehensive Projection of Climate Change Impacts. 2008. *Global Warming Impacts on Japan—Latest Scientific Findings*. Tokyo: Ministry of the Environment Japan.

Putnam, Robert D. 1988. "Diplomacy and Domestic Politics: The Logic of Two-Level Games." *International Organization* 42 (3): 427–460.

Raghunandan, D. 2012. "India's Official Position: A Critical View Based on Science." In *Handbook of Climate Change and India: Development, Politics and Governance*, edited by Navroz K. Dubash, 170–179. Abingdon: Earthscan.

Rayner, Tim, and Brendan Moore. 2016. "Climate Policy." In *The EU Referendum and the UK Environment: An Expert Review. How Has EU Membership Affected the UK and What Might Change in the Event of a Vote to Remain or Leave?*, edited by Charlotte Burns, Andrew Jordan, and Viviane Gravey, 15–25. Available from http://ukandeu.ac.uk/wp-content/uploads/2016/04/Expert-Review_EU-referendum-UK-environment.pdf.

Reilly, John M., Jerry Melillo, Yongxia Cai, David Kicklighter, Angelo Gurgel, Sergey Paltsev, Timothy Cronin, Andrei Sokolov, and Adam Schlosser. 2012. "Using Land to Mitigate Climate Change: Hitting the Target, Recognizing the Trade-Offs." *Environmental Science & Technology* 46 (11): 5672–5679.

Reuters. 2017. "California and China Have Signed an Agreement to Develop Clean Energy Technology." *Fortune*, June 6.

Roman, Mikael, and Marcus Carson. 2010. *Shifting Ground: Brazil Tackles Climate Change and Deforestation, But Rapid Growth, Energy Needs Undermine Progress*. Stockholm: Stockholm Environmental Institute.

Rong, Fang. 2010. "Understanding Developing Country Stances on Post-2012 Climate Change Negotiations: Comparative Analysis of Brazil, China, India, Mexico, and South Africa." *Energy Policy* 38 (8): 4582–4591.

Schlossberg, Tatiana. 2017. "What to Know about Trump's Order to Dismantle the Clean Power Plan." *New York Times*, March 27.

Schreurs, Miranda A., and Yves Tiberghien. 2007. "Multi-Level Reinforcement: Explaining European Union Leadership in Climate Change Mitigation." *Global Environmental Politics* 7 (4): 19–46.

SEEG. 2014. *Greenhouse Gas Emission Estimate System 1990–2014*. Brasilia: Climate Observatory.

Sengupta, Sandeep. 2012. "International Climate Negotiations and India's Role." In *Handbook of Climate Change and India: Development, Politics and Governance*, edited by Navroz K. Dubash, 101–117. Abingdon: Earthscan.

Sethi, Nitin. 2016. "Paris Agreement to Constrain India's Energy Policy." *Business Standard*, September 28.

Silva, Eduardo Fernandez. 2012. "Rio+20 and Brazil's Policy on Climate Change." *Nature Climate Change* 2 (6): 379–380.

Skjærseth, Jon Birger. 2015. "EU Climate and Energy Policy: Demanded or Supplied?" In *The Domestic Politics of Global Climate Change: Key Actors in International Climate Cooperation*, edited by Guri Bang, Arild Underdal, and Steinar Andresen, 71–94. Cheltenham: Edward Elgar.

Skjærseth, Jon Birger, Guri Bang, and Miranda A. Schreurs. 2013. "Explaining Growing Climate Policy Differences between the European Union and the United States." *Global Environmental Politics* 13 (4): 61–80.

Skocpol, Theda. 2013. "Naming the Problem: What It Will Take to Counter Extremism and Engage Americans in the Fight against Global Warming." Paper presented at the Politics of America's Fight against Global Warming symposium, Harvard University, Cambridge, MA, February 14, 2013.

Skodvin, Tora. 2010. "'Pivotal Politics' in US Energy and Climate Legislation." *Energy Policy* 38 (8): 4214–4223.

Skodvin, Tora, Anne Therese Gullberg, and Stine Aakre. 2010. "Target-Group Influence and Political Feasibility: The Case of Climate Policy Design in Europe." *Journal of European Public Policy* 17 (6): 854–873.

Skovgaard, Jakob. 2014. "EU Climate Policy after the Crisis." *Environmental Politics* 23 (1): 1–17.

Sprinz, Detlef F., Håkon Sælen, Arild Underdal, and Jon Hovi. forthcoming. *The Effectiveness of Climate Clubs under Donald Trump. Climate Policy.* Available from https://doi.org/10.1080/14693062.2017.1410090.

Sprinz, Detlef F., and Tapani Vaahtoranta. 1994. "The Interest-Based Explanation of International Environmental Policy." *International Organization* 48 (1): 77–105.

Sprinz, Detlef F., and Martin Weiß. 2001. "Domestic Politics and Global Climate Policy." In *International Relations and Global Climate Change*, edited by Urs Luterbacher and Detlef F. Sprinz, 67–94. Cambridge, MA: MIT Press.

Stensdal, Iselin. 2012. "China's Climate-Change Policy 1988–2011: From Zero to Hero?" *FNI Report 9/2012.* Lysaker: Fridtjof Nansen Institute.

———. 2015. "China: Every Day Is a Winding Road." In *The Domestic Politics of Global Climate Change: Key Actors in International Climate Cooperation*, edited by Guri Bang, Arild Underdal, and Steinar Andresen, 49–70. Cheltenham: Edward Elgar.

Stocker, Thomas F., Dahe Qin, Gian-Kasper Plattner, Melinda Tignor, Simon Allen, Judith Boschung, Alexander Nauels, Yu Xia, Vincent Bex, and Pauline M. Midgley.

2013. *Climate Change 2013. The Physical Science Basis. Working Group I Contribution to the Fifth Assessment Report of the Intergovernmental Panel on Climate Change.* Cambridge: Cambridge University Press.

Stokes, Bruce, Richard Wike, and Jill Carle. 2015. *Global Concern about Climate Change, Broad Support for Limiting Emissions.* Washington, DC: Pew Research Center.

Tiberghien, Yves, and Miranda A. Schreurs. 2007. "High Noon in Japan: Embedded Symbolism and Post-2001 Kyoto Protocol Politics." *Global Environmental Politics* 7 (4): 70–91.

Tsebelis, George. 2002. *Veto Players: How Political Institutions Work.* Princeton, NJ: Princeton University Press.

UNFCCC. 2009. *Copenhagen Accord Appendix II.* Copenhagen: United Nations Framework Convention on Climate Change.

US Global Change Research Program. 2014. *National Climate Assessment.* Washington, DC: US Global Change Research Program.

Viola, Eduardo, and Matías Franchini. 2014. "Brazilian Climate Politics 2005–2012: Ambivalence and Paradox." *Wiley Interdisciplinary Reviews: Climate Change* 5 (5): 677–688.

White House. 2014. *US-China Joint Announcement on Climate Change.* Beijing: White House.

———. 2017. *Statement by President Trump on the Paris Climate Accord.* Washington, DC: White House Press Office.

WHO. 2016. *WHO's Urban Ambient Air Pollution Database—Update 2016. Version 0.2.* Geneva: World Health Organization.

WRI. 2014. *Climate Analysis Indicators Tool (CAIT) 2.0.* Washington, DC: World Resources Institute.

Wurzel, Rüdiger K. W., and James Connelly, eds. 2011. *The European Union as a Leader in International Climate Change Politics.* London: Routledge.

Ydersbond, Inga M. 2016. "Where Is Power Really Situated in the EU? Complex Multi-Stakeholder Negotiations and the Climate and Energy 2030 Targets." *FNI Report 3/2016.* Lysaker: Fridtjof Nansen Institute.

Yu, Hongyuan. 2008. *Global Warming and China's Environmental Diplomacy.* New York: Nova Science.

Zhang, Zhong Xiang. 2011. *Energy and Environmental Policy in China: Towards a Low-Carbon Economy.* Cheltenham: Edward Elgar.

8 Nonstate Actors in International Policy Making: The Kyoto Protocol and Beyond

Tora Skodvin

8.1 Introduction

Since the 1970s, we have witnessed a significant increase in the participation of nonstate actors in international policy-making processes. While fewer than four hundred nongovernmental organizations (NGOs) were registered in the UN system before 1970 (Willetts 2006), more than seventeen hundred NGOs were officially recognized and accredited within the UN system at the turn of the century (Willetts 2000). Today there are more than four thousand UN-accredited NGOs (UNDESA 2016). Current estimates of the total number of international NGOs vary, but this group now likely counts tens of thousands (Finger and Princen 1994; Tallberg 2010).

Nonstate actors make their mark on processes within all issue areas of international relations (Risse 2002; Tallberg 2010), but the increase is particularly evident in issues of international environmental and resource management (Betsill 2008). NGO participation in international climate negotiations reflects this trend: since the first meeting of the COP to the UNFCCC, the number of UN-accredited nongovernmental observers increased from 175 at COP 1 in 1995 to 1949 at COP 21 in 2015 in Paris (UNFCCC 2016b). At the Copenhagen meeting (COP 15) in 2009, there were about 1.3 nongovernmental observers for every state participant (party or observer). Since then, the number has decreased somewhat, but still almost 30 percent of all participants (state parties, state and nonstate observers, and media) were nongovernmental observers at COP 21 in Paris (UNFCCC 2016a).

Today, nonstate actors perform in a number of roles and serve a broad spectrum of functions in relation to international decision making and politics. On the one hand, they are often key providers of technical as well as political information of significant importance to state parties in their decision making. On the other hand, we find nonstate actors operating as resourceful lobbyists that use their human, technical, and material resources to influence international policy making according to their own goals in a broad spectrum of policy areas. Nonstate actors, moreover, operate at all levels of decision making from the local to the international and global. Policies developed at the international arena may very well be influenced by nonstate activities that have primarily taken place at the regional, national, and/or local levels.

It is difficult to do justice to this multifaceted nature of nonstate actors in international relations within the framework of this chapter. I focus on two key roles nonstate actors may serve in international policy making: (1) their role as advocacy or lobbying groups, whose main objective is to influence international policy making according to their own goals, and (2) the functions they may serve after international agreements have been made, particularly those related to enforcement of compliance. This dual focus enables us, first, to explore conditions for nonstate influence in general, and in the negotiations of the 1997 Kyoto Protocol in particular. The Kyoto Protocol constituted the core of the international climate regime for almost twenty years, from its adoption at COP 3 in 1997 until the adoption of the Paris Agreement at COP 21 in 2015. Second, this approach also permits a discussion of the role nonstate actors may play in inducing compliance through "naming and shaming." The bottom-up approach of the Paris Agreement combined with the lack of an enforcement mechanism enhances the significance of the functions nonstate actors may serve to enforce the agreement through various forms of stakeholder pressure.

The term *nonstate actor* refers to any actor that does not act on behalf of or represent a government. The term includes "transnational actors" (Risse 2002; Tallberg 2010) or "transnational advocacy networks" (Keck and Sikkink 1998), as well as NGOs. In my analysis of nonstate influence in the negotiations of the Kyoto Protocol, my key focus is on the competitive relationship between environmental and business groups both at the international and domestic levels as exemplified by domestic climate policies in the United States.

The analysis proceeds as follows: in the next section, analytical perspectives on nonstate influence in international policy making are discussed with a main focus on the exchange model. In section 8.3, this perspective is used to highlight key patterns of nonstate influence in the negotiation of the Kyoto Protocol with particular emphasis on the competition between nonstate actors and the significance of their strategy choice. With a point of departure in analyses of "naming and shaming" as a strategy to enforce international human rights treaties and norms, section 8.4 discusses the situation after the Paris Agreement and the potential function nonstate actors may serve to enhance compliance and as component in a process of norms transformation toward norm-based rather than interest-based behavior. Section 8.5 concludes.

8.2   Analytical Perspectives on Nonstate Influence in International Policy Making: The Exchange Model

The literature on nonstate actors is fragmented and diverse and has suffered from selection bias (Risse 2002). More recently, however, nonstate influence has been subjected to more systematic analysis in large-N studies, followed by the development of a more coherent analytical perspective to capture the diversity of nonstate actors on the international arena (Tallberg et al. 2013, 2014, 2015). With a point of departure in analyses of interest-group influence in domestic politics, Tallberg et al. (2015) suggest that an exchange relationship exists between state and nonstate actors in international policy making in which "decision-makers grant interest groups access to the policy process, while interest groups in return provide information that is useful to decision-makers" (Tallberg et al. 2015, 3; see also Bouwen 2002; Dür 2008; Gullberg and Skodvin 2011; Pappi and Henning 1998; Skodvin, Gullberg, and Aakre 2010).

Since the early 1970s, we have seen a development where nonstate actors increasingly are given access to international decision-making arenas, and that has puzzled scholars: Why would states surrender "the monopoly they previously enjoyed on participation and influence in international institutions" (Tallberg 2008, 2; see also Krasner 1995; Raustiala 1997)? Several scholars highlighted the question by pointing to resources nonstate actors can bring to bear on processes of international decision making and that may be used as leverage in their relationship with state actors on the international arena. Thus, Princen, for instance, suggests that "NGOs use their bargaining leverage first to gain access to decision-making ... and second to engage directly in the formation and reform of international institutions" (1994, 36). Resources suggested to contribute to NGO bargaining leverage include "expertise, grass-roots support, a transnational base or network, the ability to rectify information imbalances, and, above all, public legitimacy" (Princen 1994, 36). Similarly, Raustiala argues:

States have incorporated NGOs because their participation enhances the ability, both in technocratic and political terms, of states to regulate through the treaty process. The terms of that incorporation reflect the resources, skills, and domestic influence of NGOs: NGO participation provides policy advice, helps monitor commitments and delegations, minimizes ratification risks and facilitates signaling between governments and constituents. (1997, 720)

This relationship of interdependence between state and nonstate actors is crucial not only to understand why (some) nonstate actors are granted access to international decision-making arenas (Tallberg et al. 2014), but also to understand variations in the influence they exert. As argued by Tallberg et al. (2015, 2), "there is broad consensus in the existing literature that NGOs sometimes succeed in their efforts to shape [international organization] policies," while less scholarly attention has been given to why "NGOs sometimes [are] successful in influencing political decisions in global governance and sometimes not" (see also Skodvin and Andresen 2003; Rietig 2016).

Many scholars have pointed to the resources nonstate actors control to understand variations in their influence. Gulbrandsen and Andresen (2004, 58), for instance, distinguish between an NGO's "intellectual base" (including issue-specific knowledge and capacity to provide expert advice and analysis) and "political clout" (including membership, access to policy makers in positions, and financial resources) and emphasize that "resources are characteristics associated with an environmental organization that may or may not translate into political influence." An important point, however, is not only *which* resources nonstate actors control, but also the *relevance* of these resources to policy makers. The literature on the role of interest groups in domestic and regional (EU) policy making suggests that the relevance of a particular resource likely depends on the extent to which it helps policy makers fulfill their political goals, that is, to make good policy choices and to enhance the likelihood of their own reelection (or otherwise remain in power) (see, e.g., Bouwen 2002; Dür 2008; Gullberg and Skodvin 2011; Pappi and Henning 1998; Princen and Kerremans 2008; Skodvin, Gullberg, and Aakre 2010). This means that even if a nonstate actor can provide extremely specific and advanced expert knowledge, this resource is unlikely to be transformed into influence if the knowledge is viewed by policy makers as irrelevant for the particular decision situation they are in. Furthermore, influence is always exerted in relationships. Thus, the significance of a particular resource for nonstate influence is also relative. Even if a nonstate actor is "rich" on a particular resource, this resource is not necessarily convertible into influence if another actor with conflicting interests is "richer" on the same resource or is "rich" on a resource with higher relevance to policy makers. This points to the sometimes competitive relationship that exists between nonstate actors and the possibility that the failure of one nonstate actor to influence policy-making outcomes may be related to the success of another (Skodvin and Andresen 2003).

The image of states as gatekeepers of nonstate access at international decision-making arenas sometimes leaves the impression that states also control nonstate influence; that is, they *allow* nonstate actors to influence policy making in (wanted) directions. Raustiala, for instance, argues:

The biases of most major NGOs are fairly well known to the governments involved. The result is that governments gain reasonably accurate, efficacious, and creative policy advice from many independent sources, and are able to move these research costs "off-budget." (1997, 727)

In contrast, Tallberg et al. argue that there will always remain a risk of information bias given the costs for governments to control the information provided by interest groups, but that:

decision makers are likely to accept the remaining risk of bias, given the benefits of outsourcing information collection to interest groups. The result will be policy decisions that are different than if interest groups had not been involved. (2015, 3)

While analyses of nonstate actors in international policy making tend to primarily focus on what goes on at the international decision-making level, it is important to recognize that nonstate actors very well may have a significant impact on international policy making via the domestic political level. Risse-Kappen, for instance, suggests that domestic decision-making structures are "likely to determine both the availability of channels for transnational actors into the political systems and the requirements for 'winning coalitions' to change policies" (1995, 6; see also Gullberg and Skodvin 2011; Milner 1997; Skodvin 2007; Skodvin, Gullberg, and Aakre 2010). If nonstate actors can influence the domestic policies of parties that are pivotal in forming a winning (or blocking) coalition in support of (or against) a particular policy at the international level, nonstate actors may have significant impact on the spectrum of politically feasible policy options at the international level without ever having set foot at the international decision-making arena.

Whether or not an actor is "pivotal" depends, among other things, on the institutional setting within which decisions are made. Actor capabilities are always "filtered" through an institutional setting that may serve to empower some actors over others. Decision-making rules are of particular importance because they ultimately determine which policy makers have a decisive impact on decision-making outcomes (Underdal 1992). For nonstate actors, decision rules are significant in the sense that they determine the extent to which policy makers (for which nonstate resources are relevant) are also in a pivotal position in the decision-making system. A nonstate actor is less likely to exert influence if it controls a resource that is relevant to policy makers that are *not* in a pivotal position.

At the international level, decisions are often made by consensus or unanimity. This decision rule implies that all (state) actors are "pivotal" in the sense that they, by denying their support of a given proposal, can block that proposal from being adopted. In principle, therefore, nonstate actors may acquire influence in international policy making via the domestic level of any participating state party. However, even in international consensus-based policy making, some actors are more pivotal than others. For instance, international policies adopted in a consensus-based decision-making process typically reflect the position of the parties whose compliance is (most) critical for the success of the adopted policies. Thus, the United States is normally more pivotal in most issue areas than, say, Luxembourg, even if both states technically have veto power as a function of the consensus principle.

To what extent can this perspective on nonstate influence in international relations contribute to highlighting key patterns of nonstate influence in the making of the Kyoto Protocol?

8.3 Nonstate Competition and Strategy in the Negotiations of the Kyoto Protocol

Academic analyses of nonstate participation and influence in processes of international policy making often tend to treat the group of nonstate actors as if it were one unified group of actors with common interests that either have or do not have influence in confrontation with state actors. While nonstate actors may have a common interest in being heard and being granted access to international decision-making arenas, their substantive positions on a given issue area may be in conflict. In that sense, competition is often a key characteristic of the relationship between many nonstate actors. Moreover, while nonstate influence certainly is related to the extent of access nonstate actors enjoy and the resources nonstate actors control, a key determinant of nonstate influence is also the actor's own strategy to acquire influence (see, e.g., Rietig 2016). Both these aspects of nonstate influence in international decision making—the significance of competition and strategy—are illustrated in the negotiation process leading up to the adoption of the Kyoto Protocol.

During the early phases of the climate negotiations, the question of climate governance and greenhouse gas (GHG) emissions regulations pitted environmental and business interests against each other. In the development of the Kyoto Protocol, environmental organizations pursued four main goals via the umbrella organization for environmental NGOs, the Climate Action Network (CAN):

1. Twenty percent GHG emissions reduction targets from 1990 levels for industrialized countries
2. Strong review and compliance mechanisms
3. No admittance for industrialized countries to meet commitments through emissions trading
4. No credits for emissions absorbed by sinks (Betsill 2008, 58)

In contrast, the prospect of international regulations of GHG emissions rattled business interests, who saw such regulations as a potential threat to the welfare of their industries. As observed by Falkner, "despite transatlantic differences in corporate outlook and lobbying style, leading businesses from the major industrialized countries were largely united in opposing a strong international climate treaty with mandatory GHG emissions reductions" (2010, 107).

It should be noted, however, that at the time of the Kyoto negotiations, neither of these groups were completely unified around these positions. Among business interests, cracks had begun to appear between the fossil fuel industry that had dominated the climate business lobby in the early phase, and other industry groups, such as the insurance industry. Disagreements within the fossil fuel industry were also becoming apparent between the European and the American branches (Falkner 2010; Skjærseth and Skodvin 2003). Similarly, environmental groups disagreed on the question of emissions trading, with the Environmental Defense Fund being much more positive on emissions trading than most other environmental NGOs (Betsill 2008; Gulbrandsen and Andresen 2004). Despite some cracks in otherwise unified positions, the main competition for policy makers' attention and support nevertheless existed between, rather than within, environmental and business lobby groups.

Environmental and industry lobby groups both control resources that are important for policy makers. Environmental NGOs represent civil-society organizations whose participation in international policy making by some is seen as important to abate the "democratic deficit" of international institutions (Tallberg 2010). The extent to which environmental NGOs represent "the public" or "public opinion" is debatable, but they often represent a counterbalancing force in international policy making, not only to governments but also to business organizations. Environmental groups, moreover, often can provide expert information, which may be scientific and political, as well as technical, in nature. In some cases, environmental NGOs have local knowledge that may be useful for policy makers. The business community is often viewed as a privileged nonstate actor in international policy making because "corporations play a critical role in the economy, as providers of employment and sources of growth and innovation, and their consent is needed if profound changes to the working of the global economy are to be achieved through international regulation" (Falkner 2010, 101). Business and industry groups, moreover, also very often control technical competence that is essential in the development of solutions to collective problems.

Both environmental and business groups were, of course, granted access to the international climate negotiations process. In fact, the rules of procedure for the UNFCCC establish that "any body or agency, whether national or international, governmental or nongovernmental, which is qualified in matters covered by the Convention" may be admitted as observers at COP-sessions, "unless at least one third of the Parties present at the session object." Further, observers may, "upon invitation of the President, participate without the right to vote" (UNFCCC 1996). While the rules guiding nonstate access to the decision-making arenas of climate negotiations may be seen as liberal in the sense that organizations and networks that want to take part in the process generally are permitted to do so, observers are not granted access to the arenas where the negotiations actually take place and the decisions are made. In that sense, observers to climate negotiations generally have found the door to the actual negotiation room closed.

Nonstate actor strategies to circumvent this obstacle seem to have played a role for their ultimate success at influencing the decisions that were made, and the Kyoto negotiations display interesting differences between environmental and business groups in this regard. When the climate issue surfaced on the international political agenda, fossil fuel industry organizations participated in gradually increasing numbers at international negotiation meetings (Carpenter 2001). The US-based Global Climate Coalition (GCC), a major business organization through which the fossil fuel industry position on climate change was pursued, was accredited as observer to the international negotiation process. The organization was also granted a more direct channel of influence at the international level via sympathetic government delegations and representatives. Newell reports that "the fossil fuel lobbies have been able to advance their minimal action agenda during negotiations, through support for the negotiating position of oil exporting states such as Saudi Arabia and Kuwait" and members of both the GCC and of the other major (also US-based) fossil fuel lobby group during this phase of the process, the Climate Council. These "were reported to have drafted a number of US–Saudi amendments designed to stall negotiations on a protocol to the convention" (Newell 2000, 108) (for more details, see chapter 9 in this volume).

Still, representatives of the fossil fuel industry seem to have viewed the domestic channel as more effective for exerting influence. In an interview with Newell, Christoph Bourillon (formerly) of the World Coal Institute stated "most of the work has to be done on a national level before the negotiations, because governments go to New York or Geneva with a brief" (cited in Newell 2000, 102). Newell finds that "influence over the scope of the agenda depends in part on the ability of lobbyists to locate sympathetic individuals in government administrations who will articulate their interests in policy debates" (Newell 2000, 103; see also Falkner 2010). In the H. W. Bush administration, for instance, one such "gatekeeper" was White House Chief of Staff John Sununu, "who was in a position to decide which views on the costs of abatement action President Bush should be exposed to" and who could "gut legislation that threatened fossil fuel interests" (Newell 2000, 103). Another mechanism through which the fossil fuel lobby acquired influence at the domestic level was through the "revolving door," described by the Center for Responsive Politics[1] as the door "that shuffles former federal employees into jobs as lobbyists, consultants, and strategists just as the door pulls former hired guns into government careers" (Center for Responsive Politics 2012). For instance, John Schlaes, who was the director of the GCC, "also held a senior position in the executive office of the White House as director of communications under John Sununu" (Newell 2000, 107; see also Levy and Egan 1998).

In contrast, even US-based environmental organizations seem to have focused their lobbying efforts primarily at the international level. In interviews with Betsill, "some American ENGO representatives acknowledge that they erred in not focusing more directly on the domestic political arena in the United States during the Kyoto Protocol negotiations" (Betsill 2008, 64). While US environmental NGOs "spent countless hours" at the international arena, they "virtually ignored Congress and the general public; a void quickly filled by representatives of the fossil fuel industry who ultimately succeeded in framing the climate change issue in the United States" (Betsill 2008, 64). Agrawala and Andresen (1999) observe a trend in the United States that environmental NGO influence decreased concurrently with increased mobilization by the fossil fuel industry against GHG regulations. Skjærseth and Skodvin find support for this observation in that "Greenpeace-U.S. resigned from its efforts to lobby U.S. ratification [of the Kyoto Protocol] even before George W. Bush was elected president" (Skjærseth and Skodvin 2003, 170).

Ultimately, neither environmental nor business lobby groups had a very significant impact on the design of the Kyoto Protocol. Almost none of the goals pursued by the environmental NGOs were reflected in the text of the Kyoto Protocol. Rather, the Kyoto Protocol aimed for an approximate 5 percent reduction in GHG emissions from 1990 levels (compared with the environmental NGOs' goal of 20 percent), and both emissions trading and sinks were included in the agreement (despite environmental NGOs' opposition). Thus, Betsill (2008, 58) concludes, "ENGOs had little effect on the outcome of the Kyoto Protocol negotiations during the period from 1995 to 1997."

Given that the business and industry lobbies wanted to block the adoption of an international climate agreement in Kyoto, the fact that the Kyoto Protocol was adopted indicates that they did not succeed. On the other hand, it seems fair to assume that the anticlimate campaigns of the fossil fuel industry in the United States may have contributed to the fierce opposition against the Kyoto Protocol among a majority of legislators in the US Congress during this period. Ultimately, this opposition discouraged the Clinton administration to the extent that the agreement was never submitted to the Senate for advice and consent concerning ratification. Thus, even if they were unable to prevent the adoption of a climate agreement in Kyoto, the failure of the United States to ratify the Protocol represents a "mission accomplished" for the US-based fossil fuel lobby. Given the pivotal position of the United States, its ratification failure was an outcome with significant negative implications for the prospects for effective international mitigation of climate change in the years (and decades) to come.

Nonstate actors may serve key roles in international relations, not only as advocacy or lobbying groups, which has been discussed so far, but also in terms of the functions they may serve after international agreements have been made. With a key focus on the Paris Agreement, we now turn to the potential role nonstate actors may serve to induce enforcement and compliance.

8.4   After Paris

In the 2015 Paris Agreement, the "top-down" approach of the Kyoto Protocol is replaced by a "bottom-up" approach. Whereas the goals of the policies are decided collectively through negotiations, emissions targets for each individual party are decided by the party itself in "Nationally Determined Contributions" (NDCs). Moreover, while the Paris Agreement as such is legally binding, the NDCs are not.

A key factor for the agreement's success is the extent to which the pledged emissions reduction targets actually will be fully implemented. In many cases, particularly when collaboration problems such as the climate problem are concerned, compliance depends on the presence of enforcement measures (e.g., Aakre, Hovi, and Skodvin 2013). While a compliance mechanism is included in the Paris Agreement, it will almost certainly not include measures to actively discourage or sanction noncompliance. Rather, the Paris Agreement states explicitly that the compliance mechanism shall be "non-adversarial and non-punitive." Bang, Hovi, and Skodvin observe, "Because NDCs are not legally binding, enforcement through domestic legal action is also unlikely. Moreover, judged by Canada's experience after its withdrawal from Kyoto, we should not expect much informal enforcement by other members if a country fails to deliver on its NDC or even withdraws from the Paris Agreement" (2016, 4). This leaves stakeholder pressure as a main compliance mechanism, for example, by various civil society organizations and politicians at the domestic level and/or by national, transnational, and international NGOs.

The main tool of nonstate enforcement is "naming and shaming" (e.g., Hafner-Burton 2008). By drawing negative public attention to "normatively objectionable practices" target states suffer reputational damages that put pressure on them to alter this practice (Murdie and Urpelainen 2015, 355). Further, while nonstate actors "usually cannot directly punish states for what they regard as bad behavior," their "naming and shaming" can serve to "mobilize other actors, such as industrialized democracies or intergovernmental organizations, to punish their targets" (Murdie and Urpelainen 2015, 253). Naming and shaming is particularly associated with enforcement of international human rights treaties and norms, but it is also used in other issue areas such as environmental politics (Murdie and Urpelainen 2015).

While naming and shaming has received a fair amount of scholarly attention, evidence of its effectiveness is somewhat mixed. Hafner-Burton, for instance, has done a large-N study of naming and shaming in which she investigates whether the impact of "international publicity by NGOs, the news media, and the UN" is followed by a reduction in human and political rights violations (Hafner-Burton 2008, 690). She finds that "naming and shaming is not all cheap talk. On the one hand, governments named and shamed as human rights violators often improve protections for political rights after being publicly criticized.... On the other hand, naming and shaming rarely is followed by the cessation of political terror and, paradoxically, sometimes is followed by more" (690–691).

Naming and shaming is also seen as a key component in processes of norms transformation (Mitchell 2015; Solbakken 2016). Thus, Mitchell (2015) discusses the role of "norm entrepreneurs" in several historical incidents of norms transformation such as the end of slavery, the demise of colonialism and more contemporary examples such as the banning of land mines. "Norm entrepreneurs" are understood as actors (e.g., nonstate actors) "drawing attention to an existing social practice, prompting an explicit discussion of that practice, and doing so via a discursive strategy and framing that reflects a logic of appropriateness rather than a logic of consequences" (Mitchell 2015, 31). The question is whether such a norms transformation is possible for climate change, and particularly whether such a major change can be induced by the Paris Agreement (or even an amended version of the Paris Agreement).

While there have been efforts at naming and shaming in climate politics, effects of this strategy have been meager. As noted by Bang, Hovi, and Skodvin, "the risk of reputational costs does not seem to have significantly influenced the United States' decision not to ratify Kyoto 1, Canada's decision to withdraw from it, or the decision of countries such as Belarus, Japan, New Zealand, Russia, and Ukraine not to sign on to Kyoto 2" (2016, 6).

The apparent ineffectiveness of naming and shaming in climate politics is also a reminder of what is at stake in the climate issue and what is required for a norms transformation to take place: "The major obstacle to such an effort is the rejection of the underlying and implicit assumption that it is legitimate to trade off environmental protection—and particularly climate protection—against economic growth" (Mitchell 2015, 32). This is all the more difficult taking into consideration that GHG emissions are currently increasing the most in those developing countries, such as India, where significant and continuous economic growth is essential to lift a large share of the population out of poverty. Is it even ethically admissible for (likely Western) NGOs to "name and shame" a country, like India, for not taking radical measures to control its GHG emissions?

While nonstate actors may serve an important function in enhancing compliance with the Paris Agreement through naming and shaming, the effect of this strategy is uncertain. Nonstate actors' role may be seen in a longer-term perspective as an important component in a process of norms transformation toward norm-based rather than interest-based behavior. But even if a norms transformation in climate politics eventually does take place, will it do so in time to "prevent dangerous anthropogenic interference with the climate system" (UNFCCC 1992, art. 2)?

8.5   Concluding Remarks

The relationship between state and nonstate actors in international policy making is often characterized by exchange: nonstate actors provide decision makers with needed information in exchange for access to the decision-making process. Nonstate influence is assumed to be associated with nonstate actors' resources. The relationship between nonstate actors, however, is often characterized by competition. Thus, the failure of one nonstate actor to influence policy-making outcomes may be related to the success of another.

These mechanisms are illustrated in the negotiations leading to the adoption of the Kyoto Protocol, particularly in the competitive relationship that existed between the business lobby and environmental NGOs. The negotiations of the Kyoto Protocol also illustrate the significance of the domestic level for nonstate influence in international policy making. If nonstate actors influence the domestic policies of parties that are pivotal at the international level, they can exert influence on international policies without ever having set foot on the international policy-making arena. In the Kyoto negotiations, this is illustrated by the success of the fossil fuel industry's strategy to influence US climate policies. The anticlimate campaign of the fossil fuel industry in the United States likely contributed to US legislators' strong opposition to the Protocol, which ultimately led to the US failure to ratify the Kyoto Protocol.

With the 2015 Paris Agreement, a top-down approach is replaced by a bottom-up one. Combined with the lack of an enforcement mechanism, this enhances the significance of the role nonstate actors may play at the domestic level in inducing compliance through naming and shaming. As a strategy for enforcement of international human rights treaties and norms, however, naming and shaming has achieved mixed results. Nonstate actors could also play a role as norm entrepreneurs in a longer-term process of norms transformation on climate policies. The question remains, however, whether a transformation toward more norm-based behavior in international climate policies is possible at all, and in time to prevent "dangerous anthropogenic interferences with the climate system."

Notes

I gratefully appreciate comments to previous drafts from two anonymous reviewers, Matthew Paterson, Jon Hovi, and Detlef F. Sprinz.

1. The Center for Responsive Politics is a nonpartisan, independent and nonprofit US-based research group that "tracks money in U.S. politics and its effect on elections and public policy" (Center for Responsive Politics 2012).

References

Aakre, Stine, Jon Hovi, and Tora Skodvin. 2013. "Can Climate Negotiations Succeed?" *Politics and Governance* 1 (2): 138–150.

Agrawala, Shardul, and Steinar Andresen. 1999. "Indispensability and Indefensibility-The United States in the Climate Treaty Negotiations." *Global Governance* 5 (4): 457–482.

Bang, Guri, Jon Hovi, and Tora Skodvin. 2016. "The Paris Agreement: Short-Term and Long-Term Effectiveness." *Politics and Governance* 4 (3): 209–218.

Betsill, Michele Merrill. 2008. "Environmental NGOs and the Kyoto Protocol Negotiations: 1995 to 1997." In *NGO Diplomacy: The Influence of Nongovernmental Organizations in International Environmental Negotiations*, edited by Michele Merrill Betsill and Elizabeth Corell, 67–100. Cambridge, MA: MIT Press.

Bouwen, Pieter. 2002. "Corporate Lobbying in the European Union: The Logic of Access." *Journal of European Public Policy* 9 (3): 365–390.

Carpenter, Chad. 2001. "Businesses, Green Groups and the Media: The Role of Non-Governmental Organizations in the Climate Change Debate." *International Affairs* 77 (2): 313–328.

Center for Responsive Politics. 2012. *Revolving Door*. Available from https://www.opensecrets.org/revolving/.

Dür, Andreas. 2008. "Interest Groups in the European Union: How Powerful Are They?" *West European Politics* 31 (6): 1212–1230.

Falkner, Robert. 2010. "Business and Global Climate Governance: A Neo-Pluralist Perspective." In *Business and Global Governance*, edited by Morton Ougaard and Anna Leander, 99–117. London: Routledge.

Finger, Matthias, and Thomas Princen. 1994. *Environmental NGOs in World Politics: Linking the Local and the Global*. London: Routledge.

Gulbrandsen, Lars H., and Steinar Andresen. 2004. "NGO Influence in the Implementation of the Kyoto Protocol: Compliance, Flexibility Mechanisms, and Sinks." *Global Environmental Politics* 4 (4): 54–75.

Gullberg, Anne Therese, and Tora Skodvin. 2011. "Cost Effectiveness and Target Group Influence in Norwegian Climate Policy." *Scandinavian Political Studies* 34 (2): 123–142.

Hafner-Burton, Emilie M. 2008. "Sticks and Stones: Naming and Shaming the Human Rights Enforcement Problem." *International Organization* 62 (4): 689–716.

Keck, Margaret E., and Kathryn Sikkink. 1998. *Activists beyond Borders: Advocacy Networks in International Politics*. Ithaca, NY: Cornell University Press.

Krasner, Stephen D. 1995. "Power Politics, Institutions, Transnational Relations." In *Bringing Transnational Relations Back In: Non-State Actors, Domestic Structures and International Institutions*, edited by Thomas Risse-Kappen, 257–279. Cambridge: Cambridge University Press.

Levy, David L., and Daniel Egan. 1998. "Capital Contests: National and Transnational Channels of Corporate Influence on the Climate Change Negotiations." *Politics & Society* 26:337–362.

Milner, Helen V. 1997. *Interests, Institutions, and Information: Domestic Politics and International Relations*. Princeton, NJ: Princeton University Press.

Mitchell, Ronald B. 2015. The Problem Structure of Climate Change: Obstacles to Cooperation and the Need for a Discursive Transition (Working Paper).

Murdie, Amanda, and Johannes Urpelainen. 2015. "Why Pick on Us? Environmental INGOs and State Shaming as a Strategic Substitute." *Political Studies* 63 (2): 353–372.

Newell, Peter. 2000. *Climate for Change: Non-State Actors and the Global Politics of the Greenhouse*. Cambridge: Cambridge University Press.

Pappi, Franz Urban, and Christian H. C. A. Henning. 1998. "Policy Networks: More Than a Metaphor?" *Journal of Theoretical Politics* 10 (4): 553–575.

Princen, Sebastiaan, and Bart Kerremans. 2008. "Opportunity Structures in the EU Multi-Level System." *West European Politics* 31 (6): 1129–1146.

Princen, Thomas. 1994. "NGOs: Creating a Niche in Environmental Diplomacy." In *Environmental NGOs in World Politics: Linking the Local and the Global*, edited by Thomas Princen and Matthias Finger, 29–47. London: Routledge.

Raustiala, Kal. 1997. "States, NGOs, and International Environmental Institutions." *International Studies Quarterly* 41 (4): 719–740.

Rietig, Katharina. 2016. "The Power of Strategy: Environmental NGO Influence in International Climate Negotiations." *Global Governance: A Review of Multilateralism and International Organizations* 22 (2): 268–288.

Risse, Thomas. 2002. "Transnational Actors and World Politics." In *Handbook of International Relations*, edited by Walter Carlsnaes, Thomas Risse, and Beth A Simmons, 255–274. London: Sage.

Risse-Kappen, Thomas, ed. 1995. *Bringing Transnational Relations Back In: Non-State Actors, Domestic Structures and International Institutions*. Cambridge: Cambridge University Press.

Skjærseth, Jon Birger, and Tora Skodvin. 2003. *Climate Change and the Oil Industry: Common Problems, Different Strategies*. Manchester: Manchester University Press.

Skodvin, Tora. 2007. Exploring the Notion of Political Feasibility in Environmental Policy. In *Working Paper 2007:03: CICERO*.

Skodvin, Tora, and Steinar Andresen. 2003. "Nonstate Influence in the International Whaling Commission, 1970–1990." *Global Environmental Politics* 3 (4): 61–86.

Skodvin, Tora, Anne Therese Gullberg, and Stine Aakre. 2010. "Target-Group Influence and Political Feasibility: The Case of Climate Policy Design in Europe." *Journal of European Public Policy* 17 (6): 854–873.

Solbakken, Simen Sørbøe. 2016. *The Dynamics of a Green Transition. An Agent-Based Analysis*. Master's thesis in Political Science, Department of Political Science, University of Oslo.

Tallberg, Jonas. 2008. "Explaining Transnational Access to International Institutions." Paper Presented at the Annual Convention of the International Studies Association, San Francisco, March 26–29.

———. 2010. "Transnational Access to International Institutions: Three Approaches." In *Transnational Actors in Global Governance: Patterns, Explanations, and Implications*, edited by Christer Jönsson and Jonas Tallberg, 45–66. Basingstoke, UK: Palgrave Macmillan.

Tallberg, Jonas, Lisa M. Dellmuth, Hans Agné, and Andreas Duit. 2018. "NGO Influence in International Organizations: Information, Access and Exchange." *British Journal of Political Science* 48 (1): 213–238.

Tallberg, Jonas, Thomas Sommer, Theresa Squatrito, and Christer Jönsson. 2013. *The Opening Up of International Organizations: Transnational Access in Global Governance*. Cambridge: Cambridge University Press.

———. 2014. "Explaining the Transitional Design of International Organizations." *International Organization* 68 (4): 741–774.

Underdal, Arild. 1992. "Designing Politically Feasible Solutions." In *Rationality and Institutions*, edited by Raino Malnes and Arild Underdal, 221–254. Oslo: Scandinavian University Press.

UNDESA. 2016. *NGO Branch*. Department of Economic and Social Affairs of the United Nations. Available from http://csonet.org/.

UNFCCC. 1992. *United Nations Framework Convention on Climate Change*. New York: United Nations.

———. 1996. *UNFCCC Rules of Procedure, Article V, Rule 7, Paragraphs 1 and 2*. Edited by United Nations. Geneva: United Nations Framework Convention on Climate Change.

———. 2016a. *Observer Organization Statistics*. Available from http://unfccc.int/files /documentation/submissions_from_non-party_stakeholders/application/pdf /participation_break_down_cop1-cop_21.pptx.pdf.

————. 2016b. *Statistics about Observer Organizations in the UNFCCC Process.* Available from http://unfccc.int/parties_and_observers/observer_organizations/items/9545.php.

Willetts, Peter. 2000. "From Consultative Arrangements to Partnership: The Changing Status of NGOs in Diplomacy at the UN." *Global Governance* 6:191–212.

————. 2006. "The Cardoso Report on the UN and Civil Society: Functionalism, Global Corporatism, or Global Democracy?" *Global Governance* 12 (3): 305–324.

9   Business

Matthew Paterson

9.1   Introduction

Business is widely regarded as crucial in responses to climate change for a number of reasons. First, it accounts for substantial proportions of global greenhouse gas (GHG) emissions. Large multinational companies produce between them around 50 percent of global GHG emissions (for an elaborate analysis of this process, see Morgera 2004). Second, it is responsible for much of the investment which leads either to increased emissions or, potentially, to reduced emissions (Forsyth 2005). Investments in large energy projects typically are either largely private sector investments or organized through partnerships between public and private sectors. Technical innovation that drives the uptake of renewable energy and energy efficiency is organized through private sector or public-private partnerships. Third, these investments are also transnationally organized—so business actions have effects across borders. Business investments that might switch energy systems toward decarbonization or alternatively entrench "carbon lock-in" (Unruh 2000, 2002) will not be limited to single states, but might rather trigger changes across the global economy. So the actions of business are integral to the pursuit of decarbonization.

But business is not only important because of its role in shaping the investment patterns that are pivotal to the shift away from fossil fuels that is central to successful long-term responses to climate change. It has also been important in political terms because of its power in constraining, shaping, and driving the character of responses to climate change at a variety of levels, from global to local. This arises out of its more general power in the global economy, and perhaps more specifically its structural power within a capitalist economy (e.g., Jessop 1990). Because of its control over investment and production, states recognize the need to accommodate business preferences and this has clearly shaped the character and extent of responses to climate change, such as in the Kyoto Protocol, the Paris Agreement, other international agreements, national policy responses, or a range of subnational and transnational governance projects (see generally Falkner 2008; Newell and Paterson 2010; Pinkse and Kolk 2009; Schreuder 2009).

Nevertheless, business does not have homogenous interests in relation to climate change. A good deal of the politics of climate change thus plays out in terms of conflicts and coalitions among different sectors of business, that compete to get "the voice of business" regarding climate change defined in terms of their own sectoral interests and have become organized through different business international NGOs (BINGOs). This chapter starts with unpacking these different business interests regarding climate change and exploring how they have changed over time. After this, it will return to the question of business power in climate politics and governance, focused on how business has shaped and constrained the overall level of ambition in climate change action, on what types of policies have been introduced in response to business pressure or to accommodate business interests, and on how business has engaged in a wide range of "private governance" activities to govern climate change directly.

9.2   Theorizing the Role and Power of Business

Theoretically, it is useful to highlight two sorts of approaches within International Political Economy that give us conceptual resources to understand the power of business. The first is the historical materialist approach outlined by Rowlands (2001). The second is a neo-institutionalist approach that is more prevalent within comparative political economy (e.g., Hall and Soskice 2001), but that could be consistent with either a realist or a liberal institutionalist approach. In order to set the scene for what follows, I elaborate here on these two approaches to draw out their differences and implications for studying business in climate change politics.

For a historical materialist approach going back to the thought of Marx, the starting point is what is regarded as a certain number of structural features of capitalist societies. Central to all such accounts of capitalism as a social form, capitalist society is defined principally by a combination of the specific commodification of human labor—the emergence of wage labor as the principal means by which most people meet their subsistence needs—and the way that capitalists confront each other in competition in the marketplace. These fundamental features create a number of contradictory consequences. First, they generate endemic class conflict as wage laborers and capitalists face each other with antagonistic interests. Second, the interests of individual capitalists and those of capitalists collectively are in contradiction with each other. Specifically, individual capitalists tend to want to keep workers' pay to the minimum necessary to enable the reproduction of their labor power, while collectively, capitalists (at least once the productive capacity of society has got beyond the point where all production can be consumed by a minority of the rich) increasingly need wages to rise to facilitate consumption of the products of industry. Thus a tendency for underconsumption/overproduction is built into the structure of capitalist society. This tendency is used to explain the boom-slump cycles endemic to the history of capitalist society. At various points in a business cycle, the tendency produces a crisis of overproduction, an inability to realize profits, and a recession that shakes out productive capacity and "surplus labor" until profits can again be realized. Third, another feature of this dynamic is that capital tends, over time, to substitute labor for machinery, in order to reduce wage bills. This is one of the principal reasons why capitalist society is so enormously dynamic as a system, but it also exacerbates underconsumptionist tendencies as workers are made unemployed and wage levels are kept depressed as workers compete not only with each other but also with machinery.

Finally, and most immediately important to understanding the power of business, the modern state as a political institution has emerged that attempts simultaneously to secure the rule of capital (through the principal institutions of private property and contract, as well as through specific laws to discipline labor and through occasional violence and repression), to manage class conflict, and to secure the conditions under which accumulation might continue reasonably smoothly—specifically through intervention to mitigate the problems caused by capitalism's underconsumptionist tendencies.[1] Promoting economic growth or capital accumulation is therefore a fundamental imperative from which states cannot escape, and business derives its power from this structural condition that state managers face. Business power in climate politics derives from these structural conditions and the historically specific forms capitalism has taken at the moment climate change came on the agenda. Marxist analyses of climate change emphasize in this context the role of fossil energy in both capital accumulation and climate change (Clark and York 2005; Malm 2015) and thus the power of fossil fuel companies, as well as the role of neoliberalism and financialization in structuring responses to climate change (Klein 2014; Newell and Paterson 2010).

The institutionalist approach (for general accounts, see Hall and Taylor 1996; Lecours 2005; March and Olsen 1984) understands business power differently in at least two important ways. First, it is not rooted in a structural account of capitalist societies but rather in the specific sorts of resources—financial, technological, organizational—available to business actors. These enable business actors to pursue strategies to achieve their goals. Most writers in this perspective do, however, tend to regard business as a privileged actor—holding resources that other social actors (e.g., environmental NGOs) do not possess, and thus are politically powerful in their bargaining with states. Second, business power is understood as variable across different societies. While the Marxist approach does recognize the variation in capitalist formations, reflecting historically specific trajectories, the "varieties of capitalism" approach (Hall and Soskice 2001) arguably goes further in insisting on the nationally or regionally specific character of capitalisms. The variation is mostly understood in terms of different traditions of state-business relations, and thus the different "embeddedness" (a term drawn from Polanyi) of business in social and political institutions. A common distinction is made here between Liberal Market Economies and Coordinated Market Economies (LMEs and CMEs, respectively). In the former (notable examples are the United States, the UK, or Australia), states and businesses tend to have fairly antagonistic relations, with businesses regarding state intervention with hostility, and states seeking to regulate, where necessary, via strict legislative requirements. In the latter (e.g., Japan, Germany, or Sweden), states and businesses tend to have much more collaborative relations, and regulation frequently takes the form more of voluntary agreements, while businesses adapt themselves to pressure from states rather than resisting it. Indeed in some instances, key industries for climate change (in the energy sector) are under government ownership or control in CMEs. While inevitably oversimplifying these differences, they nevertheless help us understand the variations in the patterns of business activity over climate change as is shown below. A number of scholars have started exploring these "varieties of climate capitalism," showing important variations in state performance on climate change as a result of these different business-state interactions (Harrison and Mikler 2014; Lachapelle, MacNeil, and Paterson 2017; Lachapelle and Paterson 2013; Mikler and Harrison 2012).

But these two perspectives share a number of themes that they emphasize in their analyses of business-politics relations. They both point to the power of business actors to pursue their interests. This power can be understood in terms of all three of the standard "faces of power" (Lukes 1974). It is behavioral in that business is able to exert direct pressure on states to achieve their goals; it is structural in that states internalize expectations about business interests and needs in their decision making; and it is discursive or ideological in that key elements in business interests are internalized in broad social terms. Second, they would share a focus on, although not entirely a shared perspective on, the mobility of capital as a source of business power. Marxists might emphasize this more than institutionalists, suggesting that the globalization of financial capital is a particular source of structural power (e.g., Levy and Newell 2005), while institutionalists would emphasize the variety of and continued embeddedness of capital in distinct national economies (e.g., Gill 2002; Hirst and Thompson 1996; Weiss 1997). Third, although for different theoretical reasons, they would share a focus on the diversity of business interests both within and across economies (e.g., Falkner 2008; Van der Pijl 1998) and thus conflict among these different business interests is an important component of climate change politics. It is to this diversity and shifts over time that we now turn.

9.3 Business Interests Regarding Climate Change[2]

As suggested above, businesses have diverse interests in relation to climate change (see notably Levy and Newell 2005). Three broad sets of interests can be identified. Some anticipate being hurt by measures to limit GHG emissions. Conversely, others see opportunities in developing new technologies or investment strategies. Finally, some expect to be hit badly by climate change impacts (for a similar set of distinctions, see, e.g., Falkner 2008, 97–100). Table 9.1 outlines these positions and some of the industries that are associated with each, along with the BINGOs representing those positions.

These general interests can be seen to have broadly affected the positions of businesses in relation to climate change—the way they have lobbied governments, their preferences for different levels of action and types of policy, and so on. But the diversity of business positions also operates at a more

Table 9.1

Different business positions on climate change.

Position on Climate Change	Example Industries	Organizations Representing These Interests (Examples)
Climate change action as threat to interests	Coal, oil, heavy manufacturing, automobiles	Global Climate Coalition, Climate Council
Climate change action as opportunity	Renewable energy, energy efficiency, new insurance products (catastrophe bonds), finance (if policy is emissions trading)	International Emissions Trading Association, Carbon Markets and Investors Association, World Business Council for Sustainable Development, Climate Action Partnership
Climate change impacts as threat to interests	Insurance, some agriculture	UNEP Finance Initiative

nuanced level once we get to individual company responses. As Pinkse and Kolk (2009, 92–98), in particular, point out individual company strategies are affected not only by these general interests but also by three extra elements. They refer to these as the following:

• "External, issue-related factors," which include their physical location and thus vulnerability to climate impacts, their relations with specific governments, and broader social relations and pressures on them

• "Industry-related factors," such as the structure of competition between firms in a sector, the rates of growth, and the level of concentration in a sector

• "Company-specific factors," including their corporate culture and management perceptions, capacity for risk management, and the history of technological innovation and diversification (Pinkse and Kolk 2009, 93)

These factors all combine to mean that even firms within a specific sector may vary in their strategies toward climate change. To take a well-known example, oil companies have varied in their strategies toward climate change. All the oil majors were members of the Global Climate Coalition (GCC) through 1997, but from then on a split emerged, with the European major companies (Shell and BP, notably, but smaller European companies like Statoil have had similar approaches), leaving and developing more "constructive" engagement with policy makers. They accepted climate change as an important issue, and recognized the need for emissions reductions, while attempting to build up their portfolio in renewable energy such as wind and solar (at least for a time), as well as playing a leading role in developing emissions trading (Meckling 2011). BP notably attempted to rebrand itself for a while as "beyond petroleum," presenting itself as an innovative company seeking to contribute to a broad social decarbonization. While it has withdrawn from this level of ambition, it remains significantly less hostile to action on climate change than US-based companies such as Exxon or Chevron, which remained in the GCC much longer and still argue against emissions reductions and, at times, argue that there are many remaining scientific uncertainties that need to be resolved before action on climate change was justified. These difference in strategies are often accounted for in terms of firm-specific features such as different corporate cultures, different histories of innovation, and different access to natural gas on the one hand or oil sands on the other,[3] as well as external factors such as different histories of government-company relations in North America and Europe. These variations reflect the "varieties of capitalism" point made above, concerning the distinction between LMEs and CMEs. Among the latter, therefore, companies like Shell and BP (and even more government-owned industries) have tended to adopt cooperative relations with governments over climate change as opposed to the combative approach of a company like Exxon (for detailed comparisons of these companies' strategies, see Rowlands 2000; Skjærseth and Skodvin 2001).

Similar diversity can be found in other companies. Some insurance companies, for example, Munich Re or Swiss Re have been highly activist, while others are relatively inactive, and even at times ignore climate change. Again, a North American–European distinction can be made at a general level, although the distinction appears to have less to do with government-industry relations and more to do with different ownership structures: European companies are very large and the sector is highly concentrated, while in the United States companies are much smaller, often just operating in one state, and themselves are thus at times relatively dependent on one or two owners. European companies have more operating freedom than US ones (see, e.g., Paterson 2001).

Over time, the representation of business interests in relation to climate change has shifted. In the early period of climate negotiations, the GCC managed to present itself fairly successfully as "the voice of business" on climate change (see, e.g., Gelbspan 2004; Gelbspan and O'Riordan 1997; Leggett

1999; Newell 2000). Skodvin (see chapter 4 in this volume) details the activities of the GCC and there is no need to repeat them. But in the mid- to late 1990s the ability of the GCC to present itself as the single or primary voice of business started to fracture. Four processes unfolded to undermine its dominance.

First, some of the "sunrise" industries, representing renewables and energy efficiency interests in particular, began to become more organized. They had been attending climate negotiations from early on, but were always small compared with the GCC companies. However, they became progressively more organized during the 1990s. Nevertheless, their ability to gain a stronger voice has been dependent on the other two processes.

Second, the insurance companies, joined at times by other financial companies (banks worried about bad investments in climate-risky sites, like low-lying deltas or in hurricane zones), became organized during the 1990s. The major reinsurers, Munich Re and Swiss Re (the world's two largest reinsurers) and Lloyds of London, had made noises during the UNFCCC negotiations in 1991–1992 (Leggett 1999), and insurers were courted by Greenpeace International shortly afterward with a view to bring them into a coalition lobbying for emissions reductions (Paterson 2001).[4] In 1995 UNEP created an Insurance Industry Initiative to bring together insurers to generate action on climate change. While only a small number of companies were involved for most of the late 1990s, the work done in UNEP Finance Initiative (as it became later on) was an important background for the explosion of investor-led activities during the 2000s, notably the Carbon Disclosure Project (see below for details).

Third, some of the companies associated with the GCC left it. Early leavers were the European oil companies like BP and Shell, who left in 1997 and 1998, respectively, as well as automobile manufacturers (the US big three left in 1999–2000), and some major manufacturing companies like DuPont, who left in 1997. By 2000 the GCC was hemorrhaging members, and it shut down in 2002. Behind this shift were to an extent the differences in corporate culture and government-industry relations outlined above, which led to an increasing number of companies shifting position on climate change to being more proactive about emissions reductions. Notably, a number of companies started to realize business opportunities in energy efficiency and investment in renewable energy, as well as to respond to shareholder and broader social pressures for "responsible" behavior.

Fourth, once emissions trading and carbon offset markets had become entrenched as a central element in the policy response to climate change, many financial companies started to get interested in climate change as a business opportunity for both substantive investments (for example, in Clean Development Mechanism [CDM] projects) or simply in the financial aspects of emission trading. The three key moments here are the negotiation of the flexibility mechanisms in the Kyoto Protocol (see chapter 2 in this volume), the decision by the EU between 1998 and 2003 to use emissions trading (what became the EU Emissions Trading System [ETS]) as its main internal policy mechanism for meeting its Kyoto goals, and the EU's subsequent decision to link its ETS to the CDM, by enabling companies regulated under the EU ETS to purchase credits (certified emissions reductions, CERs) through the CDM and count them against their EU ETS obligations.

These decisions created very significant opportunities for a range of business actors who could benefit from these policies. These beneficiaries include the lawyers who draw up ETS and CDM contracts, the auditing firms that verify emissions calculations and proposals for CDM projects, the project developers themselves who gain an extra income stream for their projects, and the consultants who brought the whole process together or advised those getting into a new and unfamiliar line of business (e.g., Newell and Paterson 2010; Schneider, Hendrichs, and Hoffmann 2010). These latter have been particularly important in building CDM activities in many countries (e.g., Hultman et al. 2012; Kang and Park 2013; Pulver, Hultman, and Guimarães 2010). The firms regulated under the EU ETS also gain by having lower compliance costs in meeting their obligations. But the main beneficiaries are arguably the financial companies who engage in the direct and derivative trading in emissions allowances and credits. An elaborate secondary market has emerged in both the CDM and the EU ETS market (that still account for around 85 percent of trading in global carbon markets), with futures, options and swaps, as well as a smaller number of more complex financial instruments, emerging. Some of the world's largest financial houses, such as Merrill Lynch or Barclays Capital, are highly involved in this trading. As a result of both the policy design itself and the entrepreneurial activities of these firms, carbon markets were the fastest growing financial markets in the 2000s, at least through to the onset of the recession in 2009.

Business has engaged in promoting emissions trading since at least the emergence of the Kyoto Protocol (see also Meckling 2011). In 1997 the International Emissions Trading Association (IETA) was formed, as an association both of firms that might be regulated by emissions trading systems, and of those involved in the trading and investment itself. IETA has played a significant role in shaping the design of emissions trading systems, as well as lobbying hard in relation to questions of reform in the CDM processes. In 2007 the Carbon Markets and Investors Association was formed, which represents only trading firms, partly out of a recognition of the different interests of regulated firms and traders (Paterson 2012).

The emergence of these different sectors has created the sort of diversity of business interests represented in international climate change politics. This shift can be explained in a variety of ways. One prominent one from within both perspectives outlined above would be to focus either on fractions of capital (Newell and Paterson 2010; Paterson 2012), on business conflict between specific sectors (Falkner 2008; Meckling 2011), or on different national business strategies.

The notion of fractions of capital would highlight in particular the differences between finance, manufacturing, and raw materials extraction as forms of capital accumulation. In the early period, the two latter fractions (notably oil and coal, automobiles and heavy industry, including electricity) issues. Then a shift occurred which should be understood principally in terms of the emergence of financial interests in climate politics, initially with the insurers. It was consolidated once emissions trading becomes the policy of choice, combined with the structural dominance of finance within neoliberal forms of capitalism (Newell and Paterson 2010). The notions of business conflict would have a similar broad narrative as to the conflicts between different sectors but would not situate these sectors in relation to broad structures of capital accumulation, but conversely would place more emphasis on the nuances of different interests of specific sectors.

But the institutionalist perspective, in its "varieties of capitalism" form, would explain the shift in terms of conflicts between LMEs and CMEs. They would point to the US dominance of early business activism surrounding climate change, and how the strategies adopted reflected the combative traditions of state-business interaction prevalent in LMEs. Then, as businesses from Europe and Asia started to become active in the mid-1990s, they brought with them the more collaborative and adaptive approaches from CME countries. For example, in Japan, the Keidanren, the main business organization, developed a set of voluntary GHG targets for its members in 1997, reflecting this sort of relation with government—avoiding direct regulation by developing industry self-regulation (Pinkse and Kolk 2009, 35).

Broadly, one can understand this history as a shift from "threat" to "opportunity" in how business has interpreted climate change (Falkner 2008, 99; Newell and Paterson 2010, chap. 3), although both interpretations of the implications of climate change are still represented, as evidenced by the recurrent backlashes in the United States against action on climate change in particular. The nature of the opportunities that climate change presents, however, are themselves diverse, impeding the emergence of a homogenous view from "progressive" business about the level and type of action on climate change that should be pursued. Some firms see opportunities in specific technologies, others in broad adoption of energy efficiency, others simply in the financial aspects of carbon markets. Others are still adopting positive noises about climate change while dragging their feet about the implementation of measures to mitigate it.

9.4 Business and International Climate Governance

Despite the diversity of business interests and strategies regarding climate change, it has had a number of important effects on international climate change governance. The strategies adopted by business are therefore important to determining climate policy outcomes in three important ways that are explored in the chapter. First, it has been important in shaping the overall level of ambition that policy makers can achieve, at various levels from local to global. Second, it has been powerful in shaping the types of policies that emerge, as businesses seek to promote policies that are consistent with business interests and prevent from emerging those that they disfavor. Third, in many contexts, business has started to be able to develop transnational climate change governance directly, only loosely connected to governmental action (see section 9.5). I now turn to these three in turn.

9.4.1 Shaping the Level of Ambition

First, it is important to shape the overall level of ambition that policy makers can achieve, at various levels from local to global. The inadequacy of existing action by states individually or collectively is well known. The international process has only been able to generate minimal action to limit the rate of global emissions growth, and the gap between that action and what is usually regarded to be required to limit climate change to the 2°C that is now routinely regarded as a desirable target (let alone the 1.5°C included in the Paris Agreement as an aspirational goal) is enormous: the International Energy Agency's projections of future fossil energy consumption and thus GHG emissions suggest a world that is 6°C warmer, unprecedented in human history (IEA 2011). Only a few states have been able to develop plans that have some chance of leading to decarbonization and even there the progress does not always match the ambition (see chapter 7 in this volume).

There are lots of reasons for this, notably the exceptionally complex nature of the collective action problem involved in coordinating the actions of all the world's states to completely transform the global energy economy. But the role of business has also been important in limiting this ambition and blocking progress, both because of the role of business in shaping a broad discourse about overriding imperatives for states (economic growth, notably) and because of lobbying that shapes the incentives of states to collaborate with each other. This is arguably the case even despite the shifts in business activity, as argued by Buxton (2016) and Spash (2016) in relation to the Paris Agreement.

First, the impacts of emissions reductions on economic growth have been more or less universally taken as the primary consideration in determining the level of abatement that is considered. All states, industrialized or developing, have focused almost wholly on GDP impacts when considering climate policy action. While this can be seen to reflect broader concerns with societal welfare and state legitimacy, it is also the case that maintaining the conditions for growth is fundamentally about maintaining the conditions for profitable investments by business in general. To the extent that climate policy measures increase energy prices, these may well have significant impact on a range of businesses that see their materials and process costs go up, and may dampen consumption of a range of goods and services. So this is a structural background condition within which the importance of business in more or less all states limits the scope for climate policy intervention. In most states, and despite rhetoric about "ecological modernization," it is still routinely assumed that climate policy intervention entails limiting the rate of GDP growth.

Second, in a number of contexts, businesses have lobbied actively to prevent the emergence of climate policy measures. The activities of the GCC discussed above have been particularly important, although not the only instance. A particularly important effect of the GCC was its importance in the United States during the run-up to the Kyoto Protocol, with significant pressure both through direct lobbying and through advertising campaigns and "Astroturf" groups. These contributed to the unanimous adoption of the Byrd-Hagel resolution in the US Senate that effectively prevented any possibility of US ratification of the Kyoto Protocol. US corporate funding of neoconservative think tanks has also been crucial to those organizations maintaining the pressure on climate policy in that country (and by extension internationally, given the particular importance of the United States to global climate policy) (e.g., Jacques, Dunlap, and Freeman 2008). While the proportion of businesses that are still actively hostile to climate policy has declined over time (see above), those that remain have nevertheless been very effective in continuing to prevent ambitious action in the world's most powerful state and by extension globally.

The variation within capitalist organization also plays an important role here. Among industrialized countries, LMEs have had significantly poorer performance in terms of the trajectory of their emissions than CMEs, even controlling for other relevant variables (Lachapelle and Paterson 2013). This reflects in part the point made above that in CMEs, major businesses anticipate and adapt more to climate policy than in LMEs, where they tend to be more antagonistic.

9.4.2 Shaping the Types of Policies

Second, and perhaps more important, business interests have both directly and indirectly affected the character of the policies that have been implemented to respond to climate change. Most prominent of these have been the emergence of carbon markets—both cap and trade and offset markets—as a centerpiece of many states responses as well as of the Kyoto Protocol. While the Kyoto Protocol was in crisis and no successor treaty was in place to come into force in 2012, it was for a long time not clear if carbon markets would play a role in a future climate agreement (e.g., Stephan 2012). The CDM was temporarily propped up by the EU and the Durban Platform established at COP17 in 2011. There was also much activity to promote the idea of markets for REDD+ in a future agreement. In the end, the Paris Agreement had more mention of carbon markets than many expected. The Paris

Agreement (UNFCCC 2015, art. 6) leaves the door open for the development of new markets, envisaging trading of "internationally transferred mitigation outcomes," but how this will be institutionalized is far from clear.

The story of the relationship between business interests and carbon markets is complex. Meckling (2011) suggests that business coalitions were central to the emergence of emissions trading in the climate regime. Others, however, suggest the link is more indirect (e.g., Newell and Paterson 2010; Paterson 2012). They suggest that the emergence of carbon markets was a confluence of a number of factors in which direct business activism played a relatively minor role. Only in the UK pilot scheme did business play a very direct role in shaping the political debate in favor of emissions trading (Paterson 2012). Elsewhere, such as in the United States, the Kyoto negotiations, the EU, the Regional Greenhouse Gas Initiative (RGGI) in the northeast United States, New Zealand (Bullock 2012), or in emerging carbon markets in Japan, South Korea, China, or India, a general ideological preference for markets was diffused through transnational policy networks (Paterson et al. 2014). Most of the actors involved are better characterized as policy experts working in think tanks, research institutes, government agencies, and some in private sector organizations (either individual firms such as BP or via consultancy firms).

At most individual venues, the dynamic seems to have been led by relatively small groups of enthusiastic officials. While this could be explored in other contexts such as Japan or South Korea, the EU is illustrative and the case on which there is the most research. In the EU, the shift to emissions trading was triggered by an important shift in personnel in the Environment Directorate, with a group of three or four individuals, characterized by Skjærseth and Wettestad (2008) as the "Bureaucrats for Emissions Trading," or BEST group, moving into their posts in early 1998, directly after the Kyoto negotiations, and pushing hard for the development of emissions trading (ET) as a core part of EU climate policy. Business interests, however, did not lobby hard directly in the development of the EU ETS (Paterson 2012).

Nevertheless, the emergence of ET and carbon-offset markets cannot be understood without reference to the power and interests of business actors. It needs to be understood in terms of notions of structural or discursive power—that those actors developing ET understood implicitly that a range of business interests would benefit from ET as a policy design and that this would make it relatively easy to sell ET politically as a climate policy compared with other proposals on the table, notably a carbon tax and simple direct regulatory measures. European business did lobby extremely hard against an EU-wide carbon tax (Newell 2000; Paterson 1996).

These benefits are primarily in relation to two groups of actors. First, those firms regulated under ET would have significantly lower compliance costs than with direct regulations, and more regulatory flexibility than for a carbon tax. They would be able to make decisions about whether or not to reduce emissions or buy permits, about what sorts of strategies to use to reduce emissions, and so on. Some would be able to make money from the sale of emissions permits if they found it relatively cheap to reduce emissions compared to their competitors or to firms in other sectors. They may also be able to get windfall profits either because of the information asymmetry between them and regulators, or because they can pass on costs directly to consumers—outcomes that have certainly occurred in the EU ETS (Sijm, Neuhoff, and Chen 2006; Skjærseth 2010).

In the UK during the 1990s, there was an active business network promoting emissions trading for precisely these reasons (Paterson 2012). International associations like IETA have similarly promoted ET using the same sorts of arguments.

But there was a second group that has also benefited from carbon markets as a climate policy, which is the financiers who organize the trading and investment via these markets. These industries have seen an entirely novel financial market grow, worth US$142 billion in 2010, and have experienced roughly a doubling in size every year since 2005, up until the recession of 2009 onward (Linacre, Kossoy, and Ambros 2011, 9). This figure measures only the size of the financial trading involved; beyond that are the legal contracts, the project developers, the verifiers, and others, who found entirely novel lines of business being created.

Neither of these groups of beneficiaries has lobbied hard for the creation of carbon markets. Indeed in many contexts their lobbying started only after the markets were already created—the lobbying by IETA of the CDM administrative system, to get it "streamlined" in IETA's view is a case in point. However, policy makers clearly implicitly understood that these policies would create vested interests in climate policy and thus could sustain a virtuous policy cycle, enabling policy makers to overcome opposition from other business groups. As carbon market policies were developed from the late 1990s onward, they saw the emerging enthusiasm of market actors for these policies, recognized their potential, and this sustained the momentum for policy development. For a more elaborate description of this process, see Paterson (2012) and also Meckling (2011), who, however, places more emphasis on business lobbying than the interpretation offered here. The UK is perhaps paradigmatic: UK policy makers recognized, implicitly for the most part but occasionally explicitly, that developing the UK pilot scheme would give the City of London a sort of first-mover advantage in developing financial strategies around carbon markets. London rapidly became and remains absolutely dominant in carbon markets—well over half of all carbon market trades are organized in that city's financial district.

Carbon markets are not the only form of climate policy that has been designed to promote business interests. Another aspect has been the way that technological innovation has been promoted. Here, the United States is perhaps paradigmatic. While formal legislation on climate change has been stymied in the US federal system, the United States has developed an elaborate range of measures to promote technological innovation to limit emissions. These measures typically operate through government-funded research institutes, either in universities or directly government operated, which are mandated to work closely with private sector organizations in the development and uptake of clean energy technologies. These initiatives were given a huge lift by the stimulus packages in the wake of the financial crisis and recession from 2008 onward. In the US case, this pattern is mostly the legacy of the military-industrial complex form of state intervention to maintain US military dominance, then added to by the sorts of intervention developed in the Reagan era in response to fears about decline in US competitiveness. Business now benefits from huge subsidies in technological innovation from federal funds, which since the Clinton administration has increasingly been turned to address the question of climate change and clean energy development (for an elaborate analysis of this process, see MacNeil 2013; MacNeil and Paterson 2012). Sectors that have seen significant activity in this regard include the focus on Carbon Capture and Storage, the emergence of smart grids in electricity markets, and geo-engineering or solar radiation management. In all of these areas, the focus on new technologies to reduce emissions or otherwise limit the impacts of climate change fosters the interests of specific firms and particular relationships between states and firms that attempt to generate a spiral of technological innovation, investment, and the deployment of the technology.

9.5   Private Climate Governance

The third role of business in international climate change governance has been in its initiatives to develop climate governance directly, either on its own, in partnership with environmental nongovernmental organizations (ENGOs) of various sorts (see also chapter 8 in this volume), or in public-private partnership with governments. Since the early 2000s, there has been a veritable explosion of these initiatives.[5] A number of common explanations are that business organizations may be trying to step into the gap provided by the absence of interstate governance in order to use their market or investor power to shape more adequate responses to climate change. Conversely, they may be attempting to either forestall state or interstate regulation by providing self-regulation as an alternative, or attempting to make sure that (inter)state regulation follows practices already established (such as carbon reporting rules) in the private sector. Finally, they may be acting to secure club goods—benefits to the participating firms, such as access to particular markets, that are not available to nonparticipating firms (Andonova 2010). Of course all these dynamics may be operating in specific instances.

9.5.1   Investor-Led Governance

Three specific areas where such governance activities are particularly prominent are worth highlighting. First, institutional investors have developed a set of initiatives to develop reporting and disclosure systems for GHG emissions by other firms. The two best known of these are the Investor Network on Climate Risk (INCR) and the Carbon Disclosure Project (CDP) (on these generally, see Harmes 2011; Kim and Lyon 2011; Kolk, Levy, and Pinkse 2008; MacLeod and Park 2011; Newell and Paterson 2010, 60–77).

The logic of these initiatives is that the organization concerned sends a survey to companies requesting information on their GHG emissions, their exposure to climate risks, and their exposure to climate policy risks. The CDP, for example, sends such a survey annually to the largest companies listed globally, such as the S&P500 or the FTSE500, as well as to companies within specific country contexts. The request states that it is on behalf of the CDP signatories that are in effect a group of the world's largest investors. In 2011, for example, the CDP claimed it was backed by 551 companies collectively holding US$71 trillion of assets (Carbon Disclosure Project 2011), representing around 90 percent of all assets under management by institutional investors.[6] The clear intent is to display a sense of investor power as a means of pressuring companies first into reporting their emissions and climate risk exposures, with a secondary effect being either that management starts to change its practices in this area, or that investors may seek to exert other pressure more directly either via management or via investment practices that punish high-carbon or recalcitrant firms. The CDP has also more recently branched out into specific reports—such as reports on water as a specific climate risk that firms may be exposed to, or extending the scope of reporting to include companies' supply chains rather than simply direct emissions.

Reporting rates to the CDP have become very high—81 percent of companies in the Global500 report responded to the survey (Carbon Disclosure Project 2011, 9). Hopes for the CDP have been very high among those involved. Nevertheless it would be impossible to say that to date the CDP has definitively led to emissions reductions. Two issues limit its effectiveness to date. First is the accuracy and comparability of reporting practices by companies. If investors were to use the information to either pressure management or switch investments, they need to know that the reporting is consistent and reliable across firms. There have been a number of reporting initiatives, notably within the International Organization for Standardization and in the WRI/WBCSD-developed Greenhouse Gas Protocol (on the latter, see Green 2010). A large number of firms reporting now use the GHG Protocol in developing their responses to the CDP. Nevertheless, the reports remain not sufficiently standardized to help investors. The CDP is currently working with others through an organization called the Carbon Disclosure Standards Board to develop reporting rules that are similarly robust as regular accounting standards (Thistlethwaite 2011).

Second, and perhaps more fundamental, is the disconnect between investors' participation in the CDP and their actual investment practices (Harmes 2011). There are two issues. On the one hand, large institutional investors are complex organizations and the parts that participate in the CDP or INCR may have no authority or significant influence over those making the day-to-day investment decisions. There is little evidence that investment managers have shifted their practices to take account of carbon disclosure reporting. On the other hand, arbitrage (short-term investment practices to profit from small but rapid changes in relative share prices between different assets) is pervasive in financial markets, such that if CDP members started to shift investments in response to fears about a company's climate risk exposure or carbon intensity in such a way as to reduce that company's share price, other investors not sensitized to climate risks would simply see the company's shares as undervalued, buy them up and the share price would be restored (Harmes 2011). The incentive effect on the company to manage its carbon or climate risks better would not thus operate.

Nevertheless, there is more evidence that the CDP has had more effect on company management through the information that CDP reporting has produced for managers. Certainly, the CDP has showcased a number of companies where this effect seems to have occurred, such as Walmart, which has innovated in terms of the carbon management of its supply chain, or the Dutch-based delivery company TNT, which has worked heavily on its vehicle fleet to maximize fuel efficiency of its operations (Newell and Paterson 2010).

9.5.2   Carbon Market Certification

The second area where business has engaged in direct climate governance is in their focus on developing certification systems in carbon offset markets. These are systems through which someone developing a carbon offset project can claim that their project does in fact reduce emissions. They involve all the same sorts of processes involved in getting a CDM project approved—the development of a project design document, the validation of the claims in that document, and the verification of emissions reductions after the project is developed (see chapter 2 in this volume). Largely, but not solely, on the back of the CDM, a "voluntary carbon market" emerged with companies purchasing carbon credits not for compliance in the EU ETS or elsewhere but for a mix of strategic, Corporate Social Responsibility, and simple "green marketing" reasons (see Bayon, Hawn, and Hamilton 2007; Newell and Paterson 2010).

There are now around twenty certification systems in operation. They have emerged to fill particular niches—some deliberately exclude all projects except in renewable energy and energy efficiency (such as the Gold Standard) while others focus specifically on forestry and on broad sustainable development benefits (the Climate Change and Biodiversity Alliance, or Social Carbon, for example). While some of these systems are developed by environmental or development NGOs, many have been developed by business groups, and most of these involve some sort of collaboration between business and ENGOs. The Social Carbon standard, for example, was produced by a collaboration between the Brazilian ENGO called Social Carbon and the carbon market company Cantor CO2e. IETA initiated the development of what has become one of the most widely used systems, the Voluntary Carbon Standard (VCS), which it did in collaboration with the Climate Group, an ENGO dedicated to persuading companies and cities to develop carbon reduction strategies. In the carbon market certification arena, there is a reasonable amount of evidence that businesses have developed standards to compete with those developed by ENGOs on their own, much like in the forestry standards area (Bumpus and Liverman 2008; Lovell 2010; Lovell and Liverman 2010).[7]

The legitimacy and effectiveness of carbon market certification is also contested. There is good evidence that over time progressively more project developers use certification systems and third-party verification processes. There is also some evidence that developers are using, or purchasers are requiring, "more stringent" certification systems, and that such systems receive a higher market price than "laxer" ones. But these questions are also bound up more generally with the contested legitimacy of carbon offsetting per se (see Bumpus and Liverman 2008; Lohmann 2006; Newell and Paterson 2010; Paterson 2010; Smith 2007).

9.5.3 Technology Partnerships

Third, there is a rapidly developing number of public-private partnerships operating transnationally in relation to climate change (Andonova 2010; Bäckstrand 2008; Kolk, Pinkse, and Van Houten 2010; Pattberg 2010). Many of these partnerships on climate change focus on the development of specific technologies to reduce emissions. They focus, for example, on eliminating methane losses in natural gas production and distribution in the Methane2Markets partnership (see De Coninck et al. 2008) or the promotion of renewable energy and energy efficiency partnership (REEEP) (see Parthan et al. 2010), in general, or in relation to electricity production, more specifically the Green Power Market Development Group (see Andonova 2010).

9.6 Conclusion

This chapter has focused on the main ways that business is connected to international climate change politics and governance. It has shown the power of business to shape the extent and types of policies that governments adopt, both individually and collectively, as well as to generate novel types of governance initiatives themselves. It has shown that for the most part, business interests have served to constrain the ambition of climate mitigation efforts, as continued corporate lobbying both at national and international levels has served to constrain the ambition of most states as well as be able to focus on particular states in order to undermine action in multilateral fora relying on consensus rules. It has also shown that they have directed such efforts particularly toward the commodification of carbon in carbon markets, resulting in the flexibility mechanisms in the Kyoto Protocol and the expansion of ETS and carbon offset systems since then.

Nevertheless, businesses do not have homogenous interests in relation to climate change. There are plenty of businesses who are now actively working for more ambitious climate change mitigation efforts and who see business opportunities in the decarbonization of the global economy. Such efforts have in some states led to the emergence of pro-decarbonization coalitions that have sustained the political momentum toward emissions reductions. This is the case more in states with a tradition of collaborative relationship between states and business than in more laissez-faire states (Lachapelle and Paterson 2013). Many of these businesses have also become involved in private governance initiatives to attempt to pursue decarbonization transnationally, either bypassing or working in complementary fashion to state policy and multilateral processes. It remains, however, an open question whether the nature of capitalist economies and the power of business with them could lead to this result in all states or could deliver the sociotechnical transformation involved in decarbonization.

The chapter has also outlined theoretically how we might understand the ability of business to shape responses to climate change. Given that climate change mitigation necessarily entails constraints on some types of business activities—coal extraction and combustion, for example—policy has in many contexts been designed to create alternative sorts of business opportunities. From one perspective, we can understand how this has operated by reference to the specific types of resources that business has—its financial muscle, its control over key technologies, for example—that give it an advantage over other groups (see chapter 8 in this volume). Alternatively, we might understand it as a result of the structural importance of businesses within a capitalist economy. Such economies are growth dependent, going into systemic crises of legitimacy when growth fails, and the actors that generate growth thus gain structural power as policy makers need to create cycles of investment and growth to secure their own legitimacy. Finally, we might combine this insight with an understanding of the variety of forms of capitalism to see why some states might be able to more easily collaborate with business to promote decarbonization (because, for example, they are dependent on fossil fuel imports, or they have businesses that might benefit from GHG emissions reductions), while others experience much more resistance from business to climate change policy measures.

In terms of the pursuit of successful climate change governance, the challenge posed by the material discussed in this chapter is to attempt to articulate patterns of investment and growth that can in fact generate decarbonization of the global economy, rather than simply novel sorts of financial instruments. The focus of governance activity, whether at local, national, international, or transnational scales, needs to be on identifying coalitions of businesses, combined with other actors that can see benefits from climate policy not only in terms of emissions reductions but also in terms of stable cycles of growth of technologies and products which they can profit from. We can already identify some sorts of coalitions among business and other actors that have been able to generate positive momentum in climate policy. In some cases, it has been alliances between ENGOs and financial actors that have generated significant momentum around carbon markets and carbon finance. In others, it is coalitions formed around the investment in renewable energy sources and energy efficiency. The logic of the argument is that there are multiple possible pathways to these sorts of coalition building, but they share in common the presence of both powerful business actors (typically financiers and/or major manufacturers) that see investment benefits in low carbon transitions, combined with ENGOs and some state actors seeking entrepreneurially to mobilize this investment potential. As a consequence, we can expect the political dynamics facing governments in international negotiations to shift, undermining the blocking power of coalitions opposing emissions reductions and enabling policy makers to identify opportunities in a way that becomes self-reinforcing over time.

Notes

1. As well as skirting many controversies, this brief account of Marxist political economy draws on a huge literature. For two accounts similar to the one shown here, see Held (1987) or Harvey (1990, 121–141). This draws also on my account

in *Automobile Politics* (Paterson 2007). One of the key controversies is whether the emergence of Fordism, or welfare capitalism, in industrialized countries, since the 1930s onward, means that these underconsumptionist dynamics no longer exist. I would take the dominant argument within Marxist political economy to be that as tendencies they remain, and that a common interpretation (e.g., that of Harvey) of Fordism is precisely a strategy by capital to overcome these tendencies by providing for high wages, full employment, and using state power as a consumer of last resort. However, this fix was only temporary and limited, and the rollbacks since the early 1980s have meant a reappearance of underconsumption crises.

2. It is worth acknowledging that this empirical survey focuses mostly on European and US companies, albeit ones with a global reach. This limits the conclusions we can draw, but it also reflects what the vast bulk of existing literature focuses on.

3. Natural gas often coexists in deposits with oil, but not uniformly. Natural gas also has a noticeably lower CO_2 coefficient than oil, and thus is often seen as a "bridge" technology in the process of decarbonization. Oil sands are a form of oil where the bitumen has to be extracted from sand, a process that is much more emissions-intensive than "conventional" oil. The largest oil sands projects are in Alberta, Canada. Some European companies are involved, notably Statoil and BP, but most of the companies involved are Canadian or from the United States.

4. A reinsurer is a company that insures primary insurers, that is, acts as a risk-pooling mechanism for particularly large-scale but low-frequency risks like hurricanes, flooding, or earthquakes. Reinsurers are thus particularly exposed to changes in the intensity or frequency of extreme weather events that most believe are already increasing as part of climate change.

5. For the fullest overview, see Bulkeley et al. (2012), although the focus there is on "transnational" governance rather than on strictly private sector governance. About 25 percent of the sixty initiatives surveyed by Bulkeley and her colleagues have been initiated by private sector actors—either individual or groups of companies, or by business associations.

6. In 2010, institutional investors had US$79.3 trillion under management (The City UK 2011).

7. On this process in the forests sector, see Cashore, Auld, and Newsom (2004).

References

Andonova, Liliana B. 2010. "Public-Private Partnerships for the Earth: Politics and Patterns of Hybrid Authority in the Multilateral System." *Global Environmental Politics* 10 (2): 25–53.

Bäckstrand, Karin. 2008. "Accountability of Networked Climate Governance: The Rise of Transnational Climate Partnerships." *Global Environmental Politics* 8 (3): 74–102.

Bayon, Ricardo, Amanda Hawn, and Katherine Hamilton, eds. 2007. *Voluntary Carbon Markets: An International Business Guide to What They Are and How They Work*. London: Earthscan.

Bulkeley, Harriet, Liliana Andonova, Karin Bäckstrand, Michele Betsill, Daniel Compagnon, Rosaleen Duffy, Ans Kolk, Matthew Hoffmann, David Levy, and Peter Newell. 2012. "Governing Climate Change Transnationally: Assessing the Evidence from a Database of Sixty Initiatives." *Environment and Planning C: Government and Policy* 30 (4): 591–612.

Bullock, David. 2012. "Emissions Trading in New Zealand: Development, Challenges and Design." *Environmental Politics* 21 (4): 657–675.

Bumpus, Adam G., and Diana M. Liverman. 2008. "Accumulation by Decarbonization and the Governance of Carbon Offsets." *Economic Geography* 84 (2): 127–155.

Buxton, Nick. 2016. "COP 21 Charades: Spin, Lies and Real Hope in Paris." *Globalizations* 13 (6): 934–937.

Carbon Disclosure Project. 2011. *CDP Global 500 Report 2011: Accelerating Low Carbon Growth*. London: Carbon Disclosure Project.

Cashore, Benjamin William, Graeme Auld, and Deanna Newsom. 2004. *Governing through Markets: Forest Certification and the Emergence of Non-State Authority*. New Haven, CT: Yale University Press.

Clark, Brett, and Richard York. 2005. "Carbon Metabolism: Global Capitalism, Climate Change, and the Biospheric Rift." *Theory and Society* 34 (4): 391–428.

De Coninck, Heleen, Carolyn Fischer, Richard G Newell, and Takahiro Ueno. 2008. "International Technology-Oriented Agreements to Address Climate Change." *Energy Policy* 36 (1): 335–356.

Falkner, Robert. 2008. *Business Power and Conflict in International Environmental Politics*. Basingstoke: Palgrave Macmillan.

Forsyth, Tim. 2005. "Enhancing Climate Technology Transfer through Greater Public-Private Cooperation: Lessons from Thailand and the Philippines." *Natural Resources Forum* 29 (2): 165–176.

Gelbspan, Ross. 2004. *Boiling Point: How Politicians, Big Oil and Coal, Journalists, and Activists Have Fueled the Climate Crisis—and What We Can Do to Avert Disaster*. New York: Basic Books.

Gelbspan, Ross, and Tim O'Riordan. 1997. *The Heat Is On: The High Stakes Battle over Earth's Threatened Climate*. Reading, MA: Addison-Wesley.

Gill, Stephen. 2002. "Constitutionalizing Inequality and the Clash of Globalizations." *International Studies Review* 4 (2): 47–65.

Green, Jessica F. 2010. "Private Standards in the Climate Regime: The Greenhouse Gas Protocol." *Business and Politics* 12 (3).

Hall, Peter A., and David W. Soskice. 2001. *Varieties of Capitalism: The Institutional Foundations of Comparative Advantage.* Oxford: Oxford University Press.

Hall, Peter A., and Rosemary C. R. Taylor. 1996. "Political Science and the Three New Institutionalisms." *Political Studies* 44 (5): 936–957.

Harmes, Adam. 2011. "The Limits of Carbon Disclosure: Theorizing the Business Case for Investor Environmentalism." *Global Environmental Politics* 11 (2): 98–119.

Harrison, Neil E., and John Mikler. 2014. *Climate Innovation: Liberal Capitalism and Climate Change.* Basingstoke: Palgrave Macmillan.

Harvey, David. 1990. *The Condition of Postmodernity.* Oxford: Blackwell.

Held, David. 1987. *Models of Democracy.* Cambridge: Polity.

Hirst, Paul, and Grahame Thompson. 1996. *Globalization in Question: The International Economy and the Possibilities of Governance.* Cambridge: Polity.

Hultman, Nathan E., Simone Pulver, Leticia Guimarães, Ranjit Deshmukh, and Jennifer Kane. 2012. "Carbon Market Risks and Rewards: Firm Perceptions of CDM Investment Decisions in Brazil and India." *Energy Policy* 40:90–102.

IEA. 2011. World Energy Outlook 2011. Paris: International Energy Agency.

Jacques, Peter J., Riley E. Dunlap, and Mark Freeman. 2008. "The Organisation of Denial: Conservative Think Tanks and Environmental Scepticism." *Environmental Politics* 17 (3): 349–385.

Jessop, Bob. 1990. *State Theory: Putting the Capitalist State in Its Place.* Cambridge: Polity.

Kang, Moon Jung, and Jihyoun Park. 2013. "Analysis of the Partnership Network in the Clean Development Mechanism." *Energy Policy* 52:543–553.

Kim, Eun-Hee, and Thomas P. Lyon. 2011. "The Carbon Disclosure Project." In *Handbook of Transnational Governance: New Institutions and Innovations,* edited by Thomas Hale and David Held, 213–218. Cambridge: Polity.

Klein, Naomi. 2014. *This Changes Everything: Capitalism vs. the Climate.* Toronto: Knopf Canada.

Kolk, Ans, David Levy, and Jonatan Pinkse. 2008. "Corporate Responses in an Emerging Climate Regime: The Institutionalization and Commensuration of Carbon Disclosure." *European Accounting Review* 17 (4): 719–745.

Kolk, Ans, Jonatan Pinkse, and Lia Hull Van Houten. 2010. "Corporate Responses to Climate Change: The Role of Partnerships." In *The Social and Behavioral Aspects of*

Climate Change: Linking Vulnerability, Adaptation and Mitigation, edited by Pim Martens and Chiung Ting Chang, 48–67. Sheffield: Greenleaf Publishing.

Lachapelle, Erick, Robert MacNeil, and Matthew Paterson. 2017. "The Political Economy of Decarbonisation: From Green Energy 'Race' to Green 'Division of Labour.'" *New Political Economy* 22 (3): 311–327.

Lachapelle, Erick, and Matthew Paterson. 2013. "Drivers of National Climate Policy." *Climate Policy* 13 (5): 547–571.

Lecours, André. 2005. *New Institutionalism: Theory and Analysis.* 1st ed. Toronto: University of Toronto Press.

Leggett, Jeremy K. 1999. *The Carbon War: Dispatches from the End of the Oil Century.* London: Penguin.

Levy, David L., and Peter J. Newell. 2005. *The Business of Global Environmental Governance.* Cambridge, MA: MIT Press.

Linacre, Nicholas, Alexandre Kossoy, and Philippe Ambros. 2011. *State and Trends of the Carbon Market 2011.* Washington, DC: World Bank.

Lohmann, Larry. 2006. "Carbon Trading: A Critical Conversation on Climate Change, Privatization and Power." *Development Dialogue* 48:1–356.

Lovell, Heather C. 2010. "Governing the Carbon Offset Market." *Wiley Interdisciplinary Reviews: Climate Change* 1 (3): 353–362.

Lovell, Heather C., and Diana Liverman. 2010. "Understanding Carbon Offset Technologies." *New Political Economy* 15 (2): 255–273.

Lukes, Steven. 1974. *Power: A Radical View.* London: Macmillan.

MacLeod, Michael, and Jacob Park. 2011. "Financial Activism and Global Climate Change: The Rise of Investor-Driven Governance Networks." *Global Environmental Politics* 11 (2): 54–74.

MacNeil, Robert. 2013. "Seeding an Energy Technology Revolution in the United States: Re-Conceptualising the Nature of Innovation in 'Liberal-Market Economies.'" *New Political Economy* 18 (1): 64–88.

MacNeil, Robert, and Matthew Paterson. 2012. "Neoliberal Climate Policy: From Market Fetishism to the Developmental State." *Environmental Politics* 21 (2): 230–247.

Malm, Andreas. 2015. *Fossil Capital: The Rise of Steam-Power and the Roots of Global Warming.* London: Verso.

March, James G., and Johan P. Olsen. 1984. "The New Institutionalism: Organizational Factors in Political Life." *American Political Science Review* 78 (3): 734–749.

Meckling, Jonas. 2011. *Carbon Coalitions: Business, Climate Politics, and the Rise of Emissions Trading*. Cambridge, MA: MIT Press.

Mikler, John, and Neil E. Harrison. 2012. "Varieties of Capitalism and Technological Innovation for Climate Change Mitigation." *New Political Economy* 17 (2): 179–208.

Morgera, Elisa. 2004. "From Stockholm to Johannesburg: From Corporate Responsibility to Corporate Accountability for the Global Protection of the Environment?" *Review of European Community & International Environmental Law* 13 (2): 214–222.

Newell, Peter. 2000. *Climate for Change: Non-State Actors and the Global Politics of the Greenhouse*. Cambridge: Cambridge University Press.

Newell, Peter, and Matthew Paterson. 2010. *Climate Capitalism: Global Warming and the Transformation of the Global Economy*. Cambridge: Cambridge University Press.

Parthan, Binu, Marianne Osterkorn, Matthew Kennedy, St. John Hoskyns, Morgan Bazilian, and Pradeep Monga. 2010. "Lessons for Low-Carbon Energy Transition: Experience from the Renewable Energy and Energy Efficiency Partnership (Reeep)." *Energy for Sustainable Development* 14 (2): 83–93.

Paterson, Matthew. 1996. *Global Warming and Global Politics*. London: Routledge.

———. 2001. "Risky Business: Insurance Companies in Global Warming Politics." *Global Environmental Politics* 1 (4):18–42.

———. 2007. *Automobile Politics: Ecology and Cultural Political Economy*. Cambridge: Cambridge University Press.

———. 2010. "Legitimation and Accumulation in Climate Change Governance." *New Political Economy* 15 (3): 345–368.

———. 2012. "Who and What Are Carbon Markets For? Politics and the Development of Climate Policy." *Climate Policy* 12 (1): 82–97.

Paterson, Matthew, Matthew Hoffmann, Michele Betsill, and Steven Bernstein. 2014. "The Micro Foundations of Policy Diffusion toward Complex Global Governance an Analysis of the Transnational Carbon Emission Trading Network." *Comparative Political Studies* 47 (3): 420–449.

Pattberg, Philipp. 2010. "Public–Private Partnerships in Global Climate Governance." *Wiley Interdisciplinary Reviews: Climate Change* 1 (2): 279–287.

Pinkse, Jonatan, and Ans Kolk. 2009. *International Business and Global Climate Change*. London: Routledge.

Pulver, Simone, Nathan Hultman, and Leticia Guimarães. 2010. "Carbon Market Participation by Sugar Mills in Brazil." *Climate and Development* 2 (3): 248–262.

Rowlands, Ian H. 2000. "Beauty and the Beast? BP's and Exxon's Positions on Global Climate Change." *Environment and Planning C* 18 (3): 339–354.

———. 2001. "Classical Theories of International Relations." In *International Relations and Global Climate Change*, edited by Urs Luterbacher and Detlef F. Sprinz, 43–65. Cambridge, MA: MIT Press.

Schneider, Malte, Holger Hendrichs, and Volker H. Hoffmann. 2010. "Navigating the Global Carbon Market: An Analysis of the CDM's Value Chain and Prevalent Business Models." *Energy Policy* 38 (1): 277–287.

Schreuder, Yda. 2009. *The Corporate Greenhouse: Climate Change Policy in a Globalizing World*. London: Zed Books.

Sijm, Jos, Karsten Neuhoff, and Yihsu Chen. 2006. "CO_2 Cost Pass-through and Windfall Profits in the Power Sector." *Climate Policy* 6 (1): 49–72.

Skjærseth, Jon Birger. 2010. "EU Emissions Trading: Legitimacy and Stringency." *Environmental Policy and Governance* 20 (5): 295–308.

Skjærseth, Jon Birger, and Tora Skodvin. 2001. "Climate Change and the Oil Industry: Common Problems, Different Strategies." *Global Environmental Politics* 1 (4): 43–64.

Skjærseth, Jon Birger, and Jørgen Wettestad. 2008. *EU Emissions Trading: Initiation, Decision-Making and Implementation*. Aldershot: Ashgate.

Smith, Kevin. 2007. *The Carbon Neutral Myth: Offset Indulgences for Your Climate Sins*. Amsterdam: Carbon Trade Watch.

Spash, Clive L. 2016. "This Changes Nothing: The Paris Agreement to Ignore Reality." *Globalizations* 13:928–933.

Stephan, Benjamin. 2012. "Bringing Discourse to the Market: The Commodification of Avoided Deforestation." *Environmental Politics* 21 (4): 621–639.

The City UK. 2011. *Fund Management. October 2011*. London: TheCityUK.

Thistlethwaite, Jason. 2011. *Planet Finance: The Governance of Climate Change Risks in Financial Markets*. Ontario: University of Waterloo.

UNFCCC. 2015. *Paris Agreement*. Paris: United Nations.

Unruh, Gregory C. 2000. "Understanding Carbon Lock-In." *Energy Policy* 28 (12): 817–830.

———. 2002. "Escaping Carbon Lock-In." *Energy Policy* 30 (4): 317–325.

Van der Pijl, Kees. 1998. *Transnational Classes and International Relations*. London: Routledge.

Weiss, Linda. 1997. "Globalization and the Myth of the Powerless State." *New Left Review* 225:3–27.

10 Equity and Development: Developing Countries in the International Climate Negotiations

Katharina Michaelowa and Axel Michaelowa

10.1 Introduction

Developing countries' preferences and positions are central to the debate on global climate change. As the global South is expected to suffer most from the consequences of anthropogenic climate change, the salience of the issue in this world region is extremely high. With unchanged emission trends, Tuvalu and the Maldives are expected to become uninhabitable before 2100, and largely covered by water (Gemenne 2011). Sahel countries are likely to face strong problems of progressing desertification, and countries drawing their water from Himalayan and Central Asian glaciers will suffer severe water shortages. These are just a few examples, but they are sufficient to illustrate that the impact on developing countries is key to the moral imperative to find solutions for global climate change. Such examples are also referred to frequently by reform-oriented politicians and NGOs to make their point and gain public support for their positions. Owing to this peculiar situation, some of the smallest and poorest countries of the world have been astonishingly important players in the international climate negotiations for the last twenty years (Betzold, Castro, and Weiler 2012).

At the same time, other developing countries have experienced strong economic growth during the last decades, going hand in hand with a strong increase in emissions. Since 2007, China has become the world's largest CO_2 emitter in absolute terms, leaving behind even the United States. While of course Chinese per capita emissions remain well below the US level, they have crossed the world average level in the late 2000s. Traditionally, a number of Middle Eastern countries have been found at the top of the per capita emissions ranking (see table 10.1).

Table 10.1
Per capita emissions from fossil fuel combustion, 1990 and 2013 (t CO_2).

Country	UNFCCC Status	1990	2013
Qatar	Developing	26.1	33.6
Kuwait	Developing	13.5	25.0
United Arab Emirates	Developing	28.7	17.9
Saudi Arabia	Developing	9.3	16.4
US	*Industrialized*	*19.2*	*16.2*
South Korea	Developing	5.4	11.4
Russia	*Industrialized*	*14.6*	*10.8*
OECD	*Mixed*	*10.3*	*9.6*
Singapore	Developing	9.5	8.6
Israel	Developing	7.0	8.5
South Africa	Developing	6.9	7.9
China	Developing	1.9	6.6
Ukraine	*Industrialized*	*13.3*	*5.8*
Chile	Developing	2.2	4.7
World	*Mixed*	*3.9*	*4.5*
Mexico	Developing	3.0	3.8
Brazil	Developing	1.2	2.3
India	Developing	0.6	1.5

Source: International Energy Agency (2015).
Note: Selected countries, sorted by per capita emissions in 2013; industrialized countries, OECD and world total in italics.

This has increased awareness that developing (or emerging) countries will also have to play an active role in any sustainable solution to the problem of global climate change. Emerging economies have therefore become major players in the international climate change negotiations (see also chapter 7 in this volume). In addition, during the last decade, the widening of the range of emissions between developing countries along with the concurrent differences in the impact of climate change has led to a differentiation of preferences and hence to a split of the hitherto monolithic negotiation block of the G77 and China into a number of different negotiation groups. Moreover, the differentiation of emissions paths of developing countries has brought up a new debate on the relationship between economic growth and emissions, as well as on related questions on the right to economic development.

In this chapter, we first discuss the central positions of developing countries in the international climate negotiations (section 10.2). In section 10.3 we further differentiate between different types of developing countries, and different (regional or socioeconomic) groups within developing countries that put in perspective the seemingly uniform positions presented before. Section 10.4 uses the diversity among developing countries to provide a concrete empirical basis for the debate on the link between economic development and the growth of per capita emissions. Section 10.5 considers the requirement of transfers between rich and poor countries, both to help vulnerable countries to adapt to the consequences of climate change, and to support economically growing countries to adopt a sustainable growth path. Section 10.6 provides some final remarks and conclusions.

10.2   Central Positions of Developing Countries in International Climate Negotiations

Ever since the UN Conference on the Human Environment in 1972, developing countries have stressed that environmental protection always needs to be seen in the light of the development imperative (UNEP 1972). This stance has guided developing country strategies in key environmental treaty negotiations such as the Montreal Protocol. In the same vein, negotiating the contributions of countries to the prevention of dangerous anthropogenic climate change has been a challenge right from the beginning of international climate policy in the late 1980s. Developing countries have stressed that their contribution to greenhouse gas (GHG) emissions is limited while they are likely to disproportionally suffer from climate change impacts (UNFCCC 2007). They have thus argued that their role in combating climate change and mitigation of greenhouse gases should be different from that of industrialized countries, and that equity principles should determine the allocation of responsibilities and rights. The key elements of developing country positions developed in the few years leading up to the signature of the UN Framework Convention on Climate Change (UNFCCC) in 1992; they have not changed substantially since then. They include (1) the principle of common but differentiated responsibilities and respective capabilities, (2) responsibility for historical emissions, (3) the allocation of emissions budgets on a per capita basis, and (4) compensation for climate damages. A number of these elements are linked to the theoretical approaches to justice, that is, distributive and retributive justice, respectively (Paterson 2001). Distributive justice aims to achieve a fair distribution of burdens of mitigation and thus relates to approaches (1) and (3) while retributive justice aims to compensate victims of damages, that is, is linked to approach (4). Schlosberg (2004) shows the limits of distributive justice approaches when taking into account various circumstances such as cultural backgrounds. In the following section, these central positions will be explained and discussed referring to the different debates they have provoked.

10.2.1 Common but Differentiated Responsibilities

The concept of common but differentiated responsibilities emerged during 1990–1991 in the negotiations of the UNFCCC. Particularly India and Saudi Arabia (which defines itself as a developing country) strived to enshrine this principle, which they interpreted in a way that industrialized countries should take the lead in greenhouse gas mitigation and finance mitigation activities in developing countries. The Indian focus on this issue was triggered by a heated debate between the Indian NGO Centre for Science and Environment and the US think tank World Resources Institute regarding the Indian GHG emissions level (Agarwal and Narain 1991), which stressed the difference between lifestyle versus needs—related emissions—or in more drastic terms *luxury* versus *survival* emissions.

In the UNFCCC, the principle is reflected in the preamble and led to the definition of a list of industrialized countries in the Convention's Annex I. The list of industrialized countries was derived from OECD membership and non-OECD countries in transition in Eastern Europe. Annex I countries agreed to stabilize CO_2 emissions at 1990 levels by 2000. A subset of Annex I countries, the Annex II countries, would provide financial support to developing countries in order to finance national emissions inventories. Despite rapid changes in country circumstances that led a significant number of non-Annex I countries to achieve higher per capita incomes and emissions than the poorest Annex I countries, the differentiation between Annex I and non-Annex I countries was retained (with few exceptions) in the context of the Kyoto Protocol. Industrialized countries listed in Annex B of the Kyoto Protocol (see chapter 2 in this volume) took up legally binding emissions commitments. Non-Annex B countries had no commitments but were able to generate emissions credits through the Clean Development Mechanism (CDM) that they could sell to Annex B countries. Ever since, the country lists in these annexes have not seen any adjustment. In 1998 Argentina declared its willingness to take up emissions commitments, but was ostracized by the other developing countries. Simultaneously, industrialized countries, especially the United States, have tried to weaken the principle of common but differentiated responsibilities. In 2007 the Bali Action Plan almost floundered due to conflicts regarding the interpretation of Nationally Appropriate Mitigation Actions (NAMAs) in developing countries. While industrialized countries focused on developing countries' participation in mitigation action, developing countries stressed that they would only engage in NAMAs if financial and technological support were granted by industrialized countries. A main reason for the failure of Copenhagen in 2009 was the stalemate between the United States and China regarding the uptake of emissions commitments by the latter.

Subsequently, the focus of international climate negotiations shifted toward a "bottom-up" solution, where governments would specify their mitigation targets and international rules would focus on transparency regarding emissions levels reached by each country. The Durban platform in 2011 stated that a new treaty would involve "all parties," and in December 2015, the bottom-up approach became the cornerstone of the Paris Agreement that found universal acclaim. Under the Paris Agreement all countries are called to submit Nationally Determined Contributions (NDCs) with mitigation targets. Bodansky (2016) stresses that countries representing 95 percent of global submissions submitted their intended NDCs, and thus argues that the Annex I/non-Annex I differentiation is essentially over. This is not fully the case as least developed countries and small island states get special treatment with regard to the timeframe of their NDCs. Developing countries do not have to take up economy-wide absolute reduction targets. Moreover, with regard to the provision of mitigation finance, the old differentiation is still there, as NDCs of developing countries are generally made conditional on receiving financial support from industrialized countries. There is a significant risk that a replay of the Annex I/non-Annex I stalemate happens in the area of climate finance.

Generally, the persistence of the principle of common but differentiated responsibilities in its static form as embodied by the Annexes of the

UNFCCC and the Kyoto Protocol over twenty years is noticeable. Since 1992, there has been a marked differentiation of developing countries, as some countries have embarked on rapid industrialization. This is most marked in the case of China whose per capita emissions increased above the global per capita average in the late 2000s. Only the Paris Agreement managed to reach a breakthrough by introducing the concept of the NDCs that will lead to contributions by countries without commitments under the Kyoto Protocol from 2020 onward and thus overcome the rigid differentiation based on the 1992 Annexes.

While the principle of "common but differentiated responsibilities" is immediately plausible in principle, linking it to an unchangeable country list was much less so. The definition of fixed country lists in the UNFCCC in 1992 and the Kyoto Protocol in 1997 was highly problematic. It let to strong path dependencies and negatively affected negotiation dynamics by reinforcing existing divides (Castro, Hörnlein, and Michaelowa 2011) to the point that the international negotiation process almost collapsed.

Ideally, rather than fixed country lists, there should be clear and easily measurable criteria on which differentiation could be based. Pan's (2005) assessments of emissions allocation on a need basis or Baer et al.'s (2008) Greenhouse Development Rights approach present some possible options. A system of "Graduation and Deepening" (Michaelowa, Butzengeiger, and Jung 2005) would be a way to use such objective criteria for a more dynamic attribution of differentiated responsibilities. The approach of the Paris Agreement to "ratchet up" NDCs every five years allows such a deepening, but only provided there is sufficient public and peer pressure on governments.[1]

10.2.2 Responsibility for Historical Emissions

A central criterion proposed by developing countries to define a country's responsibility for global climate change is accumulated historical emissions. Given that CO_2 and most other greenhouse gases remain in the atmosphere for hundreds of years, this criterion is immediately plausible. As a consequence, industrialized countries would have to bear all the cost of mitigation (and, in fact, adaptation) and even emerging economies like the BASIC countries (Brazil, South Africa, India, and China) would not need to participate in the common effort for many decades to come.

The "Brazilian Proposal" of July 1997 formally introduced the notion of historical responsibility in the UNFCCC negotiations. At the same time, it acknowledged that industrialized countries alone would not be able to reduce emissions sufficiently to reach the objective on cumulative emissions that would avoid dangerous climate change. For this reason, Brazil proposed that a penalty should be paid for emissions above this level. Revenues from the penalty would be spent on the development of mitigation technologies in the hope that this would further speed up the international mitigation process (La Rovere, Valente de Macedo, and Baumert 2002). After Copenhagen, further proposals similar to the Brazilian one have been made by experts from BASIC countries (Winkler et al. 2011). However, in the context of the Paris Agreement this concept was not applied.

If historical emissions were to be taken seriously as a criterion for the attribution of responsibilities, there would also be a need to determine the date from which the accumulation of emissions would be accounted for. In this context, it appears appropriate to consider the time when governments were first made aware of the consequences of GHG emissions. Given that the science of anthropogenic climate change only fully emerged during the 1980s and the first IPCC report was published in 1990, the year 1990 could be a sensible start date for a cumulative approach (see also La Rovere, Valente de Macedo, and Baumert 2002).

10.2.3 Allocating Emissions Budgets on a Per Capita Basis

Another crucial element of equity demanded by developing country negotiators has been to consider all criteria on a per capita basis. While essentially identical, the political debate was typically not framed in terms of criteria for attributing responsibility, but in terms of the allocation of per capita emissions rights. Accounting for population size so as to give every person the same right to pollute has a strong moral appeal and has, as such, never been openly and formally contested. Yet discussions about large polluters like China and India that should take up their share of the responsibilities as launched by the United States in recent years indirectly or directly refer to absolute emissions, at least as far as India is concerned. On a per capita basis, talking of India as a large polluter would not make any sense, given that its per capita emissions are only a third of the world average. Highly populated countries like India thus underscore the relevance of the per capita approach.

The per capita approach is frequently associated with the idea of an identification of a common level of emissions per person toward which all countries could converge. While this point was raised by Agarwal and Narain (1991), it was fully elaborated only in the concept "Contraction and Convergence" in the mid-1990s (Meyer 2000). Industrialized countries would converge from above (i.e., would need to contract) while developing countries would converge from below. However, with rapid emissions growth in a number of developing countries, particularly in the Middle East and East Asia, per capita emissions of more and more countries increased above commonly discussed convergence levels. Apart from the definition of the level of per capita emissions toward which the system should converge, the approach requires the agreement on a date at which contraction should start and on a date at which the pre-agreed convergence level should be reached.

Some developing countries, notably China, have argued, however, that if the timing and level of emissions reductions were stringent enough to reach a limitation of warming to less than 2°C compared with the pre-industrial level, which is often seen as akin to avoiding dangerous climate change (the Paris Agreement now even considers 1.5°C), developing countries would not have sufficient leeway for economic development (Conrad 2012). If the objective was stringent enough while, at the same time, developing countries were given more rights to pollute, this would imply that either industrialized countries would need to converge earlier or (at least temporarily) to a lower level of per capita emissions. In a way, this would account for their historical responsibility discussed above, which is not considered in the simple version of the contraction and convergence approach. The concept of convergence is only indirectly visible in article 4.11 of the Paris Agreement, which specifies that developing countries have more time for peaking of their emissions than industrialized countries.

10.2.4 Compensation for Climate Damages

Impacts of climate change on developing countries are currently due mainly to accumulated GHG emissions by the industrialized world. Therefore, and in line with the idea of responsibility for historical emissions, developing countries have been arguing that they should be compensated for such damages. This request, while somewhat sidelined after the Copenhagen conference, resurfaced in Cancun and Durban with the decision to embark on a work program on "loss and damage." The Warsaw conference in 2013 introduced an international mechanism to address "loss and damage" with the United States stressing that this cannot lead to compensation payments through the mechanism. The decision accompanying the Paris Agreement states clearly that "the Agreement does not involve or provide a basis for any liability or compensation" (UNFCCC 2015, para. 52).

Challenges regarding the compensation approach are the differentiation between impacts from climate change and impacts due to insufficient resilience against natural climate variability. Under current knowledge of the effect of climate change on meteorological extreme events, this differentiation is virtually impossible, albeit attempts have been made in this direction (Jaeger et al. 2008). Paying for all impacts that actually accrue from meteorological extreme events would not be fair to those countries that have invested substantial sums to achieve a high resilience against current climate variability. Therefore, a heuristics has to be developed to deduct a "standard" volume of "natural" meteorological impacts given certain general country characteristics including latitude and length of coastline.

Another thorny issue in the context of such compensation is the value of human life. Economists have traditionally valued human life according to its insurance value, which is usually proportional to GDP (Miller 2000). Thus, a life lost in a least developed country would effectively account for only a small fraction of a life in the industrialized world. This is normatively unacceptable. At the same time, using a valuation of human life in the context of climate related risks that is substantially higher than the valuation of human life and related risks in other sectors within the same country generates an undue incentive to shift toward avoidance of climate-related losses of life (i.e., to taking more risk in this area than would otherwise appear acceptable in this economy). During the writing of the Second Assessment Report of the IPCC, a controversy over these arguments erupted between certain economists and NGO representatives. Eventually, the latter prevailed and the report did not differentiate the values of human life across countries (Tol 1997).

In essence, the issue may be considered as a question of equity across, as opposed to equity within countries. The consequence of the decisions taken goes beyond their relevance for calculating potential compensations. They are relevant for the calculation of damages in general, including expected future damages, and thereby also affect the cost-benefit analysis of intertemporal mitigation and adaptation decisions. The valuation of human life may thus affect the concrete specification of all the above discussed principles and criteria.

Equally affecting the value of emissions reduction, and thereby—at least indirectly—much of the above discussion, is the estimation of a plausible discount rate. This discount rate should reflect time preference under consideration of increasing income levels and a related decrease in marginal utility over time. Nordhaus' (2007) estimation of the discount rate at 4.5 percent is a typical example of the corresponding neoclassical economic analysis based on observable consumer behavior. However, Stern (2006) and—much earlier—Cline (1992) challenge the assumption that such long-term intertemporal allocation decisions can be appropriately modeled on the basis of the time preferences observed for individual consumers. Based on a normative analysis of fairness with respect to future generations (intertemporal equity) they suggest a much lower discount rate (1.4 percent in the Stern Review).

Finally, Dasgupta (2007) argues that even when accepting Stern's intergenerational equity assumption the overall discount rate should be higher. He notes that Stern makes use of this assumption only for the parameter representing "pure" time preference, but not for the parameter that weighs the expected additional income of future generations. Dasgupta is of the opinion that intragenerational equity is not sufficiently addressed by Stern. Thus, the parameter addressing differences in the income distribution should be much larger. Overall this would lead to discount rates that come close to the 4.5 percent suggested by Nordhaus.[2]

At such a high rate, mitigation today has a relatively low priority, because its costs arise immediately while benefits can be expected only in the future. From this perspective, for the next couple of decades, mitigation action should be limited while there should be investments in human capital and technology development in order to increase growth rates and to enable future generations to settle the problem. Moreover, there should be adaptation to the consequences of climate change.

Given that poor countries—just like poor people—are supposed to have discount rates that may be far beyond the average, this result might match their preferences. Indeed, funding for both adaptation and technology development has frequently been demanded by their representatives (for the latter, see, e.g., the Brazilian proposal discussed above in the subsection on historical responsibilities). However, at least as long as they are not required to contribute to the cost of mitigation action, their strong time preference also implies that they should strongly prefer global mitigation action today to mitigation action tomorrow. As opposed to that, for those countries requested to shoulder the cost, time preference (even if it is much lower than for developing countries) implies that they would rather push these expenses toward the future. Therefore, the real challenge of the Paris Agreement consists in the willingness of industrialized countries to finance the conditional parts of developing country NDCs.

10.3   Whose Preferences and Whose Positions? On the Difficulties to Represent a Large Variety of Countries and the Differentiated Needs of Their Citizens

The group of developing countries is no monolith; it features substantial differences in their economic structures and income distributions both among and within countries. This also implies strong differences in preferences when it comes to climate change mitigation objectives, in needs for adaptation to the consequences of climate change, and in the capacity with respect to the implementation of either of these. While the above discussed objectives are widely considered to reflect a common developing country perspective, they mask these important differences. To go beyond a very superficial discussion, these differences need to be taken into account.

10.3.1   Differences in Developing Country Characteristics and the Fragmentation of Developing Country Groups in UNFCCC Negotiations

Over the last two decades, developing countries as defined within the UNFCCC (i.e., not belonging to Annex I) have become increasingly differentiated with regard to development indicators. A number of countries have reached a level of industrialization which in the past would have clearly led to their inclusion in the group of industrialized countries. Chile, Israel, Mexico, and South Korea have joined the OECD, the club of industrialized countries. Several oil exporting countries of the Gulf region belong to the top performers in terms of per capita gross national income (GNI). The lowest-positioned Annex I country, Ukraine, is now situated in the bottom half of that ranking, preceded by large countries like Brazil, China, and South Africa (see table 10.2). At the same time, a large number of least developed countries remains dominated by subsistence economies.

The wide range of interests of countries has not remained without effect on the international climate negotiations. Despite trying to act as a block

Table 10.2

"Developing countries" in high gross national income ranks.

Country	UNFCCC Status	Ranking in GNI Per Capita	GNI Per Capita 2015 (PPP)
Qatar	Developing	1	140,720
Singapore	Developing	2	81,190
Kuwait	Developing	3	79,970
United Arab Emirates	Developing	5	70,570
Saudi Arabia	Developing	10	54,730
Israel	Developing	29	34,940
South Korea	Developing	30	34,700
Russia	*Industrialized*	*47*	*23,790*
Chile	Developing	51	21,740
Mexico	Developing	59	17,150
Thailand	Developing	70	15,210
Brazil	Developing	71	15,020
China	Developing	76	14,160
South Africa	Developing	81	12,830
*Ukraine**	*Industrialized*	*109*	*7,810*

Source: World Bank (2016).

Note: Selected countries, sorted by GNI per capita 2015.

*Industrialized country with the lowest per capita GNI.

in the UNFCCC negotiations, already in the early years of the international climate negotiations, developing countries have consisted of several subgroups. The small island states set up the Alliance of Small Island States (AOSIS), and were extremely successful, at least initially. AOSIS got a special seat on every institution of the international climate regime and was able to influence the negotiations much more than the small share of its members in world population and economic production would have suggested (Betzold, Castro, and Weiler 2012). Another important player has been the Organization of the Petroleum Exporting Countries (OPEC). Oil-exporting countries successfully slowed down negotiations through procedural tricks. For example, the opposition of Saudi Arabia led to the blocking of voting rules in the UNFCCC regime (Depledge 2008). The resulting requirement to achieve consensus has been a heavy burden on the negotiation process, before creative interpretations of consensus emerged after the Copenhagen conference. Nevertheless, for almost twenty years the Group of 77 managed to find a common voice in the UNFCCC process. Copenhagen then served as catalyst to lead to the final split. The negotiation coalition "BASIC" emerged, consisting of the large advanced developing countries Brazil, China, India, and South Africa. This group played a crucial role in the negotiation of the Copenhagen Accord with the United States, sidelining the EU. Further groups, such as the Group of Least Developed Countries, the African Group and the Alliance of Rainforest Countries have come up, often overlapping in membership. It is obvious that many of these groups have differing, or even outright contradicting preferences. While OPEC tries to slow down the international negotiation process, AOSIS strives for fast and substantial agreements leading to significant mitigation action. BASIC in turn seems to be primarily concerned by reaching agreements without own mitigation commitments.

At the Doha conference in 2012, fragmentation accelerated. China and India mobilized a group of twenty "Like Minded Developing Countries" that includes traditional hardliners (Bolivia, Philippines, Saudi Arabia, Sudan) but also past progressives (Argentina, Egypt, Thailand). It supports the traditional interpretation of developing country negotiation positions. In a direct reaction, progressive Latin American countries (Chile, Colombia, Costa Rica, Guatemala, Panama, and Peru) set up the Alliance of Independent Latin American and Caribbean States (AILAC). Overall, the fragmentation of developing countries leads to sidelining of smaller countries and regional alliances, as the final deals are done by the "heavyweights." However, collaboration between progressive developing and industrialized countries becomes easier. This was very visible at the Paris conference, where a "High Ambition Coalition" emerged whose members came equally from industrialized and developing countries. Moreover, some advanced developing countries have started to seriously engage in mitigation (with regard to South Africa and Indonesia, see Michaelowa and Michaelowa 2015), which is reflected in relatively ambitious Nationally Determined Contributions under the Paris Agreement.

10.3.2 Differences within Developing Countries

The major characteristic of the last decade is the increasing emergence of large middle classes in developing countries that start to develop a consumerist lifestyle. This is linked to an accelerated urbanization and buildup of transport infrastructure, which in turn triggers demand for energy-intensive products like steel and cement, and a rapid takeoff in GHG emissions (Michaelowa and Michaelowa 2009). So far, this trend has mainly been found in China, but it now starts in Brazil and India as well. At the same time, large swathes of rural populations remain engaged in subsistence agriculture in these countries. For example, in India a significant share of rural population still does not have access to electricity and modern fuel, thus using "dung cakes"—that is, dried livestock manure—for cooking and heating. In urban agglomerations, water and electricity cuts are often inversely correlated with average income of the area's inhabitants, frequently leaving the poor without access.

It is obvious that the different parts of the population have different interests when it comes to national and international climate policy. Just as in the cross-country perspective, the poor must be expected to be much more vulnerable to climate change. For instance, because of glacier melting, they will face even bigger problems of access to drinking and irrigation water. In rural areas, their basic breadwinning activity may be endangered. While the poor will have a high time preference leading to a priority for adaptation as compared to mitigation, they will not be against mitigation as long it is paid by rich countries or rich citizens of their own country.

Similar differences may arise between different sectors in the economy. For instance, the renewable energy sector in a country like China or India might benefit from serious national mitigation targets, and the modern industrial sector in India might favor the abolition of energy subsidies in competing traditional industries. Moreover, individual sectors can benefit from more specific issue areas agreed upon within the package of an international deal on climate policy. In particular, many firms in emerging economies have benefited from new income opportunities in the context of the CDM, and these countries have fought strongly to keep a window for market mechanisms in the Paris Agreement. More recent topics like Reducing Emissions from Deforestation and Forest Degradation (REDD) can also support certain industries.

Finally, even regional differences within a country may lead to different preferences regarding national and international climate policy. In large developing countries, the exposure to climate change impacts can vary substantially. An instructive example is China, whose cold northeastern regions benefit from warming—at least up to a certain intensity of climate change. In fact, agricultural policy has actively promoted adaptation to this warming by promoting a northward expansion of rice cropping (Yang et al. 2007). At the same time, southern regions will be subject to increased extreme precipitation events. Similar differences across regions arise in any large country with different climatic zones.

Given these differences in preferences across, but also within developing countries, one may wonder what—or rather whom—the so-called developing country positions discussed in section 10.2 actually represent. This leads us to some more theoretical considerations in the next section.

10.3.3   Lack of Information, Vested Interests, and the Aggregation of Preferences

International relations theory suggests that decisions on international agreements can be explained by a two-level process that considers both, decision making in the individual countries concerned, and—as a second, albeit simultaneous step—decision making in the international arena (Putnam 1988). Similarly, we can assume that positions are shaped both by the political process within each country, and by the international exchange between the different country delegations at the international level. At the national level, public choice theory (esp. Olson 1965) suggests that government positions will typically be driven by the urban middle classes rather than by the masses of the rural poor (Jaeger and Michaelowa 2015). This is because governments tend to provide more attention to those actors in the economy who are more vocal, organize better, protest more easily, or have the relevant financial means to support politicians who defend their preferences. Moreover, the urban middle class tends to benefit from a higher level of education, which is relevant indirectly, for the factors listed above (e.g., organizational capacity), but also directly for understanding the relevant problems in the first place, and for being able to compare the effect of alternative policies.

Drawing from the theory of public goods provision, government bias toward these groups to the detriment of more marginalized and vulnerable parts of the population can be expected to be particularly strong in non-democracies (Bueno De Mesquita et al. 1999; Mueller 2003, 412). Indeed in India—the world's largest democracy—a public debate has erupted on whether the country's poor are (mis)used in the international climate negotiations to shield the rich against international criticism (Chakravarty and

Ramana 2012). Is the requested leeway for development that provides the argument for refusing mitigation commitments effectively used for those in need (e.g., for the electrification of the rural poor) or does it only provide a pretext for the upper or middle class to increase their own "luxury" emissions? In countries where these questions are not openly discussed, they may be even more prevalent.

It is more difficult to make a general theoretical argument about the impact of vested interests within different industries. As the expected role of each industry depends on its specific structure and relevance within the country, this requires an in-depth case study analysis. The same is true for an assessment of the relative influence of the interests of different regions. In a country like China, some regions—notably those driving the current growth process—are widely known to be quite powerful within the national setting, but these differences are much more difficult to determine in many other countries.

At the international level, country representatives do not only need to consider the preferences of their home constituencies with respect to the subject matter, but also how their positions and strategies will be received by their peers at the UNFCCC and by the international media (which will eventually also be observed by their own national citizens). Just as for industrialized country governments, at least for some of the large emerging economies, in this context, not only the position itself is of importance, but also the demonstration of leadership abilities. This applies, for example, to India in the context of the G77 and/or BASIC. Its role as a speaker for the poor is deeply rooted in the country's history and seems to be regarded as a moral duty. Moreover, India appears as a natural international leader for developing countries, as it is a large and economically (increasingly) important country and can select its negotiators from a large and well-trained civil service with strong command of English as the language of negotiations. The majority of the delegates will themselves have an upper-middle-class background since their professional activity requires university education and good language skills. At the same time, India's own rapid economic development increasingly leads to different priorities and to some difficulties to reconcile the objective of international leadership and national development priorities. This is well expressed in a statement by the former Indian Minister of the Environment Jairam Ramesh, when he refers to pressure by Bangladesh and the Maldives to justify his more proactive negotiation strategy in the context of the UNFCCC negotiations in Copenhagen in 2009. For a complete case study on India in the international climate negotiations, see Michaelowa and Michaelowa (2011b; see also Vihma 2011, 15).[3]

Many of the smaller developing countries do not even command the necessary human capital to generate the relevant knowledge of the concrete effects of different climate policy options (including both mitigation and adaptation), or even appropriate estimations of the expected damages due to climate change. This makes them rely on some other delegations whom they trust to be more knowledgeable and representing their needs.

In a number of cases, international NGOs have stepped in to provide special support to particularly vulnerable countries, already at an early stage of the UNFCCC negotiations. The case of Tuvalu leading the AOSIS group backed by well-trained international lawyers within their delegation is a key example (Betzold 2010, 141).

10.4   Reconciling Mitigation Action and Economic Development

The above discussion has shown that apart from exceptional cases such as AOSIS, we must expect relatively well-off developing countries to shape *the* "developing country position" internationally. Moreover, we must expect this position to be influenced significantly by these countries' urban elites (even if it may, at times, be readjusted under the pressure of other, poorer and more vulnerable countries).[4] Unless they see a clear advantage in mitigation or adaptation policies, it will thus be very difficult to reach any agreement on the international level that could include a commitment from developing countries.

In addition, just like in industrialized countries, those policy alternatives need to be highlighted that may allow them to reconcile their preferences for further economic development with a sustainable emissions path. This is most easily done by comparing the emissions paths of different countries.

10.4.1   Exploring Different Development and Emission Pathways

Development success is commonly measured in terms of economic growth or, in order to obtain a more complete picture including non-economic dimensions of development (such as health and education), in terms of changes in the UN Human Development Index (HDI).[5] In Michaelowa and

Michaelowa (2009) we looked at all countries that managed to achieve an increase in the HDI of over ten percentage points between 1975 and 2005 and assessed whether and to what extent this development success was accompanied by an increase in per capita emissions. We find substantial differences between different country groups. While some countries—especially the oil-exporting states of the Persian Gulf—have shown an extremely emissions-intensive development path throughout, others have reached a similarly high level of development with much less emissions. For certain countries, we observe a shift from an emissions-extensive to an emissions-intensive development path once they have reached a certain level of development. This can indeed be attributed to the strongly increasing energy requirements related to the rising middle class, their consumption needs (e.g., cars and air-conditioning), and related developments of urban infrastructure. However, there are some country examples that illustrate that this shift to an emissions-intensive path is not unavoidable.

These observations can be confirmed based on more recent data. Figure 10.1 provides a comparison of countries that succeeded in increasing their HDI by twenty or more percentage points over the last thirty years. Overall these strong development performers include eleven countries. We exclude Nepal which, despite the impressive improvements in recent decades, still remains at a low level of development (below 0.5)—suggesting that a broader middle class has not yet been built up in the country. Indeed, with per capita emissions of less than 0.15t CO_2 for any year in the period observed, the country's contribution to global climate change remains negligible. We also exclude the United Arab Emirates (UAE)—for the simple reason that its extremely high CO_2 emissions per capita would have dwarfed all other emissions data so that the differences between other countries would not have been visible any more in our graph.

The remaining set of countries is spread across all continents. The North African countries Tunisia, Algeria, Egypt, and Morocco, as well as Turkey, and also the Latin American country El Salvador, have managed to combine substantial HDI growth with a very limited increase in emissions. In fact, for most of these countries, CO_2 emissions per capita actually stabilized or even slightly declined. As opposed to that, China and Iran are examples of those cases where, at an HDI of about 0.6 (reached in China in the year 2000 and in Iran in 1995), emissions took off rapidly and disproportionately as

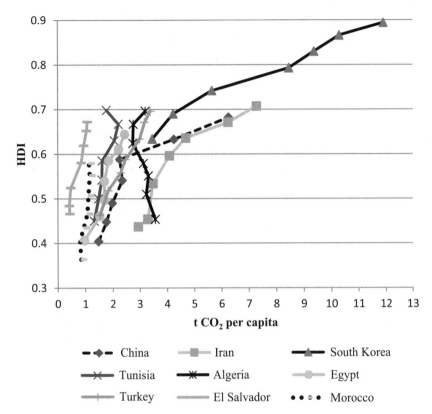

Figure 10.1
Emissions-extensive versus emissions-intensive development paths, 1980–2010.
Sources: Energy Information Administration (2012); Human Development Report Office (2011).
Note: The lines for each country connect the information on HDI and emissions in five-year steps starting with 1980 for the lowest point on the line.

compared to further improvements in the HDI. They now seem to follow the emissions-intensive development path South Korea started way back in the 1980s. Today already, they have reached the lower end of the range of per capita emissions in traditional industrialized countries (e.g., Switzerland or France) (see Energy Information Administration 2012).

Why do some countries embark on an emissions-intensive development path while others do not? How can the shift to an emissions-intensive development path be avoided? These questions are highly relevant especially as other large emerging economies like India and Indonesia are about to reach the level of development where emissions must be expected to take off if they follow the examples of China and Iran.

Currently, the main explanation for why a country can be found in the emissions-extensive category is a low carbon energy system, dominated by hydropower. Moreover, heavy industry and fossil fuel production is absent or very limited—at least relative to population size. India, for instance, has a sizeable heavy industry and a highly carbon-intensive electricity generation system. However, at least for the moment, these sectors remain small when compared to its huge population. This is different for South Korea, whose per capita emissions increased from 3.5 to 12 t CO_2 between 1980 and 2010 (see figure 10.1). Basic chemicals and shipbuilding were the two pillars of its industrial growth, and only recently, higher-value-added productions were added, possibly leading to a slowdown in future emissions growth. Other countries like Tunisia, which also reached a HDI as high as in China or Iran, have focused more on services, notably in the context of tourism. Admittedly, the low emissions figures for this country do not account for emissions arising in the context of foreign tourists flying to their holiday destinations. Yet, in general, growth based on service industries reduces emissions. This also provides some reason for optimism with respect to the future development in India, which is already known for its strong service sector (notably IT services).

Apart from the choice of the energy mix and the industrial orientation, appropriate incentives for consumer behavior seem to play a relevant role in directing the economy toward an emissions-extensive development path. The disastrous role of distorting incentive structures is best seen when considering economies based on fossil fuel exports, such as the monarchies of the Persian Gulf. In all these countries, in 2010, per capita emissions were at least as high as those of the United States (18t), and in some cases a multiple of these (Energy Information Administration 2012). They all provided their local population with energy at production cost rather than at market price, which leads to a loss of export revenues and thus public resources that could have otherwise been invested into other development activities. It may also be noted that the benefit incidence of such (untargeted) energy subsidies tends to accrue disproportionally to the wealthier parts of the national population because of their higher energy consumption. This may be a concern when considering equity within countries. At the same time, given the arguments on the strong political role of the urban middle class in section 10.3.3, this will make the abolition of such subsidies very difficult.

10.4.2   National Voluntary Action versus International Obligations

While the choice of a low emissions development path may not always be politically feasible, some factors enhance the chances for some positive dynamics in this direction. Increasingly availably information on climate change related risks may have a certain role to play (for the Indian case, see Michaelowa and Michaelowa 2011b). Much more important, however, countries seem to be driven toward less emissions-intensive development by much more direct economic incentives. These incentives are generated, primarily, by shortages in traditional energy supply that could significantly curtail growth in countries like China and India in the future. In today's India, the lack of high-quality coal and gas sources has led to problems in expanding thermal power plants sufficiently to cover the rapidly rising electricity demand (Michaelowa and Michaelowa 2011b); the July 2012 blackout depriving over six hundred million Indians of electricity for several days has highlighted this. In China, the expansion of coal power capacity has so far been able to keep pace with rising demand but it has led to massive air pollution problems. While the mandated closure of small, obsolete plants and their replacement by large-scale supercritical plants has somewhat reduced the pressure, it is clear that a significant contribution to solving the air pollution challenge can only be achieved by reducing the share of coal power.

In China and India, these problems have given rise to significant domestic policy initiatives. In the second half of the 2000s, both countries have introduced substantive greenhouse gas mitigation programs. In 2008, India announced a National Action Plan on Climate Change that consists of several "missions" involving an expansion of renewable energy, as well as a trading system for energy efficiency credits. China, which suffered from a reversal of the multidecade decline of energy intensity during the first half of the 2000s, introduced several vigorous energy efficiency improvement policies for large companies. Moreover, the introduction of a countrywide feed-in tariff for wind and solar energy in the second half of the 2000s led to a massive increase in wind and solar capacity, with China becoming the world leader in both technologies. In addition, there was a conversion of industries from coal to gas in a number of provinces in Eastern China, and the development of nuclear power (including highly innovative research on thorium reactors)—which is, of course, a more ambiguous measure from an environmental sustainability perspective.

All in all, the policies adopted by China and India are more vigorous than those of many industrialized countries. Interestingly, until Copenhagen, they have not been brought up in the context of the international climate negotiations. In fact, referring to the principle of common but differentiated responsibilities as well as related ideas discussed in section 10.2, India and China ferociously fought against emissions commitments for developing countries until the post-Durban emergence of the bottom-up process. As described by Dubash (2012) for the Indian case, the international position reflects an adherence to general moral principles, and does not hinder self-determined national mitigation action. At Copenhagen, both countries announced a commitment to specific national energy efficiency targets. In the run-up to Paris, both countries submitted an intensity-based intended NDC. The level of mitigation ambition has been ranked by the Potsdam Institute for Climate Impact Research, Climate Analytics and Ecofys as being "medium", comparable to that of key industrialized countries. For other developing countries as diverse as Bhutan, Costa Rica, Ethiopia, and Morocco, even the high rank of "sufficient" is awarded. Other key developing countries like Indonesia, South Korea, Singapore, and South Africa, however, score "inadequate," comparable to Australia, Canada, and Russia (Climate Action Tracker 2015).

10.5   Financial Support by the Industrialized World

While the last section showed that certain mitigation policies are in the self-interest of emerging economies, and that economic development can also be achieved on an emissions-extensive growth path, the measures induced by domestic incentives may not be considered sufficient for the participation of developing countries in global mitigation activities. However, to go beyond these measures requires funding, and the arguments discussed in section 10.2 provide some solid ground for the request that such funding should be provided by the industrialized world. In addition, those arguments—and notably the historical responsibility argument—can be used to make a case for additional funds from industrialized countries to finance developing countries' adaptation measures and even compensation for damages already experienced. As argued by Sprinz and von Bünau (2013), financial compensation might not just lead to more equity but that it could also be efficient in the sense that it, if properly implemented, is in the interest of both developed and developing countries. Moreover, given the lack of human capital in many developing countries, external funding may be required to support their informed participation in the negotiation process itself.

Consequently, from the outset of international climate negotiations, developing countries have called for financial support, and over the years several forms of such support have been granted. National reports of developing countries within the UNFCCC framework have always benefitted from financial assistance. Since the early 1990s, the Global Environment Facility (GEF) has financed mitigation and adaptation projects in developing countries. Bi- and multilateral aid has also flown into such activities. In the following section, we discuss the existing financial commitments, as well as certain interests by both donors and recipients that may impede their effectiveness and efficiency.

10.5.1   Equity through Burden Sharing: Recent Developments in Climate Finance

While activities related to climate change have been financed by the GEF and by bi- and multilateral development cooperation for many years, the Copenhagen Accord of 2009 provided the first substantial agreement on development finance within the framework of the UNFCCC. The Copenhagen Accord specified that industrialized countries should provide US$30 billion of "fast start finance" during 2010–2012 to developing countries. From 2020 onward, annual climate finance flows should reach US$100 billion. This figure is substantial and corresponds to almost 80 percent of net official development assistance (ODA) (see OECD/DAC 2012, 3). However, it is not supposed to be taken out of existing development funds since it was agreed in several climate decision texts that financial support should be "new and additional." Given that most industrialized country governments have committed to substantial increases in their general aid budgets over and over again for the last decades without ever getting close to their objective (i.e., to reach a share of 0.7 percent of GDP), one might wonder whether these new commitments are credible in any way. One loophole could be that the new climate finance may encompass private flows.

Even several years after the end of the fast start finance period, while formally the full amount has been pledged, only a small share has actually been disbursed. In addition, even whether the full amount of the pledges has actually been reached is a matter of debate. In fact, this would only be the case if low-carbon foreign direct investment could be taken into account (Buchner et al. 2011; Stadelmann, Roberts, and Michaelowa 2011a). OECD and Climate Policy Initiative (2015) have developed an accounting approach for international climate finance that calculates a volume of about US$60 billion for 2013 and 2014. These numbers have been contested by India as being exaggerated (Ministry of Finance 2015). An uncontested means of international climate finance is the Green Climate Fund (GCF) which has been allocated US$9.6 billion and has started to select project proposals for funding in late 2015. However, the Paris Agreement remained silent on short-term climate financing, just repeating the reference to US$100 billion by 2020. The accompanying decision states that this level shall be exceeded from 2025 onward, but does not specify numbers.

With growing flows of private finance from advanced developing countries to industrialized countries, the question arises whether only the net volume of North-South flows should be counted. However, this would have the somewhat paradoxical implication that the more an emerging country is able to invest in the North, the more "support" it would have to receive from the North.

10.5.2 Input Assessment, Leverage, and Additionality

The above discussion clearly shows that the agreement on climate finance for developing countries lacks the clear definitions necessary for its implementation. Moreover, it is not clear what the additionality requirement is supposed to mean in practice. Is climate finance "new and additional" when it leads to increased ODA, but still less so than even prior ODA commitments would have required? International negotiations have never agreed on any definition what "new and additional" support means, leading to substantial uncertainty and mistrust by developing countries (Stadelmann, Roberts, and Michaelowa 2011b).

While we have looked at the political economy in developing countries in section 10.3, we need to look at the political economy in industrialized countries to understand this type of agreement. Obfuscation (i.e., the deliberate lack of clarity) is vital to reconcile the different interests within national constituencies. On the one hand, the issue of global climate change had gained important media coverage around Copenhagen, and environmental preferences were strongly articulated. On the other hand, at a time of financial and economic crisis, governments hardly wanted to take the political risk of increasing taxes to finance such measures. At least in the short run, an agreement with high and easily publishable numbers like the US$100 billion figure pleases the environmental community, while the lack of clear definitions reduces accountability and enables the government to eventually continue with business as usual. If anything at all really happens beyond business as usual, these financial flows are prone to be counted under several headings. For example, revenues from carbon market mechanisms could be counted as climate finance even if they just serve to reach the NDCs of industrialized countries. And other funds can be counted as additional ODA. The whole process then tends to become primarily an exercise of creative accounting.

Similar developments have already been observed within ODA. In the late 1990s, the OECD introduced a so-called Rio marker for mitigation related aid activities (followed by a Rio marker for adaptation a decade later). As shown by Michaelowa and Michaelowa (2011a), a strong environmental constituency within the donor country (measured by the share of parliamentarians from environmental parties) leads to an incentive for bilateral donor agencies to increase the attribution of these markers for a given project portfolio. All in all, this results in substantial overreporting: At the time of the study, the number of aid activities with a mitigation marker exceeded the number of activities actually related to mitigation by about 30 percent.

These problems would certainly be less prevalent if it were easier to directly assess the impact of mitigation and adaptation activities. The lack of reliable impact evaluations drives the focus toward inputs rather than outputs, assuming that more activities and increased funding will automatically lead to better results. This is, of course, a highly questionable assumption. To some extent, this assumption may also explain the current fashion to "assess" the efficiency of government funding by the share of complementary private funds it was able to mobilize, i.e., the "leverage" of private funding. Inclusion of private funds into "climate finance" again only changes the statistics on the input side but does not guarantee enhanced outputs, as many private funds would probably have been invested anyway. Moreover, a focus on projects with high leverage of private investments may distort public funding from its initial climate priorities toward private business interests, for example, projects with high income from electricity sale. Therefore, a focus on private finance leverage may reduce effectiveness of public climate finance, even when the private sector is more efficient in implementation (Stadelmann, Castro, and Michaelowa 2011).

10.5.3   Learning from Half a Century of Development Assistance

Similar problems have been faced in the context of development aid for many decades and have been widely discussed in the literature on the political economy of aid (see, e.g., Lahiri and Michaelowa 2006). The tendency of gearing aid toward the needs of domestic firms rather than toward development priorities has been widely discussed in the literature on aid allocation decisions (e.g., Berthélemy 2006) and gave rise to a long-term debate about the inefficiency of aid tied to exports of goods and services at the level of the OECD's Development Assistance Committee (DAC) in the early 1990s.

More generally, policy coherence has been a continuous discussion in the context of aid. As many different policy areas affect the developing prospects of the South, there is a high risk that policies in domains with a less development-oriented constituency wipe out any positive effects that aid may have. The broad scope of the Sustainable Development Goals (SDGs) adopted by the UN in September 2015 and the related Agenda 2030 for Sustainable Development can be seen as an attempt to bring the different development-relevant dimensions under a common framework to overcome such coherence problems (United Nations 2015).

For many years, a central aspect of the coherence debate has been the contrast between aid policy, on the one hand, and protectionist trade policy, on the other hand. Similarly, today, industrialized country governments are increasingly worried about potential production shifts to developing countries attracted by the lower cost of production. To avoid such shifts, they consider the introduction of policy instruments such as subsidies or border tax adjustments that would reduce the price advantages of developing country producers. If the higher production cost in industrialized countries is only due to environmental regulation to reduce CO_2 emissions, policy measures to avoid bypassing of the regulation (and thus ensuring actual emissions reductions) may be well founded. However, in many cases, higher cost will be driven by a variety of factors, including wage preferences of domestic workers. In this case, compensating policy measures may well entail a significant part of pure protectionism. Different policy areas need to be considered simultaneously to identify potential conflicts of interest and to assess the overall impact on developing countries.

The problem of using inputs rather than impact as a measure of success has also been widely discussed in half a century of experience with development assistance. In this context, it has become clear that increasing inputs do not only fail to be a sufficient condition for development impacts, but that in fact, they may at times even set wrong incentives and do more harm than good (see, e.g., Easterly 2006). Therefore, a successful aid intervention does not only require a valuable purpose, but also an in-depth consideration of the different actors and interests that will be affected. In particular, successful projects are usually associated with effective local ownership and some degree of good (political, institutional, and economic) governance. The situation may be so complex that aid agency staff, confronted with an unexpected increase in funding, frequently report difficulties in identifying enough promising projects. With respect to climate finance, these issues seem to have been given much less attention so far. Given the national political economy in many developing countries (section 10.3.3), it can, for instance, not be expected that external funds to compensate for damages or to support adaptation will necessarily be provided to those in need. In the context of development assistance, the attempt to effectively achieve benefits for the poor has led to an extensive policy discussion of issues such as targeting, policy and process conditionality, and project versus sector or budget aid. While no consensus has been reached so far, many arguments within this discussion deserve close consideration.

To sum up, it appears that many questions now coming up in the context of climate-change-related transfers from industrialized to developing countries have already come up earlier in the area of development cooperation. These experiences should be taken into account when designing a system for the allocation of climate finance, be it bilateral or in the context of the multilateral GCF.

10.6 Conclusion

Combining insights from international climate negotiations, development cooperation, and political economic analysis of the decision making processes in both developing and industrialized countries, this chapter has provided a discussion of developing country positions, their implications for different groups of the population, the potential to reconcile development with a low-emissions path, and challenges regarding financial support by the industrialized world. It turns out that developing country positions with their emphasis on the primary responsibility of industrialized countries have a strong moral appeal, while the definition of the fixed dividing line between "developing" and "industrialized" became more and more debatable until it started to dissolve in Paris.

Equity understood in terms of equal rights to development can be established when those who have benefitted from free emissions to build up their economies now are held accountable for the related negative externalities. While this is at least theoretically unambiguous, thorny technical details such as the estimation of damages, the choice of an appropriate discount rate, and the decision about a useful starting point for the calculation of cumulated historical emissions have a huge impact on the practical consequences resulting from this general statement. A narrow focus on equity embodied in an ossified categorization of countries slowed down international negotiations over the last decade.

Equity issues have to be considered not only between but also within countries, and between different types of countries within the overall developing country group. Much of the discussion related to differentiated responsibilities between countries could, in principle, be applied to different groups within the developing countries. A political economic analysis reveals that the most vulnerable tend to benefit least from the positions their governments adopt at the international level, notably when this means to block international progress by disagreeing with any kind of own commitments to be borne by the urban middle class in emerging economies. Fortunately, at least in the large emerging economies of China and India, this middle class has other incentives, unrelated to the international negotiation process, to accept mitigation policies. These are related primarily to a shortage of energy supplies and to problems with local pollution. Thus despite their relatively intransigent stance at the international level, the governments of both India and China have introduced substantial mitigation policies in recent years. Therefore we are likely to see significant mitigation action in the emerging economies. A cross-country comparison of the emissions path of a couple of fast developing economies from different continents also suggests that, as opposed to perceived knowledge, rapid economic development does not necessarily require a substantial increase in emissions. As the Paris Agreement shows, developing countries of varying sizes and circumstances are willing to underwrite mitigation under the "bottom-up" system of NDCs.

When looking at financial support by the industrialized world, we highlight the challenges due to the different interests not only between North and South but also within developing and within developed countries. For instance, industrialized countries' business interests may play a strong role when climate finance is heavily leveraged by private funds. This may divert priorities from emissions reductions. Moreover, industrialized country governments that try to reconcile environmental interests and budgetary concerns tend to resort to vague agreements that state impressive numbers with no clear attribution of responsibilities. Eventually, this tends to end in an exercise of creative accounting. This has also been shown in the context of development aid. More generally, many of the questions relating to climate finance for developing countries have already come up earlier in the context of development cooperation. This also concerns issues of appropriate targeting and conditionality. The often sobering experience of half a century of development assistance should be given due consideration within the context of international climate policy.

While the Paris Agreement has the ambition to reach an emissions path that keeps warming "well below" 2°C, it remains open whether any real mitigation action will be taken. If developing countries wait for climate finance from industrialized countries to reach the level on which NDCs have been made conditional, the ambitious goal of the Paris Agreement will remain out of reach.

Notes

1. For a more detailed discussion of CBDR and the development of its interpretation over time, see Michaelowa and Michaelowa (2015).

2. For a comprehensive overview of the heated debate between economists in the second half of the 2000s following the Stern Review, see Godard (2008).

3. For China as well, being seen as an important partner in international negotiations appears to be a foreign policy objective in itself. According to Conrad (2012), Copenhagen was a disaster for the Chinese delegation, and apparently less so for its limited substantive outcomes than for the reason that the country was largely presented as the major culprit of blocking the process.

4. Whether and to what extent the interests of urban elites or poorer strata of the society prevail is discussed in a case study for India by Jaeger and Michaelowa (2015).

5. More specifically, the HDI is a geometric mean of three sub-indices based on life expectancy at birth, years of schooling, and gross national income (GNI) per capita. Its scale ranges from 0 (lowest) to 1 (highest human development). See UNDP (2011).

References

Agarwal, Anil, and Sunita Narain. 1991. *Global Warming in an Unequal World: A Case of Environmental Colonialism*. New Delhi: Centre for Science and Environment.

Baer, Paul, Tom Athanasiou, Sivan Kartha, and Eric Kemp-Benedict. 2008. *The Greenhouse Development Rights Framework*. Berlin: Heinrich-Böll Stiftung.

Berthélemy, Jean-Claude. 2006. "Bilateral Donors' Interest vs. Recipients' Development Motives in Aid Allocation: Do All Donors Behave the Same?" *Review of Development Economics* 10 (2): 179–194.

Betzold, Carola. 2010. "'Borrowing' Power to Influence International Negotiations: AOSIS in the Climate Change Regime, 1990–1997." *Politics* 30 (3): 131–148.

Betzold, Carola, Paula Castro, and Florian Weiler. 2012. "AOSIS in the UNFCCC Negotiations: From Unity to Fragmentation?" *Climate Policy* 12 (5): 591–613.

Bodansky, Daniel. 2016. "The Paris Climate Change Agreement: A New Hope?" *American Journal of International Law* 110 (2): 288–319.

Buchner, Barbara, Angela Falconer, Morgan Hervé-Mignucci, Chiara Trabacchi, and Marcel Brinkman. 2011. *The Landscape of Climate Finance*. Venice: Climate Policy Initiative.

Bueno De Mesquita, Bruce, James D. Morrow, Randolph M. Siverson, and Alastair Smith. 1999. "Policy Failure and Political Survival: The Contribution of Political Institutions." *Journal of Conflict Resolution* 43 (2): 147–161.

Castro, Paula, Lena Hörnlein, and Katharina Michaelowa. 2011. "Path Dependence of Negotiation Structures in International Organizations: The Impact of Annex I Membership on Discussions within the UNFCCC." CIS Working Paper 67, edited by Center for Comparative and International Studies. Zurich: ETH Zurich and University of Zurich.

Chakravarty, Shoibal, and M. V. Ramana. 2012. "Hiding behind the Poor Debate: A Synthetic Overview." In *Handbook of Climate Change and India: Development, Politics and Governance*, edited by Navroz K. Dubash, 218–229. New Delhi: Oxford University Press.

Climate Action Tracker. 2015. *Tracking INDCs*. Available from http://climateaction tracker.org/indcs.html.

Cline, William R. 1992. *The Economics of Global Warming*. Washington, DC: Institute for International Economics.

Conrad, Björn. 2012. "China in Copenhagen: Reconciling the 'Beijing Climate Revolution' and the 'Copenhagen Climate Obstinacy.'" *China Quarterly* 210 (1): 435–455.

Dasgupta, Partha. 2007. "Commentary: The Stern Review's Economics of Climate Change." *National Institute Economic Review* 199 (1): 4–7.

Depledge, Joanna. 2008. "Striving for No: Saudi Arabia in the Climate Change Regime." *Global Environmental Politics* 8 (4): 9–35.

Dubash, Navroz K., ed. 2012. *Handbook of Climate Change and India: Development, Politics and Governance.* New Delhi: Oxford University Press.

Easterly, William. 2006. *The White Man's Burden: Why the West's Efforts to Aid the Rest Have Done So Much Ill and So Little Good.* New York: Penguin.

Energy Information Administration. 2012. *International Energy Statistics.* Available from http://www.eia.gov/cfapps/ipdbproject/iedindex3.cfm?tid=90&pid=45&aid =8&cid=regions&syid=1980&eyid=2010&unit=MTCDPP.

Gemenne, François. 2011. "Climate-Induced Population Displacements in a 4 C+World." *Philosophical Transactions of the Royal Society A: Mathematical, Physical and Engineering Sciences* 369 (1934): 182–195.

Godard, Olivier. 2008. "The Stern Review on the Economics of Climate Change: Contents, Insights and Assessment of the Critical Debate." *Surveys and Perspectives Integrating Environment and Society* 1 (1): 23–41.

Human Development Report Office. 2011. *International Human Development Indicators.* Available from http://hdr.undp.org/en/data.

International Energy Agency. 2015. CO_2 *Emissions from Fuel Combustion.* Paris: International Energy Agency.

Jaeger, Carlo C., Jette Krause, Armin Haas, Rupert Klein, and Klaus Hasselmann. 2008. "A Method for Computing the Fraction of Attributable Risk Related to Climate Damages." *Risk Analysis* 28 (4): 815–823.

Jaeger, Mark Daniel, and Katharina Michaelowa. 2015. "Global Climate Policy and Local Energy Politics: Is India Hiding behind the Poor?" *Climate Policy* 16 (7): 940–951.

La Rovere, Emilio, Laura Valente de Macedo, and Kevin Baumert. 2002. "The Brazilian Proposal on Relative Responsibility for Global Warming." In *Building on the Kyoto Protocol: Options for Protecting the Climate,* edited by Kevin Baumert, 157–173. Washington, DC: World Resources Institute.

Lahiri, Sajal, and Katharina Michaelowa. 2006. "Editorial: The Political Economy of Aid." *Review of Development Economics* 10 (2): 177–178.

Meyer, Aubrey. 2000. *Contraction and Convergence: The Global Solution to Climate Change.* Devon: Green Books.

Michaelowa, Axel, Sonja Butzengeiger, and Martina Jung. 2005. "Graduation and Deepening: An Ambitious Post-2012 Climate Policy Scenario." *International Environmental Agreements: Politics, Law and Economics* 5 (1): 25–46.

Michaelowa, Axel, and Katharina Michaelowa. 2009. "Does Human Development Really Require Greenhouse Gas Emissions?" In *Rethinking Development in a Carbon-Constrained World*, edited by Eija Paluoso, 170–183. Helsinki: Finnish Ministry of Foreign Affairs.

Michaelowa, Katharina, and Axel Michaelowa. 2011a. "Coding Error or Statistical Embellishment? The Political Economy of Reporting Climate Aid." *World Development* 39 (11): 2010–2020.

———. 2011b. "India in the International Climate Negotiations: From Traditional Nay-Sayer to Dynamic Broker." *Working Paper No.70*, edited by Center for Comparative and International Studies. Zurich: ETH Zurich and University of Zurich.

———. 2015. "Do Rapidly Developing Countries Take Up New Responsibilities for Climate Change Mitigation?" *Climatic Change* 133 (3): 499–510.

Miller, Ted R. 2000. "Variations between Countries in Values of Statistical Life." *Journal of Transport Economics and Policy* 34 (2): 169–188.

Ministry of Finance. 2015. Climate Change Finance, Analysis of a Recent OECD Report: Some Credible Facts Needed. Discussion Paper Climate Change Finance Unit. Department of Economic Affairs. New Delhi.

Mueller, Dennis C. 2003. *Public Choice III*. Cambridge: Cambridge University Press

Nordhaus, William D. 2007. "A Review of the Stern Review on the Economics of Climate Change." *Journal of Economic Literature* 45 (3): 686–702.

OECD/DAC. 2012. *Development Aid at a Glance: Statistics by Region*. Available from http://www.oecd.org/dac/aidstatistics/42139479.pdf.

Olson, Mancur. 1965. *The Logic of Collective Action: Public Goods and the Theory of Groups*. Cambridge, MA: Harvard University Press.

Pan, Jiahua. 2005. "Meeting Human Development Goals with Low Emissions: An Alternative to Emissions Caps for Post-Kyoto from a Developing Country Perspective." *International Environmental Agreements: Politics, Law and Economics* 5 (1): 89–104.

Paterson, Matthew. 2001. "Principles of Justice in the Context of Global Climate Change." In *International Relations and Global Climate Change*, edited by Urs Luterbacher and Detlef Sprinz. Cambridge, MA: MIT Press. 119–126.

Putnam, Robert D. 1988. "Diplomacy and Domestic Politics: The Logic of Two-Level Games." *International Organization* 42 (3): 427–460.

Schlosberg, David. 2004. "Reconceiving Environmental Justice: Global Movements and Political Theories." *Environmental Politics* 13:517–540.

Sprinz, Detlef F., and Steffen von Bünau. 2013. "The Compensation Fund for Climate Impacts." *Weather, Climate, and Society* 5 (3): 210–220.

Stadelmann, M., P. Castro, and A. Michaelowa. 2011. *Is There a Leverage Paradox in Climate Finance? Efficiency of the CCD and the GEF in Leveraging Funds and Reducing CO2*. Cambridge: Climate.

Stadelmann, M., J. Timmons Roberts, and A. Michaelowa. 2011a. *Accounting of Private Climate Finance: Types of Finance, Data Gaps and the 100 Billion Dollar Question*. Cambridge: Climate Strategies.

Stadelmann, Martin, J. Timmons Roberts, and Axel Michaelowa. 2011b. "New and Additional to What? Assessing Options for Baselines to Assess Climate Finance Pledges." *Climate and Development* 3 (3): 175–192.

Stern, Nicholas. 2006. *Stern Review on the Economics of Climate Change*. London: HM Treasury.

Tol, Richard S. J. 1997. "The Social Cost Controversy: A Personal Appraisal." In *Proceedings of the International Symposium Prospects for Integrated Environmental Assessment: Lessons Learnt from the Case of Climate Change*, edited by Andrew Sors, Angela Liberatore, Silvio Funtowicz, Jean-Charles Hourcade, and Jean-Louis Fellous, 35–42. Brussels.

UNDP. 2011. *Human Development Report: Sustainability and Equity: A Better Future for All*. New York: United Nations Development Program.

UNEP. 1972. *Declaration of the United Nations Conference on the Human Environment*. Stockholm: United Nations Environment Program.

UNFCCC. 2007. *Climate Change: Impacts, Vulnerabilities and Adaptation in Developing Countries*. Bonn: UNFCCC.

———. 2015. *Paris Agreement*. Paris: United Nations.

United Nations. 2015. *Transforming Our World: The 2030 Agenda for Sustainable Development*. Available from https://sustainabledevelopment.un.org/post2015/trans formingourworld.

Vihma, Antto. 2011. "India and the Global Climate Governance: Between Principles and Pragmatism." *Journal of Environment & Development* 20 (1): 69–94.

Winkler, Harald, T. Jayaraman, Pan Jiahua, Adriano Santhiago de Oliveira, Zhang Yongsheng, Girish Sant, José Miguez, Thapelo Letete, Andrew Marquard, and Stefan Raubenheimer. 2011. *Equitable Access to Sustainable Development: Contribution to the Body of Scientific Knowledge*. Beijing: BASIC Expert Group.

World Bank. 2016. *World Development Indicators 2016*. Washington, DC: World Bank.

Yang, Xiu, Erda Lin, Shiming Ma, Hui Ju, Liping Guo, Wei Xiong, Yue Li, and Yinlong Xu. 2007. "Adaptation of Agriculture to Warming in Northeast China." *Climatic Change* 84 (1): 45–58.

11 Implementation, Compliance, and Effectiveness of Policies and Institutions

Jon Hovi and Arild Underdal

11.1 Introduction

Environmental governance can be analyzed as an extended and iterative process—an evolving sequence of connected events (see figure 11.1). Grossly simplified, we may distinguish three main stages: describing and diagnosing problems, developing and adopting policy "cures," and implementing these cures. Each stage serves a particular function, which may be referred to as "cognitive," "regulatory," and "behavioral," respectively. When students of international environmental governance measure the *effectiveness* of regimes and regulations, they usually focus on the end product. Thus, a regime is considered to be effective insofar as it solves or alleviates the problem it has been established to cope with (Mitchell 2008). Understanding governance as an evolving sequence of connected events opens for a more refined approach whereby we can differentiate achievement by stages or functions (see Stokke 2012). Such differentiation can be an important tool for improving diagnostics and fine-tuning policy designs. For example, instead of just assigning a low overall effectiveness score to the UNFCCC regime, we would give a fairly high score to the IPCC for its contributions to developing a science-based, broadly accepted description, as well as diagnosis of the problem, but a significantly lower score for the regime's achievements in adopting policy cures and bringing about behavioral change (Clark et al. 2001).

In this chapter, we examine the third phase more closely (this phase consists of the last three boxes in figure 11.1), and ask to what extent the UNFCCC regime (1) has succeeded in inducing the parties to the agreements reached to fulfill their commitments,[1] and (2) has been equipped with, or succeeded to acquire, the means needed to accomplish that task. To

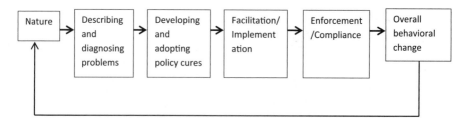

Figure 11.1
The governance process.

answer these questions, we must consider the implementation capacity of
the regime agencies themselves and their implementation efforts, and the
incentives, capabilities, and behavioral responses of the actors involved in
the activities that are subject to regulation. We should also recognize that
international regimes and organizations can shape member states' policies
not merely through brokering agreement but also through serving as arenas
for unilateral *learning* (from more "advanced" peers) and *adaptation* (to the
consequences of important others' actions). Moreover, global conferences
tend to generate their own stakes for participants. Such process-generated
stakes will sometimes lead governments to promise more than they had initially planned to promise. The net effect on implementation will depend on
the governments' trade-off between the (economic) costs of full compliance
and the (political) costs of failing to honor the "pacta sunt servanda" norm.

We begin (in section 11.2) by identifying two main conditions for effective compliance (beyond mere coincidence): willingness and ability. A brief
review of the research literature (section 11.3) shows that students of compliance disagree over which of these two conditions is the less likely to be met;
the enforcement school sees willingness as the more serious concern, while
the managerial school points to ability. Their policy prescriptions diverge
accordingly. We find (in section 11.4) that the Kyoto Protocol very explicitly
combines elements of enforcement with elements of facilitation. In contrast,
the Paris Agreement explicitly denounces enforcement and concentrates on
facilitation alone. We also conclude, however, that Kyoto's enforcement system is fundamentally flawed and that critical questions can be raised about
the effectiveness of important facilitation mechanisms. In the final section,
we briefly explore how the enforcement system might be strengthened in a
new climate change mitigation agreement, should Paris fail.

11.2   Implementation

Implementation involves efforts to bring a certain policy (decision, agreement) into effect. Since international agreements are, at least in principle, *voluntary* exchanges of commitments, one may assume that the parties signing and ratifying agreements have carefully considered the consequences of alternative options and promised no more than what they are willing and able to deliver. In fact, the situation will often be more complicated, particularly in complex settings of multilateral cooperation.

Consider first a party's *willingness* to deliver. As Simmons (2010), Hathaway (2002), and others have pointed out, international agreements are sometimes signed (and, if required, ratified) even by governments that seem to have no intention of making the changes required to comply. These "false positives" join for other reasons, such as harvesting reputational benefits or escaping political or economic sanctions.[2] In addition, governments that sign (ratify) a treaty or protocol in good faith may later come to conclude that compliance costs outweigh the benefits they can obtain from the deal. In the hectic last-ditch efforts to conclude a global conference on an upbeat note, some governments may decide to throw their support behind the emerging consensus by signing an agreement in which they see no significant benefits for themselves. For these "reluctant positives," a minor increase in compliance costs or a small reduction in benefits may be sufficient to turn the balance negative. Even a government that has enthusiastically promoted the agreement and signed with the best intention of complying may get cold feet if important circumstances change. Bad news, such as economic recession, may cause governments and societies to change their priorities, at least temporarily. Good news in the form of discoveries of major new deposits of oil or coal will likely increase a country's relative costs of meeting its mitigation targets. In the global climate change negotiations, even the largest countries have sound reasons for being concerned with reciprocity. Failure by other countries to participate with deep commitments or to honor these commitments will likely reduce a country's benefits from the agreement and trigger complaints about unfair exploitation by free riders. Even if circumstances do not change, all governments have multiple goals and programs to attend to, and with limited funds of political capital, they will sometimes have to give up one in order to secure sufficient support for another. In these and several other situations, "the best policy currently planned for some future period is no longer the best when that period arrives" (Cukierman 1992, 15). In dealing with the extremely demanding challenge of climate change mitigation, time-inconsistent policies are likely to be common (Hovi, Sprinz, and Underdal 2009). The take-home message is simply that even governments that have signed and ratified a climate change mitigation agreement in good faith may stall at some point when the time to deliver arrives.[3]

Compliance failure may also be due to limited *ability* to contribute as promised. In trying to honor its commitments, a government may find itself constrained by limited control at two levels. First, governments depend—to varying degrees—on some form of domestic approval of the international agreements they negotiate (Putnam 1988). In democratic political systems, domestic ratification can be a major hurdle. President Clinton's acknowledgment that the US Senate would not have ratified the Kyoto Protocol had it been asked to do so is a case in point. The more demanding the decision rule and the weaker the government's position, the more the cards are stacked against ratification. Even if an agreement is formally approved, effective implementation cannot be taken for granted. Governments are complex organizations consisting of multiple agencies, each with its own mandate, agendas, and repertoires (Allison 1971). In business-as-usual circumstances, the involvement of sector agencies and organizations tends to increase as the governance process moves into the implementation stage. Moreover, since specific measures will in most cases affect particular activities, sectors, or groups more than others, the problem itself will to some extent be reframed along the way. Thus, what started out as "climate change mitigation" policy may increasingly come to be seen as matters of, for example, energy policy, industrial policy, or land use policy. Evaluated in terms of such sectorial frameworks, at least some of the specific measures that could be important components of a comprehensive and ambitious mitigation policy are likely to be seen by many as less attractive. Consequently, policies emerging from the implementation stage will often be characterized by a particular kind of *vertical disintegration*, where the aggregate thrust of micro-decisions falls short of delivering what professed policy goals and principles require (Underdal 1987).

Second, the human impact on the global climate system can be traced to a wide range of activities, from burning fossil fuels to land use and land-cover change. No government can control all these activities or the underlying driving forces (population, income, technology). Consequently, mitigation policies may fail to produce the effects desired and expected. This failure applies not merely to general regulatory instruments such as a carbon tax or a cap-and-trade system; even specific projects in which a government invests substantial amounts of money and political prestige sometimes fail. Norwegian Prime Minister Stoltenberg's "moon landing" carbon capture and storage program for a Norwegian gas refinery owned and operated by a state-owned company (Statoil) is an interesting case in point.

11.3   Research on Implementation and Compliance

Students of implementation and compliance agree that, for all practical purposes, both willingness and ability to deliver can be considered necessary conditions for a party to honor—except by coincidence—its (deep) commitments under an international agreement. They disagree, however, about which condition is less likely to be met. Over time, two distinct schools of research have emerged, one seeing *will* as the more serious concern (the enforcement school), the other pointing to *ability* as the critical factor (the managerial school).

Both schools start from the premise that—because of the international system's anarchical nature—countries cannot guarantee to honor their commitments (Axelrod and Keohane 1986; Oye 1985). Hence, both schools see it as essential to study how countries can bind themselves to mutually beneficial courses of action. They also agree that compliance with multilateral environmental agreements (MEAs) has generally been high although most MEAs lack a potent enforcement system (Chayes and Chayes 1993; Downs, Rocke, and Barsoom 1996; Weiss and Jacobson 1998).

However, the two schools disagree over three main issues (Aakre et al. 2016; Tallberg 2002). The first is whether enforcement influences compliance. The managerial school considers MEA enforcement to be largely irrelevant, arguing that efficiency concerns, national interests, and regime norms give states a "general propensity to comply" (Chayes and Chayes 1995, 3). In contrast, the enforcement school contends that we should expect high compliance only with shallow MEAs, that is, MEAs that commit countries to little more than business as usual. Such shallow treaties entail little incentive for non-compliance. *Deep* MEAs, on the other hand, require substantial behavioral change and will therefore often entail large incentives for free riding. These incentives must be offset by potent enforcement measures. According to the enforcement school, the observed extensive MEA compliance without enforcement is unsurprising because most MEAs are shallow. States tend to avoid commitments they are unable or unwilling to meet. The enforcement school argues that we would be mistaken to expect high compliance for *deep* treaties without enforcement because high compliance is common for *shallow* treaties without enforcement (Downs, Rocke, and Barsoom 1996).

Second, the two schools offer contrasting explanations for the rather rare cases of MEA noncompliance that we *do* observe. The managerial school views cases of noncompliance *not* as attempted free riding, but rather as a result of: (1) MEAs' ambiguity and indeterminacy, (2) technical and financial constraints on states' capacity to comply, and (3) changed social and economic circumstances between when states make commitments and when they must implement them. In contrast, the enforcement school considers incentives for free riding as the root cause of noncompliance; in essence, states fail to comply when they expect the benefits of noncompliance to outweigh the costs of being detected and disciplined.

Finally, the two schools disagree on how MEAs can best avoid noncompliance and reestablish compliance. The managerial school recommends that MEAs focus on: (1) refining mechanisms for dispute resolution, (2) providing technical and financial assistance, and (3) increasing transparency. It considers the role of MEAs is to modify preferences, generate new options, persuade parties to comply with regime norms, and strengthen the overall normative structure's compatibility with overall MEA objectives (Chayes and Chayes 1995, 229). In contrast, the enforcement school recommends that MEA parties construct enforcement systems that make clear to would-be free riders that cheating will trigger potent punishment, thereby making cheating unattractive to them (Downs, Rocke, and Barsoom 1996, 385).

11.4 The UNFCCC Regime

11.4.1 Facilitation and Enforcement

From the very beginning, the global climate change negotiations have been embedded in a broader context of stark asymmetries between guilt for causing the problem and capacity to alleviate it on the one hand, and socioecologic vulnerability to climate change on the other (see also Sprinz et al. in this volume). In agreeing on the formula "common but differentiated responsibilities and respective capabilities," the parties to the Framework Convention explicitly recognized that the rich industrialized countries would have to bear responsibility for most of the emission cuts required to achieve the goal set in the Convention: "stabilization of greenhouse gas concentration in the atmosphere at a level that would prevent dangerous anthropogenic interference with the climate system" (UNFCCC 1992, art. 2). Moreover, the Framework Convention includes a set of broad guidelines for supporting capacity building in less developed countries (UNFCCC 1992, art. 4) and a "Financial Mechanism" (UNFCCC 1992, art. 11) designed to provide the resources required (see also chapters 2 and 10 in this volume).

This dual-track approach has been pursued in later negotiations and is further specified in the Kyoto Protocol, concluded at COP 3 in 1997. "Quantified emission limitation and reduction commitments" are limited to a group of thirty-eight countries and the European Union (labeled "Annex I Parties"). Moreover, "developed (country) Parties" agree to "provide new and additional financial resources to meet the agreed [full/full incremental] costs of developing country Parties in advancing the implementation of existing commitments" under the Framework Convention (UNFCCC 1998, art. 11).[4] The Kyoto Protocol also introduced a clean development mechanism (CDM), designed to help developing countries achieve sustainable development and to help developed countries meet their emission control targets at lower costs (UNFCCC 1998, art. 12). The latter arrangement involves development assistance and purchase of mitigation services—a combination that probably stretches the managerial school's notion of facilitation beyond its original meaning. Yet the CDM is a mechanism for enabling and inducing developing countries to contribute (more) to global mitigation efforts, and significant funds are being transferred to support a large number of projects. The basic idea behind the CDM is to increase the global sum of mitigation through lowering mitigation costs. COP decisions in 2010 and 2011 established a new financial mechanism under the Framework Convention—the Green Climate Fund (GCF)—to support adaptation as well as mitigation measures in developing countries. An overall target of US$100 billion per year by 2020 has been suggested. A steep increase in developed countries' pledges will be required to meet that target (see also chapter 10 in this volume).

Several other international arrangements provide support and inducement for poor countries to contribute toward the goals set in the Framework

Convention and for rich countries to honor the principle of *differentiated* responsibilities. Such arrangements include climate investment funds (one of the most important being the Clean Technology Fund), established agencies (such as the International Renewable Energy Agency), and public-private partnerships (for example, the World Bank's Prototype Carbon Fund). Most of these have no formal link with the UNFCCC, but they are nonetheless relevant in this context as components of a broader international drive to mitigate the impact of human activities on the climate system.

The Kyoto Protocol does not include specific provisions for a compliance system. However, in 2001 at COP 7 in Marrakesh, the parties reached agreement on a compliance system for Kyoto.

The Marrakesh Accords describe the compliance system in detail.[5] In keeping with articles 5, 7, and 8 of the Kyoto Protocol, the Accords provide arrangements for estimating, reporting, and reviewing the parties' emissions of greenhouse gases (GHG emissions). First, each party must have in place a national system for estimating emissions of GHG emissions by various sources and a system for removals by sinks. Second, each party must annually report inventories of its GHG emissions and provide national communications at regular intervals.[6] Finally, expert review teams examine these inventories and national communications, and make in-country visits. Expert review-team members shall serve in "their personal capacities," have "recognized competence in the areas to be reviewed," and "refrain from making any political judgments" (UNFCCC 2005, 179).

To promote, control, and enforce compliance with member countries' commitments, the Marrakesh Accords also establish a Compliance Committee with two branches.

First, the Facilitative Branch provides advice and facilitation to parties concerning their implementation of the Protocol, thereby promoting parties' compliance with their Kyoto commitments (UNFCCC 2005, 131). It shall provide for early warning of potential noncompliance, formulate recommendations, and facilitate financial and technical assistance—including technology transfers and capacity building for non-Annex I parties. Finally, the Facilitative Branch is also responsible for reviewing the parties' reports to ensure that their uses of the flexibility mechanisms are "additional" to domestic measures. It does not, however, have its own financial resources to *provide* material assistance to parties that are unable to meet their obligations.

Second, the Enforcement Branch is responsible for determining whether Annex I Parties comply with their Kyoto commitments, and for inducing noncompliant parties to return to compliance. The enforcement "consequences" to be applied if a party fails to meet its obligations are the punitive (or "hard") elements of Kyoto's compliance regime. These consequences "shall be aimed at the restoration of non-compliance [sic] to ensure environmental integrity, and shall provide for an incentive to comply" (UNFCCC 2005, 132).

Two main types of noncompliance exist—failure by a party to meet its assigned emissions target, and failure by a party to fulfill the eligibility requirements for participating in Kyoto's flexibility mechanisms.[7] Should a party fail to meet its assigned emissions target, three consequences are at the Enforcement Branch's disposal. First, the noncompliant party must present its compliance restoration plan. Second, in the next commitment period, it must cover its surplus emissions from the first commitment period, *plus* an additional 30 percent of that surplus. The additional 30 percent comes on top of whatever its emissions reduction target for the next period would be. Finally, it loses its eligibility to sell emission permits.

Should a party fail to meet the eligibility requirements for participating in the Kyoto flexibility mechanisms (emissions trading, joint implementation, or the CDM), the Marrakesh Accords state that the eligibility of the noncompliant party shall be suspended in accordance with relevant provisions under articles 6, 12, and 17 of the Kyoto Protocol (UNFCCC 1998). These articles offer provisions for joint implementation, the CDM, and emissions trading, respectively.

The Enforcement Branch has no discretion to choose which punitive consequences are to be applied. It shall only ascertain whether a party is in noncompliance (either for failing to meet its emissions target or for failing to meet the eligibility requirements for participating in Kyoto's flexibility mechanisms). Second, the punitive consequences are also *automatic*. Once it determines that a party is in noncompliance, the Enforcement Branch is "responsible for applying the consequences." Decisions made by the Enforcement Branch can be appealed to the COP/MOP, but this possibility is very limited.[8]

The Enforcement Branch is composed of one member from each of the five regional groups of the United Nations, one member from the group of Small Island Developing States, two (other) members from Annex I Parties, and

Table 11.1
The composition of the enforcement branch (numbers refer to the number of members
from each category).

	Annex I	Non–Annex I
Africa		1
Asia and Oceania		1
Latin America and the Caribbean		1
Western Europe and others	1	
Eastern Europe	1	
Small Island Developing States		1
Annex I	2	
Non–Annex I		2
Total	**4**	**6**

Source: Ulfstein and Werksman (2005, 47).

two (other) members from non–Annex I Parties. Thus, although the punitive
consequences can be applied only to Annex I Parties, non–Annex I Parties
have a majority of the votes in the Enforcement Branch (see table 11.1).

If possible, decisions shall be made by consensus, but can, if necessary,
be made by a double qualified majority, that is, *both* a three-fourths majority among all members of the Enforcement Branch *and* (simple) majorities
among both the Annex I members and the non–Annex I members. Therefore, a decision can be blocked by a coalition consisting of two of the four
Annex I members. In contrast, a coalition consisting of two of the six non–
Annex I members, or a coalition consisting of one Annex I member and one
non–Annex I member, will *not* be able to block a decision.

11.4.2 Evaluation of the Compliance System

Facilitation Over the past fifteen years, substantial support for investment
in low carbon energy systems has been provided through international
mechanisms such as the CDM and the Global Environmental Facility (GEF)
and through a number of bilateral official development assistance (ODA)
programs. The World Bank (2010, 262) estimated that about US$95 billion
in clean energy investment benefited from CDM support over the 2002–
2008 period, while official development assistance directed toward mitigation was on the order of US$19 billion (2002–2007). Most of these transfers
do not enhance *compliance* by recipients, simply because most recipients

have no specific mitigation targets. In fact, the only significant effects on compliance, strictly interpreted, will likely be found on the side of rich countries that take advantage of the CDM system to reduce their mitigation costs. This is, of course, not to say that the CDM and other transfer mechanisms do not contribute to fulfilling the UNFCCC regime's main goal. Overall, the net effect seems to be positive. The *effectiveness* of these instruments in enhancing mitigation, however, is contested. In particular, critical questions have been raised about the extent to which the CDM leads to emission cuts that would not otherwise have occurred. Victor (2011, 93) suspects that the CDM system provides "massive numbers of credits for emission reductions that were nearly costless to implement and would have happened anyway." And the World Bank (2010, 265–266) admits that "the CDM contains some inherent inefficiencies," and lists questionable "additionality" (mitigation effect), insufficient contribution to sustainable development, weak governance, and limited scope as four main concerns.

The root of the additionality problem may be that neither side has truly strong incentives to make sure that credits go to projects where the additional funding makes a critical difference (see also chapter 10 in this volume). For most recipient countries, economic development will be higher on the priority list than climate change mitigation. For the Annex I countries, the CDM provides opportunities to fulfill some of their obligations at lower costs than those that would be incurred were all mitigation measures to be taken at home. Independent and critical assessment of projects is therefore an essential function for achieving the CDM's official purpose. Reports indicate that international organizations and agencies in charge struggle to provide that kind of assessment—partly due to the kind of data available, the limited human resources, and structural constraints. An effective "cure," at the very least, must provide a more effective mechanism for generating reliable data.

Enforcement   Kyoto's enforcement system could be commended for having a relatively advanced institutional structure (including a review system and the possibility of drawing attention to individual cases of noncompliance), compared to the enforcement systems of other environmental treaties.

Note, however, that the climate change problem entails much stronger incentives for free riding than other collective action problems do. Offsetting these incentives requires very potent enforcement measures. Unfortunately, both major punitive consequences in Kyoto's enforcement system suffer from significant flaws, making it unlikely that they will have much bearing on the member countries' compliance.[9]

Additional emissions reductions Implementing additional emissions reductions (see above) in a noncompliant member country is beyond the climate regime's control and beyond the control of individual, compliant members, too. In fact, only the punished party *itself* can implement such additional reductions (Halvorssen and Hovi 2006). It follows that this consequence is essentially a type of *self-punishment* (Barrett 2003). Enforcement based on self-punishment would not be particularly troubling if the system had provided a secondary punishment for failure to implement the required additional emissions reductions. Many compliance systems depend on punishments that require some degree of cooperation by the punished subject. For example, a taxpayer who fails to pay the full amount of tax on time may be required to pay a penalty, which is essentially self-punishment. An important difference exists, however: if the taxpayer fails to pay voluntarily, the government will collect by force both the outstanding tax and the penalty, at additional costs to the taxpayer. In contrast, Kyoto's compliance system includes no secondary punishment for failure to implement additional emissions reductions (Barrett 2003).

Even this objection might not have been too damaging had there existed a sufficiently strong *norm* saying that a noncompliant party should cooperate with the climate regime by implementing required additional emissions reductions. Many scholars rightly emphasize the importance of norms for enhancing international compliance (e.g., Chayes and Chayes 1993; Checkel 2001; Franck 1990). However, parties to the Kyoto Protocol had it in their power to reinforce compliance norms by making the requirement to implement additional emissions reductions *legally binding*. They chose *not* to use this power. In fact, not only did the Conference of the Parties choose *not* to make legally binding the perhaps most important consequence of noncompliance, it also created several hurdles that made it difficult to *change* this state of affairs.[10] We do not suggest that only legally binding norms influence behavior; however, making a norm legally binding may generally be expected to strengthen its effect on behavior.

At least three other troubling aspects of the consequence concerning additional emissions reductions deserve mention (Barrett 2003). First, even if a punished party does not refuse outright to implement required additional emissions reductions, it could easily *delay* such implementation. Uncertainty concerning whether the climate regime's architecture will persist over time (see chapter 2 in this volume) might make such delay particularly tempting. We now know that the Kyoto architecture based on a series of five-year commitment periods proved unviable already after the first period. Delay may ultimately enable a noncompliant country to escape punishment entirely.

Second, suppose a noncompliant country expects to be punished and intends to cooperate by implementing required additional emissions reductions in the next commitment period. Such a country would have a strong incentive to insist on a lax emissions limitation target for the next commitment period, because a lax target could water down the punishment.

Third, a country that has been a party to Kyoto for at least three years is entitled to withdraw by giving the depositary written notification (UNFCCC 1998, art. 27). Such withdrawal will take effect one year after the date of the notification or on such later date as may be specified in the notification. In essence, the withdrawal option means that a noncompliant country can escape the Enforcement Branch's punishment by withdrawing from Kyoto,[11] as Canada did when it gave notification of its withdrawal on December 12, 2011. Withdrawal will unlikely be cost-free, because it will bar the country in question from participating in Kyoto's flexibility mechanisms. It might also reduce its influence in future climate negotiations and perhaps damage its reputation. Nevertheless, the withdrawal option remains a way for the noncompliant country to escape the Enforcement Branch's punishment. We return to this point later.

Suspension of the right to sell emissions permits   Now consider suspension of the right to sell emissions permits, the second major punitive consequence available to the Enforcement Branch. Initially, this consequence would seem to have more teeth than the first because it does not rely on self-punishment. The climate regime controls its implementation; indeed, trading emissions permits makes little sense without the regime's approval.

Nevertheless, this second punitive consequence, too, has a serious flaw. A member that has already failed to reach its emissions target would be little affected by losing its right to sell emissions permits, because such a member would simply not have any permits to sell. Suspending the noncompliant member's right to *buy* permits would make more sense.[12] Although originally included in the draft text, the latter type of consequence was removed from the final agreement because its impact was considered potentially damaging to the environment (it would increase the noncompliant country's cost of getting back into compliance).

At best, therefore, this second punitive consequence will prevent a noncompliant member from illegally selling permits it does not have ("overselling"). Nevertheless, even if its right to sell permits is suspended, the member country could continue its noncompliance by refraining from buying enough permits to meet its emissions target ("underbuying").

The unfairness of the compliance system   Kyoto's compliance system has one additional flaw that deserves mentioning: it is *unfair* in the sense that the consequences can be imposed only for noncompliance, not for nonparticipation. The Enforcement Branch can punish an Annex I country that has accepted a binding emissions limitation target and yet fails to comply with this target. In contrast, it *cannot* punish a country that has ratified Kyoto *without* a binding emissions limitation target (non–Annex I Parties), a country that has declined to ratify Kyoto (the United States), or a country that has ratified and withdrawn before the first commitment period ended (Canada). Ironically, the Enforcement Branch is empowered to impose punitive consequences on certain member countries that do *something* (perhaps even a great deal) to curb emissions, but is not empowered to impose punitive consequences on any nonmembers, including nonmembers that do little or even *nothing* to curb emissions. Understandably, some countries dislike this lack of empowerment.

Some readers might object that the right to withdraw stems not from flawed design of the Kyoto protocol or its enforcement system but rather from international law. However, the right to withdraw from treaties is *not* a general feature of international law. Rather, this right is confined to treaties that expressly permit withdrawal (like the Kyoto Protocol does). Other treaties either expressly *forbid* withdrawal or are silent on the matter. Concerning the latter category, the Vienna Convention on the Law of Treaties (United Nations 1969, art. 56) states that such treaties cannot be unilaterally denounced unless (1) it can be demonstrated that the parties intended to admit withdrawal, or (2) the right of withdrawal can be implied from other treaty terms.[13]

Despite the many flaws of the compliance system, Kyoto 1 achieved full compliance.[14] Some countries did not meet their targets through domestic emissions reductions (Shishlov, Morel, and Bellassen 2016); however, even those countries reached compliance through sufficient use of the flexibility mechanisms.[15] The perfect compliance rates may be explained by a combination of seven main factors: (1) the "hot air" of Economies in Transition (EIT); (2) the United States' nonparticipation and Canada's withdrawal; (3) reduced economic activity owing to the financial crisis; (4) the member countries' policies and measures to reduce emissions; (5) the fact that the targets were relatively shallow; (6) a very low permit price; and (7) the fact that the vast majority of the Annex I countries are EU countries.[16]

11.5   Toward a More Effective Compliance System?

Compared with Kyoto, the 2015 Paris Agreement achieved a sharp increase in the number of parties with an emissions reduction or limitation commitment. Particularly striking is the support of a large majority of developing countries that consistently refused to accept own commitments in the Kyoto agreement. Much of the explanation for this change is to be found in an important procedural change made in the UNFCCC negotiations—from a "top-down" approach that had often spurred heated bargaining over the distribution of mitigation duties as a function of "guilt" and "capabilities," to a "bottom-up" approach in which each party determines what will be its own "nationally determined contribution (NDC)." Important is also the status of these NDCs as "pledges" that are not legally binding and (therefore) not subject to international enforcement.[17] While work is currently under way to develop a compliance system, the Paris Agreement expressly states that any compliance measures should be "facilitative in nature and function in a manner that is transparent, non-adversarial and non-punitive" (UNFCCC 2015). Two components of such a system are open reviews and updating of pledges every fifth year, events introduced in order to encourage states to upgrade their commitments.

Most observers agree that the changes made in approach and procedures are important—arguably even critical—to the survival of UNFCCC conference diplomacy (see, e.g., Keohane and Oppenheimer 2016; Victor 2011, 2016). Yet it remains an open question whether the Paris Agreement will develop to become significantly more effective than its predecessors (Hovi et al. 2016). On the positive side, the bottom-up approach acknowledges that countries differ in important respects and therefore can more effectively mobilize a wider range of domestic actors and motivations if allowed to choose contributions that make sense from their own perspectives (Victor 2016, 135). On the negative side, Keohane and Oppenheimer (2016, 142) are right that the "actual impact of the Paris Agreement will depend on whether it can be used by domestic groups favoring climate action as a point of leverage in domestic politics." If the pessimists are right, parties might soon begin to search for an alternative design that is based on binding commitments and that includes incentives for both participation (with deep commitments) and compliance.

At least two good reasons exist for considering alternative enforcement systems for a (future) global climate treaty. First, because nearly all economic activities entail GHG emissions, free-rider incentives are considerably stronger for climate change than for most (if not all) other environmental problems (Barrett 1999). Second, because of these strong free-rider incentives, and because effectively combating climate change will require participation by all major countries, a new global climate agreement may well have to include incentives for participation (i.e., participation enforcement). Recent research involving one of the authors has shown that compliance enforcement is largely pointless *without* participation enforcement, yet can be very effective *with* participation enforcement (Aakre, Helland, and Hovi 2016; Aakre and Hovi 2010). Reluctant actors (would-be free riders) that are induced to participate may be expected to drag their feet concerning their compliance unless deterred from doing so by potent compliance enforcement. Thus, should Paris fail, designing a new agreement that provides incentives for countries to participate with deep commitments and to comply with these commitments might be the next step in the UNFCCC negotiations.

While good ideas should be welcomed for improving both facilitation and enforcement, we here focus on the enforcement aspect. The reason is partly that mechanisms for capacity building and for other types of facilitation are more loosely connected to the concepts of compliance and participation (perhaps even to the UNFCCC regime as such), yet we simply have more to say about the enforcement aspect.

Exactly what will be a good enforcement-system design for the next climate agreement will depend on other characteristics of that agreement, such as whether it will be quantity-based (e.g., cap-and-trade), price-based (taxes), or technology-based (R&D, transfers, standards). Clearly, however, enforcement measures requiring extensive cooperation by punished parties should be avoided.

At least four types of enforcement measures have received widespread attention in the recent research literature (Hovi et al. 2012; see chapter 4 in this volume): issue-specific reciprocity, linkage to club goods, trade restrictions, and deposit-refund systems. Issue-specific reciprocity means that punishment for noncompliance consists of some or all compliant countries temporarily switching to less ambitious emission reduction schedules. Scholars have extensively studied such an enforcement system, using infinitely repeated games and focusing on weakly renegotiation-proof equilibria (e.g., Asheim et al. 2006; Asheim and Holtsmark 2009; Barrett 2003; Froyn and Hovi 2008; Heitzig, Lessmann, and Zou 2011). A major problem with issue-specific reciprocity is that investments in GHG abatement technology (e.g., windmill parks, heavily insulated buildings, or public transportation systems) have long lead times. Countries cannot sensibly stop using such technologies simply because another country fails to fulfill its GHG emissions reduction commitments. At best, they might cancel or postpone new emissions-reducing investments. Moreover, such cancellation or postponement may not be politically feasible, because environmental NGOs and green businesses would likely voice strong opposition (Hovi et al. 2012). A second potential problem with issue-specific reciprocity is that lowering the aggregate level of emissions reductions will hurt the environment. However, this problem can be solved by requiring noncompliant countries to undertake additional emissions reductions that compensate for switching to less ambitious schedules in compliant countries, so that aggregate emissions reductions remain unaffected in the punishment period (Heitzig, Lessmann, and Zou 2011).

Another important strand of the MEA enforcement literature examines conditions for stable coalitions (e.g., Finus 2008; see chapter 4 in this volume). While stable coalitions are generally small, scholars have shown that coalition size may be enhanced by linking cooperation on climate change to cooperation on some club good such as R&D knowledge or free trade (see, e.g., Hovi et al. 2016). A similar system could be invoked to enforce compliance. However, controlling knowledge produced by R&D is demanding, because knowledge often diffuses through channels beyond governmental control. Moreover, it may not be in a country's best interest to deny other countries new, green technology; after all, domestic firms holding patent rights benefit from worldwide sales of such technology, and green technology diffusion causes emissions reductions that benefit *all* countries (Buchner et al. 2005). Hence, this second type of enforcement measures is also likely to be politically infeasible.

Several MEAs permit use of trade restrictions for enforcement; for example, some observers claim that such restrictions have been instrumental in the Montreal Protocol's success (Barrett 2002; Benedick 1999; Brack 2003). In a new climate treaty, trade restrictions could be used both to increase participation and to deter noncompliance (e.g., Stiglitz 2006), at least in principle without violating GATT rules (WTO 2002; see chapter 6 in this volume). However, enforcing a new climate treaty would likely require much more extensive trade restrictions than those required to enforce Montreal. As a result, trade sanctions are much less likely to be politically feasible for a climate change agreement than for an agreement on ozone-depleting substances. A related argument is that frequent threats to use (or frequent use of) extensive trade restrictions could entail frequent trade disputes that would likely cause damage to the world trade system (WTO 2002). Yet another downside is that to be credible, trade restrictions must avoid hurting sender countries of trade restrictions. Such avoidance might require that the trade restrictions reduce carbon *leakage*, which ensues when a country's noncompliance improves its competitiveness and therefore increases its emissions. Barrett (1999) argues that the capacity for reducing leakage by trade restrictions may not suffice to make credible the threat of such restrictions in a climate change context. The reason is that for the countries imposing them, trade sanctions will often be more costly than the extra externalities caused by the leakage.

Finally, inspired by Finus (2008), Gersbach (2008), and Gerber and Wichardt (2009), several recent papers have considered the possibility of basing a new climate agreement on a deposit-refund system. Such a system's design must take into account the type of climate agreement in question. Here we briefly consider a design for a cap-and-trade type of agreement.[18] Essentially, each member country must deposit a significant sum of hard currency upon ratifying the agreement and must make additional yearly deposits until the commitment period begins. If a member country declines to make further required deposits or fails to reach its emissions limitation target, it will forfeit all or part of its existing deposits (depending on the degree of noncompliance). In contrast, a country that makes all required deposits and meets its target will receive a full refund when the commitment period ends. A deposit-refund system will effectively deter noncompliance, provided that each country's deposits exceed its abatement costs. Abatement costs, and hence the required deposit size, vary significantly across countries. For example, based on the assumption that emission reduction targets equal the pledges made in the Copenhagen Accords, Hovi et al. (2012) find that major permit buyers must make deposits around 1 percent of GDP, whereas other countries must make only small deposits or even none at all.

As a compliance enforcement tool, a deposit-refund system has a number of advantages (Hovi et al. 2012). First, it is simple. Whereas Kyoto's compliance enforcement system is complex, a system whereby noncompliance entails lost deposits is straightforward. Second, implementation of punishment does not require cooperation by noncompliant countries, because the climate regime will control deposits. This second advantage provides another contrast to Kyoto's enforcement system, which relies on self-punishment. Third, assuming that deposits exceed compliance costs, the threatened punishment will be potent, in the sense that fulfilling one's commitments will be better than being noncompliant *and* forfeiting one's deposits. Fourth, the threatened punishment will be credible. Under a deposit-refund system, punishing a noncompliant party will benefit the other parties individually as well as collectively. Finally, whereas under Kyoto a noncompliant country could escape punishment by withdrawing from the treaty, a deposit-refund system can easily be designed to make such escape unfeasible. For example, the treaty could specify that withdrawal before the commitment period ends will entail forfeiture of deposits.

In theory, deposit-refund systems may also be designed to induce countries to ratify. For example, in a symmetric setting (i.e., all countries are identical), the treaty could state that entry into force will not occur until *all* countries have ratified and made the required deposits. Such a clause would make free riding by not ratifying infeasible. Consequently, the so-called relative-gains problem would also be reduced. When free riding through nonparticipation is infeasible, relative-gains concerns no longer provide a motive for nonparticipation (at least not in a symmetric setting).

In practice, however, a deposit-refund system is implausible as an instrument for inducing countries to ratify. First, the climate change problem is entangled in many serious asymmetries (e.g., Victor 2011), which makes the requirement that *all* countries must participate extremely impractical:

If even a single country declines to make required deposits, the treaty cannot enter into force. Second, relaxing the requirement that *all* countries
must ratify would undermine the incentive to join the agreement; indeed,
if the agreement requires only partial participation, and does not provide
other incentives for participation, a deposit-refund system may even be dis-
ruptive (Cherry and McEvoy 2013). Third, it may not be credible that if
one country declines to make required deposits, other countries will abstain
from cooperating among themselves. The incentive to participate and make
deposits critically hinges on such credibility. Finally, countries facing serious
liquidity problems may be particularly reluctant to participate in a climate
treaty based on a deposit-refund system.

In conclusion, a deposit-refund system could—at least in principle—solve
many problems associated with Kyoto's enforcement system; however, it can
primarily be used for enforcing compliance. Thus, one would need other
measures to ensure broad participation; for example, one might encourage
countries to participate through norms, issue linkages, or trade restrictions.[19]

11.6   Conclusion

If a new (future) climate agreement is to truly alleviate the climate change
problem, it must entail broad participation, deep commitments, *and* high
compliance rates, a very demanding combination that will likely require
ambitious facilitation as well as potent enforcement of both participation and
compliance. As we have seen, Kyoto's enforcement system addresses only
compliance (not participation), and does so through a seriously flawed system.

To what extent are the flaws in the enforcement system responsible
for Kyoto's relative lack of success? It is obvious that a climate treaty can
accomplish very little if it imposes binding emissions reduction or limitation commitments only on countries responsible for as little as about
20 percent (Kyoto 1) or even 10 percent (Kyoto 2) of global emissions. A
treaty having enforcement measures able to induce all (major) countries to
ratify with deep commitments and to comply with them would no doubt
accomplish much more.

Of course, the problem is that such potent enforcement measures will
unlikely be politically feasible—especially in the UNFCCC context where
decisions are made by consensus, so that countries expecting to be subjected to enforcement have the final word. Whether more exclusive groups

outside the UNFCCC might fare substantially better in developing an effective climate agreement remains an open question (Aakre, Hovi, and Skodvin 2013; Hovi et al. 2017).

In conclusion, we expect future negotiations (inside or outside the UNFCCC) to struggle in arriving at an effective agreement on climate mitigation. In particular, attempts to design a potent enforcement system will likely encounter harsh resistance. Nevertheless, if the Paris Agreement eventually fails and countries embark on negotiating and designing a new climate agreement, the flaws in Kyoto's enforcement system should at least be taken seriously.

Notes

1. We here focus on commitments concerning mitigation. However, the climate regime also faces challenges concerning implementation of other commitments, such as those related to climate finance (e.g., reaching US$100 billion by 2020). See chapter 10 (in this volume) for more details on the latter.

2. Simmons (2010) also finds examples of "false negatives," that is, of governments not signing and ratifying an international agreement and nevertheless behaving largely as prescribed in that agreement. In the climate change domain, the United States is an interesting case in point; a remarkable conversion to shale gas has cut emissions sufficiently to make its Kyoto Protocol target a realistic prospect.

3. This all indicates that—although the distinction between willingness and ability is useful in identifying necessary conditions—both willingness and ability will depend heavily on assessments of costs and benefits.

4. "Full costs" are set as the appropriate standard for some commitments, "full incremental costs" as the appropriate standard for others.

5. For a more detailed presentation of the compliance system, see, for example, Ulfstein and Werksman (2005, 41–49) and chapter 2 (in this volume).

6. National communications provide information on topics such as: (1) national circumstances relevant to emissions and removals, (2) inventories, (3) policies and measures (including their projected effects), (4) vulnerability assessments, (5) climate change impacts and adaptation measures, (6) financial resources, and (7) technology transfers. For an example of a national communication, see Danish Ministry of the Environment (2005).

7. A third type of noncompliance is failure by a party to meet its requirements regarding estimation, reporting, and review of both emissions by sources and removals by sinks.

8. See Marrakesh Accords, Decision 24/CP.7, Annex, section XI (UNFCCC 2005).

9. We ignore the third consequence, that a noncompliant party must present a compliance restoration plan. This consequence entails very limited economic costs; however, it might imply a "shaming" effect.

10. The Kyoto Protocol states that "any procedures and mechanisms ... entailing binding consequences shall be adopted by means of an amendment to this Protocol" (UNFCCC 1998, art. 18). Moreover, if such an amendment is proposed, the parties "shall make every effort to reach agreement ... by consensus." Only if "all efforts at consensus have been exhausted, and no agreement reached," can the amendment, as a last resort, "be adopted by a three-fourths majority vote of the Parties present and voting" (UNFCCC 1998, art. 20). If adopted, the amendment will enter into force ninety days after it has been ratified by three-fourths of the parties. However, it will enter into force *only for those parties that chose to ratify the amendment*. Parties expecting to exceed their emissions target for the first commitment period could hardly be expected to ratify an amendment making legally binding the obligation to implement *additional* emission reductions.

11. Actually, it could obtain the same effect by withdrawing from the Framework Convention. According to the Kyoto Protocol, "any Party that withdraws from the Convention shall be considered as also having withdrawn from this Protocol" (UNFCCC 1998, art. 27.3).

12. However, suspending a noncompliant party's right to buy permits might give it an additional incentive to delay implementation, or even to withdraw from the Kyoto Protocol.

13. When North Korea declared its intention to withdraw from the International Covenant on Civil and Political Rights, the United Nations Secretary-General stated that the original signatories of the Covenant had not *overlooked* the possibility of explicitly providing for withdrawal; they had deliberately *chosen* not to provide for it. Accordingly, withdrawal was not possible (United Nations 2003, 112).

14. The Enforcement Branch has nevertheless considered a number of cases, often triggered by questions relating to the reports of expert review teams (see UNFCCC 2016).

15. The first four of these factors are emphasized by Shishlov, Morel, and Bellassen (2016).

16. The EU controls powerful incentives for inducing its member countries to comply (Aakre and Hovi 2010).

17. Comparative research on international environmental regimes more generally indicates that legally binding agreements tend to enhance *compliance* but not *effectiveness* (see, e.g., Breitmeier, Underdal, and Young 2011; Downs, Rocke, and Barsoom 1996).

18. A design for an agreement based on carbon emission taxes is analyzed by Gersbach and Winkler (2012).

19. In addition, domestic groups that remind governments of their moral and legal obligations might be able to facilitate participation and compliance (e.g., Dai 2007).

References

Aakre, Stine, Leif Helland, and Jon Hovi. 2016: "When Does Informal Enforcement Work?" *Journal of Conflict Resolution* 60 (7): 1312–1340.

Aakre, Stine, and Jon Hovi. 2010. "Emission Trading: Participation Enforcement Determines the Need for Compliance Enforcement." *European Union Politics* 11 (3): 427–445.

Aakre, Stine, Jon Hovi, and Tora Skodvin. 2013. "Can Climate Negotiations Succeed?" *Politics and Governance* 1 (2): 138–150.

Allison, Graham T. 1971. *Essence of Decision: Explaining the Cuban Missile Crisis.* Boston: Little Brown.

Asheim, Geir B., Camilla Bretteville Froyn, Jon Hovi, and Fredric C. Menz. 2006. "Regional versus Global Cooperation for Climate Control." *Journal of Environmental Economics and Management* 51 (1): 93–109.

Asheim, Geir B., and Bjart Holtsmark. 2009. "Renegotiation-Proof Climate Agreements with Full Participation: Conditions for Pareto-Efficiency." *Environmental and Resource Economics* 43 (4): 519–533.

Axelrod, Robert, and Robert O. Keohane. 1986. "Achieving Cooperation under Anarchy: Strategies and Institutions." In *Cooperation under Anarchy*, edited by Kenneth A. Oye, 226–251. Princeton, NJ: Princeton University Press.

Barrett, Scott. 1999. "Montreal versus Kyoto. International Cooperation and the Global Environment." In *Global Public Goods: International Cooperation in the 21st Century*, edited by Inge Kaul, I. Grungberg, and Marc A. Stern, 192–219. Oxford: Oxford University Press.

———. 2002. "Towards a Better Climate Treaty." *Working Paper No. 54/2002.* Milan: Fondazione Eni Enrico Mattei.

———. 2003. *Environment and Statecraft: The Strategy of Environmental Treaty-Making.* Oxford: Oxford University Press.

Benedick, Richard Elliot. 1999. *Ozone Diplomacy: New Directions in Safeguarding the Planet.* Cambridge, MA: Harvard University Press.

Brack, Duncan. 2003. "Monitoring the Montreal Protocol." In *Verification Handbook*, edited by Trevor Findlay, 209–226. Available from www.vertic.org/media/Archived _Publications/Yearbooks/2003/VY03_Brack.pdf.

Breitmeier, Helmut, Arild Underdal, and Oran R. Young. 2011. "The Effectiveness of International Environmental Regimes: Comparing and Contrasting Findings from Quantitative Research." *International Studies Review* 13 (4): 579–605.

Buchner, Barbara, Carlo Carraro, Igor Cersosimo, and Carmen Marchiori. 2005. "Back to Kyoto? US Participation and the Linkage between R&D and Climate Cooperation." *Advances In Global Climate Change Research* 22:173–204.

Chayes, Abram, and Antonia Handler Chayes. 1993. "On Compliance." *International Organization* 47 (2): 175–205.

———. 1995. *The New Sovereignty*. Cambridge, MA: Harvard University Press.

Checkel, Jeffrey T. 2001. "Why Comply? Social Learning and European Identity Change." *International Organization* 55 (3): 553–588.

Cherry, Todd L., and David M. McEvoy. 2013. "Enforcing Compliance with Environmental Agreements in the Absence of Strong Institutions: An Experimental Analysis." *Environmental and Resource Economics* 54 (1): 63–77.

Clark, William C., Jill Jäger, Josee van Eijndhoven, and Nancy Dickson. 2001. *Learning to Manage Global Environmental Risks*. Cambridge, MA: MIT Press.

Cukierman, Alex. 1992. *Central Bank Strategy, Credibility, and Interdependence: Theory and Evidence*. Cambridge, MA: MIT Press.

Dai, Xinyuan. 2007. *International Institutions and National Policies*. Cambridge: Cambridge University Press.

Danish Ministry of the Environment. 2005. *Denmark's Fourth National Communication on Climate Change under the United Nations Framework Convention on Climate Change*. Copenhagen: Danish Ministry of the Environment.

Downs, George W., David M. Rocke, and Peter N. Barsoom. 1996. "Is the Good News about Compliance Good News About Cooperation?" *International Organization* 50 (3): 379–406.

Finus, Michael. 2008. "The Enforcement Mechanisms of the Kyoto Protocol: Flawed or Promising Concepts?" *Letters in Spatial and Resource Sciences* 1 (1): 13–25.

Franck, Thomas M. 1990. *The Power of Legitimacy among Nations*. New York: Oxford University Press.

Froyn, Camilla Bretteville, and Jon Hovi. 2008. "A Climate Agreement with Full Participation." *Economics Letters* 99 (2): 317–319.

Gerber, Anke, and Philipp C. Wichardt. 2009. "Providing Public Goods in the Absence of Strong Institutions." *Journal of Public Economics* 93 (3): 429–439.

Gersbach, Hans. 2008. "A New Way to Address Climate Change: A Global Refunding System." *Economists' Voice* 5 (4): 1–4.

Gersbach, Hans, and Ralph Winkler. 2012. "Global Refunding and Climate Change." *Journal of Economic Dynamics and Control* 36 (11): 1775–1795.

Halvorssen, Anita, and Jon Hovi. 2006. "The Nature, Origin and Impact of Legally Binding Consequences: The Case of the Climate Regime." *International Environmental Agreements: Politics, Law and Economics* 6 (2): 157–171.

Hathaway, Oona A. 2002. "Do Human Rights Treaties Make a Difference?" *Yale Law Journal* 111 (8): 1935–2042.

Heitzig, Jobst, Kai Lessmann, and Yong Zou. 2011. "Self-Enforcing Strategies to Deter Free-Riding in the Climate Change Mitigation Game and Other Repeated Public Good Games." *Proceedings of the National Academy of Sciences of the United States of America* 108 (38): 15739–15744.

Hovi, Jon, Mads Greaker, Cathrine Hagem, and Bjart Holtsmark. 2012. "A Credible Compliance Enforcement System for the Climate Regime." *Climate Policy* 12 (6): 741–754.

Hovi, Jon, Detlef F. Sprinz, Håkon Sælen, and Arild Underdal. 2016. "Climate Change Mitigation: A Role for Climate Clubs?" *Palgrave Communications* 2.

——. 2017. "The Club Approach: A Gateway to Effective Climate Cooperation." *British Journal of Political Science*. Published online first: 15 June 2017.

Hovi, Jon, Detlef F. Sprinz, and Arild Underdal. 2009. "Implementing Long-Term Climate Policy: Time Inconsistency, Domestic Politics, International Anarchy." *Global Environmental Politics* 9 (3): 20–39.

Keohane, Robert O., and Michael Oppenheimer. 2016. "Paris: Beyond the Climate Dead End through Pledge and Review?" *Politics and Governance* 4 (3): 142–151.

Mitchell, Ronald B. 2008. "Evaluating the Performance of Environmental Institutions: What to Evaluate and How to Evaluate It?" In *Institutions and Environmental Change: Principal Findings, Applications, and Research Frontiers*, edited by Oran R. Young, Leslie A. King, and Heike Schroeder, 79–114. Cambridge, MA: MIT Press.

Oye, Kenneth A. 1985. "Explaining Cooperation under Anarchy: Hypotheses and Strategies." *World Politics* 38 (1): 1–24.

Putnam, Robert D. 1988. "Diplomacy and Domestic Politics: The Logic of Two-Level Games." *International Organization* 42 (3): 427–460.

Shishlov, Igor, Romain Morel, and Valentin Bellassen. 2016. "Compliance of the Parties to the Kyoto Protocol in the First Commitment Period." *Climate Policy* 16 (6): 768–782.

Simmons, Beth A. 2010. *Mobilizing for Human Rights: International Law in Domestic Politics*. Cambridge: Cambridge University Press.

Stiglitz, Joseph. 2006. "A New Agenda for Global Warming." *Economists' Voice* 3 (7).

Stokke, Olav Schram. 2012. *Disaggregating International Regimes: A New Approach to Evaluation and Comparison.* Cambridge, MA: MIT Press.

Tallberg, Jonas. 2002. "Paths to Compliance: Enforcement, Management, and the European Union." *International Organization* 56 (3): 609–643.

Ulfstein, Geir, and Jacob Werksman. 2005. "The Kyoto Compliance System: Towards Hard Enforcement." In *Implementing the Climate Regime: International Compliance,* edited by Olav Stokke, Jon Hovi, and Geir Ulfstein, 39–62. London: Earthscan.

Underdal, Arild. 1987. "What's Left for the MFA? Foreign Policy and the Management of External Relations in Norway." *Cooperation and Conflict* 22 (2): 169–192.

UNFCCC. 1992. *United Nations Framework Convention on Climate Change.* New York: United Nations.

———. 1998. *Kyoto Protocol to the United Nations Framework Convention on Climate Change.* Kyoto: United Nations.

———. 2005. *The Marrakesh Accords and the Marrakesh Declaration.* Marrakesh: United Nations.

———. 2015. *Paris Agreement.* Paris: United Nations.

———. 2016. *Compliance under the Kyoto Protocol. United Nations Framework Convention on Climate Change 2016.* Available from http://unfccc.int/kyoto_protocol/compliance /items/2875.php.

United Nations. 1969. *Vienna Convention on the Law of Treaties.* Edited by United Nations. Done at Vienna: United Nations.

———. 2003. *Final Clauses of Multilateral Treaties Handbook.* New York: Treaties Section of the Office of Legal Affairs, United Nations.

Victor, David G. 2011. *Global Warming Gridlock: Creating More Effective Strategies for Protecting the Planet.* Cambridge: Cambridge University Press.

———. 2016. "What the Framework Convention on Climate Change Teaches Us about Cooperation on Climate Change." *Politics and Governance* 4 (3): 133–141.

Weiss, Edith Brown, and Harold Karan Jacobson. 1998. *Engaging Countries: Strengthening Compliance with International Environmental Accords.* Cambridge, MA: MIT Press.

World Bank. 2010. *The World Development Report 2010.* Washington, DC: World Bank.

WTO. 2002. "GATT/WTO Dispute Settlement Practice Relating to GATT Article XX, Paragraphs (B), (D), and (G), WT/CTE/W/203." In *Committee on Trade and Environment.* Geneva: World Trade Organization.

12   Our Conclusions

Detlef F. Sprinz

12.1   The Trump Withdrawal from the Paris Agreement

This book focuses on what political scientists and related social sciences can contribute to better understand the international response to global climate change. The Paris Agreement—concluded a quarter century after international negotiations began on the UNFCCC—has been considered a major hallmark of global climate diplomacy. It was meant to be a long-term, flexible architecture to guide global climate policy through the twenty-first century. As many of the specific obligations are not particularly onerous, it is a document of good intent whose major specifications and its effectiveness have yet to be proven in the future (Bang, Hovi, and Skodvin 2016).

On June 1, 2017, President Trump announced in the White House's Rose Garden that the United States of America intends to withdraw from the 2015 Paris Agreement. He declared the agreement not to be fair to the American people, in particular the most economically disadvantaged ones, and a giveaway of funds, principally the Green Climate Fund, to emerging economies that are still allowed to increase their GHG emissions (*New York Times* 2017). President Trump suggested that the USA will continue domestically to be a global climate leader, and that a new global agreement as a replacement of the present Paris Agreement be forged that is fair to the United States; the possibility of no future climate agreements being successfully concluded was explicitly mentioned (White House 2017). Given his announcements during the presidential election campaign of 2016, the decision to withdraw from the Paris Agreements was not surprising.

The decision historically echoes the Byrd-Hagel resolution of the US Senate, concluded prior to the finalization of the Kyoto Protocol in 1997, which suggested two benchmarks to be fulfilled for US engagement in global climate agreements: (1) emerging economies should limit their GHG emissions in addition to industrialized countries, and (2) the measures taken should not have negative consequences for the US economy (US Senate 1997). While the first point is accommodated under the Paris Agreement by all countries submitting nationally determined contributions (NDCs) (see chapter 2 in this volume), the second point is up to the domestic policy design chosen by any US government. The US withdrawal from the Paris Agreement also echoes the decision by former president George W. Bush to remove the US signature from the Kyoto Protocol (never implemented; UNFCCC 2017) and to not submit the protocol to the US Senate for advice and consent (see chapter 2 in this volume). In response to President George W. Bush's decision in the early 2000s, the rest of the world rallied around the climate flag to collect sufficient support to allow the Kyoto Protocol to come into force. While the Paris Agreement is in force since 2016, it remains unclear how the withdrawal by the historically largest emitter of GHG emissions and the second largest current emitter will energize or retard the ambitions of other countries. Moreover, what challenge does the decision by President Trump pose to the international relations of global climate change?

In the run-up to and in the immediate response to the decision by President Trump, the G6 (the G7 minus the United States) and China, as well as France, Germany, and Italy and an EU/China resolution (European Commission 2017), suggested that they will stick to the architecture and goals of the Paris Agreement. California's Governor Brown signed an agreement with China on June 6, 2017, on joint climate policy efforts (Reuters 2017). All politically demanding obligations at Paris were included in the concluding decision of the UNFCCC's Conference of the Parties (COP), yet all legally binding and not onerous obligations were included in the Paris Agreement. The latter was annexed to the final COP decisions (UNFCCC 2015, 2016). As a consequence of its commitments in both documents, the USA was not obliged, in practice, to take additional policy steps.[1] It could even have watered down the US NDC without fearing international enforcement. As President Obama largely used executive orders and specifically the Clean Power Plan as well as a ruling by the US Environmental Protection Agency (Environmental Protection Agency 2015) to pursue his domestic climate policy rather than let the US Congress pass new laws or amend existing ones, policy reversal was always feasible by executive fiat.

The US withdrawal from the Paris Agreement should be seen against the backdrop of global GHG emissions that appeared to be leveling off, yet is projected to increase again in 2017 (Global Carbon Project 2017). This book is geared to understand how international relations can help us better understand global climate policy and the Paris Agreement. In the following, I describe the Paris Agreement in analytical terms (section 12.2), turn to the main actors engaged in global climate policy (section 12.3), select concepts and theories used (section 12.4), and provide a brief concluding outlook (section 12.5).

12.2   The Paris Agreement as a Sandwich Solution

In response to the failed attempt to conclude a successor to the Kyoto Protocol and its first compliance period at Copenhagen in 2009, this author developed the so-called "sandwich solution" (Sprinz 2010). While the architecture of the Kyoto Protocol was often perceived as a "top-down" agreement, the Copenhagen Accord opened the way to collect what were originally called intended nationally determined contributions (INDCs), now NDCs, to become a "bottom-up" agreement.[2]

A sandwich solution metaphorically resembles a double-faced sandwich with the top part reflecting the top-down architectural part, and the lower part the bottom-up part. The top part suggested to comprise the ultimate goal, such as an ambition to reach the 2°C goal of global mean temperature change, as well as "monitoring, reporting, and verification of emissions and impacts … [as well as] reviews of policies and the analysis of alternative future pathways" (Sprinz 2010, 72). Complementing from the bottom, inventions and innovations of breakthrough technologies to get closer to a low-GHG transition were envisioned. Appropriate frameworks should be established to increase the probability of such innovations (Sprinz 2010, 73). In a fundamental sense, the Paris Agreement very much resembles such a double-faced sandwich, with the 1.5–2°C goal serving as the overall focal point of ambition; the reporting and assessment mechanisms needing fuller development in the future; and the NDCs—and thereby ambitions—being under the full control of national governments (see chapter 2 in this volume). While article 3 of the Paris Agreement stipulates that "[t]he efforts of all Parties will represent a progression over time," article 4 stipulates that upgrading is expected from each country (UNFCCC 2015). Given that the Paris Agreement only enshrines a facilitative noncompliance system (see chapter 2 as well as chapter 11 in this volume), the Paris Agreement metaphorically represents the sandwich solution of coordination of basic directions at the top with decentralized efforts that give life to such ambition by way of domestic policies.

12.3 Actors That Matter

Given that fossil fuels are engrained in many aspects of daily life, international climate policy is unthinkable without a domestic foundation. Beginning with Robert Putnam's seminal conceptualization of international negotiations as a two-level game (Putnam 1988), international negotiations have subsequently been analyzed as the confluence or divergence between domestic (level 2) and international (level 1) negotiation positions. Depending on the configuration of positions across levels, treaties can be either (1) successfully negotiated and implemented or (2) may fail at the level of agreement at the international level or at the stage of ratification or implementation at the domestic level. Various chapters in this volume attest to the importance of domestic and transnational actors (see, e.g., chapters 3, 8, 9, and 10 in this volume), and President Trump invoked domestic political reasons for leaving the Paris Agreement.[3] While a systematic weighting of the importance of actors is beyond the scope of this chapter, it is worthwhile to recall the broad set of actors covered in this book.

By their sheer size of emissions, at least eight countries (Brazil, China, the EU28, India, Indonesia, Japan, Russia, and the United States) merit continuing attention (see chapter 7 in this volume). Together with the other members of the UNFCCC, they are the main subjects of international law as recognized state governments. Countries negotiate and potentially become parties to (or abstain from) signing, ratifying, implementing, and complying with multilateral environmental agreements. In view of the UNFCCC, the Paris Agreement, and to a lesser degree the Kyoto Protocol, global climate agreements show limited "bite" in terms of being the pivotal agents of emission reductions, although the Kyoto Protocol clearly sent the signal that the price for carbon emissions will henceforth be positive and has to be taken into account in business decisions. Since few multilateral environmental agreements (MEAs) concentrate power and resources at the international level, the onus of implementing commitments largely rests with the domestic level.

Three actors stand out at the domestic level: environmental nongovernmental organizations (ENGOs), business, and a social climate movement. Since the Paris Agreement is mostly an agreement about laudable aims, architecture, and processes—as is the UNFCCC—much of naming and shaming to keep and upgrade commitments will rest with ENGOs. In particular, ENGOs will be charged with keeping the long-term policy of climate policy high on the list of national policy priorities. Lack of attention to the domestic side of a potential Kyoto Protocol, for example, afforded climate-skeptic and industry structure-preserving business NGOs opportunities to influence the political mainstream and the public to a substantial degree in the USA (see chapter 8 in this volume). But business can also be seen as the potentially greatest transmission belt for transformational change. Some of the lead in resisting the decision by President Trump to leave the Paris Agreement comes from industries that either espouse green goals as part of their core business or that wish to avoid to be perceived as "dirty" by consumers (Shear and Smale 2017; Thompson and Bajaj 2017; Victor 2017). As many businesses are not protected by monopoly rents and have to keep an eye on consumers that support their business model and changes in consumer sentiment, choices by companies to "go green" are both promising and sometimes fickle. As Paterson (chapter 9 in this volume) shows, climate markets are also a business opportunity, and higher prices for carbon offsets allow for more generous profit margins for companies operating in the carbon markets. Given the ability of business to stimulate lifestyle changes among customers and at emulating greener business models among fellow competitors, greener business sectors could hold a key multiplier and mainstreaming position in a transition to low-GHG economies. If this were amplified by technological advances and assisted by domestic legal provisions that link continued emissions to responsibilities, business could be part of a virtuous cycle toward lower emissions while also being profitable.

Science, as an actor, has not received very detailed attention in this book—although all authors are scientists and contribute themselves to and build on scientific advances by others. The degree of climate skepticism—that is, the suggestion that humans do not cause an appreciable share of the greenhouse effect—has been receding following five waves of reports by the

Intergovernmental Panel on Climate Change (IPCC) that were published since 1990. While scientists are an important source of knowledge, gaps in knowledge, innovative ideas, and political awareness raising, their reputation ultimately rests on their approval by their peers or taking courageous positions such as Copernicus did. Scientists are ultimately most likely to serve as midwives for policies that they may have helped shape but ultimately are not responsible for. In practical terms, their influence will be mostly reflected in the country positions during international negotiations.

Roughly half a century ago, the environmental movement started to gain momentum, initially in the United States, subsequently in many other industrialized and also in developing countries. There is little doubt that environmental movements have enabled environmental policies and legislation to become policy priorities, and the impact on existing parties and the creation of green parties in many countries is quite discernible. Avaaz, an Internet petition and mobilization platform, claims to have nearly forty-five million members (Avaaz 2017a) and to have mobilized four hundred thousand members to march for climate change in New York City and three hundred thousand elsewhere in the world in 2014—the year preceding the Paris Agreement (Avaaz 2017a,b; see also Alter 2014). At present, it is difficult to discern whether these are sustained efforts beyond more traditional ENGOs as mobilization shows discernible spikes. Furthermore, petition platforms often cover climate, environmental, and other concerns. As extreme climate impacts become increasingly discernible and stronger in magnitude, and combined with an evolving sustainability and sustainable development agenda, social movements must be reckoned with especially if officeholders wish to be reelected.

12.4 Concepts and Theories

Research on mitigation, adaptation, and compensation constitute the three main concepts of climate science, both in the social and in the natural sciences. The major emphasis in this book is on what political scientists and related social sciences can contribute to better understand the international response to global climate change over the past three decades.

The grand theories of international relations, neorealism, neoliberal institutionalism and constructivism have only limited explanatory power. Instead, we may wish to focus on domestic foundations and even the micro-foundations of policies that enable experimentation and potential diffusion across countries (see chapter 3 in this volume). The conceptions of equity, embraced especially in the chapter by Michaelowa and Michaelowa (chapter 10 in this volume), underlie much of where responsibility ought to rest, yet the various preferences over particular equity norms eschew general support for one specific guiding norm. The situation is, moreover, complicated by the fact that different countries have followed different emissions trajectories at comparable levels of economic development. Whenever it comes to taking over substantial financial obligation, such as the goal for developed countries to provide US$100 billion per year beginning 2020—and subsequently increase such amounts over time—will necessitate either creative accounting or a new willingness in domestic political systems of developed countries to spend major amounts of climate-related assistance on not yet developed countries. Given the announcement of the US exit from the Paris Agreement—and, thereby, the withdrawal of a major financier—mobilizing large amounts of funding continuously on the international level appears quite optimistic. Perhaps more prudent are current undertakings by Bangladesh and a few other countries to develop special-purpose climate impact compensation funds, endow them domestically to some degree, espouse good and transparent governance, and entice bilateral and multilateral donors to bring domestic climate compensation funds to critical size. Rather than creating an international system of compensation on the international level (Sprinz and von Bünau 2013), we may witness a federation of decentralized solutions that work by way of diffusion. As compensation for wrongs is a standard solution in the domestic context of countries under the rule of law, there is no good reason why compensation cannot be part of the solution at the international level.

Can such voluntarism thrive? This is both a conceptual and an empirical question, yet should also build on present experience with the world that we know. As chapter 4 in this volume has shown, only moderate-sized coalitions are renegotiations-proof, and experiments with punishment show that incentives to avoid punishment—and thus encouraging contributions—might work. If major polluting businesses and major polluting countries become convinced that the days of liability-free pollution are coming to an end—and markets price this into company and country valuations (such as asset prices and bond ratings)—it may not be too far-fetched to believe that a virtuous cycle may have commenced.

And since much economic growth is associated with international trade, it appears prudent to explore more courageously how the benefits from international trade can be combined with benefits from avoided climatic damages (see also chapter 6 in this volume). Nearly no constitutional provision is beyond careful reconsideration at the domestic level in democratic systems under the rule of law—and the same should apply to the world trading system. The Montreal Protocol to protect the stratospheric ozone layer has quite well managed to exclude trade with nonmembers on stratospheric ozone-depleting substances, and it does not take much imagination that this small wheel can be writ large in the context of climate change.

12.5   Outlook: Creative Destruction or Climate Clubs?

There is no guarantee that the world at large will be able to avoid the worst climatic impacts, that is, the possibility that only part of Planet Earth will be inhabitable as we presently know it and with the amenities and the richness of plants, animals, glaciers, high seas, soils, and so on, that many of us appreciate and consider worth protecting. If, however, doomsday outcomes are to be avoided, the present fossil fuel based world economy will have to be confronted with a substantial amount of "creative destruction" (Schumpeter 1994 [1942]) (i.e., innovations that may deliver comparable amenities that we presently enjoy) and avoiding a range of disutilities (such as high particle levels in inner cities or high GHG emissions) that we may not miss. We may be only a couple of decades away from renewable energies to deliver energy on a competitive level with existing coal-fired power plants. Missing the train has had large implications for German power providers E.ON and RWE that had to split themselves up during the past years (including a renewable branch) and lose substantially more than half of their historical top stock market valuation. Creative destruction may be painful in the short run, yet rewarding in the longer term. Increases in technology may certainly be helpful (Levi et al. 2010; see chapter 3 in this volume), yet any investment and diffusion opportunity generates probabilistic rather than deterministic outcomes.

While especially natural scientists see abundant problem pressure and a need to successfully cope with the climate challenge, it is important to keep an eye on and push the boundaries of what is feasible. Simply asking for political will to be concentrated on climate change, a "man to the moon" or a climate Marshall Plan to be initiated, shortsightedness be replaced by farsightedness in political decision making, and other single-issue solutions have all been mentioned over the past decades, yet they carry more rhetorical vigor than offer politically feasible guidance.

In keeping with the bottom-up architecture reviewed above, Hovi, Sprinz, Sælen, and Underdal explored in a range of articles the possibility for and limits to incentive-driven, voluntary, bottom-up strategies among countries (Hovi et al. forthcoming, 2016; Hovi, Sprinz, and Underdal 2014). Inspired by Victor (2011, 2015), they explored the feasibility of climate mitigation clubs in the presence or absence of members-only club goods, such as enhanced trade possibilities. The club idea mostly centers on some large emitters, either by themselves or in coordination with other large emitters, to form an initial coalition of members to each spend 1 percent of GDP annually to reduce its GHG emissions (enthusiasts). Other (reluctant) countries are invited to join if they are willing to also spend 1 percent of their GDP on membership in the climate mitigation club. Reluctant members leave the club if there is no net benefit to their membership, while enthusiasts compare the net benefits of the existence of the club with the net benefits when all countries are outside the club. Our findings show that under a range of alternative sets of enthusiastic countries, climate mitigation clubs can be started, sustained, and grow to reach appreciable size by covering about half of global GHG emissions. The success of forming such clubs not only rests with the specific configuration of enthusiasts, but also the level of additional (yet profitable) conditional commitments by enthusiasts and the level of provision of the members-only club good. In some configuration of enthusiasts, clubs can even emerge in the absence of members-only club goods and without additional, conditional commitments by the enthusiasts (Hovi et al. forthcoming). Alternatively, side-payments (essentially targeted subsidies of the membership fee for reluctant countries) also prove an efficient and effective way to enable climate clubs, yet might be politically less easily feasible as countries would be enticed into the club on a one-by-one basis (Sælen 2016).

What can be learned from the idea of climate clubs? First and foremost, if some of the largest emitters club together as enthusiasts, prospects for mitigation are quite optimistic if a level of club members–only benefits can be reached comparable to a transatlantic trade and investment agreement (Hovi et al. forthcoming). Second, assuming that enthusiasts can top up their initial offers (conditional commitments), this leads to enhancements of investment into climate mitigation. And third, many of these outcomes are robust to alternate assumptions about affinity or conflict between countries (Hovi et al. forthcoming). Fourth, even as the United States eschews such a climate club arrangement, the prospects for climate mitigation clubs become more limited, but the incentives to build such clubs among remaining countries largely endures—even as the scope of GHG emissions covered shrinks somewhat (Sprinz et al. forthcoming). Larger incentives based on climate impacts avoided combined with members-only benefits could be a winning formula, yet the automatism assumed by our model ought to be refined with the help of a domestic politics model which accounts for the within-countries forces that work in favor of or against such policies.

Overall, countries face a threefold challenge that makes global climate policy a formidable challenge: time inconsistency, domestic fragmentation, and international anarchy (Hovi, Sprinz, and Underdal 2009). First, time inconsistency is the challenge of persevering on promises when conditions have changed and revised policies could counteract the promise made earlier. As a consequence, long-term credible commitment to long-term policy becomes an enduring challenge, both within countries and across countries. Second, domestic fragmentation with its many interactions among and across domestic political forces that wish to favor or retard protection against climatic impacts is difficult to aggregate, especially if interacted with the time inconsistency challenge. And, third, international anarchy, that is, the absence of binding and enforceable central authority in international relations, leaves it to those willing to undertake costly sanctioning to enforce international agreements. The history of weakening the enforcement branch of global climate agreements from the Kyoto Protocol to the Paris Agreement is instructive. Furthermore, only countries that participate in international agreements are subject to potential enforcement under the Kyoto Protocol, while nonparties can eschew such action (see chapter 11 in this volume). The Paris Agreement "solved" the participation challenge by allowing each country to define its own goals in Nationally Determined Contributions (NDCs), yet given that the progression of NDCs over time cannot be enforced if a country is immune to naming and shaming, the

Paris Agreement is a good illustration of all three aspects highlighted by Hovi, Sprinz, and Underdal (2009).

Perhaps the international relations of global climate change by way of MEAs is, in practice, an illustration of the weak link between countries to try to overcome the tripartite challenge of time inconsistency, domestic fragmentation, and international anarchy. Governments can offer framework policies (*Ordnungspolitik*) that encourage creative investment into low-GHG futures, yet markets, domestic constituents, and transnational actors may be the ones that bring it to fruition.

Notes

I greatly appreciate comments by Alexandra Goritz and Jon Hovi on an earlier draft of this chapter.

1. While even the Sierra Club of the USA thinks that a watering down of the Obama era NDC would not be enforceable in US courts (Levitz 2017), President Trump decided in favor of leaving the international agreement that his predecessor helped to shape.

2. Equating the Kyoto Protocol with a top-down architecture is inaccurate as no country could be forced to sign up to join any of the developed or developing country lists of obligations or that countries had to take over specific emission limitations against their will. Even if the foregoing were wrong, parties not satisfied with the negotiated text could opt not to ratify the protocol or withdraw later. As of June 7, 2017, Canada has withdrawn its ratification of the Kyoto Protocol, and the United States signed but never ratified it (UNFCCC 2017).

3. There are strong indications that few geographic areas of the United States would support his decision (Marlon et al. 2016).

References

Alter, Charlotte. 2014. "Hundreds of Thousands Converge on New York to Demand Climate-Change Action." *Time*, September 21.

Avaaz. 2017a. *Avaaz: The World in Action*. Available from https://secure.avaaz.org.

Avaaz. 2017b. *Victory! The End of Fossil Fuels Has Begun*. Available from https://secure .avaaz.org/en/climate_story_loc/.

Bang, Guri, Jon Hovi, and Tora Skodvin. 2016. "The Paris Agreement: Short-Term and Long-Term Effectiveness." *Politics and Governance* 4 (3): 209–218.

Environmental Protection Agency. 2015. "Carbon Pollution Emission Guidelines for Existing Stationary Sources: Electric Utility Generating Units; Final Rule." In *40 CFR Part 60*.

European Commission. 2017. *EU-China Summit: Moving Forward with Our Global Partnership*. Brussels: European Commission.

Hovi, Jon, Detlef F. Sprinz, Håkon Sælen, and Arild Underdal. 2016. "Climate Change Mitigation: A Role for Climate Clubs?" *Palgrave Communications* 2:16020.

———. forthcoming. "The Club Approach: A Gateway to Effective Climate Co-Operation?" *British Journal of Political Science*, https://doi.org/10.1017/S0007123416000788.

Hovi, Jon, Detlef F. Sprinz, and Arild Underdal. 2009. "Implementing Long-Term Climate Policy: Time Inconsistency, Domestic Politics, International Anarchy." *Global Environmental Politics* 9 (3): 20–39.

———. 2014. "Bottom-Up or Top-Down?" In *Toward a New Climate Agreement: Conflict, Resolution and Governance*, edited by Todd L. Cherry, Jon Hovi, and David M. McEvoy, 167–180. London: Routledge.

Le Quéré, C., Andrew, R. M., Friedlingstein, P., Sitch, S., Pongratz, J., Manning, A. C., ... Zhu, D. (2017). Global Carbon Budget 2017. Earth System Science Data Discussions, 2017, 1–79. doi:10.5194/essd-2017–123

Levi, Michael, Elizabeth C. Economy, Shannon O'Neil, and Adam Segal. 2010. "Globalizing the Energy Revolution: How to Really Win the Clean-Energy Race." *Foreign Affairs* (November/December).

Levitz, Eric. 2017. "Trump Reportedly Leaning toward Exiting Paris Climate Deal." *New York Magazine*, May 3.

Marlon, Jennifer, Peter Howe, Matto Mildenberger, and Anthony Leiserowitz. 2016. Estimated % of Adults Who Support Setting Strict CO_2 Limits on Existing Coal-Fired Power Plants, 2016. Yale Climate Opinion Maps—US 2016.

New York Times. 2017. "President Donald Trump on Paris Climate Accord Withdrawal." Available from https://www.youtube.com/watch?v=deTcuNgKN-E.

Putnam, Robert D. 1988. "Diplomacy and Domestic Politics: The Logic of Two-Level Games." *International Organization* 42 (3): 427–460.

Reuters. 2017. "California and China Have Signed an Agreement to Develop Clean Energy Technology." *Fortune*, June 5.

Sælen, Håkon. 2016. "Side-Payments: An Effective Instrument for Building Climate Clubs?" *International Environmental Agreements: Politics, Law and Economics* 16 (6): 909–932.

Schumpeter, Joseph A. 1994 [1942]. *Capitalism, Socialism and Democracy*. London: Routledge.

Shear, Michael D., and Alison Smale. 2017. "Leader Lament US Withdrawal, but Say It Won't Stop Climate Efforts." *New York Times*, June 2.

Sprinz, Detlef F. 2010. "The 'Sandwich Solution' to Global Climate Policy." In *Delivering Tomorrow: Towards Sustainable Logistics*, edited by Deutsche Post, 71–74. Bonn: Deutsche Post AG.

Sprinz, Detlef F., Håkon Sælen, Arild Underdal, and Jon Hovi. forthcoming. *The Effectiveness of Climate Clubs under Donald Trump. Climate Policy*, https://doi.org/10 .1080/14693062.2017.1410090.

Sprinz, Detlef F., and Steffen von Bünau. 2013. "The Compensation Fund for Climate Impacts." *Weather, Climate, and Society* 5 (3): 210–220.

Thompson, Stuart A., and Vikas Bajaj. 2017. "Why Are These CEOs Still Standing with Trump on Climate?" *New York Times*, June 2.

UNFCCC. 2015. *Paris Agreement*. Paris: United Nations.

———. 2016. *Report of the Conference of the Parties on Its Twenty-First Session, Held in Paris from 30 November to 13 December 2015/Add.1/Part Two: Action Taken by the Conference of the Parties at Its Twenty-First Session*. Paris: United Nations.

———. 2017. *Status of Ratification of the Kyoto Protocol*. Available from http://unfccc .int/kyoto_protocol/status_of_ratification/items/2613.php.

US Senate. 1997. Senate Resolution 98. Congressional Record, Report No. 105–5412. Washington, DC.

Victor, Daniel. 2017. "'Climate Change Is Real': Many US Companies Lament Paris Accord Exit." *New York Times*, June 1.

Victor, David G. 2011. *Global Warming Gridlock: Creating More Effective Strategies for Protecting the Planet*. Cambridge: Cambridge University Press.

———. 2015. *The Case for Climate Clubs*. Geneva: International Centre for Trade and Sustainable Development and World Economic Forum.

White House. 2017. *Statement by President Trump on the Paris Climate Accord*. June 1. Washington, DC: White House Press Office.

Contributors

Michaël Aklin is assistant professor of Political Science, University of Pittsburgh, United States.

Guri Bang is research director at CICERO—Center for International Climate Research, Norway.

Daniel Bodansky is foundation professor at Sandra Day O'Connor College of Law, Arizona State University, United States.

Thierry Bréchet is professor at the Center for Operations Research & Econometrics (CORE) and Louvain School of Management (LSM), Université catholique de Louvain, Belgium.

Lars Brückner is professional staff member of the Center for Controlling & Management at the Institute of Management Accounting and Control, WHU—Otto Beisheim School of Management, Vallendar, Germany.

Frank Grundig is lecturer in international relations at the School of Politics and International Relations, University of Kent, Canterbury, United Kingdom.

Jon Hovi is professor in the Department of Political Science at the University of Oslo, Norway.

Yasuko Kameyama is deputy director at the Center for Social and Environmental Systems Research, National Institute for Environmental Studies, Tsukuba, Japan.

Urs Luterbacher is professor emeritus at the Centre for Environmental Studies and Centre for Finance and Development, Graduate Institute of International and Development Studies, Geneva, Switzerland.

Axel Michaelowa is head of research on International Climate Policy and department chair of Political Economy and Development at the Center for Comparative and International Studies (CIS), University of Zurich, Switzerland.

Katharina Michaelowa is professor of political economy and development at the Center for Comparative and International Studies (CIS), University of Zurich, Switzerland.

Carla Norrlof is associate professor in the Department of Political Science at the University of Toronto, Canada.

Matthew Paterson is professor of International Politics, University of Manchester, United Kingdom.

Lavanya Rajamani is professor at the Centre for Policy Research, New Delhi, India.

Tora Skodvin is professor in the Department of Political Science at the University of Oslo, Norway.

Detlef F. Sprinz is senior scientist at PIK—Potsdam Institute for Climate Impact Research, Germany, Rice faculty fellow and visiting professor at Yale University, United States, senior fellow at Käte Hamburger Kolleg, Centre for Global Cooperation, University of Duisburg-Essen, Germany, and professor at the University of Potsdam, Germany.

Arild Underdal is professor emeritus in the Department of Political Science at the University of Oslo and Professor at CICERO—Center for International Climate Research, Norway.

Jorge E. Viñuales is Harold Samuel Chair of Law and Environmental Policy, University of Cambridge, and director of the Cambridge Centre for Environment, Energy and Natural Resource Governance (C-EENRG), United Kingdom.

Hugh Ward is professor in the Department of Government at the University of Essex, United Kingdom.

Index

Global Environmental Accord: Strategies for Sustainability and Institutional Innovation

Nazli Choucri, series editor